The Problem of Political

Also by Michael Huemer

ETHICAL INTUITIONISM
SKEPTICISM AND THE VEIL OF PERCEPTION

The Problem of Political Authority

An Examination of the Right to Coerce and the Duty to Obey

Michael Huemer
University of Colorado at Boulder, USA

palgrave
macmillan

First published 2013 by
PALGRAVE MACMILLAN.

Palgrave Macmillan in the UK is an imprint of Macmillan Publishers Limited,
registered in England, company number 785998, of Houndmills, Basingstoke,
Hampshire RG21 6XS.

Palgrave Macmillan in the US is a division of St Martin's Press LLC,
175 Fifth Avenue, New York, NY 10010.

Palgrave Macmillan is the global academic imprint of the above companies
and has companies and representatives throughout the world.

Palgrave® and Macmillan® are registered trademarks in the United States,
the United Kingdom, Europe and other countries.

ISBN: 978–1–137–28164–7 hardback
ISBN: 978–1–137–28165–4 paperback

A catalogue record for this book is available from the British Library.

A catalog record for this book is available from the Library of Congress.

10 9 8 7 6 5 4 3 2 1
22 21 20 19 18 17 16 15 14 13

Transferred to Digital Printing in 2014

Contents

Analytical Contents

Part II Society without Authority

it could succeed in a limited area, assuming most people accepted anarchism. They need not argue that people are likely to accept the theory.

Moderate political theories can be utopian. Statists must not merely assume that governments will act as they should nor that government officials are exempt from human nature.

Hobbes argued that anarchy would be a state of war of all against all but that a single absolute ruler would create peace.

It is normally prudentially irrational to start fights with others, even in the absence of government.

The prevalence of violence is affected by cultural values, prosperity, and technology.

Interstate violence is not deterred as easily as interpersonal violence.

Absolute rulers have little cause to care about their subjects' rights or welfare and often commit horrible abuses.

In a democracy, the majority may oppress the minority.

The government may ignore the rights and interests of nonvoters, including foreigners affected by the government's policies.

Voters tend to be politically ignorant and irrational, since each voter knows his own vote will have no impact.

Figures

Preface

This book addresses the foundational problem of political philosophy: the problem of accounting for the authority of government. This authority has always struck me as puzzling and problematic. Why should 535 people in Washington be entitled to issue commands to 300 million others? And why should the others obey? These questions, as I argue in the following pages, have no satisfactory answers.

Why is this important? Nearly all political discourse centers on what sort of policies the government should make, and nearly all of it – whether in political philosophy or in popular forums – presupposes that the government has a special kind of authority to issue commands to the rest of society. When we argue about what the government's immigration policy ought to be, for example, we normally presuppose that the state has the right to control movement into and out of the country. When we argue about the best tax policy, we presuppose that the state has the right to take wealth from individuals. When we argue about health care reform, we presuppose that the state has the right to decide how health care should be provided and paid for. If, as I hope to convince you, these presuppositions are mistaken, then nearly all of our current political discourse is misguided and must be fundamentally rethought.

Who should read this book? The questions addressed herein are relevant to anyone interested in politics and government. I hope my fellow philosophers will profit from it, but I also hope it will reach beyond that small group. I have therefore tried to minimize academic jargon and to keep the writing as clear and straightforward as possible. I do not presuppose any specialized knowledge.

Is this a book of extremist ideology? Yes and no. I defend some radical conclusions in the following pages. But although I am an extremist, I have always striven to be a reasonable one. I reason on the basis of what seem to me common sense ethical judgments. I do not assume a controversial, grand philosophical theory, an absolutist interpretation of some particular value, or a set of dubious empirical claims. This is to say that although my *conclusions* are highly controversial, my *premises* are not. Furthermore, I have striven to address alternative viewpoints fairly and reasonably. I consider in detail the most interesting and initially plausible attempts to justify governmental authority. When it comes to my own political view, I address all the important objections found in the literature and the oral tradition. Politics being as it is, I cannot expect to persuade committed partisans of other ideologies. My aim, however, is to persuade those who have kept an open mind regarding the problem of political authority.

What is in this book? Chapters 2–5 discuss philosophical theories about the basis of state authority. Chapter 6 discusses psychological and historical evidence regarding our attitudes about authority. Chapter 7 asks the question, if there is no authority, how ought citizens and government employees to behave? It is here that the most immediately practical recommendations appear. Part II of the book proposes an alternative social structure not based on authority. Chapters 10–12 address the most obvious practical problems for such a society. The last chapter discusses whether and how the changes I recommend might come about.

I wish to acknowledge some friends and colleagues who helped me with this book. Bryan Caplan, David Boonin, Jason Brennan, Gary Chartier, Kevin Vallier, Matt Skene, David Gordon, and Eric Chwang provided invaluable comments that helped eliminate mistakes and improve the text in numerous places. I am grateful for their generosity. If any mistakes remain, the reader may look these professors up and ask them why they did not correct them. The work was completed with the assistance of a fellowship from the Center for the Humanities and the Arts at the University of Colorado in the 2011–12 academic year, for which assistance I am also grateful.

Part I
The Illusion of Authority

1

The Problem of Political Authority

1.1 A political parable

Let us begin with a short political story. You live in a small village with a crime problem. Vandals roam the village, stealing and destroying people's property. No one seems to be doing anything about it. So one day, you and your family decide to put a stop to it. You take your guns and go looking for vandals. Periodically, you catch one, take him back to your house at gunpoint, and lock him in the basement. You provide the prisoners with food so they don't starve, but you plan to keep them locked in the basement for a few years to teach them a lesson.

After operating in this way for a few weeks, you decide to make the rounds of the neighborhood, starting with your next door neighbor. As he answers the door, you ask, 'Have you noticed the reduction in crime in the last few weeks?' He nods. 'Well, that is thanks to me.' You explain your anticrime program. Noting the wary look on your neighbor's face, you continue. 'Anyway, I'm here because it's time to collect your contribution to the crime prevention fund. Your bill for the month is $100.'

As your neighbor stares at you, making no apparent move to hand over the money, you patiently explain that, should he refuse to make the required payment, you will unfortunately have to label *him* a criminal, at which point he will be subject to long-term confinement in your basement, along with the aforementioned vandals. Indicating the pistol at your hip, you note that you are prepared to take him by force if necessary.

Supposing you take this tack with all of your neighbors, what sort of reception could you expect? Would most cheerfully give over their assigned share of the costs of crime prevention?

Not likely. In all probability, you would observe the following. First, almost none would agree that they *owe* you anything. While some

3

might pay up for fear of imprisonment in your basement and a few might pay up out of hostility toward the vandals, almost none would consider themselves duty bound to do so. Those who refused to pay would more likely be praised than condemned for standing up to you.

Second, most would consider your actions outrageous. Your demands for payment would be condemned as naked extortion, and your confinement of those who refused to pay as kidnapping. The very outrageousness of your conduct, combined with your deluded presumption that the rest of the village would recognize an obligation to support you, would cause many to question your sanity.

What does this story have to do with political philosophy? In the story, you behaved like a rudimentary government. Though you did not take on all the functions of a typical, modern state, you assumed two of its most central roles: you punished people who violated others' rights or disobeyed your commands, and you collected nonvoluntary contributions to finance your activities. In the case of the government, these activities are referred to as the criminal justice system and the tax system. In your case, they are referred to as kidnapping and extortion.

On the face of it, your activities are of the same kind as those of a government. Yet most people's evaluations of the government are far more lenient than their evaluations of you in the story. Most people support the state's imprisonment of criminals, feel obligated to pay their taxes, and consider punishment of tax evaders both desirable and within the rights of the state.

This illustrates a general feature of our attitudes toward government. Governments are considered ethically permitted to do things that no nongovernmental person or organization may do. At the same time, individuals are thought to have obligations to their governments that they would owe toward no nongovernmental person or organization, even if nongovernmental agents behaved similarly to a government. This is not simply a point about the law, nor is it about what sorts of actions one can get away with. The point is that our *ethical judgments* differentiate sharply between governmental and nongovernmental actions. Acts that would be considered unjust or morally unacceptable when performed by nongovernmental agents will often be considered perfectly all right, even praiseworthy, when performed by government agents. Hereafter, I shall use 'obligation' to refer to ethical obligations rather than mere legal obligations; similarly for 'rights'.[1]

---

[1] Some thinkers distinguish obligations from duties (Hart 1958, 100–4; Brandt 1964). Hereinafter, however, I use 'obligation' and 'duty' interchangeably to denote any ethical requirement.

Why do we accord this special moral status to government, and are we justified in so doing? This is the problem of political authority.

1.2 The concept of authority: a first pass

What is it in ordinary moral thinking that differentiates your actions in the above story from the actions of a government? Broadly speaking, two sorts of explanations could be given. One type of explanation is that, despite appearances, the two *behaviors* are different, that the government is not really doing the same thing as the vigilante. For instance, suppose one thought the crucial difference was that the vigilante (you in the story) does not give the vandals fair jury trials, as the government (in some countries) does to those it seeks to punish. That could explain why the vigilante's behavior is less legitimate than that of the government.

The other type of explanation is that the two agents are different.[2] That is, the government may be doing the same things as the vigilante, but *who* is doing it makes all the difference. You are to be condemned in the story, not because you are not faithfully imitating the government, but because you *are* acting like a government, though *you're not the government.*

It is this second type of explanation that I characterize as an invocation of *political authority.* Political authority (hereafter, just 'authority') is the hypothesized moral property in virtue of which governments may coerce people in certain ways not permitted to anyone else and in virtue of which citizens must obey governments in situations in which they would not be obligated to obey anyone else. Authority, then, has two aspects:

(i) *Political legitimacy*: the right, on the part of a government, to make certain sorts of laws and enforce them by coercion against the members of its society – in short, the right to rule.[3]
(ii) *Political obligation*: the obligation on the part of citizens to obey their government, even in circumstances in which one would not be obligated to obey similar commands issued by a nongovernmental agent.

---

[2] I leave the distinction between characteristics of the agent and characteristics of the action at an intuitive level. 'Characteristics of the action' must be taken somehow to exclude such characteristics as 'having been performed by an agent of such-and-such type'. Likewise, 'characteristics of the agent' must not include such things as 'being such that he performs actions of such-and-such type'.

[3] I use 'authority', 'legitimacy', and 'political obligation' in stipulated, technical senses. My use of 'authority' and 'legitimacy' roughly follows that of Buchanan

If a government has 'authority', then both (i) and (ii) exist: the government has the right to rule, and the citizens have the obligation to obey.

The having of political obligations does not mean merely that one must do the things that the law or other governmental commands require.[4] For example, the law prohibits murder, and we have a moral duty not to murder. But this does not suffice to establish that we have 'political obligations', because we would be morally obligated not to murder even if there were no law against it. But there are other cases in which, according to popular opinion, we are obligated to do things precisely *because* the law commands them, and we would not be obligated to do those things if they were not legally required. For instance, most believe that we are obligated to pay taxes on our income in countries that legally require this and that we are obligated to pay the specific amount required by the tax code. Those who think taxes are too high do not feel entitled to evade a portion of their taxes. Those who think taxes are too low do not feel obligated to send extra money to the government. And if the law changed so that income tax was not legally required, then one would no longer be obliged to pay the government this portion of one's income. So, in the popular mind, the obligation to pay income tax is a political obligation.[5]

Those who believe in political authority need not hold that political authority is unconditional or absolute, nor need they hold that *all* governments have it. One could hold, for instance, that the state's authority is contingent on its respecting basic human rights and allowing citizens a certain level of political participation; thus, tyrannical governments lack authority. One might also hold that even a legitimate government may not command a person, for example, to commit murder, nor would

---

(2002), but I do not require that political obligations be owed specifically *to* the state. The state's alleged right to rule should be understood as a justification right rather than a claim right (Ladenson 1980, 137–9); that is, it renders it permissible for the state to do certain things rather than imposing some moral demand on other agents. My uses of 'legitimacy' and 'authority' differ from those of some other theorists (Simmons 2001, 130; Edmundson 1998, chapter 2; Estlund 2008, 2).

4   Political obligation may apply not only to laws but also to other governmental commands, such as administrative edicts and court orders. This point should be understood throughout, though I shall often speak simply of obligation to obey the law.

5   Klosko's focus group research lends some support to this impression of popular attitudes (2005, chapter 9, especially 198, 212–18).

a citizen be obligated to obey such a command. A believer in authority may thus believe only that certain governments have a certain limited sphere of authority.

Despite these limitations, the authority ascribed to some governments is an impressive moral property. As we saw in Section 1.1, this authority would explain an entitlement to perform actions of kinds that would be considered very wrong and unjust for any nonauthoritative agent.

1.3 Actions versus agents: the need for authority

Does one need this notion of authority to explain the moral difference between the vigilante in Section 1.1 and the government? Or can one explain the difference by appealing only to differences between the government's behavior and the vigilante's behavior?

In the story as I described it, there were many differences between the vigilante's behavior and that of a typical government; however, none of these differences are essential. One can modify the example so as to remove any difference that might be thought relevant, and provided one does not convert the vigilante into a government, most people will still intuitively judge the vigilante much more harshly than government agents who act analogously.

Thus, consider the fact that many governments provide fair jury trials for accused criminals. The vigilante could do the same. Suppose that every time you catch a vandal, you round up a few of your neighbors and force them to sit through a trial. After the presentation of evidence, you make your neighbors vote on the guilt or innocence of the accused vandal, and you use the outcome to decide whether to punish the accused. Would this render your actions acceptable? Perhaps your treatment of the vandals would be more fair, but it hardly seems to legitimate your program as a whole. In fact, you have now added another offense to the list of your outrageous actions: your temporary enslavement of your neighbors to serve your 'justice system'.

Consider another suggestion. Government agents generally arrest people only for infractions of explicitly published rules – the laws – whereas the vigilante punishes people only according to his internal sense of right and wrong. This difference, too, can be removed. Suppose that you write down a long list of behaviors that you consider unacceptable, along with accounts of what you plan to do to people who engage in those behaviors. You post copies of your lists on a bulletin board outside your house. Again, this hardly suffices to legitimate your behavior.

A more initially plausible suggestion is that your behavior is impermissible because the community did not choose you to play that role. In contrast, in democratic countries, the citizens choose their leaders. (This account implies that only democratic governments are legitimate; so the great majority of the governments throughout history have been illegitimate, and the great majority of people have lacked political obligations. This is probably already a significant revision to common sense.) But notice that this account of the difference between the government and the vigilante is an appeal to *authority*. It does not claim that the vigilante is doing something different from what the government does; it claims that the actions in question may be performed by one agent and not another. The vigilante lacks the authority to punish criminals and collect taxes because he has not been authorized by his society. I examine this theory of authority in a later chapter. For now, the point to observe is simply that *some* account of authority is needed.

1.4   The significance of coercion and the reach of authority

The need for an account of political legitimacy arises from the moral significance of *coercion* and from the coercive nature of government. It is important to bring these principles clearly into focus so as to have a clear view of what needs explaining before trying to explain it.

First, what is coercion? Hereinafter, I use the term 'coercion' to denote a person's use of or threat to use physical force against another person. When I speak of coercing a person to do something, I shall mean using physical force or the threat of physical force to induce that person to perform the desired action. I use 'physical force' and 'violence' interchangeably. I shall not define 'physical force' here; our intuitive understanding of the notion will suffice for the subsequent arguments, and I shall not rely on any controversial judgments about what qualifies as physical force.

My definition of 'coercion' is not intended as an analysis of the term's standard use in English. It is a stipulative definition, intended to avoid repetition of the phrase 'use of or threat to use physical force'. My use of the term differs from the ordinary usage in at least two ways: first, in the *ordinary* sense of the term, when A 'coerces' B, A induces B to behave in some way desired by A; but in *my* sense, A might coerce B by physically injuring B, whether or not A influences B's behavior. Second, the ordinary sense counts a broader range of threats as coercive: in the ordinary sense, A might 'coerce' B using a threat to spread malicious rumors about *B*. This would not qualify as coercion in my sense, because the threat is not one of violence. The ordinary concept of coercion is useful in many contexts; nevertheless, I have introduced a stipulative definition because doing so enables consideration of some important and interesting arguments regarding political authority while avoiding unnecessary semantic debates.[6]

Government is a coercive institution. Generally speaking, when the state makes a law, the law carries with it a punishment to be imposed upon violators. It is possible to have a law with no specified punishment for violation, but all actual governments attach punishments to nearly all laws.[7] Not everyone who breaks the law will in fact be punished, but the state will generally make a reasonable effort at punishing violators and will generally punish a fair number of them, typically with fines or imprisonment. These punishments are intended to harm lawbreakers, and they generally succeed in doing so.

Direct physical violence is rarely used as a punishment. Nevertheless, violence plays a crucial role in the system, because without the threat of violence, lawbreakers could simply choose not to suffer punishment. For example, the government commands that drivers stop before all red lights. If you violate this rule, you might be punished with a $200 fine. But this is simply another command. If you didn't obey the command to stop before all red lights, why would you obey the command to pay $200 to the government? Perhaps the second command will be enforced by a third command: the government may threaten to revoke your driver's license if you do not pay the fine. In other words, it may command you to stop driving. But if you violated the first two commands, why would you follow the third? Well, the command to stop driving may be enforced by a threat of imprisonment if you continue to drive without a license. As these examples illustrate, commands are often enforced with threats to issue further commands, yet that cannot be all there is to it. At the end of the chain must come a threat that the violator literally cannot defy. The system as a whole must be anchored by a nonvoluntary intervention, a harm that the state can impose regardless of the individual's choices.

---

[6] Edmundson (1998, chapter 4) argues that law is typically *not* coercive in the ordinary sense. My technical usage of 'coercion' is designed to avoid Edmundson's argument while retaining the moral presumption against coercion.

[7] There are a few exceptions, such as laws against suicide, some international treaties, and a government's constitution.

That anchor is provided by physical force. Even the threat of imprisonment requires enforcement: how can the state ensure that the criminal goes to the prison? The answer lies in coercion, involving actual or threatened bodily injury or, at a minimum, physical pushing or pulling of the individual's body to the location of imprisonment. This is the final intervention that the individual cannot choose to defy. One can choose not to pay a fine, one can choose to drive without a license, and one can even choose not to walk to a police car to be taken away. But one cannot choose not to be subjected to physical force if the agents of the state decide to impose it.

Thus, the legal system is founded on *intentional, harmful coercion*. To justify a law, one must justify imposition of that law on the population through a threat of harm, including the coercive imposition of actual harm on those who are caught violating the law. In common sense morality, the threat or actual coercive imposition of harm is normally wrong. This is not to say that it cannot be justified; it is only to say that coercion requires a justification. This may be because of the way in which coercion disrespects persons, seeking to bypass their reason and manipulate them through fear, or the way in which it seems to deny the autonomy and equality of other persons.

I shall not attempt any comprehensive account of when coercion is justified. I rely on the intuitive judgment that harmful coercion requires a justification, as well as on some intuitions about particular conditions that do or do not constitute satisfactory justifications. For instance, one legitimate justification is self-defense or defense of innocent third parties: one may harmfully coerce another person if doing so is necessary to prevent that person from wrongfully harming someone else. Another justification for harmful coercion is consent. Thus, if you are in a boxing match to which both participants have agreed, then you may punch your opponent in the face.

On the other hand, many possible reasons for coercion are clearly inadequate. If you have a friend who eats too many potato chips, you may try to convince him to give them up. But if he won't listen, you may not *force* him to stop. If you admire your neighbor's car, you may offer to buy it from him. But if he won't sell, you may not threaten him with violence. If you disagree with your coworker's religious beliefs, you may try to convert him. But if he won't listen, you may not punch him in the nose. And so on. In common sense ethics, the overwhelming majority of reasons for coercion fail as justifications.

Modern states stand in need of an account of political legitimacy because modern states commonly coerce and harm individuals for reasons that would be viewed as inadequate for any nongovernmental agent. This can be illustrated by some embellishments on the story of Section 1.1.

Suppose you announce that you believe a neighboring town is building some very destructive weapons, weapons they might one day use to terrorize other villages. To prevent this from happening, you round up a few like-minded villagers and travel to the neighboring town, where you violently depose the mayor, blowing up some buildings and predictably killing several innocent people in the process.

If you behaved in this way, you would be labeled a terrorist and murderer, and calls for your execution or life imprisonment would likely abound. But when the government behaves in this way, its behavior is labeled 'war', and many support it. To be sure, there are many who reject the idea of preemptive war. But only political extremists describe soldiers or the government leaders who send them into battle as terrorists and murderers. Even among opponents of the 2003 Iraq war, for example, few went so far as to call George W. Bush a mass murderer or call for his execution or imprisonment. The notion of political authority is at work here: the feeling is that, whether its choice is good or bad, the government is the agent with the authority to decide whether to go to war. No other agent has the right to commit large-scale violence to achieve its ends in anything like these circumstances.

Suppose now that, amidst all your other unusual activities, you decide to start supporting charity. You find a charity that helps the poor. Unfortunately, you believe your village has not contributed enough to this charity voluntarily, so you take to forcibly extracting money from your neighbors and handing it over to the charity.

If you behaved in this way, you would be labeled a thief and extortionist, and calls to imprison you and compel you to personally repay those whose wealth you expropriated would be commonplace. But when the government behaves in this way, its behavior is known as conducting social welfare programs, and most people support it. To be sure, there are some who oppose social welfare programs, but even opponents rarely view the government agents administering the programs or the legislators who vote for the programs as thieves and extortionists. Very few would call for their imprisonment or their being forced to personally repay taxpayers. Again, the notion of authority is at work: we think that the government has the authority to redistribute wealth; nongovernmental organizations do not.

This should give some indication of the range of governmental activities whose justification relies on the notion of political authority. In

Chapter 7 I will discuss further how far this range extends. But even from this brief discussion, it should be clear that, without a belief in authority, we would have to condemn a great deal of what we now accept as legitimate.

1.5   The concept of authority: a second pass

In this section, I refine the notions of 'political authority', 'political legitimacy', and 'political obligation'. The following five principles are implicit in the ordinary conception of the authority of government; this is what defenders of authority would like to defend:

1. *Generality.* The state's authority applies to citizens generally. That is, the state is entitled to coercively impose rules on at least the great majority of its citizens, and the great majority of citizens have political obligations.[8]
2. *Particularity.* The state's authority is specific to its citizens and residents in its territory. That is, a government is entitled to impose rules on those in its territory in a way in which it is generally not entitled to impose rules on those in foreign countries, and citizens have obligations to their own states of a sort that they do not bear to other states.[9]
3. *Content-Independence.* The state's authority is not tied to the specific content of its laws or other commands.[10] That is, there is a broad range of possible laws such that within that range, the state is entitled to coercively impose whichever laws it chooses, and citizens will be obligated to obey them. The range of acceptable laws need not be unlimited – perhaps the state is not entitled to make or enforce certain kinds of grossly unjust laws, such as laws enforcing slavery. But the state is at least frequently entitled to enforce laws even if the laws are bad or wrong, and citizens are obliged to obey.
4. *Comprehensiveness.* The state is entitled to regulate a broad range of human activities, and individuals must obey the state's directives within that broad sphere.[11] This range need not be unlimited; for instance, perhaps the state may not regulate citizens' private

---

[8] This condition is articulated by Simmons (1979, 55–6).
[9] Simmons 1979, 31–5.
[10] Hart 1958, 104; Raz 1986, 35–7, 76–7; Green 1988, 225–6; Christiano 2008, 250; Rawls 1964, 5.
[11] Klosko 2005, 11–12.

religious practices. But modern states typically regulate and are taken to be entitled to regulate such matters as the terms of employment contracts, the trading of financial securities, medical procedures, food preparation procedures in restaurants, individual drug use, individual weapon possession, movement into and out of the country, the flying of airplanes, trade with foreign countries, and so on.

5. *Supremacy.* Within the sphere of action that the state is entitled to regulate, the state is the highest human authority.[12] No nongovernmental agent may command the state, nor has any such agent the same right to command individuals that the state has.

In advancing conditions (1)–(5), I seek to faithfully characterize the ordinary, common sense conception of political authority. A satisfying account of authority should accommodate and explain these five principles. If no plausible theory comes close to accommodating principles (1)–(5), one should conclude that no state truly has authority.

These five principles are vague, employing as they do such concepts as that of a 'broad range' and a 'great majority'. I shall not attempt to make the notion of political authority precise in these respects. The concept will be clear enough for purposes of evaluating the arguments in the remainder of the book. It is also vague how closely a theory must accommodate these principles. Again, I shall not attempt to make this precise. We should simply take note that if a theory falls very far from accommodating the intuitive conception of authority, then at some point it ceases to be a defense of authority.

A few words about what defenders of authority are *not* committed to: The idea of political obligation does not entail that the government's commanding something is by itself *sufficient* for one's having an obligation to do that thing. Those who believe in authority may hold that there are further conditions for the government's commands to be binding; for instance, that the laws should have been made in accordance with fair and democratic processes, that the present government should not have usurped an earlier, legitimate government, and so on. They may likewise hold that there are limits to the government's authority; for instance, that the laws may not be grossly unjust, that they may not invade certain protected spheres of privacy, and so on. So the idea that one must perform an action 'because the law requires it'

---

[12] Green 1988, 1, 78–83.

may really mean, roughly, that one must perform an action because the law requires it, the law was made in an appropriate way by a legitimate government, the law is not grossly unjust, and the law is within the sphere of things the government may legitimately regulate.

To illustrate the above principles, consider the case of taxation. According to popular opinion, the state may impose taxes on any and all residents in its territory, and residents are generally obligated to pay the imposed taxes (the Generality condition). The state is not entitled to tax people in foreign countries, nor need foreigners pay if the state attempts to do so (Particularity).[13] The state is generally entitled to determine what activities in its territory shall be taxed and how much, and residents are obligated to pay that amount, even if the tax is unreasonably high or low (Content-Independence). No nongovernmental person or organization is entitled either to tax the state or to tax individuals (Supremacy). Thus, if popular views are correct, the case of taxation illustrates the government's political authority.

1.6   A comment on methodology

The first part of this book is an exercise in the application of moral philosophy to politics. The central concern is the evaluation of our moral attitudes toward government: Are governments really entitled to do the things we usually take them to be entitled to do? Are we really obligated to obey governments in the ways we usually take ourselves to be obligated?

Questions of this kind are notoriously difficult. How should they be approached? One approach would be to start from some comprehensive moral theory – say, utilitarianism or Kantian deontology – and attempt to deduce the appropriate conclusions about political rights and obligations. I, unfortunately, cannot do this. I do not know the correct general moral theory, and I don't think anyone else does either. The reasons for my skepticism are difficult to communicate, but they derive from reflection on the problems of moral philosophy and on the complex, confusing, and constantly disputed literature about those problems. It is a literature in which one theory after another runs into a morass of puzzles and problems that becomes ever more complicated as more philosophers work on it. I cannot fully communicate the situation here; the best way of appreciating my skepticism about moral theory is

---

[13] An exception is tariffs, which are considered permissible because the state may set conditions on foreigners' interactions with the state's own people.

for readers to delve into that literature themselves. Here, I shall simply announce that I will not assume any comprehensive moral theory, and I think one should be very skeptical of any attempt to arrive at sound conclusions in political philosophy by starting from such a theory. Nor, for similar reasons, do I start by assuming any general political theory, though I shall arrive at a political theory in the end.

What is the alternative? I shall start from moral claims that are, initially, relatively uncontroversial.[14] This seems an obvious plan. Political philosophy is a difficult and disputed field. One who hopes to make progress cannot begin from a contentious moral theory, still less from a contentious political ideology. One's premises should be things that, for example, both liberals and conservatives would typically find obvious at first glance. One must then attempt to reason from these premises to conclusions about the contested questions that are of interest. Yet natural as it may seem, this approach is seldom taken up. Political philosophers more commonly argue for a position on some controversial issue by starting from a controversial general theory. For instance, a philosopher might seek to determine whether immigration should be restricted by applying a Rawlsian hypothetical social contract theory to the issue.[15]

Most of the moral premises on which I rely are moral evaluations of particular behaviors in relatively specific scenarios. The story of the vigilante in Section 1.1 is a case in point. It is reasonable to take it as a premise that the individual in that story acts impermissibly. The case is not a dilemma (like, say, the Trolley problem[16]), nor does it involve a moral controversy (like, say, a case of someone performing an abortion). To common sense, the negative evaluation is a straightforward, obvious verdict.[17]

Some philosophers believe that in doing moral philosophy, one should rely only upon abstract ethical principles, refusing to trust intuitive evaluations of specific cases.[18] Others believe, more or less, that only

---

[14] In philosophy, almost every claim is disputed by someone, so we cannot rely on *entirely* uncontroversial premises if we are to reach any interesting conclusions.

[15] Carens 1987, 255–62; Blake 2002.

[16] See Foot 1967.

[17] Herein, I use 'common sense' for what the great majority of people are inclined to accept, especially in my society and societies that readers of this book are likely to belong to. This is not to be confused with the technical use of 'common sense beliefs' in my earlier work (2001, 18–19).

[18] Singer 2005.

judgments about particular cases should be relied upon.[19] Still others think that no ethical judgments can be relied upon, and that there is no moral knowledge.[20] All of those views strike me as wrong. What seems right is that *controversial* ethical judgments tend to be unreliable, whereas obvious, uncontroversial ethical judgments – whether specific or general – tend to be reliable. I shall assume that we have some moral knowledge, and that our clearest, most widely shared ethical judgments are instances of such knowledge.[21]

Although my ethical premises will be relatively uncontroversial, my conclusions will not be. On the contrary, the conclusions I reach are so far from most people's initial opinions that probably no argument could convince most people to accept them. I shall ultimately conclude that political authority is an illusion: no one has the right to rule, and no one is obliged to obey a command merely because it comes from their government. But while this may be counterintuitive to most people, I do not think it reveals any mistake on my part. Bertrand Russell has said, '[T]he point of philosophy is to start with something so simple as not to seem worth stating, and to end with something so paradoxical that no one will believe it.'[22] I do not believe that this is the point of philosophy, but nor is reasoning from intuitive premises to surprising conclusions necessarily a mark of bad philosophy.

My attitudes toward common sense might seem inconsistent. On the one hand, I consider the most widely shared ethical intuitions reasonable premises on which to rely. On the other hand, I claim that some very widely shared political beliefs are fundamentally mistaken. The claim that there are some legitimate governments is not very controversial; nearly everyone, whether on the left or the right of the political spectrum, takes that for granted. Why, then, do I not accept the existence of legitimate states as a starting premise, just as I accept common sense beliefs about personal ethics?

One reason is that I have never shared other people's political intuitions, if that is what they are. I share most of the normative intuitions of my society, such as that one must not steal from, kill, or otherwise harm other individuals (except in certain special cases, such as self-defense); that one should generally tell the truth and keep one's promises; and so

---

[19] Dancy 1993, chapter 4.
[20] Mackie 1977.
[21] See Huemer 2005, especially chapter 5, for an account of moral knowledge and responses to moral skepticism.
[22] Russell 1985, 53.

on. But it never seemed to me that there were people with the right to
rule over others, and it never seemed to me that anyone was obligated
to obey a law merely because it was the law.

My intuitions are not entirely idiosyncratic. In contemporary political discourse, there is a vocal minority who advocate drastic reductions
in the size of government. Often, they defend their views in practical
terms (government programs don't work) or in terms of absolutist claims
about individual rights. But I think these arguments miss the main
issue. I believe the true, underlying motivation is a broad skepticism
about political authority: at bottom, the advocates of smaller government simply do not see why the government should be permitted to
do so many things that no one else would be permitted to do. Even
if you do not share this skeptical attitude, I would caution against
simply dismissing the intuitions of those with differing ideologies.
Human beings are highly fallible in political philosophy, and clashes of
intuitions are frequent. Objectivity requires each of us to give serious
consideration to the possibility that it is we who have the mistaken
intuitions.

Those who begin with an intuition that some states possess
authority may be brought to give up that intuition if it turns out, as
I aim to show, that the belief in political authority is incompatible
with common sense moral beliefs. There are three reasons for prefer-
ring to adhere to common sense morality rather than common sense
political philosophy: first, as I have suggested, common sense political philosophy is more controversial than common sense morality.
Second, even those who accept orthodox political views are usually
more strongly convinced of common sense morality than they are
of common sense political philosophy. Third, even those who intuitively accept authority may at the same time have the sense that this
authority is puzzling – that some explanation is required for why some
people should have this special moral status – in a way that it is not
puzzling, for example, that it should be wrong to attack others without
provocation. The failure to find any satisfactory account of political
authority may therefore lead one to give up the belief in authority
rather than to give up common sense moral beliefs.

1.7 Plan of the book

The central thesis of the first part of this book is that political authority
is a moral illusion. I show this through a critique of the leading philosophical accounts of authority (Chapters 2–5). I follow the discussion

of these theories with a discussion of the psychology of our attitudes about authority (Chapter 6), in which I suggest that philosophical accounts of authority are rationalizations for attitudes with nonrational sources, sources in which we should place little trust.

Most people believe that government is incredibly beneficial, that without it society would collapse into an unlivable state of chaos. I would ask the reader to set this belief aside for the time being. The question of the first part of this book is not whether government is good or bad. The question is whether the government has certain special rights that you and I do not have and whether we have certain special duties to the government that we do not have towards anyone else. A government, just like a private vigilante, could be highly beneficial and yet still lack authority in the sense I have defined. Most accounts of authority turn on more than the claim that the authoritative agent provides large benefits. For instance, the social contract theory claims that the citizens of some states have *consented* to their political system. The existence and validity of this consent can be examined independent of the magnitude of the benefits provided by the state. Of course, one might think that the large benefits provided by the state play a key role in establishing its legitimacy. That topic will be taken up in Chapter 5 and, in more detail, in Part II of the book. I ask the reader to leave that question aside until it is time to address it directly.

Questions about the necessity of the state and about how a society might function without a belief in authority are important. These questions will be taken up in Part II, where I address the practical consequences of abandoning the illusion of political authority. The central thesis of Part II will be that society can function and flourish without a general acceptance of authority.

My political philosophy is a form of anarchism. In my experience, most people appear to be convinced that anarchism is obvious nonsense, an idea that can be refuted within 30 seconds with minimal reflection. This was roughly my attitude before I knew anything about the theory. It is also my experience that those who harbor this attitude have no idea what anarchists actually think – how anarchists think society should function or how they respond to the 30-second objections. Anarchists face a catch-22: most people will not give anarchism a serious hearing because they are convinced that the position is crazy; they are convinced that the position is crazy because they do not understand it; and they do not understand it because they will not give it a serious hearing. I therefore ask the reader not to give up reading this book merely because of its conclusion. The author is neither stupid nor crazy nor evil; he has a reasoned account of how a stateless society might function. Whether or not you ultimately accept the account, it is very likely that you will find it to have been worth considering.

In the philosophical literature in recent years, it has become common to question the reality of political obligations. Skepticism about political obligation is now probably the dominant view. This surprising development is due mostly to the trenchant work of A. John Simmons, who tore down several leading accounts of political obligation in his *Moral Principles and Political Obligation*. I endorse most of Simmons's arguments. Some readers will already be familiar with these arguments, but many will not; thus, in succeeding chapters I explain the most important arguments against political obligation, regardless of whether they have appeared in print before. At the same time, I believe contemporary philosophers have not gone far enough. Philosophers working on political obligation have mostly faced up to the inadequacy of extant accounts of political obligation. But they have not yet faced up to the inadequacy of accounts of political legitimacy.[23] And very few philosophers today give serious attention to political anarchism. Typically, arguments about political obligation take for granted that the state is vitally needed; the dominant view has it that even though we need government and even though modern states are justified in most of their typical activities, we still are not obligated to obey the law merely as such. I hope this book will induce a deeper reflection, both on the assumption of political legitimacy and on the assumption of the necessity of the state.

---

[23] Simmons (1979, 196) denies that there are any 'legitimate' governments or that any governments have the 'right' to coerce or to punish their citizens. However, he seems to use these terms in a stronger sense than mine, because he goes on to accept that governments may be *morally justified* in their activities (199). This is confirmed by Simmons 2001, 130–1. Hence, Simmons's apparent agreement with me is only verbal; in my terminology, Simmons accepts political legitimacy, whereas I reject it.

2
The Traditional Social Contract Theory

2.1 The social contract orthodoxy

The social contract theory is the most prominent account of authority in the last 400 years of philosophy and has as good a claim as any to being America's theory of authority. The theory holds that, at least in some countries, there is a contractual relationship between the government and its citizens. The contract requires the government to provide certain services for the population, notably protection from private criminals and hostile foreign governments. In return, citizens agree to pay their taxes and obey the laws.[1] Some views of the social contract assign the government a larger role, perhaps including providing for the basic needs of indigent citizens, ensuring an equitable distribution of material resources, and so on.[2] Whatever a particular theorist takes to be the state's legitimate functions, the theorist will argue that the social contract both authorizes and obligates the state to perform those functions.

Under the terms of the traditional social contract theory, then, political obligation is a species of contractual obligation: citizens must obey the law because they have agreed to do so. The social contract would also account for political legitimacy straightforwardly. If a person agrees to be subjected to a particular form of coercion, then, as a rule, that coercion will not be wrong and will not violate his rights. For example, it is normally wrong to cut a person with a knife.

---

[1] Locke 1980. Hobbes, however, claims that the state owes nothing to the citizens because the state is not a party to the contract; instead, he takes the social contract as an agreement among citizens (1996, 122).

[2] Rawls 1999; Gauthier 1986.

But if you have hired a doctor to perform surgery on you, then it is not wrong and not a violation of your rights for him to cut you in the performance of that surgery. In the same vein, if citizens have agreed to pay the government for its services and have agreed to be subjected to coercion if they fail to pay, then it is permissible for the government to force its citizens to pay.[3]

2.2 The explicit social contract theory

Is there a social contract? At first glance the theory exhibits an impudent disregard for reality: no one has ever been presented with a contract describing how the government operates and asked for a signature. Few have ever been in a situation in which a verbal or a written statement of agreement to have a government would have been appropriate, let alone have actually made such a statement. When do the social contract theorists think this event happened?

John Locke believed that there was (in the case of at least some governments) an actual, explicit agreement made at the time the government was founded.[4] Little evidence remains of these events, Locke explained, because people in those times kept few records. He cites Rome and Venice as examples of cases in which a society was founded with an explicit social contract.

But even if there was an original social contract, how could this contract bind people born much later, who never participated in the original agreement and were never asked for their consent? Locke believed that it worked through a perpetual restrictive covenant on the land: the original contractors committed all their possessions, including their land, to the jurisdiction of the government that they were creating, so that any person to ever use that land in the future would be required to submit to that government.[5]

Despite the cleverness of this last maneuver, the entire theory is sheer mythology, and its interest today is mainly as a bit of history and as a foil for more plausible theories. David Hume painted the more realistic picture of human history, when he observed that nearly all

---

[3] An interesting question remains as to whether citizens might later withdraw their consent, as one may typically withdraw consent to other forms of coercion. This raises problems additional to those I discuss below in the text.

[4] Locke 1980, sections 100–4.

[5] Locke 1980, sections 116–17, 120–1.

governments are founded on usurpation or conquest.[6] That is, at some time in the history of any presently existing nation, either the government was forcibly taken over by a person who lacked the right to do so, as in a coup d'état, or the government (or its citizens or future citizens) seized the land it presently controls from the original inhabitants by force. Either of these events would invalidate the state's authority, on a Lockean view.

In the case of the United States and its government, for instance, the history is one of conquest. The present territory of the United States was stolen from the Native Americans and then placed under the control of the U.S. government. On a Lockean view, this history renders the U.S. government's control over the land illegitimate.

As I have said, this theory is chiefly of historical interest today; no prominent contemporary theorist endorses the explicit social contract theory. The next version of social contract theory is designed to avoid these problems.

2.3   The implicit social contract theory

Explicit consent is consent that one indicates by stating, either verbally or in writing, that one consents. By contrast, *implicit* consent is consent that one indicates through one's conduct, without actually stating one's agreement. If citizens have not embraced a social contract explicitly, perhaps they have embraced it implicitly.

How can one indicate agreement without stating agreement? In some situations, one expresses agreement to a proposal simply by refraining from opposing it. I call this 'passive consent'. Suppose you are in a board meeting, where the chairman says, 'Next week's meeting will be moved to Tuesday at ten o'clock. Any objections?' He pauses, and no one says anything. 'Good, it's agreed', the chairman concludes.[7] In this situation, it is plausible that their failure to express dissent when invited to do so indicates that the board members consent to the change.

In other cases, one commits oneself to accepting certain demands by soliciting or voluntarily accepting benefits to which those demands are known to be attached. I call this 'consent through acceptance of benefits'. For example, suppose you enter a restaurant and order a nice, tasty veggie wrap. After you eat the wrap, the waitress brings the check. 'What's this?' you say. 'I never said I was going to *pay* for any of this. If

---

[6] Hume 1987, 471.
[7] This example is from Simmons (1979, 79–80).

you wanted payment, you should have said so at the start. I'm sorry, but I don't owe you anything.' In this case, the restaurant could plausibly argue that, by ordering the food, you implicitly indicated agreement with the usual demand connected with the provision of that food: namely, payment of the price mentioned on the menu. Because it is well known in this society (and presumably known to you) that restaurants are generally only willing to provide food in order to get paid, it was *your* responsibility, if you wanted free food, to state this up front. Otherwise, the default assumption is that you agree to participate in the normal practice. For that reason, you would be obligated to pay for your meal, notwithstanding your protestations to the contrary.

A third form of implicit consent is what I call 'consent through presence', whereby one indicates agreement to a proposal merely by remaining in some location. While having a party at my house, I announce, loudly and clearly to everyone present, that anyone who wants to stay at my party must agree to help clean up afterwards. After hearing my announcement, you carry on partying. In so doing, you imply that you agree to help clean up at the end.

Finally, sometimes one implicitly consents to the rules governing a practice by voluntarily participating in the practice. I call this 'consent through participation'. Suppose that, during one of my philosophy classes, I tell the students that I am going to run a voluntary class lottery. 'Those who want to participate', I explain, 'will put their names into this hat. I will draw one name out at random. Each of the other participants will then pay $1 to the person whose name is drawn.' Suppose that you put your name into my hat. When the winner's name is drawn, you discover, alas, that the winner was not you. I come to collect $1 from you to give to the winning student. 'I don't owe you anything', you insist. 'I never *said* that I agreed to pay a dollar. All I did was drop my name into your hat. Maybe I was dropping it in just because I like putting my name into hats.' In this situation, it seems that you are obligated to hand over the dollar. Your voluntary participation in the process, when it was well known how the scheme was supposed to work, implied that you agreed to accept the possible financial burden associated with my lottery scheme.

Each of these four kinds of implicit consent – passive consent, consent through acceptance of benefits, consent through presence, and consent through participation – might be used as a model for citizens' implicit acceptance of the social contract. To begin with, perhaps citizens typically consent to the social contract merely by refraining from objecting to it (passive consent). Just as few if any of us have ever explicitly stated that we accept the social contract, few have ever stated that we do *not* accept it. (The exceptions are anarchists who have explicitly stated their rejection of government.)

Consent through acceptance of benefits would also confer a nearly universal authority. Nearly everyone has accepted at least some benefits from their government. There are certain public goods – such as national security and crime prevention – that the state provides automatically to everyone within its territory. *These* goods are not relevant to consent, because these are benefits given whether citizens want them or not. Pacifists, for instance, are given the 'good' of military defense, against their will. However, there are other goods that citizens have a choice about accepting. For example, nearly everyone uses roads that were built by a government. The government does not force people to use these roads; thus, this is a case of voluntary acceptance of a governmental benefit. Similarly, if one calls the police to ask for assistance or protection, if one takes another person to court, if one voluntarily sends one's children to public schools, or if one takes advantage of government social welfare programs, then one is voluntarily accepting governmental benefits. It can then be argued that one implicitly accepts the conditions known to be attached to the having of a government – that one should help pay the monetary costs of government and obey the laws of the government.

Consider next the case of consent through presence. This, in my experience, is the most popular theory of how citizens give their consent to the state, perhaps because it is the only account that can be applied to everyone within the state's territory. The government does not require anyone (other than prisoners) to remain in the country, and it is well known that those who live within a given country are expected to obey the laws and pay taxes. Therefore, by voluntarily remaining, perhaps we implicitly accept the obligation to obey the laws and pay taxes.[8]

Lastly, some citizens might give implicit consent through participation in the political system. If one votes in elections, it might be inferred that one accepts the political system in which one is participating. This, in turn, might obligate one to abide by the outcome of the political process, including the laws made in accordance with the rules of the system, even when these are different from the laws that one desired.

If any of these four suggestions hold up, they would account for both political obligation and political legitimacy, at least with respect to some citizens.

---

[8] Locke 1980, sections 120–1; Otsuka 2003, chapter 5.

2.4 Conditions for valid agreements

A *valid* agreement is an agreement that is morally efficacious – that is, it succeeds in rendering permissible some action to which one consents or in generating an obligation to act in a way that one has agreed to act. All the examples in the previous section were of valid agreements. But some 'agreements' are invalid. For instance, suppose a criminal holds a gun to your head and demands that you sign over the movie rights to your latest book. If you sign, the contract would be invalid, because the threat of violence made it nonvoluntary. Or suppose you agree to buy a television from a salesman, but the salesman neglects to inform you that the television is broken and does not display a picture. In this case, the sale agreement is invalid because it was elicited by fraud on the part of the salesman. Televisions are normally understood to be capable of displaying a picture, and this is essential to why people buy them. Thus, if one wishes to sell a nonworking television, one must state this condition; otherwise, the default assumption is that the television works.

I shall not attempt a complete account of when a valid agreement exists. But the following are four plausible general principles governing valid agreements:

1. *Valid consent requires a reasonable way of opting out.* All parties to any agreement must have the option to reject the agreement without sacrificing anything to which they have a right.

   Consider a modification of the boardroom example from Section 2.3. The chairman says, 'Next week's meeting will be moved to Tuesday at ten o'clock. Those who object will kindly signal this by cutting off their left arms.'[9] The chairman pauses. No arms come off. 'Good, it's agreed!' he declares. This is not a valid agreement, because the demand that board members give up their left arms as the price of dissenting from the schedule change is unreasonable. On the other hand, in the party example from Section 2.3, the demand that you leave my party if you do not agree to help clean up is reasonable, because I have the right to determine who may attend my parties.

   The important difference between the modified boardroom example and the party example is not a matter of how large the costs are; that is, it is not simply that losing your left arm is much worse

---

[9] The example is from Simmons (1979, 81).

than being expelled from a party.[10] The chairman would not be justified even in demanding that board members pay one dollar to express their objection to the schedule change. Rather, it is a matter of who has rights over the good that dissenters are asked to give up. Those who seek your agreement to some proposal may not demand that you give up any of your rights as the cost of rejecting their proposal. I may demand that you give up the use of my property if you do not accept some proposal of mine, but I may not demand that you give up the use of *your* property.

2. *Explicit dissent trumps alleged implicit consent.* A valid implicit agreement does not exist if one explicitly states that one does not agree.

Consider a modification of the restaurant example from Section 2.3. Suppose that, after being seated, you tell the waitress, 'I will not pay for any food that you bring me. But I would like you to give me a veggie wrap anyway.' If the waitress then brings you the wrap, you are not obligated to pay for it. Given your statement, she could not plausibly claim that you agreed to pay for the meal.

What about the party example? I announce that anyone who remains at my party must agree to help clean up. Suppose that after my announcement, you reply, 'I do not agree.' I then ask you to leave, but you refuse and instead remain until the end of the party. Are you then obligated to help clean up? You did not agree to clean up, since you explicitly stated that you did not agree (how much clearer could you have been?). Nevertheless, it is plausible that you are obligated to help clean up – not because you agreed to do so, but because I have the right to set conditions on the use of my house, including the condition that those who use it help clean it. This derives not from an agreement but from my property right over the house.

3. *An action can be taken as indicating agreement to some scheme, only if one can be assumed to believe that, if one did not take that action, the scheme would not be imposed upon one.*

Suppose that in the board meeting example, the chairman announces, 'Next week's meeting will be moved to Tuesday at ten o'clock, and I don't care what any of you have to say about it – the schedule change will happen whether you object to it or not. Now, does anyone want to object?' He pauses. No one says anything. 'Good, it's agreed', he declares. In this case, there is no valid agreement. Though the board members were given a chance

---

[10] As Otsuka (2003, 97) argues, consent may be valid even when failure to consent would have been very costly.

to object, they were also given to understand that if they objected, the schedule change would be imposed anyway. Their failure to express objections therefore cannot be taken to indicate agreement. It may simply indicate that they did not wish to waste their breath protesting something about which they had no choice.

4. *Contractual obligation is mutual and conditional.* A contract normally places both parties under an obligation to each other, and one party's rejection of his contractual obligation releases the other party from her obligation.

Suppose that you order food in a restaurant. There is an implicit agreement between you and the restaurant's owners: they provide food, and you pay them. If the waitress never brings the food, then you need not pay them; their failure to live up to their end of the deal releases you from the obligation to live up to yours. Furthermore, if one party simply communicates that they don't intend to live up to the agreement, then the other party is not obligated to live up to it either. Thus, if, after ordering food but before receiving it, you inform the waitress that you recognize no obligation to pay the restaurant, then the restaurant may conclude that you have rejected the agreement, and they need not bring you any food.

These four conditions belong to the common sense conception of consent and contracts. In the next section, I apply these principles to the putative social contract.

2.5 Is the social contract valid?

2.5.1 The difficulty of opting out

Begin with the first condition on valid agreements: all parties to a contract must have a reasonable way of opting out. What are the available means of opting out of the social contract? There is only one: one must vacate the territory controlled by the state.

Let us review some of the reasons one might have for failing to exercise this option. To leave one's country, one must generally secure the permission of some other state to enter its territory, and most states impose restrictions on immigration. In addition, some individuals lack the financial resources to move to the country of their choice. Those who can move may fail to do so due to attachments to family, friends, and home. Finally, if one moves to another country, one will merely become subject to another government. What should one do if one does not wish to consent to *any* government? Those seeking to avoid all governmental jurisdiction have three options: they may live in the ocean, move to Antarctica, or commit suicide.

In light of this, is the option of leaving the territory controlled by the state a *reasonable* way of opting out of the social contract? Some find it unreasonable because the demand is too onerous. In the words of David Hume,

> We may as well assert that a man, by remaining in a vessel, freely consents to the dominion of the master; though he was carried on board while asleep, and must leap into the ocean, and perish, the moment he leaves her.[11]

However, as discussed in Section 2.4, this is not the primary issue. The primary issue is whether one is being asked to give up something to which one has a right, as the price of rejecting the social contract. This certainly seems to be the case. If a board chairman cannot demand that board members pay him a dollar to express dissent from a proposed schedule change, how can someone be required to give up home and job and leave all friends and family behind to express disagreement with a contract?

Here is one answer: perhaps the state owns all the territory over which it claims jurisdiction. Thus, just as I may expel people from my house if they do not agree to help clean up at the end of the party, the state may expel people from *its* territory if they do not agree to obey the laws and pay taxes.

Even if we granted that the state owns its territory, it is debatable whether it may expel people who reject the social contract (compare the following: if anyone who leaves my party before it is over is doomed to die, then, one might think, I lose the right to kick people out of my party). But we need not resolve that issue here; we may instead focus on whether the state in fact owns all the territory over which it claims jurisdiction. If it does not, then it lacks the right to set conditions on the use of that land, including the condition that occupants should obey the state's laws.

For illustration, consider the case of the United States. In this case, the state's control over 'its' territory derives from (1) the earlier expropriation of that land by European colonists from the people who originally occupied it and (2) the state's present coercive power over the individual landowners who received title to portions of that territory,

---

[11] Hume 1987, 475.

handed down through the generations from the original expropriators. This does not seem to give rise to a legitimate property right on the part of the U.S. government.[12] Even if we overlook source (1), source (2), which applies to all governments, is not a legitimate basis for a property claim. Might does not make right; the mere fact that the state exercises power over the people in a certain region does not give the state a property right (nor any other kind of right) in all the land within that region.

If we could establish the state's *authority*, then the state could establish ownership of all its territory simply by promulgating a law assigning that property to itself. The law of 'eminent domain' (or 'compulsory purchase', 'resumption', or 'expropriation', depending on the country one lives in) may be interpreted as just such a law. But this is of no use to the social contract theorist, for the social contract is intended as a way of *establishing* the state's authority. The social contract theorist therefore may not presuppose the state's authority in accounting for how the social contract itself is established. If we do not assume that the state already has authority, then it is very difficult to see how the state can claim title to all the land of its citizens. And if we must assume that the state already has authority, then we do not need the social contract theory.

Chapter 1 included a story in which you take to punishing vandals and extorting payment for your services from the rest of your village. Imagine that, when you show up at your neighbor's door to collect payment, your neighbor protests that he never agreed to pay for your crime-prevention services. 'Au contraire', you respond. 'You have agreed, because you are living in your house. If you do not wish to pay me, you must leave your house.' Is this a reasonable demand? Does your neighbor's failure to leave his house show that he is obligated to pay you?

Surely not. If you have a tenant occupying *your* house, then you may demand that the tenant either purchase your protection services or vacate your house (provided that this is consistent with the existing contract, if any, that you have made with the tenant). But you have no right to demand that your neighbors leave *their* houses nor to place

---

[12] The problem of unjust history affects all or most of the world's land. It is unclear what ought to be done about this problem, when returning the land to its last rightful holders is impossible. I propose no solution to this ethical problem here; however, I assume that the principle 'whoever holds power over the population presently occupying the land has the right to control its use' lacks ethical force. At minimum, some prior defense of a government's legitimacy would seem required to establish its right to control the land.

conditions on their continued occupation of their property. Your demand that your neighbor leave his own house if he does not agree to pay you for protection does not represent a 'reasonable way of opting out' of buying your protective services. Unless the government really owns all the land that (as we usually say) its citizens own, the government would be in the same position as you in that example: it may not demand that individuals stop using their own property, nor may it set the conditions under which individuals may continue to occupy their own land.

I conclude that the first condition on valid contracts is violated by the social contract.

2.5.2 The failure to recognize explicit dissent

Let us turn to the second condition: you have not implicitly accepted a contract if you explicitly state that you do not accept it. In the case of the social contract, a small number of people have explicitly indicated their disagreement. These are the political anarchists, people who hold that there should be no government. Yet every government continues to impose laws and taxes on anarchists. However vociferously you protest against the social contract, the government will not refund your tax money nor exempt you from the laws.

There *could* be a state that recognized explicit dissent. The social contract for such a state would be closer to being valid – it would at least not violate this second principle of valid agreements. But actual states violate this condition and thus fail to have genuine authority over at least some of those over whom they claim authority. This does not prevent these states from having authority over *other* citizens, if those other citizens have somehow voluntarily consented. But the state's well-known refusal to recognize explicit dissent calls into question the validity of any tacit consent allegedly given even by those who have not explicitly expressed dissent. Even for those who would not in fact wish to dissent, it remains true that they were not given the *option* of explicitly turning down the social contract.

2.5.3 Unconditional imposition

The third principle about valid agreements was that an action can be taken as indicating a person's agreement to some scheme only if that person can reasonably be assumed to believe that, if he did not take that action, then the scheme would not be imposed on him. This rules out nearly all of the ways in which citizens are said to implicitly accept the social contract.

Almost everyone knows that the state will still impose the same laws and the same taxes on one, regardless of whether one objects to the government, accepts government services, or participates in the political process. Therefore, one's failure to object, one's acceptance of government services, and even one's participation in the political process cannot be taken to imply agreement to the social contract.

The one form of implicit consent not ruled out by this principle is consent through presence. If you cease to reside in the territory controlled by the state, then and only then will the state cease to impose its laws on you.[13] Unlike all the other alleged ways of implicitly consenting to be governed, remaining present in the state's territory really is a condition of having the state's laws imposed on you. Thus, only consent through presence satisfies the third principle about valid agreements. The idea of consent through presence, however, has been rejected above on other grounds.

2.5.4 The absence of mutual obligation

Finally, we come to the fourth principle concerning valid agreements: a contract imposes mutual obligations on the parties, with each party's obligation conditional on the other party's acceptance of its obligation.

In the case of the social contract, individuals are supposed to be obligated to obey the laws promulgated by the state. Sometimes citizens violate those laws, in which case the state's agents – if they are aware of the violation and can spare the resources – will punish the citizen, usually with fines or imprisonment. Given the wide and indefinite range of laws that might be created by the state and the range of punishments to which one might be subjected for violating them, an individual's concessions to the state under the social contract are quite large.

The state, in turn, is supposed to assume an obligation to the citizen, to enforce the citizen's rights, including protecting the citizen from criminals and hostile foreign governments. Does the state ever fail in this duty? What happens when it does?

In one sense, the state fails all the time. In any large society, thousands or millions of citizens are victimized each year by crimes that the state failed to prevent. But it would be unreasonable to expect the state to prevent all crimes. Perhaps the social contract only requires the state to make a *reasonable effort* to prevent crimes. But what if the state

---

[13] Even to this there are some exceptions. For instance, U.S. citizens living abroad may still be required to pay U.S. taxes on some of their income.

fails to do even that? Suppose you are a victim of a serious crime that the government could easily have prevented, at little cost, had it made a reasonable effort to do so. Would the state then have failed in its obligations under the social contract?

If the social contract means anything, then the answer to that question must be yes. If there is a contract between the state and its citizens, then the state must have some obligation to do something for the citizens. Since protection from crime is the most central and widely recognized function of the state, the state must presumably have some obligation in regard to protecting one from crime. If this obligation is meaningful at all, then there must be *something* the state could do that would count as failing to meet the obligation. And if the situation described in the preceding paragraph does not count as a failure to meet the obligation of protecting a citizen from crime, then it is hard to see what would.

In the United States, that situation has occurred many times. I describe one such instance below. Though the story is disturbing to hear, there is an important point to be learned from it.

On a morning in March 1975, two men broke into a town house in Washington, DC, where three women resided.[14] The two women upstairs heard the break-in and heard their roommate's screams coming from downstairs. They telephoned the police and were told that help was on the way. The two women crawled out of a window onto an adjoining roof and waited. They observed a police car drive by and then leave. Another officer had knocked on the front door but, receiving no answer and seeing no signs of forced entry, decided to leave. The police did not check the back entrance to the house, where the criminals had actually broken in. Going back inside, the women upstairs again heard their roommate screaming, and they again telephoned the police. They were assured that help was on the way, but in fact no officers were ever dispatched to respond to the second call. When their roommate's screams stopped, the two women upstairs thought the police had arrived. They called down to their roommate, which served only to alert the criminals to their presence. The two criminals then kidnapped the three women and took them back to one of the criminal's apartments, where they beat, robbed, and raped the women over the course of fourteen hours.

---

[14] The incident is the basis for the case of *Warren v. District of Columbia* (444 A.2d. 1, D.C. Ct. of Ap., 1981), from which derives my account of the facts.

What is notable about this case is not just that the state failed tragically in its obligation to protect some of its citizens. More important for the social contract theory is what happened afterwards. The women sued the District of Columbia in federal court, for the government's negligent failure to protect them. If the government had a contractual obligation to make a reasonable effort to protect its citizens, then the women should have had a clear-cut case. In fact, the judges dismissed the case without a trial. The plaintiffs appealed, but the dismissal was upheld.

Why? No one disputed the government's negligence, and no one disputed that the women had suffered great harm as a direct result of that negligence. What the court denied was that the government had any duty to provide protection to the three women in the first place. The Appeals Court cited 'the fundamental principle that a government and its agents are under no general duty to provide public services, such as police protection, to any particular individual citizen'. The government's duty, the court explained, was only a duty *to the public at large*, to provide a general deterrent to crime. The court worried that the recognition of a duty to protect *individuals* 'would effectively bring the business of government to a speedy halt' and 'dispatch a new generation of litigants to the courthouse over grievances real and imagined'.[15]

This was not an idiosyncratic decision. In another case, a woman telephoned the police because her estranged husband had just called her and told her that he was coming over to murder her. The police told her to call back when he arrived. When he arrived, the woman was unable to call back because her husband carried out his threat.[16] In a third case, the Department of Social Services was monitoring a man for abuse of his son. On five occasions, a DSS social worker recorded evidence of abuse, but the child was left in his father's custody. Eventually, the man beat his son so severely that the child suffered permanent brain damage.[17] These cases, too, resulted in lawsuits against the government, and these suits, too, were summarily dismissed. The child abuse case was appealed to the U.S. Supreme Court, which upheld the dismissal. Again, the courts held that the government owed no duty to protect the citizens in these cases.

---

[15] Ibid., from the majority opinion.

[16] *Hartzler v. City of San Jose*, 46 Cal.App. 3d 6 (1975).

[17] *DeShaney v. Winnebago County Department of Social Services*, 489 U.S. 189 (1989).

How do these cases bear on the social contract doctrine? The courts in these cases denied that the state has any obligation to the individual. Since a contract generally requires mutual obligation of the parties to one another, this implies that there is no contract between the individual and the state.

What of the suggestion that the state's obligation is owed to the public at large rather than to any individual? One problem with this suggestion is that it is purely arbitrary. There is no actual evidence for the suggestion, and one might be forgiven for suspecting that the state simply declares that the social contract requires only whatever the state itself wants to do. The other problem is that the social contract theory is meant to explain why individuals are obligated to obey the state. If an individual is not a party to the social contract, then the individual has no duty to the state under that contract. If the contract somehow holds only between the state and the public at large, then perhaps 'the public at large' owes something to the state, but no individual does. If, on the other hand, the social contract holds between the individual and the state, then the state must have an obligation to the individual. One cannot have it both ways: one cannot maintain that the individual owes duties to the state but that the state owes nothing to the individual.[18]

Perhaps the court opinions in these cases were mistaken. Be that as it may, opinions that are rendered by the courts, reaffirmed, and never overturned are the official positions of the government. The government, then, has officially, explicitly adopted the position that it has no obligation to protect any particular citizen. Thus, the government has repudiated the social contract. If the state rejects the social contract, then individuals cannot be taken to be obligated under that contract either.

This last argument, the argument from mutual obligation, applies specifically to the United States, where the court cases discussed occurred. Other governments might escape this particular defect if they recognize an affirmative duty to protect their citizens.

My claim in this section has not been that most people would not agree to have a government. My claim is that there is in fact no valid

---

[18] One might claim that the social contract holds between the individual and the state, but that the state's only promise to the individual was to protect society in general. Typically, however, when individuals make contracts to obtain goods or services, they obtain a promise to be personally given the good, not a promise that society in general will be more or less supplied with the good.

agreement. Perhaps you would have accepted the social contract if you had been given a choice. But you were not. This makes your relationship with the government a nonvoluntary, noncontractual one, regardless of whether you are actually happy with the relationship. Nor do I claim that all nonvoluntary relationships are morally illegitimate or unjust. The point is simply that the social contract theory is false, because it depicts a nonvoluntary relationship as voluntary.

2.6 Conclusion

The social contract theory cannot account for political authority. The theory of an actual social contract fails because no state has provided reasonable means of opting out – means that do not require dissenters to assume large costs that the state has no independent right to impose. All modern states, in refusing to recognize explicit dissent, render their relationships with their citizens nonvoluntary. Most accounts of implicit consent fail, because nearly all citizens know that the government's laws would be imposed upon them regardless of whether they performed the particular acts by which they allegedly communicate consent. In the case of those governments that deny any obligation to protect individual citizens, the contract theory fails for the additional reason that, if there ever was a social contract, the government has repudiated its central obligation under the contract, thereby releasing its citizens from the obligations they would have had under that contract.

The central moral premise of the traditional social contract theory is commendable: human interaction should be carried out, as far as possible, on a voluntary basis. But the central factual premise flies in the face of reality: whatever else may be said about it, subjection to government is obviously not voluntary. In modern times every human being is born under this subjection and has no practical means of escaping it.

3
The Hypothetical Social Contract Theory

3.1 Arguments from hypothetical consent

As we have seen, the traditional claim that individuals have consented to the state cannot plausibly be defended. Hypothetical social contract theorists turn instead to the claim that individuals *would* consent to the state under certain hypothetical conditions.[1] These conditions may involve stipulations regarding the knowledge, degree of rationality, and motivations of the parties to the social contract, in addition to the stipulation that all members of a society be given a choice as to what sort of society they shall live in. The fact that we would have agreed to a given arrangement in a particular hypothetical scenario is thought to legitimize that arrangement and generate obligations to support it. This approach has the dialectical advantage of avoiding the sort of dependence on empirical facts about the actual world that proved the downfall of the traditional social contract theory.

Defenders of any hypothetical social contract theory must complete two tasks: first, they must show that people would accept the social contract in their hypothetical scenario; second, they must show that this hypothetical consent is morally efficacious, in the sense that it generates obligations and ethical entitlements similar to those generated by valid actual consent.

---

[1] Most modern hypothetical contract theories are meant to explain something broader than political authority. Typically, they aim to account for the part of morality that concerns, in the words of Scanlon (1998, 7), what we owe to each other. For the purposes of the present chapter, I shall suppose the theories of such contemporary thinkers as Rawls and Scanlon adapted so as to account for the foundations of political authority.

3.2   Hypothetical consent in ordinary ethics

At first glance, a hypothetical agreement would seem to bear little normative import. Promises that one has made typically bind one to perform as promised, yet promises that one merely would have made under idealized circumstances do not similarly bind one. One's actual consent can give others the right to coerce one, yet consent that one merely would have given under idealized circumstances does not similarly give others the right to coerce one. Or so it seems.

However, there are circumstances under which hypothetical consent is morally efficacious, circumstances in which the fact that someone 'would have agreed' to some procedure can render it permissible to perform the procedure, where the procedure is of a type that normally requires consent. Suppose that an unconscious patient has been brought to a hospital, in need of surgery to save his life. Under ordinary circumstances, physicians must obtain the patient's informed consent before operating. In this situation, insistence on this principle would preclude the application of lifesaving medical care, as the patient is unable to either consent to or dissent from the treatment. In such a case, it is generally acknowledged that the doctors should proceed despite the lack of consent. The most natural explanation appeals to the reasonable belief that the patient *would* consent to the lifesaving procedure if he were able to do so.[2]

Might hypothetical consent have similar moral efficacy in the case of the social contract? There are two necessary conditions for the moral efficacy of hypothetical consent in such a case as that of the unconscious patient. First, the obtaining of actual consent must be impossible or unfeasible, for reasons other than the unwillingness of the other party to consent. To illustrate, imagine that a second patient arrives at the hospital, also in need of lifesaving surgery, but in this case perfectly alert and psychologically normal. If here, too, the physicians choose not to solicit the patient's consent but simply administer anesthetics and proceed with the surgical procedure they deem most beneficial, they could not justify their behavior by appealing to the likelihood of the patient's having consented had he been asked. While the truth of this hypothetical claim might mitigate the physicians' culpability,

---

[2] Waldron (1993, 49) cites this type of case in support of the moral and political relevance of hypothetical consent. Dworkin (1989, 19) discusses cases of this kind but with more skepticism about their political relevance.

it would not justify their failure to obtain actual consent, given the feasibility of doing so.

Second, when we appeal to hypothetical consent, the parties' hypothetical consent must be consistent with their relevant actual values and philosophical beliefs. Imagine that a third patient is brought into the hospital in the same condition as the first patient, unconscious and in need of surgery. But in this case the attending physician, due to his familiarity with this particular patient, is aware that the patient has strong religiously based objections to the practice of surgery, even when needed to save life. In this situation the doctor may not proceed with the surgery, in disregard of the absence of consent, on the grounds that the patient 'would have consented'. It is always possible to conceive circumstances under which any given individual would consent to any given procedure – in the present case, for example, the patient would have consented *if* he lost his religious beliefs. But hypotheticals that require alterations of subjects' fundamental beliefs and values – even if some of those beliefs and values are misguided – are irrelevant to establishing morally efficacious hypothetical consent. In the present case, the ethically controlling hypothetical judgment is the judgment that the patient would not have consented to receive surgery if he were asked in relatively normal circumstances, with his actual philosophical, religious, and moral beliefs intact.

This is not to deny that there might exist circumstances under which paternalistic coercion is justified; it is only to deny that coercion is ever justified in virtue of hypothetical consent where the hypothetical consent depends upon imagined fundamental alterations of subjects' beliefs and values.[3]

In light of these conditions, the hypothetical social contract cannot be accepted as valid. To begin with, the citizens of a given country, by and large, are neither unconscious nor mentally incompetent nor otherwise unable to either consent to or dissent from the social contract, nor is it unfeasible for the state to solicit their consent. One reason why modern states refrain from soliciting such consent may be that they are

---

[3] Mill (1978, chapter V, 95) adduces a case in which a bystander coercively restrains a man from riding across a bridge that the bystander but not the rider knows to be unsafe. Here, it seems reasonable to appeal to the judgment that the rider would probably consent to being stopped if he knew the state of the bridge – despite the fact that this hypothetical envisions an alteration of the rider's beliefs. It is in light of such cases that I have included qualifiers such as 'fundamental' and 'religious, philosophical, and moral' before 'beliefs' in this discussion.

not prepared to exempt those who would withhold their consent from the demands of taxation and other legal requirements. But this consideration surely does not license an appeal to hypothetical consent in this case, any more than a physician could legitimately dispense with a patient's actual consent to a medical procedure on the grounds that the physician was unwilling to desist in the event that the patient actually rejected the recommended treatment.

Second, agreement on any social contract would require modifications of the philosophical beliefs and values of at least some citizens. Among the individuals on whom government is imposed are some who, on philosophical grounds, oppose the general form or style of government to which they are subject in favor of some other sort of government. Others oppose all forms of government in favor of some form of political anarchism. Agreement on a social contract specifying even very general features of the sort of government to be adopted would require these individuals to renounce important philosophical beliefs and values to which they are actually committed. Perhaps some justification could be devised for imposing a form of government on these individuals without their consent, but certainly the claim that they would have consented does not succeed.

3.3 Hypothetical consent and reasonableness

3.3.1 Hypothetical agreement as evidence of reasonableness

On some philosophers' views, when a strictly voluntary system is unfeasible, an acceptable approximation may be a system about which no one has any *reasonable complaint*.[4] And the fact that a political system would be the focus of an agreement by reasonable persons under ideal conditions of deliberation might be thought to show that no one has a reasonable complaint about it.

In imagining the conditions under which this hypothetical agreement occurs, we may suppose some actual characteristics of human beings altered. For instance, we may assume that the parties to the agreement are better informed and better at reasoning than most actual people. We may assume them to be both rational and reasonable, where 'reasonable' persons are understood as being concerned to make a fair agreement with others, provided that others are likewise disposed.

---

[4] Nagel (1991, 33–40) advances this suggestion, applying Scanlon's (1998) contractual theory of morality to the problem of political legitimacy.

Reasonable persons, thus, do not attempt to insist on an agreement that serves only themselves; they are willing to take account of the claims of others to reach an agreement acceptable to all.

Nevertheless, we must not imagine the parties to the hypothetical agreement as being too different from actual human beings, lest the hypothetical agreement lose its justificatory force. For example, we should take no interest in a hypothetical agreement that could be reached only after all have converted to the one true religion. We must accept the fact that reasonable people have persistent religious differences and, more generally, persistent philosophical differences, and we must seek a focus for agreement despite those differences. Hypothetical contract theorists have explicitly embraced this point, avowing that their aim is to provide justification that applies to all reasonable people.[5]

3.3.2   Could agreement be reached?

Advocates of the sort of contract theory just described have offered no evidence or reasoning to show that some particular political system would be agreed upon by all reasonable persons. Though these theorists exert considerable effort to describe the conditions that they believe would establish the legitimacy of a political system, they make no serious effort to show that any political system satisfies those conditions. One possible explanation for this omission is that, in fact, no government satisfies the conditions for legitimacy.

Thomas Nagel provides one example of the pattern. After describing the idea of a hypothetical agreement, Nagel proceeds to the question of how much the well-off members of society should be expected to give by way of aid to the worst off. At one extreme is the view that they need give little or nothing; at the opposite extreme is the view that they must give nearly everything they have. Both of these extremes he finds unreasonable. But, he concedes, there is a substantial interme-diate range in which any principle could reasonably be rejected, either by the poor or by the wealthy; hence, no unanimous agreement would be possible with respect to the principles of distributive justice.[6] Nagel goes on to raise the possibility that we might alter our motivations in such a way that the conditions for legitimacy would become satisfiable in the future.

In his later work, John Rawls takes a view similar to Nagel's view of the conditions for political legitimacy, though he seems more sanguine

---

[5] Scanlon 1998, 5, 208–9; Nagel 1991, 36; Rawls 2005, 137.
[6] Nagel 1991, 50–2.

about the prospects for agreement. Rawls's optimism, however, is without justification.[7] He describes at length how it is conceivable that his own theory of justice should be the focus for a consensus among individuals with differing religious, moral, and philosophical views. These differing views might all turn out to support a single political conception. Following the exposition of this logical possibility, one might anticipate the presentation of evidence that the possibility is realized in some actual society. Such evidence might take the form, for example, of a series of arguments, each starting from tenets of a widely held religion, moral system, or philosophical system and each concluding in the central principles of Rawls's theory of justice. No arguments of this kind are to be found in Rawls's work, nor is any other form of evidence for the conclusion that every reasonable comprehensive doctrine supports Rawls's theory of justice.

The closest Rawls comes to arguing that some religious doctrine supports his theory is in his discussion of religious toleration, where he cites John Locke's *Letter Concerning Toleration* in illustration of why religious thinkers may support toleration.[8] In fact, Locke, while tolerant for his time, was highly intolerant by modern standards, explicitly rejecting the idea of toleration for atheists and those who profess socially destructive ideas.[9] That observation aside, the more serious difficulty is that what Rawls seeks to provide in this passage falls far short of what his theory needs. What is needed is an argument that all reasonable persons would agree to all the major tenets of Rawls's system; what Rawls provides is an explanation of a way in which a follower of one religion could reasonably support one of Rawls's principles of justice.

The closest Rawls comes to arguing that a comprehensive secular moral theory supports his political conception of justice is in his discussion of utilitarianism, where he suggests that utilitarians might consider his theory of justice to achieve an acceptable approximation to utility maximization.[10] This suggestion, however, is left as no more than that; no argument is presented to show that Rawls's theory of justice in fact provides an acceptable approximation to the maximization of utility.

Thus far, therefore, the hypothetical contract theory appears less a grounding for political legitimacy than a promissory note for such a grounding. In essence, the theory requires that all *A*s be *B*, and the

---

[7] See Huemer 1996, responding to (an earlier edition of) Rawls 2005.
[8] Rawls 2005, 145, especially note 12, citing Locke 1990.
[9] Locke 1990, 64, 61.
[10] Rawls 2005, 170.

theorist's defense consists in explaining how it is conceptually possible that there should be an *A* that is *B*.

Nagel and Rawls both addressed themselves chiefly to principles of distributive justice, a highly contentious area.[11] Perhaps we will have more success in defending hypothetical consent if we limit ourselves to the general agreement to have a government.

There is some reason to doubt that an agreement, whether hypothetical or actual, on the bare claim that society should have some form of government would suffice to confer authority on any particular government. If an individual agrees that there should be government but believes that it should be of a fundamentally different kind from the government he in fact finds himself subject to, it is doubtful that that government can adequately justify itself to that citizen by citing the mere fact that he agrees that there should be some form of government. An analogous case is one in which an individual wishes to have his house painted white, and a painter arrives and, without the consent of the homeowner, paints the house green. The fact that the individual would have consented to have his house painted some color by some painter does not entitle that painter to paint the house that color. When hiring a painter to paint his house, the homeowner need not consent to every detail of the painter's performance, but he must at least consent to the most important features thereof, including the identity of the painter, the color of the paint, and the price to be paid. Similarly, consent to the social contract need not include consent to every detail of the state's structure and operation, but it must at least include consent to the basic form and most important governing principles of the state.[12]

Unfortunately, even this basic level of agreement seems unattainable. Just as there are seemingly intractable disagreements about religion, philosophy, morality, and particular policy issues, so there are seemingly intractable disagreements about the general form, structure, and guiding principles of government. There is no reason to think that all reasonable people will achieve agreement on the basic principles of government any sooner than they reach agreement on the correct religion, the correct moral theory, and so on.

---

[11] For a preliminary indication of the diversity of conceptions of distributive justice, see Rawls 1999; Cohen 1992; Harsanyi 1975; and Nozick 1974.

[12] Gaus (2003, 216–17) argues that political legitimacy requires agreement among all reasonable persons on general principles, though disagreements on the interpretation of those principles may remain. He mistakenly assumes that agreement on general principles is common.

In fact, there remain thoughtful and reasonable individuals who believe that the optimal social organization would contain no government at all.[13] That these individuals remain a minority of society is of little comfort to hypothetical social contract theorists who aim at showing that all reasonable people would agree to the social contract. Anarchist thinkers do not, as a rule, appear particularly less rational, informed, or reasonable than partisans of other political views. They do not, for example, refuse to offer reasons for their views, refuse to consider objections, or refuse to take into account the interests of others. It is therefore difficult to identify any non-question-begging rationale for excluding them from the class of people whose agreement is sought. Unless anarchists are to be simply excluded from the agreement, hypothetical social contract theorists owe us an account of how political anarchists could be convinced to accept government.

It might be thought that I am imposing excessively strict standards for the justification of social arrangements. Surely the mere fact that someone, even a reasonable person, disagrees with a particular practice or institution does not suffice to show that the practice or institution is unjustified. The dissenter may simply be mistaken.

In reply, what I have been applying is a constraint, not on the justification of social theories in general, but on the justification of social theories *through an appeal to hypothetical consent*, and this constraint derives not from my own philosophical views but from those of my opponents, the hypothetical social contract theorists who claim that hypothetical consent establishes reasonableness. It is these theorists who have laid down as a condition of legitimacy that all reasonable people agree on a given social arrangement. It is, therefore, not I but such hypothetical contract theorists as Rawls, Scanlon, and Nagel who have in effect granted the reasonable anarchist's veto.

3.3.3 The validity of hypothetical consent

The hypothetical social contract faces another problem: even if it could be shown that all reasonable people would agree to some system of government, this fact would not establish political authority.

The legitimacy of a political system is a matter of the permissibility of imposing that system on all the members of a given society.

---

[13] See Rothbard (1978); Friedman (1989); Barnett (1998); Wolff (1998); Chomsky (2005); Sartwell (2008). In Stringham 2007, see the papers by the Tannehills, Barnett, Friedman, Hoppe, Rogers and Lavoie, Long, Hasnas, Childs, Cuzán, Caplan and Stringham, de Jasay, Leeson and Stringham, and Anderson and Hill.

It is, in part, a matter of the permissibility of intentionally, coercively harming those who disobey the rules produced by the system. The hypothetical social contract theory, on the present interpretation, offers the following candidate justification for this sort of coercion: one may coercively impose an arrangement on individuals, provided that the individuals would be unreasonable to reject the arrangement.

This principle stands in stark conflict with common sense morality. Imagine that an employer approaches a prospective employee with an entirely fair, reasonable, and attractive job offer, including generous pay, reasonable hours, pleasant working conditions, and so on. If the worker were fully informed, rational, and reasonable, he would accept the employment offer. Nevertheless, the employer is not ethically entitled to coerce the employee into working for him in the event that the employee, however unreasonably, declines the offer. The reasonableness of the offer, together with hypothetical consent, would bear very little ethical weight, at most slightly mitigating the wrongness of imposing forced labor.

Similar judgments apply to other exercises of coercion that would normally require consent: it is not permissible for a physician to coercively impose a medical procedure on a patient, even if the patient was unreasonable to refuse the treatment; nor for a vendor to extort money from a customer, even if the customer was unreasonable to refuse to buy the vendor's product; nor for a boxer to compel another boxer to fight, even if the latter was unreasonable to reject the offer of a match.

Similar remarks apply to the issue of political obligation. The unreasonableness of rejecting an arrangement does not suffice to generate an obligation to comply with the arrangement. The worker in the above example is entitled to refuse the offer of employment, unreasonable though this refusal may be.

Contrasting intuitions may be drawn from another analogy. A shipwreck has stranded a number of people on a hitherto uninhabited island. The island has a limited supply of wild game, which may be hunted for food but must be conserved against extinction. Assume that the only reasonable plan is for the shipwrecked passengers to carefully limit the number of animals harvested each week. Despite these facts, one passenger refuses to accept any such limit. It seems plausible to hold that the other passengers may coercively restrain the unreasonable passenger from excessive hunting for the benefit of all on the island. Furthermore, the reasonableness of limiting the rate of hunting and the unreasonableness of rejecting such limits seems to play a crucial role in the justification for such coercion.

What is the difference between the island case and the employment contract case? The most important difference is that the employment contract case involves the seizure of a resource, the employee's labor, to which the victim of coercion has a moral right; whereas the island case involves the protection of a resource, the wild game, over which it is plausible to ascribe a collective right, held only partly by the coercee but mostly by the coercers. The unreasonable passenger in the latter case lacks any moral right to decide unilaterally on the use or distribution of the wild game, in the way that an individual has a moral right to decide on the use of his own labor.

If we accept this account of the cases, the hypothetical social contract is more like the rejected employment contract, for the social contract concerns, perhaps among other things, the coercive redistribution of resources that individuals have rights over. Among other things, the state lays claim to a portion of all persons' earnings, whatever the source. (See Section 7.1.6 for further discussion of whether individuals have property rights independent of the state.) Nor is the state's coercion undertaken solely or even chiefly in the service of protecting collective resources. Often, the state deploys coercion in the service of paternalistic, moralistic, or charitable ends or for the sake of providing indirect economic benefits for small segments of society at the expense of others.[14] No private individual or organization would be considered entitled to use coercion for these sorts of purposes, however reasonable his plans.

Here as elsewhere, our attitudes toward government differ from our attitudes toward other agents. The unreasonableness of rejection clearly does not license a private individual to force the terms of some contract upon another individual. Yet the unreasonableness of rejecting the social contract is thought to license the state to force the terms of that contract on its citizens. What the hypothetical contract theory gives, then, is another example of the particularly lenient moral attitudes applied to government rather than a justification of those attitudes. One must begin by ascribing some special moral status to the state to believe the state morally entitled to force an arrangement on individuals merely because they would be unreasonable to reject the arrangement.

---

[14] See Section 5.4.2, for a more complete taxonomy of governmental activities.

3.4   Hypothetical consent and ethical constraints

3.4.1   Rawls's contract theory as an account of authority

John Rawls is, by far and without question, the most influential political philosopher of the last hundred years. As a rough indicator, a search for the keyword 'Rawls' in the Philosopher's Index yields more than 2,000 hits for articles and books published between 1990 and 2011. He is chiefly known for the hypothetical social contract theory of *A Theory of Justice*. It is therefore of great interest to investigate what that theory can teach us about political authority.

Rawls devises a hypothetical scenario, the 'original position', in which individuals form an agreement on the basic principles to govern their society.[15] These individuals are assumed to be motivated solely by self-interest, but they have temporarily been deprived of all knowledge of their position in society and indeed of any other personal information about themselves, including their race, sex, religion, social class, and so on.[16] This condition, known as the 'veil of ignorance', prevents the parties from tailoring the chosen political principles to their own advantage; being ignorant of what one's position in society will be, one must endeavor to devise principles that are fair to everyone. Rawls goes on to argue that people in this original position would choose two particular principles of justice to govern their society.[17] He concludes that people should in fact adopt those principles. (I omit here discussion of Rawls's two principles of justice and the reasoning leading to them. My present concern is whether Rawls's argumentative strategy can be deployed to defend political authority.)

---

[15] Rawls 1999. This sort of thought experiment was first used to derive principles of distributive justice by Harsanyi (1953; 1955), who argued that the thought experiment supported utilitarianism.

[16] Rawls (1999, 12, 111) distinguishes his assumption of 'mutual disinterestedness' from an assumption of egoism. However, his distinction rests on the mistaken assumption that only desires for such things as wealth, power, and prestige count as 'egoistic' or 'selfish'. Serious ethical egoists reject that assumption (Hunt 1999).

[17] At the end of *A Theory of Justice* (1999, 509), Rawls discusses what principles would be chosen in the original position if the parties had a more complete list of possible principles to choose from rather than the short list that Rawls considers earlier in the book: 'I doubt, however, that the principles of justice (as I have defined them) will be the preferred conception on anything resembling a complete list.' However, I shall set aside this apparent admission that Rawls's principles of justice are not supported by his own argumentative strategy.

Though Rawls does not directly address the need for government in general, one could devise a Rawlsian argument for political authority. It might be said that the parties in the original position would prefer to establish some form of government rather than accept anarchy. If one could make a compelling argument for this claim, would this suffice to establish political authority?

If a Rawlsian hypothetical contract is capable of justifying principles of justice, it is plausible to think that such a contract could also justify government in general. But how is the hypothetical contract thought to justify principles of justice? Rawls offers the following remarks:

> Since all are similarly situated [in the original position] and no one is able to design principles to favor his particular condition, the principles of justice are the result of a fair agreement or bargain.[18]

> [The chosen principles of justice] express the result of leaving aside those aspects of the social world that seem arbitrary from a moral point of view.[19]

> The idea here is simply to make vivid to ourselves the restrictions that it seems reasonable to impose on arguments for principles of justice, and therefore on these principles themselves. Thus it seems reasonable and generally acceptable that no one should be advantaged or disadvantaged by natural fortune or social circumstances in the choice of principles. It also seems widely agreed that it should be impossible to tailor principles to the circumstances of one's own case. We should insure further that particular inclinations and aspirations, and persons' conceptions of their good do not affect the principles adopted. ... At any time we can enter the original position, so to speak, simply by following a certain procedure, namely, by arguing for principles of justice in accordance with these restrictions.[20]

> It is natural to ask why, if this agreement is never actually entered into, we should take any interest in these principles. ... The answer is that the conditions embodied in the description of the original position are ones that we do in fact accept. Or if we do not, then perhaps we can be persuaded to do so by philosophical reflection.[21]

---

[18] Rawls 1999, 11.
[19] Ibid., 14.
[20] Ibid., 16–17; cf. 119–20.
[21] Ibid., 19.

These remarks merit close scrutiny, as they form the lynchpin for Rawls's version of social contract theory, by far the most influential theory in contemporary political philosophy. The passages above represent Rawls's entire account of how the hypothetical contract justifies moral or political principles.[22] It would therefore be difficult to overstate the importance to political philosophy of a clear understanding of these few passages.

At least two strands of argument can be found in those passages. The first appeals to direct constraints on putative principles of justice. Rawls mentions two important constraints of this sort: first, principles of justice should be fair to all members of society, treating all members as equals. Second, principles of justice should 'leave aside' or, more strongly, compensate for aspects of the social world that are arbitrary from a moral point of view, such as the situation of individuals' receiving benefits or burdens as a result of mere good or bad luck.

The second strand of argument appeals to constraints on *arguments* about justice. In the third quotation, Rawls suggests that, rather than envisioning a scenario involving people ignorant of their identity deliberating about the rules of their future society, one could achieve the same result simply by reasoning about justice in accordance with certain restrictions – namely, that one avoid being influenced, in the arguments or principles one accepts, by anyone's natural fortune or social circumstances; that one avoid tailoring the principles of justice that one accepts to one's own case; and that one avoid being influenced by particular inclinations or a particular conception of one's good. The original position is nothing but an imaginative device for inducing us to think in this way.[23]

Below, I shall return to the question of whether this justification for the use of the original position succeeds. For now, I consider what, if anything, would emerge from the original position.

3.4.2   Could agreement be reached?

Why does Rawls believe that the parties in the original position could reach agreement rather than persistently disagreeing, as people do in the actual world? The reason is simple: '[S]ince the differences among

---

[22] Rawls devotes §4 in *A Theory of Justice* to the argument, which he restates in Rawls 1985, 236–9, and Rawls 2001, 17–18. None of these passages contains any significant additional detail beyond the quotations reproduced in the text.

[23] Rawls emphasizes this idea more strongly in his 1985, 236–9.

the parties are unknown to them, and everyone is equally rational and similarly situated, each is convinced by the same arguments'.[24]

Rawls's conclusion does not follow from his stated premises. Rawls assumes that, once all particular inclinations and all individual characteristics (or knowledge thereof) are excised, all reasonable and rational people will be convinced by the same arguments. This assumption rests on a particular diagnosis of the phenomenon of widespread intellectual disagreement: that such disagreement is due entirely to such factors as ignorance, irrationality, and biases created by knowledge of one's individual characteristics.[25] If that diagnosis is correct, then a situation in which such ignorance, irrationality, and bias are removed should result in general agreement. But if the diagnosis is not correct and there are other sources of disagreement, then Rawls has given no reason for believing that agreement would be reached in the original position.

How plausible is Rawls's implicit diagnosis of disagreement? While much disagreement is doubtless due to irrationality, ignorance, and personal bias, it is unlikely that all disagreement is to be explained in these ways. Outside political philosophy, philosophers carry on persistent debates in epistemology, ethics, and metaphysics, some of which are millennia old. The partisans in these debates commonly appear equally rational, well informed, and intelligent. None appear to be attempting to tailor their theories to their own circumstances nor to be illicitly relying on personal information about themselves, if indeed such transgressions would be possible in these areas. Nevertheless, philosophers manifestly fail to find the same arguments convincing. It is therefore difficult to escape the conclusion that the human mind is subject to sources of differing judgment apart from irrationality, ignorance, and personal bias. And whatever these sources of disagreement may be, if they operate in epistemology, ethics, and metaphysics, it is not plausible to assume that they are absent from political philosophy.

A more plausible diagnosis of widespread and persistent philosophical disagreements is that human beings experience differing intuitions and other intellectual appearances. When we contemplate

---

[24] Rawls 1999, 120.

[25] In his later work, Rawls seems to renounce this diagnosis, recognizing disagreement as the natural result of the free exercise of human reason (2005, 36–7, 54–8). Nevertheless, the diagnosis is required by his argument in *A Theory of Justice*.

theories and arguments, we differ in the degree of plausibility we see in them, independent of whether and how our personal interests differ. Individuals with differing philosophical intuitions and plausibility judgments will, understandably and rationally, reach differing philosophical positions.[26] Nor can these intellectual appearances simply be stipulated away, since some sense of what is plausible is essential to any sophisticated thinking process of the sort involved in philosophical reasoning. A being with no philosophical intuitions would not therefore achieve a particularly unassailable philosophical position; it would simply be unable to evaluate philosophical positions.

Consider now one disagreement of particular interest, the disagreement between anarchists and statists about the necessity of government.[27] There is no reason for thinking that this disagreement would evaporate behind the veil of ignorance, because Rawls has given no reason for thinking that those who in fact hold either of these views do so only because they are relying on knowledge of their particular position in society. Anarchists do not disagree with statists because anarchists have some peculiar social position or combination of personal traits that somehow would enable them to prosper in the absence of government while the rest of society fell apart. If the anarchists are correct in their factual beliefs, then some stateless system would be better for society as a whole than a governmental system; if they are wrong, then it would be worse for everyone, anarchists included. Whatever explains this particular disagreement, it is not that someone is tailoring moral or political principles to his own advantage.

In appealing to this example, note that I do not presuppose that political anarchism is *correct*; I assume only that there are *reasonable* political anarchists (myself included, I should like to think). It is for the hypothetical contract theorist to demonstrate that there are not. Nor do I presuppose that political legitimacy requires agreement on all details of policy. But presumably agreement on whether there should be a state is the minimum that any social contract theory requires.

---

[26] In Huemer 2007, I argue that all rational beliefs are based on how things seem to the believer. See Huemer 2005, chapter 5, on the role of intuition in ethics in particular. See Huemer 2011 on the role of agent-centered epistemic norms in explaining rational disagreement. But see Hanson and Cowen (2004) for a competing view.

[27] I use 'statism' for the view that government ought to exist; that is, the alternative to political anarchism.

3.4.3 The validity of hypothetical consent, part 1: the appeal to fair outcomes

I turn next to the question of the moral efficacy of hypothetical consent. I mentioned earlier that one way of reading Rawls's justification for the original position is as an appeal to direct constraints on principles of justice, in particular the constraints that principles of justice should be fair to everyone and that they should rectify moral arbitrariness in the distribution of advantages. Can that approach be used to defend political authority?

Imagine that Sue makes an offer to buy Joe's car. Given the facts about the car's condition, Sue's and Joe's respective situations, and so on, Sue's offer is entirely fair to both parties, not biased in either party's favor. A perfectly rational, fully informed, reasonable owner would accept the offer. Nevertheless, Joe refuses to sell. Is it plausible that Joe has acted wrongly? Or that Sue may force Joe to sell?

Imagine next that by pure chance, Joe has discovered a diamond in his backyard, which confers on him a material advantage of which Sue, through no fault of her own, is deprived. Since the moral arbitrariness of the resulting distribution of wealth could be rectified by a suitable wealth transfer, is Joe morally obligated to give Sue half the value of the diamond? Is Sue entitled to force Joe to do so?

As these examples show, the fact that some hypothetical agreement is fair or rectifies moral arbitrariness does not in general create an obligation to act according to the hypothetical agreement, nor does it create an ethical entitlement to coerce others to follow the hypothetical agreement.

Perhaps Rawls would respond to my examples, as he once replied to another critic,[28] by observing that his principles of justice were meant to apply only to the basic structure of society rather than to small-scale interactions between individuals. There are two possible points of distinction Rawls could raise here. The first is a matter of scale: the examples of the two preceding paragraphs each involve only two individuals rather than an entire society. This difference, however, has no ethical relevance. If a very large corporation makes offers to a very large number of people, the corporation's sheer size will not entitle it to force individuals to accept its offers (even if they are fair offers), any more than a single individual would be entitled to do so.

---

[28] See Rawls 1974, 141–2, responding to Harsanyi's (1975) criticisms of the maximin decision rule.

The other distinction is political: my examples involve private actors, whereas Rawls's principles prescribe action by the state. This distinction, however, cannot be employed in Rawls's defense without begging the question, since the reply simply presupposes that the state possesses some special moral status such that coercion on the part of the state is more easily justified than coercion on the part of private agents. If the state possesses political authority, then this presupposition would be correct; however, since what is sought is a justification for authority, one cannot take it for granted in this manner. Without ascribing any special moral status to the state, Rawls would have no way of restricting the proposed justification for coercion to the case of state agents. And since the appeals to fairness or the rectification of moral arbitrariness would clearly fail as justifications for private coercion, they should also be rejected as a source of political legitimacy.

As these cases show, there is a wide gap between what hypothetical agreement might plausibly be taken to establish, such as the fairness or reasonableness of some arrangement, and what the defender of political authority needs to establish: the right to impose an arrangement by force, including the right to intentionally and coercively harm those who fail to cooperate and the obligation of individuals to accede to that arrangement. While an actual agreement might establish these things, a merely hypothetical agreement cannot.[29]

3.4.4   The validity of hypothetical consent, part 2: sufficient conditions for reliable moral reasoning

The dominant strand in Rawls's defense of hypothetical contract theory appeals to constraints on reasoning about moral principles: in moral reasoning, one must avoid being influenced by self-interest, particular inclinations, or any other ethically irrelevant individual traits. The original position is but a picturesque way of putting these constraints, which we already accept, into effect.

Let *C* stand for the conjunction of all of these reasonable constraints on moral reasoning; that is, all of the constraints that are held to be embodied in Rawls's original position. Let *J* stand for any principle

---

[29] Stark's (2000) recent defense of hypothetical social contract theory concedes this point. She proposes that a hypothetical contract may 'justify' political principles in some sense, yet she denies that it can show either that one is obligated to follow these principles or that the state is entitled to enforce the principles (321, 326).

emerging from the original position; that is, a principle of justice or other moral principle that the hypothetical parties would agree upon.[30] Rawls's argument in favor of *J* might be understood as follows:

1. *J* can be arrived at by reasoning that satisfies *C*.
2. If a moral principle can be arrived at by reasoning that satisfies *C*, then it is correct.
3. Therefore, *J* is correct.

We might wish to consider variations on this argument; for instance, for 'is correct', we might substitute 'is probably correct', 'is justified', or 'ought to be adopted'. My criticisms below should be taken as applying also to any such weakened version of the argument.

Premise (1) is true by stipulation. It is unclear, however, why one ought to embrace premise (2). Though it is plausible that the constraints Rawls identifies are *necessary* conditions on the reliability or rational persuasiveness of moral reasoning, Rawls makes no attempt to show that they exhaust the conditions for reliable or rationally persuasive moral arguments. Indeed, he expressly aims at keeping the assumptions of the original position as weak as possible consistent with the scenario's having a determinate outcome,[31] which coheres with the aim of ensuring that the constraints incorporated into the original position are all necessary for the acceptability of a piece of moral reasoning. But it does not fit with the aim of ensuring that they are (collectively) *sufficient* for the acceptability of a piece of moral reasoning.

A related difficulty concerns the gap between procedural acceptability and substantive correctness. Even if Rawls succeeded in identifying all of the appropriate procedural constraints on moral arguments, a person's satisfying these constraints – failing to be biased, failing to commit fallacies, and so on – would not guarantee the correctness of his conclusions. The correctness of one's conclusions, whatever one's field of inquiry, depends partly on the correctness and completeness of the information from which one reasons. This is easily seen in examples involving scientific reasoning. Isaac Newton held mistaken

---

[30] Though he initially describes his hypothetical contract theory as a way of arriving at principles of justice (1999, sections 1–4), Rawls later appeals to the hypothetical contract as a justification for ethical principles more generally (sections 18–19, 51–2).

[31] Rawls 1999, 16, 510.

theories due, not to any procedural error in his thinking about physics, but rather to the incompleteness of his information – specifically, his ignorance of relativistic and quantum mechanical phenomena.

The same principle holds good for normative theories, where the needed information is, at least in part, evaluative. That is, one's chances of arriving at acceptable moral conclusions depend in part upon the substantive correctness and completeness of one's initial values. If a person has misguided ultimate values, such as a belief that pain is intrinsically good, or if his basic values are correct but incomplete, as in the case of one who mistakenly takes pleasure to be the sole intrinsic good, then this person will most likely arrive at incorrect normative conclusions, even if all his reasoning is perfectly procedurally acceptable, devoid of self-interested biases, and so on. Thus, to ensure that the parties in the original position arrive only at correct normative conclusions, one must endow the parties with complete and correct values, stipulating that they use these correct values in coming to their decision.

One explanation for Rawls's failure to incorporate this stipulation may be that it would require him to resolve seemingly intractable debates within moral theory about what the correct values are before he could properly characterize the original position and draw conclusions from it. This difficulty, however, does not show that Rawls is justified in omitting the condition of complete and correct values from the original position; it shows only that the prospects for using the original position to justify normative principles are dim. Only if C includes a constraint of complete and correct values is it plausible to claim that premise (2) is true, and one may not, in constructing a philosophical argument, dispense with a condition necessary for the plausibility of a premise of that argument merely because that condition interferes with one's constructing the rest of the argument. An analogy is the case of the man who has lost his keys in a dark alleyway but chooses to search for them under a street lamp because the light is better there. The difficulty of identifying the correct comprehensive ethical theory and its political implications no more prevents that information from being needed to guarantee morally correct conclusions than the difficulty of seeing in a darkened alleyway prevents one's keys from being located there.

I have read the Rawlsian argument as claiming that some principle *J* is correct or ought to be adopted. Suppose that this is weakened to the claim that it is *permissible* to adopt *J* or that *J* is not illegitimate. This may render the argument more persuasive, since it may seem less implausible that Rawls has provided sufficient conditions for the permissibility of a political arrangement than that he has provided sufficient conditions for the correctness of a political arrangement. But this weakening of the argument's conclusion does not truly avoid the problem already discussed. An adequate supply of correct basic moral premises is required to identify permissible courses of action no less than obligatory ones. Suppose, for example, that individuals have rights but that Alastair is unaware of this fact. Alastair may then be led to conclude falsely that certain actions are permissible (particularly actions that in fact violate people's rights) without committing any procedural error in his thinking. My argument here does not presuppose that there are in fact individual rights; the point is simply that one would need to know the truth about such things to be assured of reliably identifying what is permissible.

In sum, the present argument for the efficacy of hypothetical consent fails because the original position embodies only certain necessary conditions for the reliability of normative reasoning rather than sufficient conditions for the correctness of normative conclusions. If the original position is modified so as to include sufficient conditions for normative correctness, it becomes difficult or impossible to determine what principles would be agreed to.

3.4.5   The validity of hypothetical consent, part 3: necessary conditions for reliable moral reasoning

There is one remaining interpretation of Rawls's argument. On this interpretation, the conjunctive constraint C represented by the original position is held to be necessary but not sufficient for the acceptability of moral arguments. If we take this view, we may argue as follows:

1. J is *uniquely* coherent with C.
2. C is correct.
3. Therefore, J is correct.

'Coherent' in (1) should be understood as referring to whatever relation enables C to support or rule out a moral principle. Thus, (1) may mean that only J can be arrived at by reasoning in accordance with C, that the correctness of J is entailed by the correctness of C, that J satisfies C to a higher degree than any competing principle, or the like. So understood, premise (1) is a very strong claim, though I have made it no stronger than the argument form demands: if C is merely necessary but not sufficient for moral correctness, then a premise to the effect that J

coheres with *C* would not show *J* to be correct; what one must show is that no alternative principles cohere with *C*.

Premise (1) is exposed to widespread and powerful counter-evidence. There are many philosophers who appear to have reached alternative conclusions by reasoning that satisfies *C*. The various thinkers who embrace utilitarianism, egalitarianism, libertarianism, or anarchism do not in general appear to have violated any widely accepted constraints on moral reasoning, nor does Rawls anywhere endeavor to show that they have.

As a case in point, consider utilitarianism, the theory that the right action (whether for an individual or for the state) is always the action that produces the greatest total net benefits, adding together benefits for everyone affected by the action. Rawls tells us that this is the theory to which he was most concerned to provide a systematic alternative.[32] He also claims that the function of the original position is simply 'to rule out those principles that it would be rational to propose ... only if one knew certain things that are irrelevant from the standpoint of justice'.[33] Utilitarianism is surely not an example of a moral principle that makes sense to propose only if one has information irrelevant from the standpoint of justice, such as information about one's race, sex, social class, and so on. Whatever else may be said about it, utilitarianism is perhaps the one ethical theory least susceptible to charges of undue partiality. The thinking of actual utilitarians therefore appears to provide a compelling counterexample to premise (1).[34]

What argument does Rawls offer in support of (1)? In motivating the original position construction, he presents arguments that the original position embodies *C*. He also argues at great length that certain principles would be chosen in the original position.[35] But neither of these things could be thought to establish premise (1). In conjunction, they may show that there is an example of reasoning satisfying *C* – namely,

---

[32] Rawls 1999, xvii–xviii.

[33] Rawls 1999, 17.

[34] It might be said that utilitarian reasoning violates the constraint of mutual disinterestedness that Rawls incorporates into the original position (1999, 12). But this can hardly be said to represent a genuine constraint on acceptable moral reasoning, since it is not the case that one's moral reasoning is defective if one takes account of others' interests. Similarly for the suggestion that utilitarianism violates the constraint that one not rely on any conception of the good.

[35] But see Harsanyi 1975 for compelling arguments that the original position actually leads to utilitarianism.

the reasoning of the parties in the original position – that leads to *J*. But it would be fallacious to infer that there is no other possible train of reasoning satisfying *C* that leads to an alternative principle (in Aristotelian logic, this is known as the fallacy of the illicit minor).[36] And indeed, as we have seen, there are examples of reasoning satisfying *C* that are inconsistent with *J*, such as the actual reasoning of utilitarians.

3.5 Conclusion

Hypothetical agreement is normally efficacious only when (i) actual agreement cannot feasibly be solicited and (ii) it is reasonable to believe that the relevant party or parties would agree, based upon their actual general beliefs and values. These conditions are unsatisfied in the case of the hypothetical social contract.

Contemporary philosophical work suggests three ways in which a hypothetical social contract might nevertheless be thought morally relevant. First, hypothetical agreement might be thought to show that a certain social arrangement could not reasonably be rejected. This argument fails because there is no reason to believe that the required hypothetical agreement could be reached. Even if such an agreement could be reached, the mere unreasonableness of someone's rejecting an arrangement does not typically render it morally permissible to coerce that person into accepting the arrangement, nor does it impose on individuals an obligation to accept the arrangement.

Second, hypothetical agreement might be thought to show that a social arrangement is fair. Again, there is no reason to believe that a general agreement on a political system could be reached, even among equally informed, rational persons who lack knowledge of their individual identities, and in any case the mere fact that an arrangement is

---

[36] In Aristotelian logic, the 'minor term' in a syllogism is the term that appears as the subject of the conclusion. If the minor term is distributed in the conclusion, then it must be distributed in at least one premise. Roughly, this means that if the conclusion makes a claim applicable to all members of a given class, then at least one premise must contain information applicable to all members of that class. In the present case, the desired conclusion is that all moral reasoning satisfying *C* is consistent with *J* (this is a paraphrase of (1)), so the minor term is 'moral reasoning satisfying *C*', and this term is distributed in the desired conclusion. Since any claims Rawls might make about the original position would concern only one case of reasoning satisfying *C*, the minor term is undistributed in the premises.

fair does not typically render it morally permissible to coerce people into accepting the arrangement, nor does it impose on individuals an obligation to accept the arrangement.

Third, hypothetical agreement might be thought to show that a set of moral principles reflects certain reasonable constraints on moral reasoning. These constraints might be intended either as collectively sufficient conditions or merely as collectively necessary conditions on the acceptability of a piece of moral reasoning. If the constraints are to be sufficient for the acceptability of moral reasoning, they must include a condition of complete and correct values on the part of the reasoner. But this condition would render the hypothetical contract theory unusable, since one would need to determine the correct comprehensive moral theory before one could determine the content of the hypothetical agreement. If, on the other hand, one relies only on necessary conditions for the acceptability of moral reasoning, then one must argue that every political theory but one somehow violates at least one necessary condition on acceptable moral reasoning. No one has argued for that claim, and the actual reasonable disagreements among theorists seem to pose powerful counterevidence.

Thus, the move to a merely hypothetical contract cannot save the social contract theory. There is no reason to believe that agreement could be reached even in the hypothetical scenarios envisioned by most theorists nor that such hypothetical consent would be morally relevant if it could be reached.

4
The Authority of Democracy

4.1 Naive majoritarianism

Once we recognize the unfeasibility of achieving unanimous consent to any nontrivial social arrangement, we might turn instead to majority consent. Can the agreement only of a majority of society's members – whether broad agreement to have a government or agreement to have specific policies or personnel – confer authority on government?

At first glance, it is unclear how this might be thought to work. The opinions or decisions of a larger group of people do not normally suffice to impose obligations on a smaller group or an individual who does not agree with the larger group, nor do they typically justify coercive behavior on the part of the larger group.

Imagine the following scenario, which I shall call the Bar Tab example. You have gone out for drinks with a few of your colleagues and graduate students. You are all busy talking about philosophy, when someone raises the question of who is going to pay the bill. A number of options are discussed. A colleague suggests dividing the bill evenly among everyone at the table. You suggest that everyone pay for his own drinks. A graduate student then suggests that *you* pay for everybody's drinks. Reluctant to spend so much money, you decline. But the student persists: 'Let's take a vote.' To your consternation, they proceed to take the vote, which reveals that everyone at the table except you wants you to pay for everybody's drinks. 'Well, that settles it', declares the student. 'Pay up.'

Are you now ethically obligated to pay for everyone's drinks? May the others collect the money from you by force? Most will answer no to both questions. Majority will alone does not generate an entitlement to coerce the minority, nor does it generate an obligation of compliance on the part of the minority. More precisely, majority will alone does not provide sufficient backing for a proposal to override an individual's private property rights (your right to your money in this example) or right not to be subjected to harmful coercion.

This sort of example places a dialectical burden on defenders of democratic authority, a burden of identifying some special circumstances that apply to the government that account for why, in the case of government, majority support provides adequate justification for coercion, even though it does not suffice for other agents.

4.2   Deliberative democracy and legitimacy

4.2.1   The idea of deliberative democracy

Recent democratic theorists have emphasized the value of decision-making procedures in a democratic society. One recent strand of thought seeks to articulate an ideal of 'deliberative democracy' – that is, an ideal of how citizens in a democratic society ought to deliberate with each other about matters of public concern.[1] Thus, according to Joshua Cohen, ideal democratic deliberation would have the following features:[2]

1. Participants take their deliberation to be capable of determining action and to be unconstrained by any prior norms.
2. Participants offer reasons for their proposals, with the (correct) expectation that those reasons alone will determine the fate of their proposals.
3. Each participant has an equal voice.
4. The deliberation aims at consensus. However, if consensus cannot be achieved, the deliberation ends with voting.

What does this have to do with political authority? In an ideal deliberative democracy, Cohen writes, 'citizens [...] regard their basic institutions as legitimate in so far as they establish the framework for free public deliberation. [...] For them, free deliberation among equals is the basis of legitimacy.'[3] Here, Cohen is not *directly* making a claim about what is a sound basis for political legitimacy. Nor is he making a psychological or sociological claim about what actual people take to be a sound basis for legitimacy. Rather, he is stipulating that citizens in an ideal deliberative

---

[1]   Cohen 2002; Habermas 2002.
[2]   See Cohen 2002, 92–3, for a fuller description of these conditions.
[3]   Cohen 2002, 91.

democracy – a purely hypothetical scenario – take deliberation as the basis for legitimacy. I will assume, however, that Cohen himself takes some suitable deliberative process to provide a sound basis for political legitimacy.

How might democratic deliberation provide a basis for legitimacy? Cohen does not clearly explain this. Perhaps the thought is that the fairness, equality, and rationality of the decision-making procedure Cohen describes confers legitimacy on its outcomes. This is a tenuous argument – why should we assume that *any* procedure, however good, confers a content-independent, exclusive entitlement for the state to coerce people to comply with the decisions produced by that procedure? Nevertheless, let us examine this line of thought more closely.

4.2.2 Deliberative democracy as fantasy

If there is one thing that stands out when one reads philosophical descriptions of deliberative democracy, it is how far these descriptions fall from reality. Of the four features of deliberative democracy that Cohen identifies, how many are satisfied by any actual society?

Begin with Cohen's first condition. Cohen writes, 'the participants regard themselves as bound only by the results of their deliberation and by the preconditions for that deliberation. Their consideration of proposals is not constrained by the authority of prior norms or requirements.'[4] This is not true of most actual people. Actual people frequently regard themselves as bound by things other than the results of public deliberation. For instance, some believe in natural law, many believe in divinely mandated moral requirements, some believe themselves bound by a constitution that was established long ago, and so on.

According to Cohen's second condition,

> Deliberation is *reasoned* in that the parties to it are required to state their reasons for advancing proposals [...] They give reasons with the expectation that those reasons (and not, for example, their power) will settle the fate of their proposal. In ideal deliberation, as Habermas puts it, 'no force except that of the better argument is exercised.'[5]

---

[4] Cohen 2002, 92. Cohen's 'first condition' contains two parts. The first part is as stated in the text. The second part is that 'the participants suppose that they can act from the results [of their deliberation].' This part seems unobjectionable.

[5] Cohen 2002, 93 (emphasis in original). The Habermas quotation is from Habermas 1975, 108. The approving quotation of Habermas suggests that the parties to the ideal deliberation not only *believe* but *correctly* believe that only stated reasons will determine the fate of their proposals.

In actual democracies, no one is *required* (by the state or anyone else) to state their reasons for advancing policy proposals. Moreover, the quality of the reasons offered for a policy proposal is only one part of what determines the fate of that proposal, and nearly everyone knows this. The fate of policy proposals in actual democracies is determined at least as much by rhetoric as by reasoning, and rhetorical appeals are heard considerably more often than sober, rational arguments. Political outcomes are also influenced by self-interest. 'Deliberation', Cohen assures us, 'focuses debate on the common good'[6] – but in reality, competing interest groups vie for control of political processes in the hopes of using state power for selfish gain.[7] It would be extremely unusual to find citizens so naive as to think that only their stated arguments, not their political power, would determine whether their policy proposals were adopted.

Cohen's third condition requires that 'parties are both formally and substantively *equal*.' He elaborates:

> [E]ach has an equal voice in the decision. [...] [T]he existing distribution of power and resources does not shape their chances to contribute to deliberation.[8]

There is of course no actual society in which these things are true. In any modern society, a small number of individuals – journalists, authors, professors, politicians, celebrities – play a large role in public discourse, while the vast majority of individuals play essentially no role in the discourse. The vast majority of people have no realistic opportunity to make their ideas heard beyond a tiny circle of acquaintances. And the existing distribution of power and resources almost completely determines one's chances to contribute to public deliberation. Wealthy citizens can buy advertising time or even own television stations or other media outlets; poor and middle-class citizens cannot. Individuals with political power can get their views aired in the national media – the President of the United States, for example, can call a press conference at any time; I cannot. It is difficult to imagine these facts changing. As

---

6 Cohen 2002, 95.

7 Carney (2006) documents numerous cases. The main point here is, not that individual voters are selfish, but that selfish special interest groups influence voters.

8 Cohen 2002, 93.

of this writing, the United States contains over 300 million citizens. How could all of those voices be heard equally? What would society be like if every one of those individuals could call a press conference to discuss their latest policy idea?

Finally, according to Cohen's fourth condition, ideal deliberation 'aims to arrive at a rationally motivated *consensus*'.[9] This, too, is false of any actual society. In the United States, for example, there is a great deal of public discussion of such issues as abortion, gun control, and health care policy. Some participants in these discussions seek to influence citizens who remain undecided on the issue in question. Most are probably just trying to express their own feelings and opinions. Hardly any are aiming at a consensus. Most know that they have no realistic hope of reaching agreement with partisans of the opposite ideological standpoint, and they make no serious attempt to do so.

As these observations remind us, Cohen's ideal deliberative democracy is a purely hypothetical scenario. Given how distant that scenario is from reality, what purpose does the imaginative exercise serve? What role can it play in justifying the actions of any actual government?

Perhaps if some actual societies at least approximated the ideal, this might confer legitimacy on their political arrangements. Cohen, however, makes no attempt to argue that any actual society even approximates his ideal, and it would be difficult to make such an argument. It isn't even *close* to being true, for example, that all individuals have an equal voice in public discourse, unaffected by their wealth or power. Nor is it anywhere close to being true that political outcomes are determined purely by rational arguments or that public discourse aims at consensus.

Cohen writes that 'the ideal deliberative procedure is meant to provide a model for institutions to mirror.'[10] Perhaps Cohen's conception of deliberative democracy provides guidance for how society ought to change. While this may provide a useful role for Cohen's construction, it brings us no closer to deriving political authority. A description of an ideal that our society ought to aim at but of which we in fact fall very far short hardly constitutes an argument that our state has political authority.

Cohen goes on to claim that 'outcomes are democratically legitimate if and only if they *could be* the object of a free and reasoned agreement

---

[9] Cohen 2002, 93 (emphasis in original).
[10] Cohen 2002, 92.

among equals.'[11] He does not argue for this thesis, nor explain exactly what it means. How should we understand the force of that 'could'?

On one reading, Cohen's principle is absurdly permissive. Imagine that you are walking down the street, when a boxer suddenly punches you in the face. 'What did you do that for?!' you demand. 'Well', the boxer explains, 'you *could have* agreed to be punched in the face.' Now suppose, analogously, that a certain law could have been the object of a free and reasoned agreement among all citizens, in the sense that citizens could have freely decided to agree to that law – but in fact no citizen has done so. It is, to say the least, unclear how this situation would give the state a moral right to impose that law by force.

Presumably, Cohen would opt for a stronger reading of 'could'. Habermas writes of what 'would meet with the unforced agreement of all those involved, if they could participate, as free and equal, in discursive will-formation'.[12] Perhaps Cohen, similarly, would say that a legitimate political system is one that we *would* agree to if we deliberated in the ideal way. On this reading, Cohen and Habermas are appealing to a hypothetical social contract theory. We have, however, already seen the problems with such theories in Chapter 3. Briefly, there were two main problems. First, there is no reason to think that the structure and principles of any actual state would in fact be agreed to after ideal deliberation. Second, even if the structure and principles of some actual state would be agreed to, there is no reason to think that this fact would confer authority on that state. Neither Cohen nor Habermas has addressed these two central problems.

4.2.3   The irrelevance of deliberation

Granted that no society satisfies Cohen's conditions for an ideal deliberative democracy, if there *were* such a society, would its government then have authority?

It is unclear why it would. Recall the Bar Tab example (Section 4.1). Your colleagues and students have voted, over your objections, to have you pay for everyone's drinks. Now add the following stipulations to the example: before taking the vote, the group deliberated. Everyone, including you, had an equal opportunity to offer reasons for or against forcing you to pay for everyone's drinks. The others advanced arguments that it would be in the best interests of the group as a whole to force you to pay. They attempted to reach a consensus. In the end, they

---

[11] Cohen 2002, 92 (emphasis added). Compare Habermas 1979, 186–7.
[12] Habermas 1979, 186.

were unable to convince you that you should pay, but everyone else agreed that you should pay. Are you now obligated to pay for everyone? Are the other members of the group entitled to compel you to pay through threats of violence?

Clearly not. You have rights – in this case, a right to choose whether and how to spend your money and a right to be free from harmful coercion – which are not negated or overridden by the mere fact that a decision to violate your rights was preceded by a fair and reasoned deliberative process. The fairness of the process does not enable it to somehow sidestep all preexisting ethical entitlements and restrictions. Likewise, it is obscure how the sort of deliberation Cohen describes, even if it were to actually occur, would confer political legitimacy on the state. Individuals have a preexisting prima facie right not to be subjected to coercion. Deliberation, however fair and reasoned, does not by itself eliminate that right. Reasons for overriding individuals' prima facie rights can of course be offered, and the offering of such reasons may be part of a deliberative process. But the deliberative process does not constitute a reason in itself for suspending individuals' prima facie rights.

4.3 Equality and authority

4.3.1 The argument from equality

I turn now to what may be the best developed contemporary argument for the claim that the democratic process confers political authority. The central idea is that we have a general obligation to treat other members of our society as equals and that this requires respecting democratically made decisions.

The argument raises questions about what counts as a democratically authorized law. A law that is the direct product of a popular referendum is the clearest case of a democratically authorized law (hereafter, 'a democratic law').[13] But what about laws that most voters do not support but that were passed by a democratically elected legislature? What if a law or political candidate is supported by a majority of *voters* but not by a majority of all citizens? What about regulations written by unelected bureaucrats? Or orders issued by unelected judges? Difficult as these questions are for democratic theorists, I shall set them aside to focus on

---

[13] Wolff (1998, 29–34) raises special problems for the legitimacy of representative democracy. Christiano (2008, 105–6) argues that representative democracy is on the whole superior to direct democracy. Nevertheless, I do not think he would doubt that laws created by referendum are legitimate.

deeper problems. Hereafter, I shall simply assume that we have a state whose laws are genuinely authorized by the people, whatever that may amount to. Even with this generous concession, as I shall argue, democratic theorists cannot establish political authority.

Thomas Christiano has developed the Argument from Equality as an argument for political obligation, roughly as follows:[14]

1. Individuals are obligated to treat other members of their society as equals and not to treat them as inferiors.
2. To treat others as equals and not as inferiors, one must obey democratic laws.
3. Therefore, individuals are obligated to obey democratic laws.

The obligation thus defended is content-independent, but it need not be taken as absolute: the advocate of the above argument can recognize the possibility of countervailing values that sometimes outweigh the obligation to obey democratic laws. One can also recognize some qualifications to principle (2): perhaps only when democratically made laws are within certain bounds – when they do not violate the constitution or blatantly oppress minorities, for example – does equal treatment of others require obedience to those laws.[15]

Why should we accept the premises of the Argument from Equality? Begin with premise (1). Christiano advances the following subargument, in paraphrase:

1a. Justice requires giving each person his due and treating like cases alike.
1b. All members of one's society have equal moral status.[16]
1c. Therefore, justice requires treating other members of one's society as equals.[17]

---

[14] Christiano 2008.
[15] See Christiano 2008, ch. 7, for discussion of the limits of democratic authority.
[16] For premise (1a), see Christiano 2008, 20. For (1b), see Christiano 2008, 17–18. For brevity, I omit discussion of exactly what equal moral status amounts to. The democratic theorist might recognize qualifications to claim (1b). Perhaps, for example, children and the insane have a different status from normal adults, such that they need not be granted equal democratic participation rights.
[17] Christiano (2008, 31) writes, 'justice as I have described it does not normally impose requirements directly on each individual person.' But the

Next, why should one accept premise (2)? There appear to be two subarguments for this. The first appeals to the idea of placing one's judgment above that of others:

2a. To disobey a democratic law is to place one's judgment above that of other members of one's society.
2b. To place one's judgment above that of others is to treat those others as inferiors.
2c. Therefore, to disobey a democratic law is to treat other members of one's society as inferiors.[18] (from 2a, 2b)

The second subargument appeals to the obligation to support democracy:

2d. Treating others as equals requires supporting the equal advancement of their interests.
2e. Democracy is crucial to the equal advancement of persons' interests.
2f. To support democracy, one must obey democratic laws.
2g. Therefore, treating others as equals requires obeying democratic laws.[19] (from 2d–2f)

Christiano spends the most time justifying (2e). He argues that to truly advance individuals' interests equally, a social system must satisfy a publicity requirement, meaning that it must be possible for citizens to see for themselves that they are being treated equally. He then argues that only democratic decision making, as a procedural form of equality, satisfies this requirement. There are other, substantive interpretations of equality – for example, that one treats others equally by equalizing their resources or that one treats others equally by granting them the same liberty rights. But these interpretations of equality do not satisfy the publicity requirement, because they are too controversial; only those who accept certain controversial ethical views could see themselves to be treated as equals in virtue of the implementation of one of these substantive forms of equality. Hence, the *public* equal advancement of interests requires democratic decision making.

---

argument for political obligation requires that justice impose requirements on individuals.

[18] Christiano 2008, 98–9, 250.
[19] Christiano 2008, 249. I have inserted premise (2f) as required for the validity of the argument, though Christiano does not explicitly state it.

4.3.2   An absurdly demanding theory of justice?

As I have interpreted it, the Argument from Equality derives a duty to obey democratic laws, in part, from a requirement of justice that one promote the equal advancement of persons' interests [premise (2d)].

Taken without qualification, this putative requirement of justice is absurdly demanding. Suppose I have $50. If I spend the money on myself, I would be advancing my interests more than the interests of others. To advance persons' interests equally, I must spend the money on something that benefits everyone, or divide the money among all the members of my society, or perhaps donate the money to help people whose interests are presently less well advanced than the average. The same reasoning applies to any resource at my disposal. It would seem, then, that I must give away nearly everything I own. In fact, since the ground of the duty to treat other members of my society as equals is their equal moral status [premise (1b)], it seems that my duty must extend to promoting equally the interests of all or most of the population of the earth.

How might we avoid an absurdly demanding theory of justice, without renouncing the Argument from Equality? One possibility is to limit the demand of justice to an obligation to promote *social institutions* that equally advance others' interests, as opposed to an obligation to directly promote equal advancement of others' interests through one's own behavior in general.

But how would such a qualification be justified? The obligation to treat others as equals is supposed to be grounded in a principle of justice requiring us to give others their due and treat like cases alike. If others are due equal advancement of their interests, then it seems that, to act justly, I must advance their interests equally; there is no ground for limiting this obligation to actions supporting general social institutions. If, on the other hand, others are not due equal advancement of their interests, then it seems that I need not support equal advancement of others' interests, whether in the promotion of social institutions or in any other sphere of action.

Perhaps individuals have an obligation of justice to promote the equal advancement of each others' interests, but this is only a prima facie obligation, which may be overridden by countervailing reasons, including prudential reasons. Perhaps I need not spend most of my resources on others, because my prudential reasons for using resources to my own benefit usually outweigh the prima facie duty to promote equal advancement of others' interests. The government, on the other hand, must devote itself more thoroughly to the equal advancement of citizens' interests, because the government, as an institution and not a person, does not have genuine prudential reasons.[20]

This last suggestion leaves it unclear to what extent individuals have political obligations. Consider two examples:

> *Charity Case:* I have $50, which I am considering either donating to a very effective antipoverty charity or spending on my own personal consumption. If I give the money to charity, it will reduce the inequality in society and bring society closer to the equal advancement of all its members' interests. However, I have already given a large amount of money to charity this year and do not wish to give more. I decide to keep the money.

> *Tax Case:* Tax laws require me to pay a large amount of money to the government. I am considering either paying all of the required taxes or cheating on my taxes in such a way as to pay $50 less than the legally required amount, in which case I will spend the $50 on personal consumption. Assume that I am certain that, if I cheat, I will not be caught or suffer any other negative personal consequences. I decide to cheat.

Advocates of democratic authority would surely wish to deny that my action is permissible in the Tax Case, yet to avoid an absurdly demanding ethical theory, they would wish to allow that my action is permissible in the Charity Case. Suppose we hold that in the Charity Case, my prudential reason outweighs my prima facie duty to promote the equal advancement of others' interests. But my prudential reason for cheating on my taxes in the Tax Case is just as strong as my prudential reason for keeping the $50 in the Charity Case. Furthermore, sending $50 to the charity is likely to promote equal advancement of persons' interests to a much *greater* degree than sending $50 to the government. Therefore, if my action is permissible in the Charity Case, how can it be impermissible in the Tax Case?

One might appeal to the idea that the *total* benefit provided by the government, vis-à-vis the equal advancement of persons' interests, is much greater than the total benefit provided by any charity organization. There are two problems with this argument. The first is that the claim need not be true. A large and efficient charity might do

---

[20] I suspect that this suggestion is closest to what Christiano has in mind when he says, '[W]e rightly impose impersonal standards on institutions that we do not *fully* impose on ourselves as individuals' (2008, 31; emphasis added).

more good than a small and inefficient state, yet defenders of political authority would still claim that the individual is obligated to pay taxes to the state and not obligated to donate to the charity. Second and more importantly, the claim is irrelevant. The total good done by an organization should not be confused with the good done by the individual's marginal contribution to that organization. It is the latter, rather than the former, that determines the strength of one's reasons for contributing. The marginal impact of $50 of my taxes on the equal advancement of persons' interests is negligible.

I have focused on the case of taxation because it is among the least controversial and least dispensable exercises of governmental authority among those who believe in political authority. If the obligation to pay taxes cannot be defended, there is no hope for defending political obligation in more controversial cases, such as the putative obligation to report for the draft when so ordered.

The upshot of this discussion is that the defender of the Argument from Equality faces a dilemma: either the obligation to promote equal advancement of interests is implausibly demanding, or it is too weak to support basic political obligations.

4.3.3   Supporting democracy through obedience

One strain in the Argument from Equality [(2d) and (2f)] claims that democracy is so crucial to the equal advancement of persons' interests that to support equal advancement of interests, one must support democracy. Furthermore, to support democracy, one must obey democratic laws. Hence, one must obey democratic laws.

The obvious problem with this inference is that a particular individual's obedience or disobedience to a particular law has no actual impact on the functioning of the state. For instance, the government persists despite a large number of people who evade a large amount of taxes every year.[21] One tax evader more will not cause the government to collapse, nor will it cause the government to become undemocratic. The same holds for nearly all other laws. Christiano tells us, 'Each person must try to realize the equal advancement of the interests of other human beings.'[22] But obedience to democratic

---

[21] The IRS estimates that over $300 billion worth of taxes are evaded annually by the 16 percent of taxpayers who cheat on their taxes (U.S. Department of the Treasury 2009, 2).

[22] Christiano 2008, 249.

laws appears to have little or no connection with this. An action that can be predicted in advance to have no impact on the attainment of a given goal is not a rational way of trying to bring about that goal.

Admittedly, while the impact of a single individual may be negligible, general obedience on the part of most of the population is a genuine requirement for the success and stability of the state. If most people regularly violated most laws, the state would likely collapse. However, most modern societies are nowhere near the threshold level of disobedience that would be required for government to collapse; thus, the individual's marginal impact on the state's survival is zero. (See Chapter 5 for discussion of whether disobedience nevertheless unfairly 'free rides' on others' obedience.)

4.3.4 Is democratic equality uniquely public?

Even if we have an obligation to try to bring about equal advancement of persons' interests, the interpretation of this goal is highly controversial. Some may believe that it requires equalizing individuals' material resources. Others may believe that it requires only granting everyone equal liberty rights. Still others may believe that it requires giving each an equal say in the political process.

Christiano argues that only the last interpretation – *democratic equality*, as I shall call it – satisfies the crucial *publicity* principle, the principle that 'it is not enough that justice is done; it must be seen to be done.'[23] There are at least two ways of interpreting this principle, one stronger than the other. On the weak interpretation, publicity requires that individuals be able to see that they are being treated in accordance with a certain conception of equality, whether or not they see that that is the correct interpretation of equality and whether or not they see that equality is essential to justice. On the strong interpretation, publicity requires that individuals be able to see that the way they are being treated *is just.*[24]

---

[23] Christiano 2008, 47.

[24] The strong interpretation is suggested by Christiano's initial remark that justice must be seen to be done, but other remarks make clear that he intends the weak interpretation; for example, '[W]eak publicity requires only that people be able to see that they are treated in accordance with what are *in fact* the correct principles of justice.' (2008, 52; emphasis added). Compare 47: '[P]ublicity demands that the principles of social justice be ones that people can in principle see to be in effect or not.' I discuss the strong principle in the text for the sake of completeness of the argument.

If we adopt the weak interpretation of publicity, then democratic decision making satisfies the publicity constraint, as do many other conceptions of equality. For instance, suppose one holds that the proper way to treat others equally is by according everyone the same liberty rights (roughly, rights to do as they wish, free of government interference). Individuals would be able to see that they were accorded the same liberty rights, even if they did not agree that this was a satisfactory way to interpret equality. So the liberty-rights interpretation of equality satisfies the publicity condition. A similar argument could be made for most other interpretations of equality.

On the other hand, if we adopt the strong interpretation of publicity, then *no* interpretation of equality or justice satisfies publicity, because there is no conception of justice that all can agree on. Not all rational thinkers have agreed even that democracy is just.[25] It thus remains unclear how one might think that democratic equality uniquely satisfies the publicity requirement.

Perhaps the idea is that democratic equality is far less controversial in its application and interpretation than other conceptions of equality of the same level of generality. Equality of rights has no uncontroversial interpretation; there is enormous disagreement on what rights individuals possess and what laws count as implementing equal rights. Similarly, equality of resources is open to interpretation. Does it require only that individuals have equal wealth? Equal incomes? Incomes proportioned to their needs? Must incomes be adjusted for differing costs of living in different locales? But equality in the decision-making process has a single uncontroversial interpretation: one person, one vote.

Or does it? Does equality of decision-making power require direct democracy, or is representative democracy sufficient? Does it require that all citizens have the same chance to stand for public office? If so, is it sufficient that all citizens are *legally permitted* to stand for public office, or must individuals also have financially and socially realistic opportunities to run for public office? If representative democracy is permitted, must representation be strictly proportional to population, or may some parts of a nation have representation in the legislature out of proportion to their population (as in the case of the representation of states in the U.S. Senate)? Is democratic equality violated if public officials draw districts in unusual shapes for voting purposes (as

---

[25] See Plato's *Republic* 1974; Oakeshott 1962, 23–6; Caplan 2006; Brennan 2011.

in the American practice of gerrymandering), with the specific intent of maximizing the representation of a particular party in the legislature? Is democratic equality violated if some persistent minorities rarely or never get their way? If so, what sort of minorities count? Do members of all third parties in the United States (parties other than the Democrats and the Republicans) count as persistent minorities who are not treated equally?

These are all controversial questions. I do not expect that anything close to unanimous agreement could be obtained on how to answer them. And all are questions about *the interpretation of democratic equality*. That is, they are not just questions about what the best way of organizing the electoral system is. They are questions about what ways of implementing the system truly treat persons equally. Thus, if the publicity constraint requires lack of controversy in the application of a given conception of equality, then the democratic interpretation of equality does not satisfy publicity.

4.3.5 Respecting others' judgments

Another strand in the Argument from Equality holds that, when one disobeys a democratic law, one thereby treats others as inferiors by placing one's own judgment above the judgments of other citizens.

In response, we must first clarify the principle that individuals ought to treat each other as equals. There are many respects in which one might take persons to be equal. One might think persons have equal rights; that their interests are of equal weight; or that they have equal capacities for moral judgment, equal intelligence, or equal knowledge. What 'treating persons as equals' amounts to depends upon the respect in which one takes persons to be equal. Presumably, one is only morally required to treat persons as equals in those respects in which persons actually are at least roughly equal.

Now suppose one disobeys a democratic law on the grounds that the law is unjust or otherwise morally objectionable. In most cases, one will thereby be expressing a rejection of the judgments of those who made the law.[26] Assume that the law was made by a referendum of

---

[26] This need not be the case. One might think that the voters or legislators made the law, not because they mistakenly believed it to be just, but because they correctly believed the law to serve their own interests, or for some other reason compatible with the fact that the law is unjust. I leave these cases aside, considering only the case most favorable to the proponent of the Argument from Equality.

all the citizens. Then one is rejecting the normative judgments of the majority of one's fellow citizens. This entails that one takes those other citizens to be unequal to oneself in at least one respect: that of having less accurate normative beliefs about this particular law. Perhaps one is also committed to some such general claim as that other citizens are less reliable than oneself at forming correct normative beliefs about the subject matter of this law. Of course, all this is perfectly compatible with one's recognizing that others have equal moral rights or that their interests are equally important as one's own.

Is there anything in this that is unjust or otherwise objectionable? This presumably depends upon whether others are in fact unequal to oneself in these respects and/or whether one is justified in believing that they are. Justice does not demand that we refrain from treating other persons as having some characteristic that we *justifiably and correctly* take them to have.

Many people are both strongly justified and correct in taking themselves to have more accurate and reliable normative beliefs about certain laws than the majority of members of their society. How does this come about? First, there are many who correctly and justifiably believe themselves to be of significantly greater than average intelligence. Second, there are many who correctly and justifiably believe themselves to have significantly greater than average levels of knowledge relevant to certain political issues. Many surveys and many casual observations have provided evidence that, for example, the average level of political knowledge in the United States is extremely low.[27] It is therefore not difficult at all to know that one has significantly exceeded it. Third, many people correctly and justifiably take themselves to have devoted significantly greater time and effort to identifying the correct positions on certain political issues than the average member of their society. All of these factors – intelligence, knowledge, time, and effort – affect one's reliability in arriving at correct beliefs. No one seriously maintains that persons are anywhere near to being equal in any of these dimensions, let alone all of them. It is therefore very difficult to see how one could argue that all persons are equally reliable at identifying correct political beliefs.

In violating a democratic law, one may well be treating others as though they were epistemic 'inferiors', in the sense of persons with less

---

[27] See Delli Carpini and Keeter 1996, chapter 2; Caplan 2007b, chapter 1.

reliable normative beliefs in a particular area. But there is nothing unjust in this if, as is very often the case, one knows this to be true.

4.3.6 Coercion and treating others as inferiors

When one violates a democratic law, one treats others as inferiors in an epistemic sense. But there are other, more serious ways of treating persons as inferiors. If a person does not agree with some plan, for example, attempting to obtain that person's cooperation through threats of violence is normally an extremely disrespectful approach, fundamentally incompatible with treating that person as an equal.

To return to an earlier example: You have gone out for drinks with some colleagues and students, and one of the students has proposed that you pay for everybody's drinks. Over your protests, the other parties at the table vote to have you pay for the drinks. You tell them that you will not agree to do so. They then inform you that, if you do not pay, they intend to punish you by locking you in a room for some time and that they are prepared to take you by force.

Apart from the fact that you need some new drinking partners, what can be said about this scenario? Who in this scenario is doing an injustice to whom? Who is treating whom as an inferior?

One might argue that by rejecting the decision of the other persons at the table, you are placing your will or normative judgment above that of the other members of the group. *They* all think you should pay, and there are more of them than there are of you. So who are you to disagree? You must think you are some sort of godlike being whose wishes take precedence over the wishes of several other people.

But that argument rings hollow. Surely it is the behavior of your colleagues and students that is disrespectful of you rather than the other way around. It is they who are unjustly setting themselves up as your superiors by using threats of punishment and physical force to obtain your cooperation with their plan.

Christiano argues that one fails to show proper respect for the judgment of other members of one's society when one refuses to go along with democratic laws. These laws normally come with threats to impose punishment on those who do not follow the law, backed up by credible threats of violence against those who attempt to avoid punishment. On the face of it, the disrespect for persons and the violation of equality involved in issuing and carrying out such threats are far more palpable than the supposed disrespect shown by those who do not comply with the laws. A majority that votes for a given law is authorizing this kind of coercion. Prima facie, therefore, it is this majority that is guilty of violating the requirement to treat other persons as equals.

The point here is that it is impossible to justify political authority if the moral principle that is supposed to generate *political obligation* also rules out *political legitimacy.* In this case, the principle is that justice prohibits treating others as inferiors. If this shows the existence of an obligation to obey democratic laws, it shows much more clearly the illegitimacy of most of those laws in the first place. Since political authority requires both political obligation and political legitimacy, it seems that political authority is impossible.

Perhaps this conclusion is drawn too quickly. It is not always objectionably disrespectful to use physical force against others. If, for example, *A* is threatening *B* with unjust violence, then *B* may use violence to stop *A* from carrying out his threat without thereby unjustly treating *A* as an inferior. This suggests that at least some laws – for example, those that prohibit unjust violence – are not rendered objectionable or unjust by the coercion required to enforce them.

But many other laws, it seems, *are* rendered objectionable by the way in which they call for coercion. I have no comprehensive theory to offer of the conditions under which coercion is objectionable. But on the surface of it, the state's collection of taxes is analogous to the collection of money from you in the Bar Tab example. In both cases a majority votes to take someone's property for the benefit of the group, and in both cases the decision is to be enforced through threats of punishment, backed up by threats of violence. One difference is that the burdens of taxation are more widely distributed than the bar tab, which we imagined being placed on a single person. One might instead suppose that, rather than placing all the burden on you, a student proposes that you pay half of the total bill, the other professors pay smaller portions, and the students each get a free ride.[28] Few will say that the wider distribution of the burdens now renders permissible the coercive imposition of this plan.

One might still worry that the Bar Tab example trades on the apparent unfairness of the student's proposal and that our intuitions

---

[28] In the United States, slightly over half of all federal taxes come from the top 10 percent of taxpayers (the full professors of society, so to speak). The poorest 20 percent (the grad students of society) pay less than 1 percent of all federal taxes and actually have a negative income tax rate (U.S. Congressional Budget Office 2009).

would change if the group had voted for an essentially fair and equitable way of paying the bar tab. But advocates of democratic authority explicitly claim that one must comply with a democratic decision regardless of whether the decision is in itself just.[29] Hence, it is perfectly appropriate to consider a hypothetical in which the majority votes for an unfair plan, as in the Bar Tab case.

4.3.7 From obligation to legitimacy?

The Argument from Equality faces serious difficulties in accounting for political obligation. But even if we could account for political obligation, there would remain the challenge of accounting for political *legitimacy*, the state's right to rule by coercively imposing rules on society. Christiano explains the origin of this right as follows:

> [T]he democratic assembly has a right to rule [...] since one treats its members unjustly if one ignores or skirts its decisions. Each citizen has a right to one's obedience and therefore the assembly as a whole has a right to one's obedience.[30]

The central problem in accounting for a right to rule is the problem of justifying coercion. Thus, if the above reasoning is to succeed, it must provide a justification for coercion. Perhaps the justification is along the following lines:

4. If justice requires (forbids) a person to do *A*, then it is permissible to coerce that person to do (not to do) *A*.
5. Justice requires obedience to democratic laws.
6. Therefore, it is permissible to coerce a person to obey democratic laws.

Premise (5) is supposed to be established by the Argument from Equality, as discussed above.

But why should we accept (4)? In many cases it is plausible that one may enforce the requirements of justice by coercion. As we have seen above, it is plausible that one may use coercion to prevent a person from unjustly harming another person. It is also plausible that one may sometimes use coercion to prevent a person from unjustly damaging

---

[29] Christiano 2008, 97; Estlund 2008, 8.
[30] Christiano 2004, 287.

or stealing another person's property or to recover stolen property or extract compensation.[31] In all of these cases, it seems that coercion is an appropriate means of inducing a person to do what justice requires or of preventing a person from doing what justice forbids. So there is some plausibility to the generalization that one may coerce persons to comply with justice.

But now consider two other sorts of alleged obligations of justice: the obligation to give equal respect to the judgments of other persons and the obligation to promote the equal advancement of persons' interests. Perhaps these are requirements of justice; perhaps not. But how plausible is it, in any case, that these particular (alleged) obligations may be enforced through coercion?

Consider an example in which I appear to violate one of these duties. I am out for drinks with some friends. Several of them are discussing what an excellent President Barack Obama is. I chime in, 'You people are fools and your opinions are worthless. I do not respect your judgment. You are all inferior to me.' I then plug my ears so I don't have to hear what they say and turn my back on them.

In this case, I have both failed to respect my friends' judgments and treated them as inferiors. This strikes me as much more evident than the claim that I fail to respect other citizens' judgments or treat other citizens as inferiors whenever I disobey a democratic law. But would my friends (or anyone else) now be justified in using physical force to impose punishment on me?

Now consider a case in which I violate the other alleged duty of justice. Suppose I have recently learned that Amnesty International is working to promote democracy in the little-known country of New Florida. AI is appealing for monetary donations and contributors to letter-writing campaigns. I think AI has a reasonable chance of being reasonably effective in this endeavor, and I recognize that I could support democratic institutions by helping AI at this time.[32] Because democracy is crucial

---

[31] Locke (1980, sections 7–12) proposed that all individuals in the state of nature have the right to punish those who transgress the natural law. In section 11, he appears to allow that even in civil society, crime victims may on their own initiative seize reparations from a criminal if the state fails to do so, and in section 20, he holds that when the state fails to collect reparations from a criminal through 'a manifest perverting of justice', then the individual may avail himself of vigilante justice.

[32] As Christiano tells us, 'each citizen has a duty to bring about democratic institutions' (2008, 249).

to the equal advancement of persons' interests, I would thereby be promoting the equal advancement of persons' interests. Nevertheless, I fail to support Amnesty International.

In this case, it is very plausible to say that I have (a) failed to promote the equal advancement of persons' interests and (b) failed to help bring democratic institutions into being. And perhaps I have done wrong. But am I now an appropriate target for threats of violence?

Not every duty is appropriately enforced through coercion. The above examples suggest that the obligation to treat others as equals by respecting their judgment and the obligation to promote equal advancement of persons' interests by promoting democracy are not obligations that one may enforce through coercion. Either these are not obligations of justice, or some obligations of justice may not be coercively enforced. In either case, Christiano's argument for political legitimacy fails.

4.4 Conclusion

Relatively speaking, democracy is admirable. In large and obvious ways, it is superior to all other known forms of government.[33] But it does not solve the problem of political authority. The fact that a majority of persons favor some rule does not justify imposing that rule by force on those who do not agree to it nor coercively punishing those who disobey the rule. To do so is, typically, to disrespect the dissenters and treat them as inferiors. Matters are not altered if one adds that the majority deliberated in a special way before deciding to impose the rule.

The need to respect the judgments of other members of one's society does not generate general political obligations in democratic countries, for at least two reasons: first, because many people know themselves to have better judgment with respect to many practical questions than the majority of citizens; second, because the obligation to respect others' judgments does not have sufficient force to override individual rights, such as an individual's right to control his property.

The obligation to promote equal advancement of interests likewise fails to establish political obligations. Among other things, it is unclear in what sense democratic equality is a uniquely publicly realizable conception of equality, and it is unclear how obedience to democratic laws constitutes meaningful support for democratic institutions. But

---

[33] See Sen 1999, chapter 6.

even if obedience to democratic laws constituted meaningful support for equality, deriving political obligation from this fact would require postulating a very strong duty to promote equality. Such a strong duty would most likely entail implausible demands requiring one to virtually devote one's life to promoting equality. In the end, democratic authorization can account for neither the obligation to obey the law nor the right to impose the law on unwilling persons by force.

5
Consequentialism and Fairness

5.1 Consequentialist arguments for political obligation

5.1.1 The structure of consequentialist arguments for political obligation

The simplest arguments for political authority are consequentialist ones. By 'consequentialist arguments for authority', I mean arguments that ascribe moral weight to the goodness or badness of an action's consequences and that appeal directly to that factor in attempting to derive political obligation and legitimacy.[1] I focus in this section on arguments for political obligation.

These arguments proceed in two stages. First, one argues that there are great values that are secured by government and that could not be secured without government. Second, one argues that this fact imposes on individuals an obligation to obey the state, on the grounds that (a) we have a duty to promote the values addressed in the first stage of the argument or at least not to undermine them, and (b) obedience to the law is the best way of promoting those values and disobedience is a way of undermining them.

5.1.2 The benefits of government

Many benefits have been claimed for government, but three are particularly prominent. The first major good ascribed to government is that of protection from crimes committed by individuals against other individuals, especially violent crimes and property crimes. The

---

[1] These arguments need not assume consequentialism, in the sense of the view that the rightness of an action is *solely* determined by its good or bad consequences.

government provides this benefit by attaching punishments to unjust acts – murder, robbery, rape, and so on – that individuals commit against each other. Without government, most people believe that unjust and harmful actions of these kinds would be far more prevalent than they are. Those who are most pessimistic about human nature fear that society would be reduced to a barbaric state of constant war of everyone against everyone.[2] There are two closely related points here. One is that government increases overall social welfare by preventing certain bad things from happening. The other is that government promotes *justice*, by reducing the number of unjust acts that occur.[3]

The second major benefit ascribed to government is the provision of a detailed, precise, and public set of rules of social conduct that apply uniformly across society. Why do we need government to provide such rules? There are natural principles of justice that exist prior to the state and that individuals can appreciate intuitively. However, these natural principles are vague and general and do not provide sufficient guidance for modern social life. For example, is it ethically permissible to release air pollution, say from one's automobile, or does this violate the rights of those who will inhale the pollutants? It is plausible that one may release certain levels and kinds of pollution but not excessive or excessively toxic pollution. But exactly how much pollution may one release and of what kinds? It is not credible that the natural principles of justice determine unique answers to all questions of this kind nor, if they do, that individuals can reliably apprehend these answers by reflection. Yet we need accepted answers to such questions for people to coordinate and to have peaceful and predictable relations with each other. A government, some argue, is the only reliable source of such a set of generally accepted rules.[4]

The third salient benefit provided by government is that of military defense. Without a means of military defense, it seems, we would easily fall prey to foreign countries seeking to enslave us or steal our resources. Given the military power of governments around the world, effective defense of a given territory seems to require an organized army with modern military technology. The only way of raising such an army seems to be to have a government of our own.

---

[2] Hobbes 1996, chapter 13. Locke (1980, chapters 2 and 9) offers a less dire assessment than Hobbes but still finds 'great inconveniencies' in the state of nature.

[3] Buchanan 2002, 703–5.

[4] Christiano 2008, 53–5, 237–8; Wellman 2005, 6–7. Christiano claims that the state 'establishes justice' by providing these uniform rules.

In Part II of this book, I challenge the widespread assumption that government is needed to provide these benefits. Nevertheless, in the present chapter I shall grant that assumption for the sake of argument. I contend that, even with this concession, one cannot derive political authority as commonly understood.

5.1.3 The duty to do good

Consequentialist arguments for political obligation claim that people have a duty to promote some value or values; for example, a duty to promote justice, to promote utility, or to aid in rescuing others from peril.[5] The duty need not be taken to be absolute or unqualified; it may be that the duty obtains only when some great harm or great injustice threatens, and it may be that even in such conditions, the duty can be overridden by sufficiently strong countervailing reasons. This is consistent with the notion that the duty to obey the law need only be a prima facie duty.

Take the case in which you see a child drowning in a shallow pond: you could easily wade in and save the child, though this would entail getting your clothes muddy and missing a class.[6] Nearly everyone agrees that in such a situation, you are morally required to help the child. We might demur in more demanding circumstances – if the child were drowning in the ocean and you had to assume a significant risk to your own life to save the child, then you would not be obligated to do so. You may properly place your own life above that of a stranger in such situations. But when some very great evil threatens another person and you can prevent it with minimal cost to yourself, it would be wrong not to do so.

There are some who would challenge even this modest ethical claim, appealing to an extreme form of individualism.[7] I do not take that approach. I seek rather to rely on broadly common sense moral views, which I take to include the modest principle of a duty to do good described in the preceding paragraph.

Proponents of the consequentialist argument for political obligation argue that general obedience to the law is necessary for the state to function. If too many citizens disobey, the state will collapse, and its

---

[5] See Rawls (1999, 295) on the duty of justice and Wellman (2005, 30–2) on the duty to rescue. Neither thinker has a generally consequentialist view, however. Rawls appeals to what parties in the original position would accept, and Wellman (2005, 33) ends up appealing to a nonconsequentialist principle of fairness.

[6] The example is Singer's (1993, 229).

[7] Rand 1964, 49; Narveson 1993, chapter 7.

enormous benefits will disappear.[8] Furthermore, they argue, the costs of obedience, while significant, are reasonable *in light of the benefits*, since most people receive substantially greater benefits than costs from the state.[9] Thus, a moderate principle of a duty to do good leads to the conclusion that we are generally bound to obey the law. Or so one might argue.

5.1.4   The problem of individual redundancy

It may be true that general obedience to the law is required for government to provide the benefits that it provides. But it is not true that *every* law must be generally obeyed; many laws are routinely flouted without the government's collapsing as a result. Nor is it true of any individual that *that individual's* obedience is required for the government to provide the benefits that it provides. It is plausible that there is some level of disobedience that would cause a governmental collapse. But as long as we are far from that level, any given individual can disobey with no consequences for the survival of government.

Of course, there are some laws that you should obey for independent moral reasons. For instance, you should not rob other people. This is not because your doing so might destroy the government. It is because robbing other people would be an injustice to the specific people robbed. This is not an example of a *political* obligation; it is simply an example of a general moral obligation to other people. Many other laws similarly correspond to independently compelling moral principles. To defend *political* obligation, one must argue that there is a content-independent obligation to obey the law because it is the law (Section 1.5) – that is, that one must obey even the laws that do not correspond to independent moral principles.

Return to the case of the child drowning in the shallow pond (Section 5.1.3). But this time, suppose that there are three other people nearby ready to save the child. They do not need help; there is no danger that the child will drown or suffer any other serious harm if you fail to assist. Furthermore, the others are going to enter the pond and muddy their clothes whether or not you also wade in. In that case must you still jump in to help save the child? To do so would simply mean assuming costs with no added benefit to anyone. Your desire to avoid getting your clothes muddy or missing a class would certainly not justify allowing a child to drown. But mightn't it justify allowing a child to be saved entirely by others rather than partly by yourself?

---

[8]   Hume 1987, 480.
[9]   Wellman 2005, 17–19.

The case of a citizen deciding whether to obey the law is more analogous to this last version of the drowning child story than to the original version: while governmental functioning requires obedience, there are already more than enough people obeying the law so that the government is in no danger of collapsing if you disobey. These other people will continue to obey whether you obey or not. In this situation, your own obedience is just as redundant as an extra rescuer jumping into the pond when there are already three rescuers wading out to save the child.

5.2 Rule consequentialism

I claim that one may break the law when what the law commands is not independently morally required and no serious negative consequences will result. This sort of suggestion is commonly met with the challenge: 'What if everybody did that?' This question is meant to suggest a moral argument against the sort of behavior at issue, but the precise content of the argument is not obvious. It does not seem to be a simple consequentialist appeal – the suggestion is not that, in breaking the law, one is likely to actually cause everybody to do the same thing (whatever exactly counts as 'the same thing'). Rather, the suggestion seems to be that the fact that it would be bad if everybody did something is by itself a strong reason not to do that thing. This idea is closely related to that of *rule consequentialism* in ethics. Rule consequentialism holds that, rather than always choosing the particular action that will produce the best consequences given the present circumstances, one should act according to general rules, and one should choose the rules that, if generally adopted, would have the best consequences.[10]

In some cases, this idea is plausible. Take the case of a newly planted lawn on a university campus. Students and professors are tempted to take short cuts across the lawn while walking from building to building. One person cutting across the lawn will have no noticeable effect. But if everybody does it, the pristine lawn will be marred by an ugly footpath running through the middle of it. Assume that the aesthetic disvalue of the path outweighs the total benefit it provides in terms of time saved. In this situation, many find it plausible that one ought not to walk across the lawn. This appears to be an illustration of the 'What if everyone did that?' principle, the principle that one ought not to do what would be bad if generally practiced.

---

[10] Brandt 1992, chapter 7.

But in other cases, the principle seems absurd. Suppose I decide to become a professional philosopher. This seems permissible. But what if everybody did this? Everyone would philosophize all day, and we would all starve. Presumably this does not show that it is morally wrong to be a professional philosopher. We will not in fact starve, because the farmers are not all going to become philosophers merely because I decide to become one. In this case, 'What would happen if everyone did what I do?' seems irrelevant.

One might try to save rule consequentialism from this objection by taking a more nuanced view of the 'rule' I am acting on. Perhaps when I decide to become a philosopher, I am not acting on the rule 'Be a philosopher' but on some more complex rule, such as 'Be a philosopher, *provided* that there are not already far too many philosophers' or 'Choose the profession best suited to you, *provided* that there are enough people in other professions that your doing so does not have serious negative consequences.' If everyone acted on either of *those* rules, then we would not all starve.

But just as I may claim to be following the rule 'Be a philosopher, provided that there are not too many philosophers' or 'provided that there will be no serious negative consequences', individuals who choose to break the law could often claim to be following some such rule as 'Break the law when what the law commands is not independently morally required, *provided* that there are not too many people breaking the law' or '...*provided* that your doing so will not have serious negative consequences.' The proviso tacked onto the end of this rule is perfectly parallel to the proviso tacked onto the 'Be a philosopher' rule, so whatever rationale allows us to include the latter proviso will almost certainly license inclusion of the former. It appears, then, that rule consequentialism itself is defensible only if it does not support a general defense of political obligation.

5.3   Fairness

5.3.1   The fairness theory of political obligation

Another account holds that one must obey the law because to disobey is *unfair* to other members of one's society, who generally obey.[11] I shall refer to this sort of obligation as an obligation of 'fair play'.

The argument is not a consequentialist one – the claim is not that one's disobedience will cause harmful consequences. Nevertheless, it

---

[11] Hart 1955, 185–6; Rawls 1964; Klosko 2005.

is easy to move from consequentialist theories to the fairness theory. Once we notice that *individual* disobedience has no harmful consequences, it is natural to move to rule consequentialism, appealing to the consequences of *general* disobedience. But we encounter many cases, such as that of a person deciding to become an academic philosopher, in which there is nothing wrong with doing something that it would be extremely bad for everyone to do. We must then explain what differentiates the cases in which it seems wrong to perform an action that would be bad for everyone to do from the cases in which it seems perfectly all right to perform such an action. The fairness theory offers an attractive answer to this question: it is a matter of whether the action treats others unfairly.

There is nothing *unfair* about my becoming a philosopher, despite the fact that it would be bad if everyone did so. In being a philosopher, I do not, for example, increase the burdens on members of other professions. On the contrary, members of other professions prefer less marketplace competition and therefore prefer that fewer others join their profession.

Contrast the following scenario. You are in a lifeboat with several other people. You are caught in a storm, and the boat is taking on water, which needs to be bailed out. Other passengers take up containers and start bailing. The other passengers' efforts are clearly sufficient to keep the boat afloat; thus, no large negative consequences will result if you refuse to bail. Nevertheless, it seems obvious that you should help bail water. Intuitively, it would be unfair to let the others do all the work.

Why would this be unfair? The important features of the situation seem to be as follows:

i) There is a large good being produced by the actions of others – in this case, that the boat remains afloat. In contrast, if the others were doing something harmful (say, scooping water *into* the boat), useless (say, praying to Poseidon), or merely of trivial value (say, entertaining each other by telling stories), then you would not be obligated to help.

ii) The others assume a cost that is causally necessary to the production of the good. In this case, the cost is the effort involved in bailing water.

iii) You receive a fair share of the benefit being produced. In this case, you avoid drowning.[12]

---

[12] Some philosophers maintain that one has an obligation of fairness to assist in a cooperative scheme only if one *freely accepts* the benefits of the scheme

iv) Your participation in the cooperative scheme would causally contribute to the production of the good.

v) The costs to you of participation would be reasonable and not significantly greater than the costs undertaken by others.

vi) Your participation would not interfere with your doing something more important. For example, suppose that instead of bailing water, you decide to tie down the supplies on the boat to prevent their being thrown overboard. Assume that this is more important than helping to bail water. In this case, it is not unfair to refrain from helping to bail water.

When these six conditions are satisfied, it is unfair to refuse to contribute to the production of the good.

Advocates of the Fair Play Account argue that to disobey the law is to treat other members of one's society unfairly. Government produces significant benefits. Other members of one's society, by paying taxes and obeying laws, have undertaken the costs required to provide these benefits. All of us share in at least some of the benefits of government, and most receive a fair share of those benefits. Each of us can causally contribute to providing the benefits by paying taxes and obeying the laws. The cost is significant, but it is typically comparable to the costs borne by others, and it is reasonable in view of the benefits. Therefore, it would be unfair not to do our part in supporting government by paying taxes and generally obeying the laws.

5.3.2   Obedience as the cost of political goods

In situations in which an obligation of fair play exists, one is not typically obligated to do whatever other participants of the cooperative scheme tell one to do merely because they tell one to do it. In the water-bailing case, suppose that one of the other bailers tells you to go and make him a sandwich. This you are not morally required to do. What you are obligated to do is only to causally contribute to providing the benefits, not to render general obedience or fealty toward anyone.

How, then, is the notion of fairness supposed to generate political obligations? The argument is that, in this particular case, obedience to the law *constitutes* sharing the cost of providing the benefits of the cooperative scheme. As discussed earlier (Section 5.1.2), the central benefits of government include protection from injustices committed by private

---

(Rawls 1964, 10; Simmons 1979, 107–8; 2001, 30–1). The water-bailing example suggests that free acceptance is not necessary.

criminals or foreign governments and the provision of predictable rules for social cooperation. So the argument must be that obedience to the law causally contributes to providing these benefits.

In the case of some laws, it is very plausible that obedience contributes to the provision of these benefits and thus counts as sharing in the costs of their provision. Consider the laws against murder and theft. By obeying these laws, I directly contribute to the good of security for other members of my society. But this does not obviously exemplify *political* obligation, because I have an obligation independent of the law to respect the rights of others. It is not clear that the existence of a law against murder *increases* my moral obligation not to commit murder nor that it increases the 'unfairness' involved in murdering someone.

Tax laws provide a more believable example. Here it is very clear how obedience contributes to the provision of governmental benefits: one's tax money will be used to hire judges, police officers, soldiers, and so on. So in paying taxes, one does one's share in providing the benefits of government. This is an instance of political obligation, for one would not be obligated to pay this money if the tax laws did not exist.

Other laws are more problematic. To take one example, in the United States and most other countries, it is illegal to smoke marijuana. In what way does obedience to *this* law constitute a sharing of the costs of providing protection from foreign governments or domestic criminals or providing predictable rules for social cooperation? How does one, by refraining from smoking marijuana, causally contribute to the security of one's society? This is no trivial or peripheral case. Enforcement of drug laws is a very large portion of law enforcement in the United States, where drug offenders account for about 25 percent of local jail inmates, 20 percent of state prison inmates, and 52 percent of federal prison inmates.[13] As of this writing, over half a million Americans are imprisoned on drug charges.[14]

---

[13] Recent statistics on incarceration of drug offenders in state and federal prisons are from U.S. Department of Justice 2010b, 37–8. The most recent statistic on drug offenders in local jails is from U.S. Department of Justice 2004, 1, reporting that 24.7 percent of jail inmates were drug offenders in 2002. Classifications are based on the most serious offense for which an inmate was imprisoned.

[14] This estimate is based on the assumption that 24.7 percent of local jail inmates are drug offenders (U.S. Department of Justice 2004, 1), together with the 2008 jail population as reported in U.S. Department of Justice 2009. Statistics for state and local prisons are from the U.S. Department of Justice (2010a, 37–8). The total number of inmates of all offense classes, including state, local, and federal institutions, is about 2.3 million.

Nor is this an isolated example. Many other laws raise similar questions. In the United States, it is illegal to provide legal advice to people without admission to the bar (even if you explicitly inform your advisees that you have not been admitted and they want your advice anyway). It is illegal to buy an hour of labor for less than $7.25. Or to buy sex for any amount of money. Or to sell packaged food without listing the number of calories it contains on the package. Or to run a private company that delivers mail to individuals' mailboxes. It is illegal to sell stevia as a food additive, though legal to sell it as a 'dietary supplement'. And so on. These are just a few of the hundreds of thousands of legal restrictions in force in the United States.

In all of these cases, it is difficult to see the connection between the legally required behavior and the sharing of costs for providing essential governmental services. It seems that the state could very well provide the goods described in Section 5.1.2 without any of the laws described in the preceding two paragraphs.[15]

Obedience to the law, according to advocates of the Fair Play Account, is analogous to helping bail water out of a lifeboat. But in view of the aforementioned laws, a closer analogy would be as follows. The lifeboat is taking on water. The passengers gather and discuss what to do about the problem. A majority (not including you) want Bob to devise a solution. Bob thinks for a minute, then announces the following plan:

i) All passengers shall start bailing water out of the boat;
ii) they shall pray to Poseidon to ask for his mercy;
iii) they shall flagellate themselves with belts to prove their seriousness; and
iv) they shall each pay $50 to Sally, who helped Bob get elected.

You know that item (i) is useful, item (ii) is useless, and items (iii) and (iv) are harmful to most passengers. Nonetheless, most other passengers participate in all four parts of Bob's plan. If you refuse to pray, self-flagellate, or pay Sally, do you thereby act wrongly? Do you treat the other passengers *unfairly*?

Failure to pray to Poseidon, whip yourself, and pay Sally is not unfair, because those actions would not contribute causally to the good of keeping the boat afloat. If other passengers feel aggrieved at

---

[15] One might argue that to effectively provide security, the state must have a certain degree of deference from the citizens – citizens must agree not to judge every individual law for themselves – and this is part of the cost of security. I address this idea in Section 7.5 below.

suffering the lash while you do not, the remedy is simple: they should stop whipping themselves. The fault lies in themselves and Bob, not in you.

Recall that political obligations are supposed to be *content-independent* (Section 1.5) – that is, it is said that one must follow the law regardless of its content (within some broad constraints) and regardless of whether the law is correct. The above discussion suggests that this is not the case. One must examine the content of a particular law to determine whether the behavior it enjoins genuinely contributes to the provision of political goods before one can say whether one has any fairness-based reason to follow that law.

Some would argue that, even if a given law is not needed to carry out the government's central functions, obedience to that law is still part of the cost of providing essential government services because disobedience risks bringing down the government and all social order. We have criticized this sort of claim above (Section 5.1.4). But if it were true, it would do as much to undermine content-independent *political legitimacy* as it would to support content-independent *political obligation*. Presumably, if individuals are obligated to help maintain social order, the state is similarly obligated. If disobedience to any law risks causing a collapse of social order, then the state, in *making* laws that are not necessary to maintaining social order and that are likely to be widely disobeyed, is itself threatening social order far more than a single individual who disobeys one of these laws. Furthermore, asking the state to renounce its desire to make such unnecessary laws is more reasonable and less onerous than asking an individual to renounce his personal liberties. Therefore, if one holds that the individual nevertheless must obey such laws when they are made, it is much clearer that the state must not make such laws. And thus, one cannot simultaneously defend political obligation and political legitimacy on this view.

5.3.3 Political obligation for dissenters

A second problem for the Fair Play Account concerns those who fail to endorse the state's activities. This includes some individuals who feel they do not need the state; for example, hermits living in the wilderness or indigenous peoples who would prefer that European colonists had never arrived on their continent. It includes those who are morally or ideologically opposed to government in general (anarchists). It includes people who, while supporting the general idea of government, believe that the proper sort of government is radically different from the government they have. And it includes people who oppose specific government programs but are nevertheless forced to contribute to them.

For instance, pacifists may not want the alleged good of a military force, yet they must pay for it just as everyone else does.

We have seen that it is difficult to account for an obligation to assist in useless or harmful projects. Here, we see that it is also difficult to account for an obligation to assist in projects to which one is sincerely opposed, whether or not one's opposition is well founded. Return to the lifeboat example. This time, suppose that the other passengers on the lifeboat believe that praying to Jehovah will assist them in staying afloat. Suppose, even, that they are correct in this belief: Jehovah exists and is receptive to petitionary prayer. Provided that a large majority pray, Jehovah will assist them. But Sally does not believe this. Sally believes that praying to Jehovah will more likely be harmful, because it will offend Cthulhu. She therefore opposes the other passengers' plan. In this situation, would it be *unfair* of Sally to refuse to pray to Jehovah?

If the existence of Jehovah and the effectiveness of petitionary prayer were easily verifiable facts, which Sally could be blamed for failing to know, then perhaps Sally would have a moral obligation to pray to Jehovah. But assume that this is not the case. Assume that these are matters on which there is reasonable disagreement and that Sally's view is rational or at least not markedly less rational than the view of the majority of passengers. In that case, it is not wrong of Sally to refrain from praying to Jehovah. She is not seeking to gain some sort of unfair advantage over others nor to profit through others' labors. If the others should try to force Sally to join in their prayers, they and not she would be acting unfairly.

In the political case, there are a number of individuals who oppose various government programs. These are not people who seek to free ride on others' efforts – they are not simply wishing for others to bear the programs' costs. They do not want these programs to exist at all. In many cases, they take governmental projects to be seriously unjust or otherwise morally unacceptable. And in many cases, their view, whether correct or incorrect, is perfectly reasonable. I should think this is the case in regard to those who oppose the U.S. presence in Afghanistan, drug prohibition, immigration restrictions, and several other controversial laws or governmental projects. There are even some who reasonably regard the institution of government itself as unjust. If one reasonably regards a project as unjust or immoral, one is hardly free riding, taking advantage of others, or treating others unfairly in refusing to support that project. Individuals thus do not act unfairly when they refuse to cooperate with laws that they reasonably regard as unjust.[16] Again, therefore, no basis for content-independent political obligations is to be found.

5.3.4 Particularity and the question of alternative goods

One of the conditions for an obligation of fair play to participate in a cooperate scheme is that one's participation should not interfere with one's doing something more important [condition (6), Section 5.3.1]. But obeying the law often interferes with doing more important things.

For instance, suppose you have the opportunity to safely evade $1,000 worth of legally prescribed taxes. It would perhaps be wrong to evade the taxes to spend the money on a new television. It would, however, be permissible to evade the taxes to use the money in a more socially valuable way than giving it to the government. And that option is almost certain to be available – the marginal social benefit of each dollar given to the government is much less than the marginal social benefit of a dollar given to any of a variety of extremely effective private charities.[17] In this case, it is not wrong to evade one's taxes to send the money to charity; indeed, doing so is praiseworthy.

Of course, most citizens pay taxes under duress from the state. This duress *excuses* the payment of taxes, but it does not render it praiseworthy or obligatory.

5.4 The problem of legitimacy

5.4.1 A consequentialist account of legitimacy

Normally, it is wrong to threaten a person with violence to force compliance with some plan of yours. This is generally true even if your plan is mutually beneficial and otherwise morally acceptable. Thus, suppose you are at a board meeting at which you and the other members are discussing how to improve your company's sales. You know that the best way to do this is to hire the Sneaku Ad Agency. Your plan will be morally unobjectionable and highly beneficial to the company. Nevertheless, the other members are not convinced. So you pull out your handgun and *order* them to vote for your proposal. This behavior

---

[16] Contrast the views of defenders of political authority, such as Rawls (1964, 5): 'It is, of course, a familiar situation in a constitutional democracy that a person finds himself morally obligated to obey an unjust law.'

[17] See http://www.givewell.org/ for charity reviews, including a list of the most effective charities.

would be unacceptable, even though you are acting for everyone's benefit and even though your plan is the right one.

But similar behavior *can* be justified in emergency circumstances. Return to the lifeboat scenario. The boat is in danger of sinking unless most of the passengers quickly start bailing water. This time, however, suppose that none of the other passengers are willing to bail water. You cannot perform the task alone, and no amount of reasoning or pleading will persuade the myopic passengers to take up their buckets. Finally, you pull your trusty Glock out of your jacket and order the other passengers to start bailing out the boat. In this situation, regrettable as the resort to force may be, your action seems justified.

Christopher Wellman offers an example with a similar lesson.[18] Amy has a medical emergency and needs to be taken to the hospital immediately. Beth is aware of this but has no vehicle with which to transport Amy. So she temporarily steals Cathy's car to take Amy to the hospital. This action violates Cathy's property rights. Nevertheless, the act is permissible, provided that there are no other ways of rescuing Amy without committing at least equally serious rights violations.

These examples suggest the following general principle: it is permissible to coerce a person or violate a person's property rights, provided that doing so is necessary to prevent something *much* worse from happening.

Thus, perhaps the state is justified in coercing people and seizing people's property through taxation, because doing so is necessary to prevent a virtual collapse of society. If the state did not coercively enforce laws, too many people would break them, and if the state did not coercively collect tax money, the state could not operate at all. In either of these cases, the state could not provide the crucial social benefits described in Section 5.1.2 above.

5.4.2   Comprehensiveness and content-independence

In the version of the lifeboat scenario discussed in Section 5.4.1, you are entitled to use coercion to save everyone on the boat. But this entitlement is neither comprehensive nor content-independent. Your entitlement to coerce is highly specific and content-dependent: it depends upon your having a correct (or at least well-justified) plan for saving the boat, and you may coerce others only to induce cooperation with that plan. More precisely, you must at least be justified in believing that the expected benefits of coercively imposing your plan on the others are very large and much larger than the expected harms. You may not coerce others to

---

[18]   Wellman 2005, 21.

induce harmful or useless behaviors or behaviors designed to serve ulterior purposes unrelated to the emergency. For instance, if you display your firearm and order everyone to start scooping water from the ocean *into* the boat, you are acting wrongly – and similarly if you use the weapon to force the others to pray to Poseidon, lash themselves with belts, or hand over $50 to your friend Sally.

Matters are similar in Wellman's car-stealing scenario. Amy is ethically entitled to violate Cathy's property right in her car. But this entitlement is highly content-specific: Amy may not violate Cathy's property right in just any way she chooses. She may not take the car and drive Beth *away* from the hospital. She may not drive Beth to the hospital and then take the car for a spin up in the mountains. She may not rifle through the glove compartment looking for valuables. Amy may use the car in one very specific way: she may drive Beth to the hospital. Nothing more.

If, therefore, we rely upon cases like this to account for the state's right to coerce or violate the property rights of its citizens, the proper conclusion is that the state's legitimate powers must be highly specific and content-dependent: the state may coerce individuals only in the minimal way necessary to implement a correct (or at least well-justified) plan for protecting society from the sorts of disasters that allegedly would result from anarchy. The state may not coerce people into cooperating with harmful or useless measures or measures we lack good reason to consider effective. Nor may the state extend the exercise of coercion to pursue just any goal that seems desirable. The state may take the minimal amount of money from its citizens necessary to provide the 'indispensible goods' that justify its existence.[19] It may not take a little extra to buy itself something nice.

How many governmental activities might be considered legitimate on this basis? Domestic laws and policies may be divided into nine categories, depending on the motivations behind them (these categories are not mutually exclusive):

1. Laws designed to protect citizens' rights; for instance, the laws against murder, theft, and fraud.
2. Policies designed to provide public goods, in the economic sense of the term; for instance, military defense and environmental protection.[20]

---

[19] On indispensable goods, see Klosko 2005, 7–8.

[20] In the economic sense of the term, a public good is a good with two characteristics: (1) it is nonrival, meaning that one person's receipt of the good does

3. Paternalistic laws, designed to prevent people from harming themselves; for instance, seat belt laws and drug laws.
4. Moralistic laws, designed to prevent behavior that is regarded as 'immoral' for some reason other than harm to self or others or violation of others' rights; for instance, laws against prostitution, gambling, and drugs.
5. Policies designed to aid the poor; for instance, welfare programs, educational subsidies, and minimum wage laws.[21]
6. Rent-seeking policies; that is, policies, other than those in category (5), designed to confer economic advantages on some people at the expense of others; for instance, subsidies given to politically powerful industries, lucrative military contracts awarded to companies with ties to government officials, and licensing requirements that protect existing workers in a profession from competition.
7. Laws designed to secure the state's monopoly and promote its power and wealth; for instance, tax laws, legal tender laws, and laws preventing private competition with government agencies such as the post office and the police.
8. Policies designed to promote other things that are regarded as good in general, apart from the goods listed above; for instance, government provision of schools, government sponsorship for the arts, and government space programs.
9. Laws and policies that appear to be motivated simply by emotion, apart from the above considerations; for instance, immigration restrictions and bans on gay marriage.[22]

When we think in the abstract about the need for law and the importance of obeying the law, we mostly have in mind laws of types (1), (2), and perhaps (7). Laws of those kinds could perhaps be justified by the sort of consequentialist argument discussed in Section 5.4.1. But as the above list suggests, there is much more to the activities of any

---

not reduce the good's availability to others; (2) it is nonexcludable, meaning that if it is provided at all, it is impossible or very costly to control who receives it.

[21] These policies are also partly paternalistic in motivation when they do something other than a straight cash transfer. For instance, when the state makes certain funds available to indigent citizens with the restriction that the money may only be used to purchase education, this is partly redistributive and partly paternalistic.

[22] See Huemer 2010b on immigration policy; see especially 460–1, on the motivations for immigration restrictions.

modern state. And those extra activities, as a rule, cannot be justified by consequentialist arguments.

Let us extend the story of the lifeboat a little further. You have forced the other passengers to bail water out of the boat, thus saving it from sinking. While you have your gun out, you decide you might as well accomplish a few other desirable goals. You see a passenger eating potato chips, which will elevate his risk of heart disease. Pointing the gun at him, you order him to hand over the chips. Then you notice a pair of passengers at the other end of the boat playing a card game. When you see that they have bet money on the game, you threaten to hurt them if they don't stop gambling. Another passenger has some expensive jewelry, so you take it from her and distribute it to some of the poorer passengers. You also collect $50 from everyone and give it to your friend Sally. You threaten to shoot any other passenger who tries to do the same things you are doing. Then you decide that it would be nice to have some art, so you force the other passengers to hand over some of their belongings so you can make a sculpture out of them. Finally, you have an uneasy feeling about one of the passengers – you don't like the way he looks – so you order the other passengers to throw him overboard.

All of these actions are indefensible. Though your initial use of coercion to preserve the lifeboat from sinking was justified, it is absurd to suggest that coercion is justified by the kinds of motives displayed in any of your later actions in this story. These motives are analogous to those displayed in policies of types (3)–(9) listed above.[23]

The specific examples I have given of policy types (3)–(9) are not important, so long as one agrees that there are (a nontrivial number of) policies of each of these types. It does not greatly matter, for instance, whether one agrees that licensing laws are motivated by rent seeking as long as one agrees that a significant number of laws are motivated by rent seeking. The point is that the state has many policies and laws

---

[23] To be explicit, here is a list of government policies analogous to your actions in the story: Stopping passenger from eating potato chips: drug laws and other paternalistic laws. Stopping the card game: laws against gambling and other moralistic laws. Confiscating jewelry: welfare and other wealth-redistribution programs. Collecting money for Sally: subsidies, no-bid contracts, and other policies motivated by rent seeking. Threatening to shoot other passengers who do the same things: prohibitions on vigilantism and setting up competing governments. Confiscating property to make sculpture: state support for the arts. Throwing a passenger overboard: immigration restriction and deportation of illegal immigrants.

whose motivations do not justify the coercion required to implement them. This is a problem because the state's authority is generally held to be *comprehensive* and *content-independent*. On a very strict reading of the comprehensiveness and content-independence conditions, the existence of just a few laws that the state is not entitled to make would preclude the state's having genuine authority. A more modest version of the comprehensiveness and content-independence conditions would hold that the state does not have genuine authority unless at least the *majority* of the things that it typically does and that it is generally considered entitled to do are in fact morally permissible. If the range of coercive actions that the state is actually entitled to take is only a small fraction of what it is generally thought to be entitled to do and of what the state in fact does, then I think the state does not truly have legitimate authority. And I think we must admit that that is in fact the case.

5.4.3 Supremacy

The state's authority is also supposed to be *supreme*, in the sense that no one else has the right to coerce individuals in the way the state does, nor does anyone have the right to coerce the state. This, too, is difficult to account for.

Modifying the lifeboat scenario once again, suppose that on the boat there are two armed passengers, Gumby and Pokey, each of whom recognizes that the lifeboat needs to be bailed out. Again, the other passengers resolutely refuse to bail. Gumby and Pokey both know that coercion is necessary to save the boat, and either of them would be justified in taking the necessary measures. But Gumby is quicker to act: he takes out his gun and forces the other passengers to start bailing. At this point, does Gumby acquire some sort of supremacy?

No, he does not. If Pokey should see some other impending disaster that can only be averted through coercion, he would be justified in using coercion to avert it. This would have been true if Gumby had never been on the lifeboat, and it remains true after Gumby has used coercion to save the lifeboat from sinking. Gumby's initial coercive act does not forestall justified coercion by others, nor does it reduce the range of circumstances in which others may use coercion, such that it becomes easier in the future for Gumby to be justified in using coercion than for anyone else on the boat. Nor would Pokey be morally barred from taking coercive actions to enforce the water-bailing scheme should Gumby's enforcement prove inadequate.

Before Gumby's initial coercive act, it would have been true that Pokey could permissibly use force against Gumby if this were necessary to prevent Gumby from seriously violating others' rights or to prevent something else very bad from happening. After Gumby's initial coercive act, this remains just as true. The mere fact that Gumby was the first to use coercion to save the boat does not somehow render him immune from being coerced in circumstances in which it would normally be permissible to coerce someone. For example, if, after saving the lifeboat, Gumby then tries to rob the passengers, Pokey would be justified in using force to defend the other passengers.

It seems, then, that the state does not, on consequentialist grounds, have supreme authority. Other agents may use force to achieve the same goals that the state would be justified in using force to achieve in the event that the state's own efforts are inadequate. For example, if the state fails to provide adequate protection from crime, there is no obvious reason why private agents may not provide security using the same methods that the state may use. Private agents may also use force to prevent disasters that the state has not taken sufficient action to avert (again, in the same circumstances in which the state may use force). And private agents may use force against the state when this is necessary to prevent the state from committing serious rights violations or to prevent something else very bad from happening.

When may one use force against others? It is plausible to hold that private individuals and organizations are justified in using force only when

i) they have strong justification for believing that the plan they are attempting to implement is correct (for instance, that it would produce the intended benefits and that these benefits would be great in comparison to the seriousness of the rights violations required to implement the plan);

ii) they have strong justification for believing that their use of force would succeed in causing their plan to be implemented; and

iii) there are no alternatives available for achieving the benefits without at least equally serious rights violations.

In reality, these conditions are quite restrictive and are seldom realized. It is plausible that most actual vigilantes violate condition (i) and that most actual rebels and terrorists violate both (i) and (ii). So most actual cases of vigilantism or terrorism should not be endorsed.

Nevertheless, the conclusion is a rejection of the supremacy of governmental authority, for the qualifications mentioned in the preceding paragraph apply equally to state actors. The state must also

have strong justification for believing that each of its coercively implemented plans is correct, that its use of coercion will be successful, and
that there are no better alternatives. If one relies on a consequentialist
account of legitimacy of the sort that has been under discussion, there
is no apparent way of escaping this conclusion. So there is no clear
sense in which the state has supreme authority; it may coerce individuals in the same sorts of circumstances, for the same sorts of reasons,
as private agents may coerce individuals. And just as most vigilante and
terrorist acts are unjustified, I think it plausible that the great majority
of state actions also violate one or more of the conditions for justified
coercion.

5.5   Conclusion

Consequentialist and fairness-based arguments come closest to
justifying political authority. Nevertheless, they cannot ground
content-independent, comprehensive, or supreme authority for the
state. The state has the right, at most, to coercively impose correct
and just policies to prevent very serious harms.[24] No one has the
right to coercively enforce counterproductive or useless policies nor
to enforce policies aimed at goals of lesser import. The state may be
entitled to collect taxes, to administer a system of police and courts to
protect society from individual rights violators, and to provide military defense. In doing so, the state and its agents may take only the
minimal funds and employ only the minimal coercion necessary.
The state may not go on to coercively impose paternalistic or moralistic laws, policies motivated by rent seeking, or policies aimed at
promoting unnecessary goods, such as support for the arts or a space
program.

---

[24] The state will lack even this right if, as argued in Part II, the state is not necessary for the provision of any vital goods.

6

The Psychology of Authority

6.1 The relevance of psychology

In this chapter, I review some evidence from psychology and history, both about the attitudes and behavior of those who are subject to others' (alleged) authority and about the attitudes and behavior of those who are in positions of authority. These findings are fascinating in their own right. They also bear, in at least two important ways, on the skepticism about political authority defended in this book. For one thing, psychological data bear on the question of how much trust we should place in our intuitions about authority. For another, psychological data bear on the question of how desirable or harmful it may be to encourage skepticism about authority. In the present chapter, when I speak of 'authorities' and 'authority figures', I mean people and institutions that are socially recognized as having authority, whether or not they have genuine authority in a normative sense. 'Positions of authority' and 'institutions of authority' should be understood similarly.

6.1.1 Is this book dangerous?

Some defenders of authority have openly worried about the consequences that might result from anarchistic ideas. If ideas like those I advance in this book were to take hold in our society, they warn, there would be much more disobedience to the government.[1] This disobedience, in turn, might lead the state to become more violent and oppressive.[2] Or, as Plato and Hume warned, it might lead to a general collapse

---

[1] Honoré (1981, 42–4) expresses this concern in regard to Simmons's philosophical anarchism, a more moderate doctrine than my own.

[2] For this reason, DeLue (1989, 1) warns that the widespread acceptance of philosophical anarchism 'would be a tragedy for liberal regimes'.

of social order.[3] Books such as this one, if not opposed sufficiently vigorously by other philosophers, might ultimately contribute to such outcomes. This would not bear directly on whether this book is *correct* in its central contentions (a correct thesis may be undesirable to advance), but it bears directly on the interesting question of whether perhaps this book is *bad* and ought not to have been written. I will address this concern in later sections of this chapter, after reviewing some important psychological findings.

6.1.2   The appeal to popular opinion

Other advocates of political authority suggest that anarchism should be rejected because it is simply too far out of the mainstream of political opinion. The belief in political obligations, writes George Klosko, 'is a basic feature of our political consciousness'.[4] He believes that we should accept common opinions as prima facie evidence in normative matters, particularly when philosophical opinion is divided. David Hume goes farther: 'The general opinion of mankind has some authority in all cases; but in this of morals 'tis perfectly infallible.'[5] If there is no political authority, it is natural to ask, then how have so many people come to have such a firm belief in it? Is it not more likely that I and the handful of other anarchists have made a mistake than that almost everyone else in the world has?

Ultimately, I disagree with that argument. All things considered, I think it more likely that others are mistaken than that I am. (Obviously, I would not hold a belief that I myself did not consider more likely true than false.) Nevertheless, the argument should not be rejected hastily or for the wrong reasons. To give the argument a fair treatment, I pause here to defend the appeal to popular opinion against overly facile objections.

There are some who reject appeals to popular opinion, in principle, as fallacious (supposedly the fallacy of *argumentum ad populum*). But

---

[3] See the *Crito* at 50d in Plato 2000, and see Hume 1987, 480. Both philosophers appear to be worried that even a small amount of disobedience, perhaps just a single act of disobedience, would lead to this result.

[4] Klosko 1992, 24. Klosko makes the point at greater length in his 2005, chapter 9.

[5] Hume 1992, section III.ii.9, 552. Hume uses this premise to reject the social contract theory, which in his time held little sway with the public. His strong thesis of moral infallibility may be explained by his antirealist metaethics (1992, Section III.i.1–2).

exactly what is supposed to be fallacious about appealing to popular opinions? The most commonly cited illustration of the alleged error is the case of Christopher Columbus; when Columbus wanted to sail around the world, it is said, his contemporaries laughed at him because they were all convinced that the earth was flat. But Columbus turned out to be right. And this, you see, shows why it is foolish to trust in the opinions of the majority.

As a historical note, the preceding account is completely inaccurate. It was Columbus who was wrong and those who 'laughed at him' who were right in the chief point of dispute. The idea that Columbus's contemporaries thought the earth was flat is a modern myth. The ancient Greeks discovered that the earth was round, and this knowledge was never lost.[6] The actual point of dispute concerned the westward distance from Europe to Asia. Columbus thought this distance small enough to sail in the kind of ships that then existed; his contemporaries thought otherwise. They were right and he was wrong: the actual distance is about four times greater than Columbus thought it was. If not for the unexpected discovery of the Caribbean Islands, Columbus and his crew would have starved to death at sea long before they came anywhere near Asia.

But that is just a side note of historical interest. There certainly are cases in which large majorities of people hold mistaken beliefs. Indeed, the false beliefs that most modern people hold about Columbus and his contemporaries are a case in point. But what interesting conclusion follows from this observation? Let us consider three conclusions one might draw.

First, perhaps the Columbus example (or some other, more genuine example of popular error) is meant to show that the existence of a very widespread belief does not provide *conclusive proof* for the thing that the majority believes, since there are *some* cases in which such beliefs are false. This is obviously correct. It is also utterly uninteresting. A belief-forming method need not be *infallible* to be useful or rational. All or nearly all belief-forming methods are fallible, including sensory observation and scientific reasoning. This does not show that we ought to eschew observation, science, and almost everything else as 'fallacious'.

---

[6] Lindberg 1992, 58; Russell 1991. In the fourth century BC, Aristotle discussed the arguments establishing the earth's sphericity (*De Caelo*, 297a9–297b20), and in the third century BC, Eratosthenes provided a reasonably accurate estimate of the earth's circumference.

Second, perhaps the Columbus argument is meant to show that the existence of a very widespread belief does not provide *any evidence at all* for the thing that the majority believes. This conclusion is much more interesting. It is also obviously unwarranted. The existence of a single error or even many errors produced by a given information source does not show that source to be completely evidentially worthless. To argue that popular opinion is evidentially worthless, one would have to argue that popular opinion does *no better than chance* – in other words, that very widely held beliefs are correct no more often than propositions drawn at random out of a hat. But the latter claim is obviously false.

Consider now the range of cases in which a small minority of people disagrees with the majority. A small minority of people today thinks that the earth is flat, that the moon landings were faked, or that perpetual motion machines are possible; the majority disagrees. A few people believe themselves to be Jesus or Napoleon or a super-hero, while all those around them disagree. In all of these cases, the majority is right, and the minority is wrong. Sometimes, in a science or mathematics class, all the students but one get the same answer to a particular problem. Sometimes, in a group of several people, all of whom witnessed some event, one person remembers the event differently from the others. In nearly all of these cases, again, the majority is right – the lone dissenter has miscalculated or misremembered. The explanation is a simple matter of probability: for the majority to be wrong, the same cognitive malfunction or cognitive malfunctions producing the same result must have occurred many times in different brains. For one person to be wrong, a cognitive malfunction need only have occurred once. The latter is generally more likely.

Third and finally, perhaps the Columbus argument is meant to show that an appeal to popular belief does not provide *strong* evidence for the thing that the majority believes. It might be argued that popular opinion, while more reliable than random guesses, is nevertheless quite unreliable.

But how are we meant to infer this? One possibility is that we are supposed to see the Christopher Columbus example and perhaps a few similar cases as constituting a large, random sample of popular beliefs in which a large percentage (100%) turn out to be false. This would provide serious evidence of unreliability. Another possibility is that we are supposed to simply recognize, on the basis of ordinary background knowledge and experience, that the Columbus example is a *typical* case of a dissenter against a majority view. But neither of these possibilities is easy to take seriously. The 'sample' of popular beliefs offered in this sort of argument typically contains only a few cases, and the sampling method is something closer to 'deliberate selection of cases with the desired trait' than 'random selection'. As to typicalness, isn't the lone conspiracy nut in the office who insists that '9/11 was an inside job' and that the U.S. government created AIDS a more typical example of a dissenter against a large majority opinion than Christopher Columbus? Based on everyday experience, how many '9/11 truthers' are there for every one Columbus?[7]

Once we see why popular opinion is to *some* degree evidentially relevant, it is difficult not to conclude that it is often *highly* relevant. Again, it is typically less likely that some cognitive malfunction occurs multiple times than that it occurs once. If that is so, then it is typically *much* less likely that a malfunction occurs *a great many* times than that it occurs a small number of times. (The principle is formalized in the Condorcet Jury Theorem.)[8] I will discuss possible exceptions to this rule below.

Appeal to popular opinion, then, is not in general fallacious. As a rule, very firm and widespread beliefs should not be lightly set aside. Considerable reflection is thus required before we set aside the common belief in political authority. We must carefully examine the most prominent and promising theories of the source of authority, as discussed in Chapters 2 through 5 above. We must also examine the likely sources of beliefs about political authority, as in the present chapter.

6.2   The Milgram experiments

6.2.1   Setup

Perhaps the most famous psychological study of obedience and authority is the one conducted by Stanley Milgram at Yale University

---

[7] See Stove (1995, 58–62) on 'The Columbus Argument' for further discussion.

[8] See McLean and Hewitt's introduction to Condorcet 1994 (35–6). Condorcet notes that when we assume individuals are 80 percent reliable and the majority outnumbers the minority by as few as nine persons, the probability of the majority being correct exceeds 99.999 percent. The Jury Theorem may be misleading, because the assumption of probabilistic independence is rarely satisfied. However, a broader qualitative point can be made; namely, that a convergence of information sources on a particular proposition probabilistically supports that proposition, to a greater degree than a single information source would, provided that (i) each source is more reliable than a random guess, (ii) neither source is *completely* dependent on the other, and (iii) one source is not more likely to agree with the other if the latter source is wrong than if the latter source is correct. It is very plausible that these conditions are commonly satisfied when the sources are individual people.

in the 1960s.[9] Milgram gathered volunteers to participate, supposedly, in a study of memory. When each subject arrived at the laboratory, he was paid $4.50 (then a reasonable payment), which he was told was his to keep just for showing up. Another 'volunteer' (actually a confederate of the experimenter) was already present. The experimenter (actually a high school teacher whom Milgram had hired to play the role) informed both of them that they would participate in a study of the effects of punishment on learning. One of them would be designated as the 'teacher' and the other as the 'learner'. Through a rigged drawing, the naive subject was selected as the teacher, and the confederate as the learner.

The experimenter explained that the teacher would read pairs of words to the learner, who would attempt to remember which word was associated with which other word. The teacher would then quiz the learner. Each time the learner gave a wrong answer, the teacher was to administer an electric shock, through an impressive-looking shock generator. With each wrong answer, the shocks would increase in intensity, starting with a 15-volt shock and increasing by 15 volts each time. The experimenter gave the teacher a sample 45-volt shock to show what it was like (and to convince subjects of the authenticity of the shock generator). The learner mentioned that he had a slight heart condition and asked whether the experiment was safe. The experimenter assured him that while the shocks might be painful, they were not dangerous. The learner was strapped into a chair in another room with an electrode attached to his wrist, supposedly connected to the shock generator.

On a fixed schedule, the learner would make mistakes, leading to increasingly severe shocks. The switches on the shock generator were labeled from 15 volts all the way up to 450 volts, along with qualitative labels ranging from 'Slight Shock' up to 'Danger: Severe Shock', followed by an ominous 'XXX' under the last two switches. Each time the learner made a mistake, the teacher was supposed to use the next switch on the shock generator. At 75 volts, the learner began grunting in pain. At 120 volts, he shouted to the experimenter that the shocks were becoming painful. At 150 volts, the learner complained that his heart was bothering him and demanded to be released. Cries of this sort continued, up to an agonized scream at 270 volts. At 300 volts, the victim refused to provide any further answers to the memory test. The experimenter

---

[9] The account that follows in the text is based on Milgram 2009. In addition to the version I describe in the text ('Experiment 5'), Milgram details several other interesting variations on the experiment.

instructed the teacher to treat a failure to answer as a wrong answer and to continue administering shocks. The victim continued to scream and insist that he was no longer a participant, complaining about his heart again at 330 volts. After 330 volts, however, nothing further was heard from the learner. When the teacher reached the final, 450-volt switch on the shock generator, the experimenter would instruct the teacher to continue using the 450-volt switch. After the teacher had administered the 450-volt shock three times, the experiment was ended.

If at any point in this process the teacher expressed reluctance to continue, the experimenter would prod the teacher with 'Please continue.' If the subject repeatedly expressed reluctance, the experimenter would prompt him with 'The experiment requires that you continue', then 'It is absolutely essential that you continue', and finally 'You have no other choice. You *must* go on.' If the subject still resisted after the fourth prod, the experiment was discontinued.

6.2.2 Predictions

The learner, of course, did not truly receive the electric shocks. The real purpose was to determine how far subjects would be willing to obey the experimenter. If you are not already familiar with the experiment, it is worth taking a moment to reflect, first, on what you think would be the right way for the teacher to behave, and second, what you think most people would in fact do.

Postexperimental interviews established that subjects were convinced that the situation was what it appeared to be and that the learner was receiving extremely painful electric shocks. Given this, a teacher clearly ought not to continue administering shocks after the learner demands to be released. To do so would have been a serious violation of the victim's human rights. At some point, the experiment would have amounted to torture and then murder. While the experimenter has some right to direct the conduct of his experiment, no one would say he has the right to order torture and murder.

What would you have done if you had been a subject in the experiment? Milgram described the experiment to students, psychiatrists, and ordinary adults and asked them to predict both how they themselves would behave if they were in the experiment and how most other people would behave.[10] Of 110 respondents, every one said that they would defy the experimenter at some point, explaining their reasons in terms of compassion, empathy, and principles of justice. Most thought

---

[10] Milgram 2009, 27–31.

they would refuse to continue beyond the 150-volt shock (when the learner first demands to be released), and no one saw themselves going beyond 300 volts (when the learner refuses to answer). Their predictions of others' behavior were only slightly less optimistic: respondents expected that only a pathological fringe of 1–2 percent of the population would proceed all the way to 450 volts. The psychiatrists Milgram surveyed thought that only one experimental subject in a thousand would proceed to the end of the shock board.

6.2.3   Results

Milgram's experiment shows something surprising, not only about our dispositions to obey but also about our self-understanding. The predictions of psychiatrists, students, and lay people fell shockingly far from reality. In the actual experiment, 65 percent of subjects complied fully, eventually administering the 450-volt shock three times to a silent and apparently lifeless victim. Most subjects protested and showed obvious signs of anxiety and reluctance – but ultimately, they did what they were told.

Milgram followed up the experiment with mailed surveys to participants. Despite the stress involved in the experiment, virtually no one regretted participating. Those who hear of the experimental design, without having participated, usually think, 'People will not do it', and then, 'If they do it they will not be able to live with themselves afterward.' But in fact, Milgram reports, obedient subjects have no trouble living with themselves afterward, because these subjects by and large rationalize their behavior, after the fact, in the same way they rationalized it in the course of the experiment: they were just following orders.[11]

6.2.4   The dangers of obedience

What lessons can we draw from Milgram's results? One important lesson, the one most prominently advanced by Milgram himself, is that of the danger inherent in institutions of authority. Because most individuals are willing to go frighteningly far in satisfaction of the demands of authority figures, institutions that set up recognized authority figures have the potential to become engines of evil. Milgram draws the parallel to Nazi Germany. Adolf Hitler, working alone, could perhaps have murdered a few dozen or even a few hundred people. What enabled him to become one of history's greatest murderers was the socially recognized position of authority into which he maneuvered

---

[11] Milgram 2009, 195–6.

himself and the unquestioning obedience rendered him by millions of German subjects. Just as none of Milgram's subjects would have decided on their own to go out and electrocute anyone, very few Germans would have decided, on their own, to go out murdering Jews. Respect for authority was Hitler's key weapon. The same is true of all of the greatest man-made evils. No one has ever managed, working alone, to kill over a million people. Nor has anyone ever arranged such an evil by appealing to the profit motive, pure self-interest, or moral suasion to secure the cooperation of others – except by relying on institutions of political authority. With the help of such institutions, many such crimes have been carried out, accounting for tens of millions of deaths, along with many more ruined lives.

It is possible that such institutions *also* serve crucial social functions and forestall other enormous evils. Even so, in light of the empirical facts, we must ask whether humans have too strong a disposition to obey authority figures. This brings us to a closely related lesson suggested by Milgram's results: most people's disposition to obey authorities is far stronger than one would have thought at first glance – and far stronger than one could possibly think justified.

6.2.5 The unreliability of opinions about authority

Another interesting lesson is this: the experience of being subjected to an authority has a distorting influence on one's moral perceptions. Everyone who *hears* about the experiment correctly perceives the moral imperative, at some point, to reject the experimenter's demands to continue shocking the victim. No rational person would think that complete obedience to the experimenter was appropriate. But once a person is in the situation, he begins to *feel* the force of the experimenter's demands. When Milgram asked one obedient subject why he did not break off the experiment, the subject replied, 'I tried to, but he [indicating the experimenter] *wouldn't let me.*' The experimenter in fact exercised no force to compel subjects to continue – yet subjects *felt* compelled. By what? By the sheer authority of the experimenter. Once a person has been subjected to this authority and has obeyed, the distortion of ethical perception often continues. The subject continues to find his actions justifiable or excusable on the grounds that he was just following orders – even though no one outside the experiment would agree.

The parallel to Nazi Germany again asserts itself. While almost all outside observers condemn the actions of the Nazis (and not just those of Adolf Hitler, who gave the ultimate orders), Nazi officers famously defended themselves with the appeal to superior orders. Was this simply an insincere ploy to escape punishment? Probably not; like Milgram's subjects, the officers probably felt that they had to obey orders. In Hannah Arendt's memorable description of the case, Adolf Eichmann thought he was doing his duty by obeying the law of Germany, which was inextricably tied to the will of the Führer; he would have felt guilty if he *didn't* follow both the letter and the spirit of Hitler's orders.[12] Even more clearly, average soldiers in the German army cannot be supposed so much more evil than typical non-Germans that they independently wanted to participate in a genocide. While anti-Semitism was rampant in Germany, it did not issue in widespread murder until the government ordered the killings. Only then did ordinary soldiers feel the killings to be justified or required.

History records many similar cases. During the Vietnam war, an American army unit carried out the massacre of hundreds of civilians at My Lai. In one of the most notorious war crimes in the nation's history, defenseless women, children, and old men were gathered together and shot en masse. Again, the soldiers involved pled that they were only following orders.[13] One soldier reportedly cried during the massacre yet continued firing.[14]

The widespread acceptance of political authority has been cited as evidence of the existence of (legitimate) political authority. The psychological and historical evidence undermines this appeal. The Nazis, the American soldiers at My Lai, and Milgram's subjects were clearly under no obligation of obedience – quite the contrary – and the orders they were given were clearly illegitimate. From outside these situations, we can see that. Yet when actually confronted by the demands of the authority figures, the individuals in these situations felt the need to obey. This tendency is very widespread among human beings. Now suppose, hypothetically, that all governments were illegitimate and that no one was obligated to obey their commands (except where the commands line up with preexisting moral requirements). The psychological and historical evidence cannot show whether this radical ethical hypothesis is true. But what the evidence does suggest is that *if* that hypothesis were true, it is quite likely that we would still by and large *feel* bound to obey our governments. That is likely, because even people who are subjected to the clearest examples of illegitimate power still typically feel bound to obey. And if we felt this requirement to obey, it

---

[12] Arendt 1964, 24–5, 135–7, 148–9.
[13] Wallace and Meadlo 1969; Kelman and Hamilton 1989, 10–11.
[14] Kelman and Hamilton 1989, 6.

is likely that this would lead us to think and say that we were obliged to obey and then – in the case of the more philosophically minded among us – to devise theories to explain why we have this obligation. Thus, the widespread belief in political authority does not provide strong evidence for the reality of political authority, since that belief can be explained as the product of systematic bias.

6.3   Cognitive dissonance

According to the widely accepted theory of *cognitive dissonance*, we experience an uncomfortable state, known as 'cognitive dissonance', when we have two or more cognitions that stand in conflict or tension with one another – and particularly when our behavior or other reactions appear to conflict with our self-image.[15] We then tend to alter our beliefs or reactions to reduce the dissonance. For instance, a person who sees himself as compassionate yet finds himself inflicting pain on others will experience cognitive dissonance. He might reduce this dissonance by ceasing to inflict pain, changing his image of himself, or adopting auxiliary beliefs to explain why a compassionate person may inflict pain in this situation.

Festinger and Carlsmith provided one of the classic illustrations of cognitive dissonance theory in an experiment conducted in the 1950s.[16] Subjects were made to perform a boring, repetitive task for an hour, which they thought was the core of the experiment they had volunteered for. At the end of the hour, one of three things happened. Subjects in the 'One Dollar' condition were paid a dollar to tell someone (supposedly another volunteer subject coming in) that the task had been fun and interesting. Subjects in the 'Twenty Dollars' condition were paid twenty dollars to say the same thing. Finally, subjects in the Control condition were not asked to say anything and did not say anything of the kind. Later, all three groups were interviewed regarding what they really thought of the repetitive task they had performed for an hour. Subjects in the Twenty Dollars condition had slightly more favorable views than those in the Control group – both of how enjoyable the task was and of how willing they would be to participate in a similar experiment in the future. Subjects in the One Dollar condition, however, had significantly more favorable views of these things than *either* the Control group *or* the Twenty Dollars group. Thus, paying the

---

[15] See Festinger and Carlsmith 1959 for a seminal defense of the theory. On the particular importance of self-image, see Aronson 1999; Aronson et al. 1999.
[16] Festinger and Carlsmith 1959.

subjects *more* had resulted in a *smaller* change in their attitudes toward the task.[17]

Festinger and Carlsmith explain the results as follows. Most people do not generally think of themselves as liars. Therefore, if they found the task they had performed boring, yet they remember that they told someone it was enjoyable, they will experience cognitive dissonance. If the task wasn't enjoyable, why had they said it was? Subjects in the Twenty Dollars condition could readily explain this to themselves: they lied to get the money. But for subjects in the One Dollar condition, this explanation was less satisfying. Because one dollar is a small amount of money, it seemed less adequate as a motivation to lie.[18] Therefore, subjects in the One Dollar condition were under more pressure to believe that the task was actually enjoyable.

In another experiment, volunteers were gathered to participate in a discussion group on sexual psychology.[19] Each volunteer was subjected to one of three conditions: subjects in the Mild condition underwent a slightly embarrassing initiation requirement to join the group (they had to read some sexual but not obscene words out loud). Subjects in the Severe condition underwent a highly embarrassing initiation requirement (they had to read obscene words out loud, followed by pornographic passages). Subjects in the Control condition had no initiation requirement. All subjects then listened to a recording, supposedly of a group discussion in progress. The discussion had been intentionally designed to be as boring and worthless as possible. Subjects were then asked to evaluate the discussion group. Intuitively, one might expect that the embarrassing initiation would have left those in the Severe condition with negative feelings, leading to harsher evaluations of the discussion group. In fact, subjects from the Severe condition had significantly higher opinions of the discussion group than those in either the Control or the Mild condition.[20]

---

[17] The largest attitude difference was between the Control group and the One Dollar group on the question of how willing they would be to participate in a similar experiment again. This was a difference of about 1.8 points on a ten-point scale.

[18] This was a 1950s dollar; the equivalent today would be about $8. The actual reason the subjects lied was probably deference to the experimenters, but the subjects did not know this.

[19] Aronson and Mills 1959.

[20] Ratings of the discussion in the Severe condition were 19% higher than in the Mild condition and 22 percent higher than in the Control condition (Aronson and Mills 1959, 179).

These and other studies show that people tend to adjust their beliefs and values so as to make themselves and their own choices appear better.[21] The same was true of Milgram's subjects. Before participating in the experiment, almost no one would regard obedience in such a scenario as morally acceptable. But afterwards, many obedient subjects found their behavior acceptable.

This psychological principle generates a bias in favor of recognizing political authority. Almost all members of modern societies have frequently submitted to the demands of their governments, even when those demands required actions that they would otherwise be strongly disinclined to perform. For example, most have paid very large amounts of money to the state in satisfaction of its taxation demands. How do we explain to ourselves why we obey? We could explain our behavior by citing fear of punishment, habit, the drive toward social conformity, or a general emotional drive to obey whoever holds power. But none of those explanations is emotionally satisfying. Much more pleasing is the explanation that we obey because we are conscientious and caring citizens, and we thus make great sacrifices to do our duty and serve our society.[22] Philosophical accounts of political authority seem designed to bolster just that image.

One reason for doubting that view of our reasons for obedience is that highly conscientious and caring individuals might be expected to donate large amounts of money to famine relief organizations and other such (nongovernmental) charity groups. The arguments for an obligation to donate to such charities are far more compelling than the arguments for political obligation.[23] Yet for most people, extremely large 'sacrifices' are typically made only when they are commanded by an authority figure and those commands are backed up by a serious threat of punishment. Very few people voluntarily give to charity anything like the amount of money they give to the state.

But whether or not our behavior is motivated by compassion and a sense of duty, it is likely that we would generally wish to believe that it is. To believe this, we must accept a basic doctrine of political obligation, and we must accept the legitimacy of our government.

---

[21] See Brehm 1956.

[22] It might be even more satisfying to believe that obedience to the state is *supererogatory* rather than obligatory, but this might strain the credulity of even the ambitious self-deceiver – most of us know that we do not generally make great supererogatory sacrifices. It is more believable that we make great sacrifices that are morally required of us.

[23] See Singer 1993, chapter 8; Unger 1996.

6.4 Social proof and status quo bias

'Social proof' is an ironic phrase meant to describe the persuasive effect on an individual of the expressed opinions of a group.[24] In one classic experiment, Solomon Asch gathered subjects for what they thought was a test of visual acuity.[25] Each subject was seated in a room with several other people, supposedly other subjects like himself. The group was shown a series of cards, each of which had a single, vertical line on the left (the 'standard line') and three comparison lines on the right. The subjects' task was to identify which comparison line was the same length as the standard. The people in the room were to report their visual judgments in series, out loud, while the experimenter recorded them.

In fact, the experimenter had spoken to all the people but one beforehand, instructing them to give identical, incorrect answers for twelve out of eighteen line comparison questions. The one naive subject was unaware of this and took the others' reported answers to express the actual beliefs of the other members of the group. The purpose was to observe how the naive subject would react to the conflict between the evidence of his senses and the unanimous opinion of the group.

The line comparisons were chosen such that, under normal circumstances, people would be over 99 percent reliable at the comparison task. Under the misleading influence of the group, however, naive subjects' reliability fell to 63 percent. Three quarters of naive subjects gave in to group pressure on at least one of the twelve questions. In postexperimental interviews, Asch identified three reasons for this. Some subjects believed the group was wrong but went along with what the group said out of fear of standing out or of looking bad in front of others. These subjects were simply lying. A very few other subjects gave every appearance of being unaware that anything had gone wrong – as far as the experimenters could tell, even after the subjects were informed of the nature of the experiment, these subjects thought that the group's answers visually appeared correct.

However, among those subjects who went along with the majority's errors at least some of the time, the most common reason was that they thought that the group must have been correct and that their own visual perception must have been somehow defective. This is not an unreasonable thing to think. It is more likely, on the face of it, that

---

[24] Cialdini 1993, chapter 4.
[25] Asch 1956; 1963.

one's own vision is somehow defective than that the seven other people in the room are all lying or misperceiving.

Our concern, however, is not with the question of what one ought to think if one finds oneself in such a bizarre situation. My aim in recounting this experiment is to make salient the very strong influence that the beliefs and attitudes of others around us have upon our own beliefs and attitudes. The Asch experiment provides a particularly striking illustration of that influence. But this sort of influence is doubtless already familiar to the reader.

Closely related to social proof is the phenomenon of bias toward the status quo. Social proof convinces us that what others believe must be true. *Status quo bias* convinces us that what our society practices must be good. The most obvious and powerful demonstration of both forces is provided by the phenomenon of *culture*. Many of the world's cultures include beliefs and practices that strike us as bizarre, absurd, or horrible, such as the belief that air and moisture mated to create earth[26] or the practice of cannibalism or human sacrifice. Yet the members of those societies generally embrace their cultures' beliefs and regard their cultures' practices as obviously correct. It would be missing the point to say, 'Well, people in other societies must be terribly benighted.' Outsiders would doubtless regard many of our culture's beliefs and practices as bizarre, absurd, or immoral (in some cases, rightly so). The conclusion to draw is that human beings have a powerful tendency to see the beliefs of their own society as obviously true and the practices of their own society as obviously right and good – regardless of what those beliefs and practices are.[27]

What does this tell us about the belief in political authority? Government is an extremely prominent and fundamental feature of the structure of our society. We know that people tend to have a powerful bias in favor of the existing arrangements of their own societies. It therefore stands to reason that, whether or not any governments were legitimate, most of us would have a strong tendency to believe that some governments are legitimate, especially our own and others like it.

---

[26] From an Egyptian creation myth, discussed in Lindberg 1992, 9.

[27] Some philosophers have elevated this bias into a theory of practical reason. MacIntyre (1986) and Murphy (1995) contend that no reason is needed for following the norms of one's society but that a reason for departing from the currently accepted practices is always needed. They do not argue for this assumption, however, and I view their taking of this position as a manifestation of status quo bias.

6.5   The power of political aesthetics

Modern governments rely on a rich collection of nonrational tools, including symbols, rituals, stories, and rhetoric, to induce in citizens a *sense* of the government's power and authority.[28] This sense of authority is emotional and aesthetic rather than intellectual, but it can be expected to influence our conscious beliefs through our intuitions.

6.5.1   Symbols

Every national government in the world has a flag. Most have national anthems. Governments adorn their currencies with various symbols; in the United States, for example, the one dollar bill bears a portrait of George Washington, the Treasury Department Seal, and the Great Seal of the United States. Statues and monuments commemorate important people and events in the nation's history.

What function do all these symbols serve? Why not convey the relevant information in a purely intellectual, aesthetically neutral way? Instead of the Great Seal of the United States, the one dollar bill could simply bear the words, 'This is American money.' Instead of flying the American flag, government buildings could display a sign reading, 'This is a U.S. government building.' In place of monuments, books could be made available that dispassionately describe the relevant historical events. Why would these alternatives be less satisfactory than the symbols actually used? The answer is that the symbols are used to create a sense of national identity through appeal to the audience's emotions.

Uniforms are another kind of symbol, used to adorn the bodies of government officials. Police officers wear uniforms with badges. Judges wear long black robes. Soldiers wear uniforms with rank insignia. All of these are symbols of the particular kind and degree of authority that the government agent is supposed to possess. It would not suffice for the agent to simply wear a sign like a name tag, reading 'judge' or 'police officer' or 'captain'. These signs would convey the cognitive content but not the emotional or aesthetic content of the special attire actually used. A judge's robes make the viewer *feel* a certain way – they engender a feeling of respect and a sense of the wearer's authority. Psychologists have found that the mere wearing of a uniform, even a

---

[28] See Wingo (2003) for extended discussion and defense of this thesis.

Figure 6.1 The Colorado state capitol building

made-up uniform with no real significance, increases the obedience of others to the wearer's commands.[29]

Architecture can also be used to symbolize power and authority. Figure 6.1 shows the Colorado state capitol building, which is typical of capitol buildings in the United States. The architecture is mostly of a traditional, classical style, with thick stone columns in the front. These columns are not needed to hold anything up; they exist for aesthetic and emotional effect, most likely to give the building a solid and traditional appearance and therefore to associate the government with stability and tradition. In front of the building is a statue of a soldier, reminding visitors of those who have fought on behalf of the state. To the left and right are (nonfunctional) cannons, symbolizing the state's military might. The building is set on a hill so that visitors look up at the building as they approach and must climb a set of stairs to reach the

---

[29] Bushman 1988. The experiment involved having a woman tell people on the street to give a nickel to a motorist for a parking meter. Subjects were more likely to comply when the woman wore an ambiguous uniform than when she was dressed in ordinary clothes (72 percent v. 50 percent compliance, $p = 0.01$).

Figure 6.2   A Colorado courtroom

door. The doors are much larger than a human being, and once inside, the visitor confronts vaulted ceilings three or four times higher than the typical human being. There are many buildings in Denver much larger than the capitol building but perhaps none that is so successful at making the visitor feel small. All of this emphasizes the power of the state and creates a disposition toward respectful submission on the part of the visitor.

Figure 6.2 shows the inside of another interesting government building, a courtroom. The judge is placed, front and center, on a platform, enabling him to literally look down on all the other occupants of the room. This is not the only conceivable way to arrange a courtroom – for instance, the witness stand could have been placed at the center, so that all attention would be focused on the witnesses. Or the judge, prosecutor, defendant, and jury could all be seated in a circle. But these alternative arrangements would not create the desired sense of the power and authority of the judge.

6.5.2   Rituals

In many societies, special rituals are felt necessary when a new leader accedes to power. When power is passed to a new U.S. president, a public swearing-in ceremony is conducted. The ceremony involves a specific, stylized series of poses and words. The new president places his left hand on the Bible, suggesting divine oversight of the proceedings, and raises his right hand with the arm bent at the elbow. He then repeats the exact words of the judge, usually the Chief Justice of the Supreme Court, administering the oath: 'I, [full name of the president-elect], do solemnly swear that I will faithfully execute the Office of President of the United States, and will to the best of my ability preserve, protect, and defend the Constitution of the United States.' Immediately after the oath, the Chief Justice addresses the new president as 'Mr. President'. The oath is followed by a speech and a parade.

What function does this ritual serve? On the surface, the function is to ensure that the new president will serve faithfully and preserve the Constitution. But this is a very weak method of attempting to ensure that outcome. If a president has it in mind to serve 'unfaithfully' or to violate the Constitution, it is unlikely that his memory of having promised not to do so will be the force that stays him. The swearing-in ceremony is mostly for emotional effect. It is like a magic spell that confers power and authority on the new president so that, just as he completes the words of the oath, the person is converted into a president.

If a government is to secure the semblance of authority, its members must be set apart from and above the ordinary run of people. They must not be seen as simply ordinary people who have somehow managed to convince the people with guns to force everyone else to obey them. Rituals like the swearing-in ceremony help to hang the necessary veil over the elites. The exact form of the rituals does not matter; what matters is that there be some recognizable rituals connected with the exercise of power. In primitive societies, these rituals are thought to actually tap magical power. Among modern viewers, the rituals have their effect on an emotional, semiconscious level.

Another context replete with symbol and ritual is the courtroom. Occupants are required to stand when the judge enters the room, symbolically recognizing the judge's superior authority. Solemn oaths are administered to jurors and witnesses, often including the words 'so help me God', invoking divine oversight of the proceedings. Witnesses sit in a special box next to the judge, dubbed 'the witness stand'. Rather than being referred to by name, the judge is referred to as 'your honor' or 'the court', the lawyers as 'counsel', and the accused as 'the defendant'. A great deal of other specialized language is used in preference to plain English. A complex set of rules must be followed regarding who is allowed to talk at any given time and what they are allowed to talk about. Everything proceeds in a specific, preordained order. None of these things is demanded by the utilitarian requirements of a procedure designed to decide whether and how to punish someone. Their function is to ritualize the whole process. Further rituals are followed when the jury returns, the verdict is read, and the judge sentences the defendant. The ceremony concludes with the bang of the judge's gavel.

Why are courts so ritualistic? Perhaps because it is here that the state is most concerned to portray its coercion as justice. It is here that the state's agents most directly confront those who have disobeyed the state and here that those agents directly order severe harms to be inflicted upon specific individuals as punishment for disobedience. The process must not be seen as just a group of people who have decided to hurt another person because they don't like something he did. The rituals create a sense of the judge's authority and of the whole process as something profound, sophisticated, and worthy of respect – and something governed by rules that go beyond the mere desires of the actual human beings carrying out the process.

6.5.3 Authoritative language

One underappreciated aspect of political aesthetics is the peculiar language used by authority figures. Consider the following paragraph from the United States Code:

> If two or more members of the same family acquire interests in any property described in paragraph (1) in the same transaction (or a series of related transactions), the person (or persons) acquiring the term interests in such property shall be treated as having acquired the entire property and then transferred to the other persons the interests acquired by such other persons in the transaction (or series of transactions). Such transfer shall be treated as made in exchange for the consideration (if any) provided by such other persons for the acquisition of their interests in such property.[30]

Admittedly, this is taken from a part of the law with a particular reputation for incomprehensibility, the Internal Revenue Code. Here is a more comprehensible law:

> No person shall place, use, keep, store, or maintain any upholstered furniture not manufactured for outdoor use, including, without

---

[30] U.S.C., Title 26, section 2702. I have no idea what the paragraph means.

limitation, upholstered chairs, upholstered couches, and mattresses, in any outside areas located in the following places:

(1) In any front yard;

(2) In any side yard;

(3) In any rear yard or other yard that is adjacent to a public street. However, an alley shall not be considered a 'public street' for the purpose of this subsection; or

(4) On any covered or uncovered porch located in or adjacent to any of the yards described in paragraphs (1) through (3) above.[31]

The writing of lawyers, judges, and lawmakers is so distinctive that it is often referred to as 'legalese', as if it were a language of its own. This language has a distinctive tone that is highly formal, dispassionate, and technical. Sentences are typically long and abstract, with multiple clauses. In the Internal Revenue Code example above, the first sentence is 69 words long (for comparison, the average sentence in this book contains 21 words). There are frequent cross-references to other laws. There are often long and seemingly redundant disjunctions and conjunctions, such as 'covered or uncovered porch' and 'place, use, keep, store, or maintain'. Technical jargon appears frequently, such as 'probable cause', 'due process', and 'term interests'. Ordinary words are sometimes used in technical senses, as with 'consideration' and 'discovery'. Archaic usages are preserved, as in the use of 'such' in 'such transfer', or terms such as 'aforementioned' and 'herewith'. The technical vocabulary frequently relies on Latin or other foreign languages, as with the terms *mens rea*, *certiorari*, and *en banc*.

What is the effect of this peculiar way of speaking and writing? First and most obviously, that laws and legal documents are frequently incomprehensible to ordinary people – one must hire a trained professional to interpret them. Our inability to understand the law may make us reluctant to question it, while the very incomprehensibility of the law confers an air of sophistication and superiority on both the law and the lawmakers. People tend to feel respect for things they cannot understand, as well as for the people who deal with those things. This sort of respect is important if one is trying to convince others to accede to one's dominion.

---

[31] Boulder Revised Code, 5–4–16. This ordinance was passed in response to a Boulder tradition of setting couches on fire after big events such as football games.

Another effect of legal language is to emotionally distance the writer, both from his subject matter and from his audience. The writer may wish to distance himself from the audience to maintain a sense of superiority. The writer may wish also to emotionally distance himself from his subject matter, because the matter at hand, in legal writing, involves commands issued by agents of the state to other human beings, backed up by threats of violence against those who disobey. Normally, ordering harm to be imposed by force on other people would be a stressful occupation (whether or not the victims deserve to be harmed). The abstract, technical language helps the audience and the author forget that this is what is happening, and it drains away the emotional impact of issuing coercive threats against other people.

Similar language is often used by theorists engaged in devising recommendations and justifications for the exercise of power. The most respected contemporary political philosophers usually employ language reminiscent of legalese. Consider a representative passage from the most celebrated political thinker of recent times, John Rawls:

> I should now like to comment upon the second part of the second principle, henceforth to be understood as the liberal principle of fair equality of opportunity. It must not then be confused with the notion of careers open to talents; nor must one forget that since it is tied in with the difference principle its consequences are quite distinct from the liberal interpretation of the two principles taken together. In particular, I shall try to show further on (§17) that this principle is not subject to the objection that it leads to a meritocratic society. Here I wish to consider a few other points, especially its relation to the idea of pure procedural justice.[32]

The tone in this sort of philosophical work is formal and emotionless. The prose is filled with solemn-sounding technical terms, such as 'pure procedural justice', 'the liberal principle of fair equality of opportunity', and so on. A great deal of attention is given to abstractly described procedures and to connections and distinctions among abstract principles. In the case of Rawls, there are frequent cross-references, as in the above reference to section 17. Some of the vocabulary is slightly archaic, as in the above use of 'henceforth'. Extra words are employed so that a statement may be made in a weaker or less direct manner, as with the above use of 'I should now like to comment...'. The entire above quotation serves as a literary throat clearing, a preparation for

---

[32] Rawls 1999, section 14, 73.

discussing what the author actually wants to discuss. All of this has the effect of draining the discussion of emotional import – or more precisely, of directing the reader's mind toward more orderly and tractable feelings.

I do not claim that Rawls or other philosophers have consciously sought to achieve these effects with their writing. What I claim is that certain styles of writing, exemplified by typical legal documents as well as some philosophical work, have the effect of softening emotional obstacles to the acceptance of state authority and of encouraging attitudes of respect and submission to conventional institutions of power. They serve to dress up the discussion of who should be subjected to violence in somber and civilized clothes.

6.6 Stockholm Syndrome and the charisma of power

6.6.1 The phenomenon of Stockholm Syndrome

Stockholm Syndrome is named after an incident that occurred in Stockholm, Sweden, in 1973. A pair of bank robbers held four bank employees hostage for six days. During the ordeal, the hostages bonded emotionally with their captors, came to side with the kidnappers against the police, and seemingly did not want to be rescued. At one point, a hostage said that the robbers were protecting them from the police. On the last day, as the police used tear gas to force everyone out of the bank, the hostages refused to leave without the kidnappers, fearing that if they did so, the police would shoot the kidnappers. After the incident was over, the victims continued to sympathize with and defend the criminals.[33] Since then, the term 'Stockholm Syndrome' has been used to describe the emotional bond that victims sometimes form with kidnappers.[34] The term is also often extended to a wider class of cases in which a person or group is subjected to the control of another.

A more extreme case was that of Patricia Hearst, who was kidnapped in 1974 by a left-wing terrorist group in California calling itself the Symbionese Liberation Army. For two months, Hearst was held prisoner in a closet and physically and sexually abused. She then joined the group and voluntarily helped them carry out crimes, including a bank robbery. She made no attempt to escape when presented with

---

[33] Graham, Rawlings, and Rigsby 1994, 1–11; Lang 1974.
[34] I follow the popular use of the expression 'Stockholm Syndrome'. My use of the word *syndrome*, however, is not intended to convey that the phenomenon is a disorder or disease.

the opportunity. Following her eventual capture by the police, Hearst claimed to have been brainwashed by the SLA.[35]

A more recent case is that of Jaycee Lee Dugard, who was kidnapped at the age of eleven by ex-convict Phillip Garrido. Garrido raped her and held her captive in a shed in his backyard. Police finally found Jaycee in 2009, eighteen years after the kidnapping. She had lived with Garrido all those years and now had two daughters fathered by Garrido. During that time, Dugard had assisted Garrido with his home business, sorting orders by phone and email. She had met customers alone at the door. She had even gone out in public. In short, Jaycee Dugard had numerous opportunities over the years to escape or seek outside help, but she never did.[36] So secure was Garrido in his relationship with Dugard that he brought her and their daughters with him to a meeting with his parole officer. At that meeting, Dugard told the officer that Garrido was a great person, and she attempted to protect him by concealing her own identity.[37]

A number of similar cases have occurred over the years. There are commonly said to be four precursors for the development of Stockholm Syndrome: first, the captor poses a credible threat to the life of the captive victim. Second, the victim perceives some form of kindness on the part of the captor. However, this 'kindness' might consist only in a relative lack of abuse or a failure to kill the victim. At one point during the Stockholm hostage crisis, one of the bank robbers was planning to shoot a hostage in the leg to make the police take his demands more seriously (the shooting never in fact occurred). At the time, the hostage who was to be shot thought that the robber was kind for planning only to shoot him in the leg and not to kill him.[38] Third, the victim is isolated from the outside world and subjected only to the captor's perspective. Fourth, the victim sees himself as unable to escape.

Under these conditions, hostages are prone to a variety of reactions that outsiders find paradoxical, including

- Emotional closeness to the kidnappers;
- Feelings of loyalty toward the kidnappers, which may continue long after the victims are freed;

---

[35] Brook 2007.

[36] Fitzpatrick 2009.

[37] Shaw 2009, 5–6. The parole officer, finding inconsistencies in their stories, separated Garrido and Dugard and continued questioning them to find out who she was. Eventually, Garrido admitted to having kidnapped Dugard, after which Dugard revealed her identity.

[38] Graham 1994, 5.

- Adoption of the captors' attitudes and beliefs;
- A perception of the captors as protectors and of outside forces trying to win the hostages' release as a threat;
- Failure to take advantage of opportunities to escape;
- Gratitude toward captors for small kindnesses and for lack of abuse. Hostages often feel that they owe their lives to their captors;
- A tendency to deny or rationalize the captors' acts of violence;
- Extreme sensitivity to the captor's needs and desires.[39]

Some have suggested that victims regress to an infantile state, with the captor serving as a parental figure.[40]

6.6.2 Why does Stockholm Syndrome occur?

There has been little academic study of the phenomenon, partly because psychologists cannot recreate it in the laboratory, and theoretical accounts are speculative. But one plausible account ascribes the syndrome to an unconscious defensive mechanism. When one is completely under the power of a dangerous person, one's survival may depend upon developing traits pleasing to one's captor. This includes a submissive dependence, as well as feelings of sympathy and liking towards the captor. Victims do not consciously choose to adopt these traits, nor do they merely pretend to adopt them. They simply find themselves having these emotions and attitudes.[41] If this is a survival mechanism, there is evidence that it is effective: after his capture, one of the Stockholm robbers reported that he was unable to kill any of the hostages due to the emotional bond he had formed with them.[42] For this reason, the FBI deliberately encourages the development of Stockholm Syndrome in hostage situations.[43]

The existence of such a defensive mechanism can be explained in evolutionary terms: during the history of the species, it has been common for a person or group to hold a great deal of power over others. Those who displeased the powerful person or group were likely to be killed or otherwise harmed. Those who pleased the powerful were

---

[39] Graham 1994, 13, 42–3.
[40] de Fabrique et al. 2007; Namnyak et al. 2008. The victim is typically unable to escape at first but often has opportunities to escape after the syndrome has developed.
[41] de Fabrique et al. 2007; Mattiuzzi 2007.
[42] Lang 1973, 126.
[43] de Fabrique et al. 2007.

more likely to survive and prosper from the powerful persons' favor. It is plausible to suppose that Stockholm-like characteristics would be pleasing to powerful persons. Therefore, evolution may have selected for a tendency to develop such traits in appropriate circumstances.

6.6.3   When does Stockholm syndrome occur?

We can explain in terms of the above theory the conditions under which Stockholm Syndrome is most likely to develop. These conditions include the following:[44]

   i) *The aggressor poses a credible and serious threat to the victim.* It is this situation that makes some defensive mechanism necessary. Stockholm Syndrome involves extreme shifts in the victim's attitudes, which have serious potential costs (for example, one might wind up joining in the aggressor's terrorist plans). We should therefore expect these changes to occur only when there is a serious threat.[45]

   ii) *The victim perceives himself as unable to escape.* Victims who could escape would prefer that option over bonding with the aggressor.

   iii) *The victim is unable to overpower the aggressor or to effectively defend himself against the aggressor.* If one has the option of neutralizing the aggressor's power, this would clearly be preferable to bonding with the aggressor.

   iv) *The victim perceives some kindness from the aggressor, even if only in the form of lack of abuse.* It is this circumstance that renders it likely that a strategy of bonding with the aggressor could succeed. Aggressors who are purely abusive are not likely to be won over if the victim develops a liking for them.

   v) *The victim is isolated from the outside world.* When a person or group of people are held captive by an aggressor, outsiders, who have no reason to develop Stockholm Syndrome, will typically view the aggressor in an extremely negative light. In any communications with the victims, outsiders are likely to express negative thoughts

---

[44] Items (i), (ii), (iv), and (v) are from Graham et al. 1994, 33–7; cf. de Fabrique et al. 2007; Namnyak et al. 2008, 5. I have added item (iii), which, though not identified as a distinct condition by Graham and others, is clearly present and of import in the classic cases of Stockholm Syndrome.

[45] Freud (1937, chapter 9) postulates that when an individual fears pain at the hands of another, the individual may cope with the anxiety by psychologically identifying with the person who poses the threat. She describes this as 'identification with the aggressor'.

and feelings about the aggressor. Stockholm Syndrome is therefore most likely to develop when this sort of contrary influence is absent.

Though the term 'Stockholm Syndrome' arose in the context of situations involving hostage taking or kidnapping, the above conditions may obtain in a variety of cases. In any situation in which these conditions obtain, we may expect to find a similar phenomenon involving identification by the victim with the aggressor. The more clearly and fully the conditions are satisfied, the more likely such an identification is. Accordingly, Stockholm-like symptoms have been observed in a variety of groups, including concentration camp prisoners, cult members, civilians in Chinese communist prisons, pimp-procured prostitutes, incest victims, battered women, prisoners of war, and victims of child abuse.[46]

6.6.4 Are ordinary citizens prone to Stockholm syndrome?

Are citizens of well-established governments susceptible to Stockholm Syndrome? Consider the above five conditions:

i) *The aggressor poses a credible and serious threat to the victim.* All modern governments control their populations through threats of violence. In some cases, their capacity for violence is astonishing. The U.S. government, for instance, may possess sufficient weaponry to kill everyone in the world. On a smaller scale, governments have an apparatus for imprisoning individuals for long periods of time, and they deploy this apparatus on a regular basis. For those who resist capture, governments have impressive tools of physical force, up to and including deadly force.

ii) *The victim perceives himself as unable to escape.* Escape from one's own government tends to be difficult and costly, typically requiring an abandonment of one's family and friends, one's job, and one's entire society. Even those willing to undertake such costs will generally then only become subject to another government. Escape from government in general is virtually impossible.

iii) *The victim is unable to overpower the aggressor or to effectively defend himself against the aggressor.* It is virtually impossible for any individual to effectively defend himself against most modern governments, to say nothing of overpowering them.

---

[46] Graham et al. 1994, 31; Graham et al. 1995; Julich 2005.

iv) *The victim perceives some kindness from the aggressor, even if only in the form of lack of abuse.* Most citizens perceive their government as beneficent in light of the social services that it provides. Some also feel that their government is good because it does not abuse its power as much as most other governments throughout history.

v) *The victim is isolated from the outside world.* In the case of citizens of a modern nation-state, perhaps the 'outside world' consists of foreign countries. Most people, particularly in advanced, liberal democracies, have access to the perspectives of the outside world in this sense, if they choose to consult those perspectives. There are, however, at least two reasons why this fact might fail to prevent the development of Stockholm Syndrome. First, our actual use of these outside perspectives is limited. Most people obtain the great majority of their information from sources within their own country. Second, the outside sources are all in a similar situation. It is as though the hostages had access only to the 'outside perspectives' of hostages and hostage takers in other places. In such a situation, it is not clear that access to these perspectives would retard the development of Stockholm Syndrome.

The general precursors for the development of Stockholm Syndrome, then, are reasonably well satisfied in the case of citizens of modern states. It is therefore not surprising to find that citizens tend to identify with their governments, adopt their governments' perspectives, and develop emotional attachments (often considered 'patriotism') to their governments.[47] Just as Stockholm victims tend to deny or minimize their captors' acts of coercion, many citizens tend to deny or minimize their government's coercion. Nearly all theorists who consider the question at all agree that government is a coercive institution,[48] yet discussions of policy issues rarely address the justification for using force to impose various policies. It is not that we fail in general to ascribe moral significance to coercion; if decisions on the part of some nongovernmental agent were under discussion, then the question of the

---

[47] One interesting manifestation of this identification with the government is the use by private citizens of the word 'we' to refer to the government, as in 'We invaded Iraq in 2003', which might be said by an American even if the speaker had personally done nothing to bring about the invasion or had actively opposed it. Since the word *we* normally includes the speaker, this suggests strong identification with the state.

[48] Edmundson (1998, ch. 4) is a rare exception.

justification for violence would take center stage. But either the reality or the moral significance of coercion fades from view when the agent involved is the state. Deferential attitudes may extend to wholesale acceptance of the state's image of itself as having a unique entitlement to coerce obedience and as capable of creating moral obligations simply by issuing commands. Due to the Stockholm dynamic, power has a self-legitimizing tendency: once it becomes sufficiently entrenched, *power* is perceived as *authority*.

Those who accept the legitimacy of government may find it difficult to believe that they are under the influence of something like the Stockholm Syndrome, since that concept is typically applied to situations in which the aggressor's role is generally socially condemned – kidnappers, bank robbers, violent spouses, and so on. All of these kinds of aggression are *bad*, and most people see their governments as *good*; therefore, the concept of Stockholm Syndrome can't apply to our feelings about government, can it?

Of course, this reaction could itself be a product of the syndrome. Fortunately, we need not first decide whether government is good or its coercion justified to decide whether the concept of Stockholm Syndrome applies. The precursors for the development of the syndrome identified in Section 6.6.3, as well as the manifestations of the syndrome described in Section 6.6.1, are nonmoral, factual conditions. The badness of the aggressor or the unjustifiedness of his coercion is not among them. And the citizens of modern states in fact tend to satisfy these descriptive conditions. This we can see regardless of whether government is ultimately justified or not.

6.7 Case studies in the abuse of power

6.7.1 My Lai revisited

Recall the case of the massacre at My Lai. Most of the soldiers who were ordered to murder civilians obeyed. A few refused to participate in the massacre, while doing nothing to stop others from doing so. According to one report, there were many more soldiers who simply avoided the area where the massacre was taking place, possibly to avoid being asked to participate.[49] Thus, the vast majority of people who were aware of the massacre, whether they participated or not, did nothing to stop it. The

---

[49] Thompson n.d., 19–20. Other details of the case are from Thompson (n.d.) and Kelman and Hamilton (1989, 1–17).

exception was one brave helicopter team, which saved a small number of villagers from being killed by flying them to safety. Everyone else in the village was killed.

Now consider the reaction on the part of U.S. government officials and other Americans. After it happened, the U.S. government attempted to cover up the massacre and to protect the soldiers responsible for it. Only after the story was leaked to the press did the government move toward prosecuting war criminals. In the end, a single person was convicted and sentenced for the massacre, Lieutenant William Calley, who ultimately spent three years under house arrest. Hugh Thompson, the heroic helicopter pilot who saved some of the civilians, was initially treated like a criminal. Thompson had landed his helicopter between a group of civilians and a group of American troops who were advancing to kill the civilians. He told his two crewmates to shoot the soldiers if they opened fire on the civilians while he was trying to save them. Fortunately, no one opened fire, and Thompson was able to save ten civilians. Back in the States, however, many regarded Thompson as a traitor. He received death threats and mutilated animals on his doorstep. One congressman stated that Thompson was the only person in the whole story who should go to jail.[50]

One lesson from the story is that even those who do not actively participate in abuses of power are often complicit in them. When members of an organization abuse their power, other members commonly look the other way. When given the chance, officials often cover up or excuse abuses. Those rare individuals with the courage to intervene to stop abuses, rather than being hailed as the heroes they are, will more often be reviled as traitors.

All of us are well aware of the atrocities committed by such regimes as Nazi Germany, the Soviet Union, and communist China. It is all too easy, in thinking about such cases, to react by congratulating ourselves on not belonging to any such barbaric and tyrannical regime. Cases like My Lai remind us that it is not only dictatorships that commit atrocities. Advanced, democratic nations commit atrocities, too, albeit with less frequency and on a smaller scale, a fact that leaves us with small ground for self-congratulation.

In focusing on this example, I do not want to leave readers with the impression that it was an isolated incident. When we read of flagrant

---

[50] Thompson n.d., 12, 27–8. Thirty years later, Thompson was honored with the Soldier's Medal and invited to speak at West Point, Annapolis, and Quantico.

abuses of power, we also usually read of the official cover-ups. But the only cases we read of are ones in which the cover-ups failed. Presumably, not all cover-ups fail. Sometimes the authorities must succeed in hiding their misdeeds. How often, we do not know. Thompson reports that, after his experience at My Lai, other soldiers told him, 'Oh, that stuff happened all the time.'[51] There is thus reason to suspect that many more massacres occurred that did not make the news.

6.7.2 The Stanford Prison Experiment

In 1971, social psychologist Phillip Zimbardo conducted an illuminating study of the effects of imprisonment on both guards and prisoners.[52] Zimbardo collected 21 volunteers, all male college students, to play the role of either prisoners or guards in a simulated prison. At the start, all the volunteers wanted to play the prisoner role; none wanted to be guards. Zimbardo randomly assigned half the subjects to be prisoners and half to be guards. The prisoners would live in makeshift prison cells for two weeks on the Stanford University campus. The guards would watch over the prisoners in eight-hour shifts, with each guard free to leave when his shift was over each day. The experimenters provided minimal guidance on the treatment of prisoners, apart from instructions concerning the provision of food and the avoidance of physical violence.

What the experimenters observed was a spiraling pattern of abuse on the part of the guards that began almost immediately and worsened each day. Prisoners were subjected to relentless verbal abuse ('You such a self-righteous, pious bastard that I wanna puke', and so on); made to perform tedious, pointless, and degrading tasks ad nauseam (doing pushups with other prisoners sitting on their backs, cleaning the toilet with their hands, and so on); required to verbally insult both themselves and each other; deprived of sleep; confined for hours in a closet with about one square yard of floor space; and finally required to perform simulated sodomy. Not all the guards approved of or participated in the abuse. But the abusive guards assumed de facto positions of dominance among the guards, which no one challenged. The 'good guards' tacitly acquiesced in the behavior of the more aggressive guards, neither doing nor saying anything against them. The ordeal was so stressful and depressing for the prisoners that five had to be released early, and

---

[51] Thompson n.d., 11.
[52] Zimbardo et al. 1973; Zimbardo 2007.

on the sixth day the experimenters found it ethically necessary to terminate the experiment.

6.7.3   Lessons of the SPE

Much worse abuses have occurred in real prisons, prisoner-of-war camps, concentration camps, and the like. The Stanford experiment differs from those real-world prisons in a number of interesting ways. First, all the participants knew themselves to be merely participating in a psychological experiment, which they thought would be over in two weeks, whereupon they would return to their normal lives. Second, the prisoners had been selected randomly, and both the guards and the prisoners knew that the prisoners had done nothing wrong. The prisoners could not have been seriously regarded as criminals or enemies in any meaningful sense. Third, the prisoners and guards had been screened beforehand. The experimenters had given questionnaires and personal interviews to an initial pool of 75 volunteers in order to select only the most normal, psychologically stable participants. Furthermore, on the basis of psychological testing, there appeared to be no significant initial personality differences between the guards and the prisoners.

Any of these conditions might have been expected to insulate the simulated prison against the sort of abuses often seen in real prisons. (Admittedly, the abuses in Stanford look mild in comparison to those seen in Abu Ghraib or the Soviet gulags; then again, the trajectory of increasing abusiveness was cut short after only five days.) One might have thought that the context of a relatively short-term psychological experiment would be insufficient to break down normal standards of decency and respect for others. One might have suspected that prisoner abuse occurs because prisoners are believed to be criminals or enemies, so that the abuse is thought justified. Or one might have thought that prisoner abuse occurs because individuals with sadistic predispositions are more likely to become guards or because prison inmates tend to be unusually aggressive and thus draw out aggressive responses on the part of guards. The Stanford Prison Experiment is of particular interest in that it puts hypotheses like these to the test.

As it turns out, none of these things was the case. There was something about the guard *role* that brought out the worst in people. Zimbardo's central conclusion, from this study and much other evidence, is that the determinants of good or evil behavior lie more in the *situations* that individuals are placed into than in those individuals' intrinsic dispositions.[53] An individual's circumstances can have dramatic corrupting or uplifting effects.

What was it about the guard role that brought out subjects' dark side? Lord Acton, I believe, had the right of it: power corrupts.[54] This has long been apparent from history; now we have experimental evidence as well. When some human beings are given great power over the lives of others, they often discover that the sense of power is intoxicating. They want to exercise their power more frequently and more fully, and they don't want to give it up. When the Stanford Prison Experiment was ended prematurely, all the prisoners were relieved. Most of the guards, however, seemed disappointed. They were enjoying tormenting their charges. As Zimbardo reports, none of the guards ever turned up late for a shift, and on several occasions they stayed late, unsolicited and without extra pay.[55] Not everyone is visibly corrupted by the exercise of power. But there are always some who are, and as the experiment suggests, even the least corrupted typically do nothing to restrain the excesses of the most corrupted.

But why inflict suffering and humiliation on the prisoners – couldn't one as well experience power in benevolent gestures? George Orwell had a key insight into this connection: 'How does one man assert his power over another...?... By making him suffer. ... Unless he is suffering, how can you be sure that he is obeying your will and not his own? Power is in inflicting pain and humiliation.'[56] It is certainly true that the Stanford guards intentionally inflicted pain and humiliation on their captives. And again, these guards were perfectly normal human beings, as far as could be ascertained beforehand. There is thus reason to believe that it is no accident that governments have so often been led by tyrannical leaders.

---

[53] See Zimbardo 2007, esp. 210–21, on the situational factors in the Stanford Prison Experiment. See his chapters 12–16 for evidence and arguments beyond the Stanford Prison study.

[54] Acton 1972, 335 (from a letter to Mandell Creighton dated 5 April 1887): 'Power tends to corrupt and absolute power corrupts absolutely. Great men are almost always bad men, even when they exercise influence and not authority: still more when you superadd the tendency or the certainty of corruption by authority.'

[55] Zimbardo, Haney, and Banks 1973, 81.

[56] Orwell 1984, 219–20. The remarks quoted are from thought police agent O'Brien, the character who captures and tortures the novel's protagonist in order to break his spirit.

Another lesson of the Stanford experiment concerns the reactions of others to authority figures. The prisoners in the experiment, initially at least somewhat resistant, were reduced to meek submission by the end of the experiment. They complied with nearly all, even the most offensive demands issued by the guards. On the face of it, this is puzzling, as the guards had no real power to compel the prisoners to obey. The guards were prohibited from using violence and in any case were, in each shift, outnumbered three to one by prisoners. If the prisoners had resolutely refused to obey the guards, it is unclear what the guards could have done. Yet the prisoners obeyed, despite the increasingly irrational and offensive nature of the guards' commands and despite the arbitrary nature of their supposed authority. Nor was this obedience to be explained as a result of a sense of contractual obligation. While the subjects had agreed to be part of a simulation of prison life, they had not agreed to obey all guard commands. And even if they thought themselves obligated to be obedient to some extent, this would not explain why the prisoners became more submissive as the study wore on and the guards' demands became more unreasonable. One lesson to draw from this is that psychologically, *power is self-validating*. Even when the 'authorities' are selected entirely arbitrarily and everyone knows this, the mere assertion of authority tends to be accepted by others.[57] Furthermore, the longer one obeys an authority figure, the more one feels 'bound' to continue to do so.

6.8   Conclusion: anatomy of an illusion

Standard intuitions about authority are not to be trusted. Whether or not one accepts the arguments advanced in the previous chapters of this book, one ought not to place much weight on the mere fact that most people believe in political authority.

Anyone who holds an unpopular view can be challenged to answer, 'How have so many others gone wrong, while you have avoided their error?' This question should be taken seriously. If one's answer is merely that human beings are fallible and that the vast majority of other people have coincidentally made the same error on this particular question, that will generally be implausible for straightforward reasons of probability.

---

[57] Milgram (2009, 139–40) notes, similarly, that mere self-designation as an authority figure normally suffices to secure others' obedience.

I do not believe that the many who accept political authority have all made this mistake by chance. I believe that there are specific features of the human mind and of the situation most people find themselves in that contribute to a moral illusion of authority. Compare the widespread belief, prior to Copernicus and Galileo, that the sun orbited the earth. This was not a chance error; it isn't that so many people *just happened* to pick the wrong answer to the question of the structure of the cosmos. There was a common explanation for the erroneous beliefs in so many minds – roughly speaking, it looks as though the sun is moving around the earth. We may characterize this as a perceptual illusion – a case in which there is a systematic tendency for things to appear, to casual observation, otherwise than how they really are. In such cases, we should expect most people to mistakenly assume that things are as they appear, unless and until they are given information to correct the illusion.

Human beings can also suffer from *cognitive* illusions, in which things appear to the mind (nonperceptually) otherwise than as they are. For instance, a medical procedure with an 80 percent success rate sounds better to most people than a procedure with a 20 percent failure rate. This difference has been shown to make a difference to people's practical judgments about realistic situations.[58] One species of cognitive illusion is of particular interest to us here: that of *moral* illusions. These are cases in which we have a systematic tendency to see something as right (or wrong) when in fact it is not. Throughout history, our forebears have been subject to widespread moral illusions – for instance, that women were inferior to men or that dark-skinned people were inferior to light-skinned ones.[59] The suggestion that we are still subject to some moral illusions today should therefore surprise no one. We need to reflect on what moral illusions we might be subject to, keeping in mind that, by the nature of the case, they will not *seem*, on casual consideration, to be illusions.

Overcoming an illusion often requires seeing why things might appear as they do even if the way they appear is false. For instance, in overcoming the belief that the sun orbits the earth, it is important to see why it would *appear* that way even if the sun was not moving but instead the earth was rotating. Likewise, in overcoming the illusion of political authority, it is important to see why it might seem to us that

---

[58] Tversky and Kahneman 1981.
[59] See Section 13.1 and Section 13.4 for further examples.

there is political authority, even if in fact no state has ever had genuine authority.

I have suggested in this chapter that human beings come equipped with strong and pervasive pro-authority biases that operate even when an authority is illegitimate or issues illegitimate and indefensible commands. As we have seen, individuals confronted with the demands of authority figures are liable to feel an almost unconditional compulsion to obey, and this may prompt them to look for explanations for why the authority is legitimate and why they are morally required to obey. People often defer instinctively to those who wield power, and there are even cases in which people emotionally bond with others (such as kidnappers) who hold great but completely unjustified power over them, adopting the perspectives and goals of those who hold the power. Once a pattern of obedience has started, the need to minimize cognitive dissonance favors continued obedience and the adoption of beliefs that rationalize the authority's commands and one's own obedience to them. Due to a general status quo bias, once a practice or institution becomes established in some society, that practice is likely to be viewed by the members of that society, almost automatically, as normal, right, and good.

None of this by itself shows that existing political institutions are illegitimate. But it strongly suggests that they would be widely accepted as legitimate even *if* they were not. Theories of authority devised by political philosophers can plausibly be viewed as attempts to rationalize common intuitions about the need for obedience, where these intuitions are the product of systematic biases.

7
What if There Is No Authority?

If there is no authority, does it follow that we ought to abolish all governments? No. The absence of authority means, roughly, that individuals are not obligated to obey the law merely because it is the law and/or that agents of the state are not entitled to coerce others merely because they are agents of the state. There might still be good reasons to obey most laws, and agents of the state might still have adequate reasons for engaging in enough coercive action to maintain a state. If the arguments of the preceding chapters are correct, the circumstances and purposes that would justify coercion on the part of the state are just the circumstances and purposes that would justify coercion on the part of private agents. It remains to be seen whether some organizations are justified in engaging in enough statelike activities to qualify as states. In the terminology of contemporary political philosophy, I have so far defended *philosophical anarchism* (the view that there are no political obligations), but I have yet to defend *political anarchism* (the view that government should be abolished).[1]

The aim of the present chapter is to discuss the practical implications of a philosophical but not political anarchism. That is, suppose one accepts the arguments of the preceding chapters, but one believes (contrary to the arguments to follow in later chapters) that government is necessary to a decent society. In that case, what practical conclusions should one draw?

---

[1] Though I have followed the established terminology here, it should be noted that the terminology is misleading, since it falsely suggests that one of the doctrines is philosophical but not political, while the other is political but not philosophical. In fact, both kinds of 'anarchism' are philosophical *and* political claims.

7.1   Some policy implications

If there is no political authority, then the vast majority of laws are unjust, because they deploy coercion against individuals without adequate justification. There are too many laws of this kind to mention them all. Here I briefly touch on some of the more prominent examples.

7.1.1   Prostitution and legal moralism

Moralistic laws prohibit some behavior on the grounds that the behavior is 'immoral', even though it does not harm anyone or violate anyone's rights. The most obvious examples are the laws against prostitution and gambling. How should we view these laws?

Political authority is a special moral status, setting the state above all nonstate agents. If we reject this notion, then we should evaluate state coercion in the same manner as we evaluate coercion by other agents. For any coercive act by the state, we should first ask what reason the state has for exercising coercion in this way. We should then consider whether a private individual or organization would be justified in exercising a similar kind and degree of coercion, with similar effects on the victims, for similar reasons. If the answer is no, then coercion by the state is not justified either.

Consider a story about three private individuals. Jon wants to have sex with Mary. But Mary does not like Jon as much as he likes her. What she does like is money, which Jon happens to have. So Mary tells Jon that she is willing to have sex with him, provided that he gives her $300. That will make it worth it to her. Jon agrees, and they complete the transaction. Later, one of their neighbors, Sam, finds out about what happened. Sam thinks people should only have sex for procreation or sensory pleasure; the thought of people having sex for money makes him angry. So Sam goes over to Mary's house with his gun. He points the gun at Mary and orders her to accompany him to his house. Once there, he locks her in his basement for the next six months.

As it turns out, Mary was not from the neighborhood; Jon had convinced her to travel from out of town to have sex with him. When Sam learns of this, he is incensed. He kidnaps Jon at gunpoint and locks him up in the basement for the next 20 years.

Whatever one thinks of Jon and Mary, Sam's behavior in this story is clearly wrong. Perhaps Mary and Jon are doing something bad (though it is unclear how); if so, it would be appropriate for Sam to explain to them what he sees as problematic about their behavior, in an effort to persuade them to stop. If he cannot persuade them, however, coercion and kidnapping are not appropriate responses.

Sam's behavior in this story is analogous to that of the government in countries where prostitution is illegal. Mary's six-month imprisonment is not unlike what a prostitute might expect to suffer. Admittedly, johns are rarely prosecuted and rarely serve prison time. Jon's 20-year imprisonment is, however, an allusion to actual U.S. federal law, which provides for a prison sentence of up to 20 years for 'enticing' someone to cross state lines for the purpose of prostitution.[2] It is worth pointing out how absurdly punitive some laws are. But the main point is not that the sentences are too high; the main point is that *no* coercion is justified at all merely to stop a pair of individuals from voluntarily exchanging sex for money.

7.1.2 Drugs and paternalism

Paternalistic laws restrict individuals' behavior for their own good. Certain drugs, for example, are outlawed, mainly because they are harmful to the user. They may damage the user's health or relationships with other people; they may cause the user to lose his job, drop out of school, or otherwise have a less successful life.

Are these adequate reasons for prohibiting drug use? The prohibition of drugs means that users and sellers are subject to coercive threats by the state. Those who are caught are often forced to spend years of their lives in prison. For most readers, being sent to prison would probably be the worst thing they ever experienced. This is of particular concern in the United States, where over half a million people are locked up for drug offenses.[3] To justify the imposition of such a large harm, the reasons for prohibition would have to be very strong.

Consider another story about Sam. Sam is opposed to cigarette smoking due to its severe health harms. Not content merely to avoid cigarettes himself, he issues a proclamation to his community that no one may smoke. After the proclamation, Sam catches you smoking, kidnaps you at gunpoint, and locks you in his basement. You share the basement with thieves, rapists, and murderers for the next year, until you are released. The person who sold you the cigarettes is locked in the basement for the next six years.

---

[2] U.S. Code, Title 18, section 2422: 'Whoever knowingly persuades, induces, entices, or coerces any individual to travel in interstate or foreign commerce, or in any Territory or Possession of the United States, to engage in prostitution, or in any sexual activity for which any person can be charged with a criminal offense, or attempts to do so, shall be fined under this title or imprisoned not more than 20 years, or both.'

[3] See Huemer 2010a, 361–2.

Did Sam act rightly? It is hard to imagine anyone saying so. The desire to prevent others from harming their health in this manner hardly seems an adequate justification for coercion and kidnapping, let alone for stealing months or years of someone's life. But Sam's action was no worse than what the government presently does to drug offenders. Tobacco is about seven times more deadly (on average, per user) than illegal drugs, so Sam has much stronger justification for what he does than the government has for what it does.[4]

Some advocates of prohibition stress the harmful nonmedical effects drugs can have on one's life. To take account of this, imagine that Sam also watches out for people in these other respects; when he learns about someone who has damaged her relationships with others without good reason, he kidnaps that person and holds her captive in his basement. Similarly for those who lose their jobs or drop out of school due to their own fault. (Add any other negative life events of the sort that drug abuse might cause.) Sam explicitly warns people against these behaviors, and he only punishes people who knowingly and willfully violate his orders. Sam's reason for punishing these people would be stronger than the reason the state has for punishing drug offenders, since drugs only have a *chance* of causing one to damage one's relationships, lose one's job, and so on, whereas Sam punishes only people who have in fact knowingly damaged their relationships, lost their jobs, and the like. Yet Sam's behavior seems outrageous. The desire to prevent people from damaging their own lives in these ways does not constitute adequate grounds for coercion.[5]

There are many other paternalistic laws about which similar arguments might be made. In general, paternalism is justified only in extreme circumstances – for instance, if a person is about to throw himself off a bridge, one might be justified in coercively preventing him from doing so, at least long enough to find out why he wants to kill himself and whether he is of sound mind. Coercion is not justified merely because another person wishes to make an unwise choice of the sort that normal people frequently make in ordinary life. Here are some other examples of legal paternalism.

– Prescription drug laws. These laws prevent one from buying certain drugs without the approval of a doctor, the apparent rationale being that patients would otherwise take dangerous and unnecessary drugs.

---

[4] See Huemer 2010a, 356–7.
[5] See Huemer 2010a for elaboration.

- Grants and low-interest loans for college education. While the salient rationale of these programs is one of wealth redistribution, they also have a paternalistic element. The recipients are not simply given money to do with as they choose, presumably because many would use the funds unwisely; hence, the funds are contingent on the recipients' attending college.
- Social Security. It is said that people must be forced to save for retirement; otherwise, they would foolishly neglect to do so. It is also sometimes said that the retirement program must be run by the government, since otherwise people would invest their money foolishly and lose it.
- Licensing laws. These laws prevent people from selling certain services without state authorization – for instance, from practicing medicine without a license or practicing law without admission to the bar. Why not instead require service providers to disclose whether they have been licensed, and allow consumers to choose whether to patronize unlicensed providers? The worry is that too many consumers would foolishly choose to buy services from unqualified doctors, lawyers, and so on.

As these examples illustrate, legal paternalism is quite widespread in modern Western society. All of these are unjustified laws.

7.1.3 Rent seeking

Rent seeking is behavior designed to extract wealth from others, especially through the vehicle of the state, without providing compensatory benefits in return.[6] The most straightforward example is a company lobbying the government for subsidies. But many of the policies that exemplify legal paternalism are also motivated partly by rent seeking. Consider the following.

- Prescription drug laws. These laws transfer money from consumers to doctors and pharmacists. If a person wishes to buy a prescription drug, he must first pay a doctor to see him and give him permission to buy it.
- Subsidies for college education. These increase the demand for college education far above the market level and thereby transfer resources to colleges and universities. (The author is grateful for the funds that you have provided him.)

---

[6] Tullock 1987.

- Social Security. I said above that Social Security could be looked upon as a program of forcing people to save for retirement. It can also be viewed, perhaps more accurately, as a system of transfer payments from the young to the old.
- Licensing. Licensing laws place an obstacle to entering a given profession, thus decreasing the competition faced by current practitioners. This raises prices and benefits existing practitioners at the expense of both consumers and those who wish to enter the profession.[7]

What is the moral status of such laws? Suppose we extend the story of Sam as follows. Sam happens to have a friend named Archer Midland. Archer asks Sam for some financial assistance, so Sam goes out, mugs some people, and gives the money to Archer. Obviously, this action is wrong. The desire to profit at others' expense is not an adequate justification for coercion.

7.1.4 Immigration

Marvin is in need of food, without which he will suffer from malnutrition or starvation.[8] He plans to travel to a nearby marketplace, where he will be able to trade for food. But before he can reach the marketplace, he is accosted by Sam, who does not want Marvin to trade in the marketplace, for two reasons. First, Sam's daughter is going to be shopping in the marketplace, and Sam fears that Marvin might bid up the price of food. Some vendors might even run out of bread if too many people come to the marketplace. Second, Marvin comes from a different culture from most people presently at the marketplace, and Sam fears that Marvin might influence other people and thus alter the culture of the marketplace. Sam decides to solve the problem by force. He points his gun at Marvin and orders Marvin to turn around. The starving Marvin is thus forced to return home empty-handed.

Sam's reasons for coercing Marvin in this story are clearly inadequate. Furthermore, Sam will be culpable for whatever harms Marvin suffers as a result of being unable to reach the marketplace; they will be harms that Sam inflicted upon Marvin. If Marvin starves to death, then Sam will have killed him. This is true even though Sam was not responsible for Marvin's initial situation of being hungry and out of food; it is true because Sam actively prevented Marvin from obtaining

---

[7] See Friedman 1989, 42–4, for discussion.
[8] This example is from Huemer 2010b, which defends the argument of this subsection at length.

more food. If a person is starving, and you refuse to give him food, then you allow him to starve. But if you take the extra step of coercively interfering with his obtaining food from someone else, then you do not merely *allow* him to starve; you starve him. The same point applies to lesser harms: if, for example, Marvin merely suffers malnutrition as a result of being unable to reach the marketplace, Sam will have inflicted this harm upon him.

The behavior of Sam in the story is analogous to that of the government of any modern country that excludes poor immigrants. Potential immigrants from developing nations come to participate in the marketplaces of wealthier countries. The governments of the wealthier countries routinely forcibly exclude these potential immigrants. As a result, many suffer greatly diminished life prospects. The government does not merely *allow* harms to befall these would-be immigrants. If the government merely stood by passively and refused to give aid to potential immigrants, then it would be allowing harms to occur. But it does not stand by passively; the government of every wealthy country in the world deliberately hires armed guards to forcibly exclude or expel unwanted persons. This coercive intervention constitutes an active infliction of harm upon them, just as Sam inflicts harm on Marvin in the story above.

The most common reasons given for immigration restriction are twofold. First, that new immigrants compete with existing Americans in the labor market, thus driving down wages for unskilled labor and making it more difficult for American workers to find jobs. Second, that if too many immigrants enter the country, they will alter the country's culture. The first concern is analogous to Sam's concern about Marvin's competing with Sam's daughter in the marketplace. It is not permissible to use force against another person simply to prevent a third party from suffering economic disadvantage through normal marketplace competition. The second concern is analogous to Sam's concern about the culture of the marketplace. It is not permissible to use force against another person simply to prevent that person from influencing the culture of one's society in undesired ways.

7.1.5 The protection of individual rights

Are there any government policies immune to the style of criticism deployed in the preceding subsections?

The policies exempt from my criticisms are generally policies that serve to protect the rights of individuals. For instance, people who wish to commit murder are subject to coercive threats by the state. Murderers who are caught are forced to spend years in confinement. But this is not at all unjust. Individuals have a right not to be murdered, and it is appropriate to defend that right by force.

Why can one not deploy here the same style of argument used in earlier subsections? Imagine that a private individual, Sam, issues a proclamation to his community that no one may murder anyone. One day, Sam discovers that someone has committed a murder. Sam takes the murderer captive at gunpoint and confines the murderer in his basement for a period of years. Has Sam acted rightly?

In this case, unlike the earlier episodes involving Sam, it seems to me that Sam's behavior is permissible, even praiseworthy.

Some are uncomfortable with this sort of vigilante action, for either of two reasons. First, one might worry about Sam's reliability in identifying the guilty. When private vigilantes exact justice, they may misidentify criminals and wind up punishing the innocent. Second, in most societies, Sam's vigilantism would be unnecessary since there are police forces and courts to punish the guilty. These are the most important reasons for opposing vigilante justice in most circumstances.

To put these concerns to rest, let us stipulate that there are no other established mechanisms for dealing with murderers in Sam's society. If Sam does not pursue the murderers, then murderers will have more or less free rein. Assume also that Sam has careful procedures for verifying the guilt of the parties whom he punishes. He has a lengthy process of reviewing evidence, in which the accused is given every opportunity to question the evidence against him and to present evidence in his own favor. The process is careful, reliable, and open to public scrutiny. In this case, I see no objection to Sam's behavior.

Sam's behavior in this last story is analogous to that of a government that pursues murderers, gives them fair and public trials, and imprisons them. There is nothing objectionable in such a practice. The same goes for policies aimed at protecting society from a number of other sorts of criminals, such as thieves, rapists, and other violent criminals.

A similar point can be made about military defense. Invaders from a foreign country are simply a large and well-organized group of thieves and murderers, and it is appropriate to use force against them in defense of oneself and one's neighbors.

I shall not attempt here to catalog all the actions that the state may justly use coercion to prevent. Particular kinds of action must be judged using our ordinary ethical intuitions and applying the general principle that it is permissible for the state to prohibit some action if and only if it would be permissible for a private individual to use force to prevent or retaliate for that sort of action, assuming the individual used reliable methods of identifying guilty parties and had no better remedies available.

7.1.6 Taxation and government finance

How may a government finance its activities? The main method now used is coercive extraction of money from the population (taxation). The prevalence of this method of finance is most likely due to the fact that it is a very reliable method of collecting very large amounts of money. But it is not normally permissible to coercively extract money from others, even if you have a very good use for the money. On the face of it, therefore, taxation appears impermissible.

That inference, however, seems to presuppose that individuals are justly entitled, prima facie, to their pretax incomes. Thomas Nagel and Liam Murphy have disputed this assumption. They believe that property rights are created by governmental laws and therefore that one only has property rights in those things to which the state's laws grant one ownership. By creating tax laws, the state shapes the property rights that individuals have such that individuals own only their after-tax incomes.[9]

In response, there are three views one might hold regarding property rights. First, one might hold that property rights are *natural*, that is, moral rights that exist prior to the state. John Locke, for example, held that individuals are justly entitled to the fruits of their labor, even in a pregovernmental society.[10] On this view, taxation would seem to be a prima facie injustice, for whatever the ethically correct way of acquiring property may be, it presumably is not forcible extraction of goods held by others.

Second, one might hold that property rights are *partly* natural, in that there are certain broad principles of property that are valid independent of governmental laws, but that there are many details of a regime of property rights that are not settled by these general moral principles. For instance, perhaps our inherent moral rights determine that we are justly entitled to the fruits of our labor, but these rights do not determine at what altitudes one may fly one's airplane over someone else's land. One might hold that state-created laws are needed to settle such matters of detail. This view still offers little comfort to a defender

---

[9] Murphy and Nagel 2002, 173–7. Compare Holmes and Sunstein 1999, chapter 3.

[10] Locke 1980, chapter 5.

of taxation, for the entitlement of one agent to coercively extract vast quantities of resources from the rest of the population is not the sort of matter of detail (like the altitude at which one may overfly others' property) that is plausibly taken to be left indeterminate by the basic moral principles of property.

Third, one might hold that there are no natural property rights. Nagel and Murphy assume that this means that property rights are created by governmental decree. This is plausible only for one who presupposes a strong doctrine of political authority. Nagel and Murphy ascribe to the state a moral entitlement, arising from its power to create property rights, to coercively enforce its chosen distribution of resources. Since no nongovernmental agent may declare a distribution of resources and a regime of property rights and then coercively enforce them, the state's right to do so would require political legitimacy. At the same time, the state's creation of a regime of property rights would presumably impose obligations on the part of citizens to respect that regime. These would be political obligations. If, therefore, the state has no authority, it has no such power of creating property rights as Murphy and Nagel suppose.

The result would seem to be that even after the state has made its laws, there still are no property rights. (If one finds this conclusion implausible, one ought to return to the view that there are natural property rights.) One might think the rejection of property rights leaves the way open for taxation: since taxpayers have no right to 'their' wealth, the seizure of some of that wealth will no longer appear as a rights violation. But by the same token, the state will have no right to that wealth either, and thus citizens do no wrong by withholding it. Meanwhile, there are the harms the state coercively imposes on those who fail to pay taxes, and these would seem to be prima facie injustices.

In short, the defender of taxation must hold that the state, rather than the taxpayers, is justly entitled to the tax revenues that the state collects. There is no plausible way to defend this view unless one assumes a doctrine of political authority.

How could a government finance its activities without taxation? One alternative is for the state to charge fees for its services. The state might charge for each service it provides or set a single fee to cover all government services. Suppose the state set a single, annual fee for its services. Those who did not pay the fee would be excluded from most government services over the course of the year – for instance, they might be unable to file lawsuits in government courts and be unable to call the government's police to protect them or to investigate crimes against them. Police protection might be provided for buildings and neighborhoods that had paid the appropriate fee, with homeowners associations collecting the funds to pay for a given neighborhood's protection. The state could establish a policy that, if a crime was committed in a building or neighborhood that had not paid the fee for governmental security, then the police and courts would do nothing about it. Provided that the state was reasonably good at its job and its fees were reasonable, most citizens, for obvious reasons, would choose to pay.

Some individuals, when first exposed to this idea, think that the proposal amounts to coercive extraction of funds from citizens, just as surely taxation does, for individuals who did not pay the state's fees would be subject to a serious risk of violence. This is a mistake. Under the present taxation scheme, the state itself inflicts harm on those who fail to pay their taxes. Under the fee-for-service scheme I have proposed, the state fails to protect from harm those who refuse to pay the necessary fee, but it does not itself inflict harm on them. Consider an analogy. Doctors provide medical care for a price. They usually do not provide care to those who do not pay them, but they are not coercing everyone who does not buy their service; if you don't hire a doctor, a doctor will not come and infect you with a disease. The fee-for-service model of government finance is like the system in which doctors provide medical care only to those who hire them. The taxation system is like a system in which doctors give diseases to those who don't hire them.

Because this alternative model of government finance has not been tried, there will undoubtedly be many questions raised about it. I cannot explore the proposal in detail here, but I will briefly mention three obvious issues. One concerns how much money the government could hope to raise through voluntary fees. In fiscal 2010, the U.S. federal government spent approximately $3.7 trillion, or about one quarter of GDP.[11] A voluntary payment scheme may be unable to support such large expenditures. The best solution to this problem would be to drastically reduce government expenditures, consistent with the very limited range of government activities we have found justified.

Another concern is that poor persons might be unable to pay the government's fees and would therefore be left with even less protection than they presently have. However, the state need not charge the same price to all citizens. Differential pricing schemes often occur even in the free market, as in the case of movie theaters that charge lower prices

---

[11] U.S. Census Bureau 2011b, 310, table 467.

for senior citizens and students. More to the point, those with expensive homes routinely pay more for property insurance than those with inexpensive homes. Along the same lines, the wealthy would be willing to pay more for protection of their persons and property than the poor would or could pay.

Another question is whether the state would be entitled to prohibit nonstate individuals or organizations from selling services similar to those of the state. For instance, could private security companies provide security for people who did not pay the government's fees? If such competition were allowed, many citizens might opt for private security, perhaps to save money or to obtain better service. If enough people behaved in this way, the government could conceivably be driven out of business. In my view, such competition should be allowed, and this provides the key to the political anarchist proposal of later chapters. However, the present chapter is for those who believe that any scheme of competing security provision with no single central authority would be socially disastrous. On that assumption, the state could justly prohibit private provision of security. It is normally wrong to coerce others, but such coercion can be justified when it is necessary to prevent something much worse from happening.

A similar point would apply if it turned out that the fee-for-service model of government finance was for some reason unworkable. If taxation were necessary to prevent a societal catastrophe, then the state would be justified in taxing. However, the fee-for-service model, if workable, has the advantage in terms of justice, since it reduces the amount of government coercion. For this reason, governments ought to at least attempt to implement this model and should resort to taxation only if serious good-faith efforts at voluntary financing fail.

7.2   The case of aid to the poor

7.2.1   Welfare and drowning children

Many government policies serve to redistribute wealth from the rich to the poor. This class of policies looms large in contemporary social theory, overshadowing every other kind of policy in discussions of social justice. I devote the present section to addressing what I consider the strongest argument in favor of wealth redistribution. This is a broadly humanitarian rather than an egalitarian argument – that is, it focuses on the problem that some people's basic needs are unsatisfied rather than on the alleged problem that people have disparate levels of wealth and income.[12]

Imagine that you are passing by a pond where you see a drowning child. If you can save the child at slight cost to yourself, then it would be wrong not to do so. This example is often deployed in the ethics literature to motivate the principle that, if one can prevent something very bad from happening at little cost to oneself, one is obligated to do so. In particular, it is often said that if we have the opportunity to save poor people from suffering from starvation, malnutrition, or other serious harms at small cost to ourselves, we must do so.[13]

But now imagine that for whatever reason, you are unable to save the child in the pond yourself. There is, however, another bystander who could save the child at slight cost to herself. This individual, however, does not care enough about the child to do so voluntarily. The only way to cause the child to be saved is to threaten the bystander with violence unless she saves the child. You do so, and she saves the child. Call this the *Drowning Child* case. In this case, regrettable as the resort to coercion may be, it seems justified.

This appears to show that it is permissible to coerce others to assist those in distress, provided that they can do so at modest cost and that there is no other way of causing the people in distress to be helped. By analogy, one may argue, the state is justified in using coercion to induce citizens to aid the poor, as in the case of government social welfare programs. In the following subsections, I suggest three objections to this conclusion.

7.2.2 The utility of antipoverty programs

Consider a variation on the Drowning Child case. Call this the *Incompetent Bystander* case: as before, there is a drowning child whom you are unable to help directly, but you can coerce a reluctant bystander into taking action. This time, however, assume that even if you coerce the bystander into entering the pond to pull the child out, it is unclear whether the child will actually be saved (whether because the child may already be too far gone, because the bystander is incompetent, or for some other reason). Second, assume that there is a fair chance that, on his way to trying to save the drowning child, the bystander will accidentally knock one or more other children into the pond who will

---

[12] See Huemer 2003 and forthcoming for arguments against egalitarianism.
[13] Singer 1993, chapter 8; Unger 1996.

then drown. You find it difficult to assess these probabilities, so it is quite unclear to you whether the net expected benefit of forcing the bystander to 'help' is positive or negative. Nevertheless, you cannot stand the thought of doing nothing, and so you whip out your trusty pistol and force the bystander to go after the drowning child.

In this case, you act wrongly. There must be some presumption against coercion. In the scenario as just described, there is no compelling case in favor of getting the bystander to take action, so the presumption against coercion stands. The conclusion is even clearer if the example is specified such that you would be justified in taking the expected benefit of coercing the bystander to be negative (that is, taking the expected harms to outweigh the expected benefits). Government antipoverty programs are justified, then, only if their expected benefits are positive *and this fact is reasonably clear* (that is, we have strong all-things-considered justification for believing it).[14]

There is a simple and well-known argument for thinking that antipoverty programs are overall beneficial: antipoverty programs redistribute money from wealthier people to poorer people. According to the well-known principle of the diminishing marginal utility of money, a given quantity of money will usually give more benefit to a poorer person than to a wealthier person (the poor need the money more). These redistributive programs should therefore do more good than harm.[15] This theoretical argument has clear prima facie plausibility. It rests on a very widely accepted and plausible economic principle, that of the diminishing marginal utility of wealth.

There are also a number of prima facie plausible arguments for the opposite conclusion. Charles Murray, the most influential critic of government antipoverty programs, argues that these programs create a moral hazard problem.[16] They lower the costs of or create benefits for certain social conditions, such as unemployment and out-of-wedlock pregnancy. This lowers people's aversion to those conditions, leading more people to behave in ways more likely to lead to those conditions.

---

[14] The formulation in terms of 'expected benefit' is intended to allow for the possibility that a coercive act might be justified by virtue of its merely reducing the risk of something very bad. It need not be clear that the coercive act *in fact prevents* the bad event; however, it must at least be reasonably clear that the coercive act reduces the risk. If the coercive act creates some other risk, it must also be reasonably clear that the reduction in the original risk outweighs the newly created risk.

[15] Lerner 1944, chapter 3; Nagel 1991, 65.

[16] Murray 1984. See also Olasky 1992; Schmidtz 1998.

Rather than helping the poor get on their feet, Murray contends, the government programs create a cycle of dependency, making it easier in the short term to engage in behaviors that are self-destructive in the long term. The general thrust of his empirical argument is that, as government antipoverty programs enjoyed enormous increases in funding and scope between the 1960s and 1980, poverty, unemployment, illegitimacy, crime, deficient education, and other social problems persisted: 'In some cases, earlier progress slowed; in other cases mild deterioration accelerated; in a few instances advance turned into retreat.'[17] Other social scientists, however, have strongly disputed Murray's empirical argument.[18]

Other arguments focus on the effects of wealth redistribution on overall economic productivity. One argument often heard in the popular discourse contends that high taxes on the wealthy reduce the incentive for people to be productive. A related, more subtle argument begins from the observation that high-income people tend to invest a much larger proportion of their income than low-income people do. Therefore, redistribution of wealth from high- to low-income persons will reduce a society's total investment rate in favor of near-term consumption. This will reduce a society's rate of economic growth. Changes in the growth rate have exponentially larger total impacts as one compounds them over longer periods of time. So the lower growth rate will make a very large difference to the material wealth of future generations.[19]

Finally, it should be remembered that government programs are not frictionless machines. It may be true that a given dollar would do more good for a poor person than for a wealthy person, but once account is taken of administrative costs and waste, government programs that take a dollar from a wealthy person are unlikely to give the poor person anything close to the whole dollar.

All of these arguments have some validity: each identifies one relevant factor tending to either promote or diminish social welfare. One important factor speaks in favor of government antipoverty programs, while other important factors speak against these programs. My guess is that in the long term, the argument from the rate of investment wins out.

I cannot attempt here to resolve the very complex question of the net effects of government antipoverty programs. On that question, I

---

[17] Murray 1984, 8–9.
[18] See Jencks 1992, chapter 2; Murray and Jencks 1985; Cowen 2002, 39–44.
[19] Schmidtz 2000; Cowen 2002, 44–9.

have nothing of import to add to the existing literature (see the notes). Nevertheless, the foregoing discussion should help to explain why the issue is controversial and why it is at best unclear that these programs are overall beneficial rather than harmful. But given the presumption against coercion, the programs are justified only if it is clear that they have a net positive expected benefit.

It is conceivable that in the future someone will devise government antipoverty programs that have clear net benefits. At that time, coercion might become justified, depending on how large the benefits were, how much coercion was required, and so on. However, bearing in mind that the theoretical arguments for the harmfulness of government antipoverty programs are based on very broad features of those programs, it is also likely that no one will devise programs devoid of these problems. I suspect that the only programs that would genuinely produce large net benefits are politically unfeasible due to widespread biases against foreigners, as suggested in the following subsection.

7.2.3   Are poverty programs properly targeted?

I turn now to another variation on the needy children theme. Call this the *Cold Child* case: there is a child who is uncomfortable because of the cold night air. She needs a jacket, but you have no jacket to give her. You do, however, have a *gun*, and you see a bystander nearby who is wearing both a jacket and a sweater. The bystander does not want to give up any of his clothing. You pull out your gun and compel the bystander to give his jacket to the girl.

Meanwhile, farther away, there is a boy who is drowning in a shallow pond. You are aware of this second child, and you could coerce the bystander to help the drowning child; however, this would interfere with his helping the cold child (the bystander has to leave shortly for very important reasons and only has time to help one child). You like the cold child better; she looks more like you, she is from your home town, and so on. So you secure help for the cold child, leaving the other child to drown.

Your behavior in this case is morally unacceptable. There are two obvious problems: first, the desire to keep a child warm is, in the absence of a medical emergency, not an adequate justification for armed robbery. Second, if you are going to use coercion to help someone, it has to be the *drowning* child, whose needs are far more urgent.

The government of a wealthy nation is in a similar position. Some of its citizens are somewhat needy. But there are much needier citizens in other countries. The American poor, for example, are only poor *relative to other Americans;* they often nevertheless own automobiles, color televisions, microwave ovens, and so on. They may be in danger of, for example, being unable to afford new clothes or being unable to send their children to college. The poor in the developing world, however, are *absolutely* poor. They are in danger of dying because of starvation, malnutrition, or easily preventable diseases. Yet for the most part, the governments of wealthy countries, such as the United States, choose to use their funds to aid people in their own countries, mostly ignoring the much needier people elsewhere. The two activities are related, because the funds that are spent on domestic poor could have been spent on foreign poor. The state could of course raise its tax rate so as to have more money available, but no matter how high the state raised its revenues within the range of plausible possibilities, it would still be the case that all or nearly all of that money would have to be spent on the foreign poor if funds were allocated in anything like a need-based manner.

As in the case of the Cold Child, most actual government wealth-redistribution programs appear to suffer from two problems. First, the needs they aim to address are not sufficiently urgent to justify coercion. The need to save a person from death or serious injury may justify a moderate level of coercion and moderate violations of property rights. But the desire to supply a person with quality clothing, a college education, or an air conditioner typically does not suffice to justify coercive seizure of the necessary funds from innocent third parties.

Second, if the government is to institute coercive aid programs at all, it surely must direct its efforts toward people whose lives are in grave danger yet who could be saved at minimal cost rather than toward people with much less urgent needs that are much more expensive to address. For example, it has been estimated that programs of vitamin A supplementation in the developing world can save lives at a cost of between $64 and $500 per life saved.[20] For comparison, when performing cost-benefit analyses, the U.S. EPA uses a figure of $6.9 million for the value of a statistical life in the United States.[21] The government could

---

[20] Horton et al. 2009. Other extremely cost-effective programs include zinc supplementation, iron and folate fortification, salt iodization, and deworming – all in the developing world (Bhagwati et al. 2009).

[21] Borenstein 2008. In other words, the EPA considers a regulation to be worthwhile if it imposes a cost of no more than $6.9 million for every American life that it is expected to save.

give its antipoverty funds to charity groups implementing extremely cost-effective, lifesaving programs in less developed countries. Surely programs of this kind must come before giving money to an American family whose income, while low by American standards, is many times greater than that of most inhabitants of the developing world.

Some would argue that the state's seemingly perverse priorities are justified because the state bears special responsibilities to its own citizens that it does not bear to foreigners.[22] This strikes me as an inadequate reply. Suppose we add to the Cold Child case the stipulation that the cold child is actually your daughter, whereas the drowning child is a stranger from some other country. If governments have special duties to their own citizens, parents have even clearer and stronger special duties to their own children. So if it were a question of saving one of the two children's lives, it would be proper to save your daughter. But you may not choose securing a jacket to keep your daughter warm over saving the life of a stranger.

The argument of this subsection does not attempt to show that no coercive antipoverty programs could be justified. What it shows is that if the state is morally justified in adopting any such programs, they would have to be very different from the programs actually found in wealthy countries. They would focus on extremely needy yet easily helped people in foreign countries. Existing programs are almost entirely aimed at the wrong people and the wrong problems.

7.2.4 A clash of analogies: drowning children and charity muggings

Is the Drowning Child case the closest analogy we can find to government antipoverty programs? Consider the *Charity Mugging* case: you have started a charity to provide monetary assistance to the poor. To collect the needed funds, you take to mugging people on the street.

This seems clearly impermissible. Now suppose for the sake of argument that your coercive action in the Charity Mugging case is *impermissible*, yet your coercive action in the Drowning Child case is *permissible*. Which case provides a closer analogy to government antipoverty programs?

On the face of it, if we are to pick one of the cases as a closer analogy, it has to be the Charity Mugging. In the Charity Mugging, the coercive

---

[22] See Goodin 1988 (but note the last sentence of the article, which comes close to taking back what the rest of the article seems to say). See also Wellman 2000.

action is taken in service of exactly the same sort of program as the government programs at issue, a program of direct economic aid to the poor. The coercive act is also of the same kind as in the government programs: forcible extraction of money. Neither of these things is true of the Drowning Child case. So, if we accept ordinary intuitions about both the Drowning Child and the Charity Mugging, we should conclude that government antipoverty programs are impermissible.

Some philosophers would argue, however, that the Drowning Child and the Charity Mugging cases have no morally significant differences: both are cases in which one coerces another person to secure aid for a needy third party, and this is all that matters. Because these cases are clearly analogous to each other, these philosophers would say, our intuitions about one of the two cases must simply be wrong.[23] Since the intuition about the Drowning Child is stronger than the intuition about the Charity Mugging, we should stick with the Drowning Child intuition, and thus, we should endorse government antipoverty programs.

Are there any relevant differences between the two cases? For those who have not previously done so, it is worth taking a moment to reflect on this question before reading on.

There are at least three differences that might be thought, either individually or in conjunction, to be morally significant:

a) In the Charity Mugging, the problem you seek to address is a *chronic social condition*, whereas in the Drowning Child, the problem is an *acute emergency*. The examples in the literature that draw forth the strongest intuitions about duties to assist others are examples of acute emergencies. The cases in which we lack strong intuitions of a duty to assist but in which philosophers try to argue us into accepting such duties are typically cases of chronic social conditions.
b) In the Drowning Child case, one can easily and quickly *solve* the problem, whereas in the Charity Mugging case, one can realistically hope only to *alleviate* the problem.
c) In the Drowning Child case, the coercion required to address the problem is a *one-time intervention*, whereas in the Charity Mugging, it is an *ongoing program* of coercion.[24]

---

[23] Though Unger does not discuss the Charity Mugging case directly, his remarks about other cases (1996, chapter 3) suggest that he would endorse the argument mentioned in the text.
[24] Unger (1996, chapter 2) discusses a similar pair of examples and considers several potentially relevant differences, including essentially (a) and (b) above. He finds (a) morally irrelevant (42). Roughly, he holds that the distinction

Government antipoverty programs align with the Charity Mugging case in all these respects. There may be other interesting differences between the two kinds of cases, perhaps including some that no one has yet identified. This is likely, since it is in general very difficult to identify the sources of our intuitions, and most people have difficulty even coming up with points (a)–(c).

There seem now to be four philosophical views about the Drowning Child and Charity Mugging cases that are worth considering:

i) The two kinds of case are relevantly alike, and in *neither* case is coercion permissible.
ii) The two kinds of case are relevantly alike, and in *both* cases coercion is permissible.
iii) One-time coercive interventions to solve acute emergencies are permissible, but ongoing programs of coercion to alleviate chronic social conditions are not. Thus, coercion is justified in the Drowning Child case but not in the Charity Mugging case.
iv) The cases are disanalogous for some other reason, and coercion is justified in the Drowning Child case but not in the Charity Mugging case.

Only on option (ii) would we conclude that government antipoverty programs are permissible. But at first glance (iii) seems much more plausible than (ii). Option (iv) also seems much more plausible than (ii), despite the failure to specify the relevant difference between the cases (it is not at all implausible to think that there may be a

---

between an 'emergency' and a 'chronic problem' consists merely in the fact that the victims of the latter have been suffering for a longer time; but this surely cannot *lessen* the reasons for helping victims of chronic problems. It is not obvious, however, that Unger's account of the distinction must be accepted.Unger considers point (b) 'confused' (41). Roughly, he would argue that in the Charity Mugging case, we can satisfy the needs of some victims of poverty. The only reason we say that our aid cannot 'solve the problem' is that we are grouping together all people suffering from poverty, and we cannot satisfy all these people's needs. But in the Drowning Child case, we could conceptually group together that particular drowning child with all the other people suffering from anything bad anywhere in the world. So here, too, our aid cannot 'solve the problem' because we cannot stop all bad things in the world. Therefore, there really is no difference between the Charity Mugging and the Drowning Child. Unger's argument here depends upon the assumption that there is no distinction between more and less natural groupings.

relevant difference that has escaped notice). Views (i) and (ii) strike me as of comparable implausibility, with (ii) less plausible than (i), though reasonable thinkers will differ on this.

Thesis (ii) has more implausible implications than just that one may extort money from others to support charity. The bystander in the Drowning Child has a stringent moral duty to assist the drowning child. If the Charity Mugging case is relevantly similar, then individuals must have stringent moral duties to donate to charity, comparable to the duty to assist a drowning child. If they did not have such duties, this would be a morally relevant difference between the two cases (it is morally relevant that in Drowning Child, one coerces the bystander only to do her duty).

Now imagine another case; call this the *Overworked Philanthropist* case. Suppose that you regularly donate 80 percent of your paycheck to charities helping poor children. On the way to work, you see a child drowning in a shallow pond. Considering how much sacrifice you have already made for others, you wonder whether you must really get your clothes wet to save yet another child.

Intuitively, the answer is yes. Even after donating 80 percent of your income to charity, you are still obligated to save a drowning child when given the chance. Now if the duty to donate to charity is comparable to the duty to save a drowning child, then it seems that we may make the same claim about donating to charity; that is, even after donating 80 percent of your income to charity, you are still obligated to donate (more) to charity when given the chance. If this is not so, then the obligation to give to charity must be somehow less stringent than the obligation to assist a drowning child. Hence, if we accept thesis (ii), it seems we must conclude that we are obligated to donate more than 80 percent of our income to charity.[25]

Furthermore, in the Overworked Philanthropist case, you would not be just slightly blameworthy if you failed to save the child. Failure to save the child would be extremely blameworthy, perhaps not much better than murder. Therefore, if the obligation to give to charity is morally comparable to the obligation to assist a drowning child, then one who fails to give away over 80 percent of his income to charity is also extremely blameworthy, perhaps not much better than a murderer. We might have to conclude that the behavior of nearly everyone,

---

[25] Compare Unger 1996, chapter 6. Of course, one need only give up to the point at which further giving threatens one's survival or one's ability to give in the future.

including, for example, philanthropists who give away only 75 percent of their income, is utterly despicable.

Some philosophers embrace just that sort of extremely demanding morality, along with its harsh judgment of nearly everyone's conduct. These philosophers point out that our strong *aversion* to giving away almost all our money is no proof that we are not obligated to do so. They may say that our reluctance to accept their demanding morality is simply due to our self-interested bias – we don't want to do what morality actually requires of us, and so we close our eyes to our obligations.[26]

The hypothesis of self-interested bias might serve as a plausible debunking explanation of one isolated datum – our reluctance to accept extremely demanding obligations of charity. But the hypothesis fares worse in explaining the larger pattern of moral attitudes that cohere with that reluctance. If we simply suffered from an egoistic bias, then we might expect this fact to be evidenced by a shift in our intuitions when we directed attention away from ourselves and toward the behavior of others or when we imagined ourselves in different positions. But this does not seem to be the case. We do not exempt ourselves from a duty of charity that we recognize for others: when we hear of someone else who gives large amounts of money to charity, we treat this as praiseworthy and supererogatory; we do not react as if we had been told of someone who merely refrains from murdering as many people as he could.

Even when we ourselves are in economic need – if, for example, we lose our job – we do not think of strangers as obligated to donate money to support us. Even those who are chronically poor do not consider strangers obligated to help them (though they may consider the state obligated to help them).

Nor do our intuitions about most other situations follow the direction of self-interest. We do not generally consider ourselves entitled to harm or exploit others for our own benefit. Even those who would be particularly good at exploiting others in a particular way do not typically hold that it is permissible to exploit others in that way.

Lastly, even those philosophers who accept extremely demanding ethical systems do not have the emotional reactions that would seem to cohere with belief in such demanding ethical systems. Utilitarian philosophers do not react with horror when you tell them that you spent $40 on dinner at a restaurant instead of sending the money to famine relief, yet they would surely react with horror if you told them

---

[26] Norcross 2003, 461; Shaw 1999, 286–7.

that you left a child to drown in a pond because you didn't want to get your clothes wet.

None of these observations *entail* that some extremely demanding morality is not correct. But they illustrate the fact that our attitudes are coherent and can be parsimoniously explained by the hypothesis that we are not in fact obligated to donate very large amounts of money to charity. It remains possible that we are suffering from a self-interested bias that blinds us to our extremely demanding obligations of charity, but this hypothesis does a poor job of explaining the pattern of judgments and attitudes that most people evince. In moral philosophy, as well as the rest of human intellectual inquiry, it is reasonable to assume that things are the way they seem until proven otherwise.[27]

The above arguments should not, however, be taken as a license for selfish disregard of those in need. Regular donation to charity groups aiding the world's least fortunate is the compassionate and decent thing to do. Virtually no one doubts this.[28] An average member of a prosperous society may be able, over the course of his lifetime, to save literally hundreds of lives by donating a small fraction of his income.[29] In view of this, it is plausible to view regular donation as a requirement of decent respect for human life (see the footnote for recommendations).[30]

7.2.5 In case the foregoing is wrong

It is often valuable to consider what the most likely alternative is, in case one's own view is mistaken. I think the most credible alternative to the position taken above is that it is permissible for the state (or a private agent) to coercively collect funds to alleviate world poverty. In doing so, the state would be obligated to prioritize people with very serious problems that can be addressed reliably and at low cost. All or nearly all of the people satisfying that description are inhabitants of the developing world. Once the state had properly targeted its poverty relief efforts, some of the objections of Section 7.2.2 would also be obviated.

---

[27] See Huemer 2005, chapter 5; 2007.
[28] See Hardin (1974) for the inevitable exception, but see Sen (1994) for refutation of Hardin.
[29] For pertinent statistics, see www.givingwhatwecan.org/resources/what-you-can-achieve.php.
[30] It is plausible that one ought to give an amount that one feels is respectful. For a review of the most cost-effective charities, see Give Well (www.givewell.org). As of this writing, Give Well gives its highest ratings to the Against Malaria Foundation (www.againstmalaria.com/donate.aspx) and Schistosomiasis Control Initiative (www3.imperial.ac.uk/schisto). Both take credit card donations through the Internet.

The view would challenge the distinction suggested above between acute emergencies and chronic conditions, arguing that some emergencies *are* chronic social conditions or components thereof. Imagine that you have been lost in the woods for several days without food, and you are in danger of starvation. You come upon a cabin in the woods. The owner is not home, but there is plenty of food inside. It seems permissible to take some food to preserve your life despite the violation of the owner's property rights. (This is permissible even if you know you will not be able to compensate the owner afterwards and even if you doubt that the owner would consent to your taking his food.) This illustrates the fact that extreme hunger can count as an emergency situation sufficient to justify the violation of another person's property rights. And if your hunger is an emergency of that sort, then the extreme hunger of a child in the Third World is an emergency of the same sort for that child. It happens that there are at any given time a great many people in that situation, so the existence of such emergencies is itself a chronic social condition. But why should that make a difference? If a certain type of rights violation would be justified when necessary to save one person from starvation, then shouldn't a program consisting of many such rights violations also be considered justified when it is necessary to save many people from starvation?

I am unsure what to make of this. Perhaps there is an ethical difference between committing an isolated theft to save oneself and starting up a regular program of extortion designed to save third parties wherever they may be. Or perhaps the conclusion of the preceding paragraph is simply correct.

Nevertheless, I want to insist on two points. First, the *actual* anti-poverty programs in wealthy countries are unjustified. They deploy coercion with inadequate justification, they are not focused on the neediest people, and they cannot be defended by appeal to analogies of drowning children and cabins in the woods. Second, the state has no special moral status. If the state may coercively seize funds for poverty relief, it is because the state would only be doing the same thing as the private parties in the examples of the Drowning Child and the cabin in the woods. If so, the same argument could be used to show why a private party would be justified in coercively seizing funds for poverty relief. One could even rob the government to provide funds to help the poor. The state has no special authority here, although the state may enjoy practical advantages in its efforts at seizing funds.

7.3 Implications for agents of the state

Government officials who are responsible for making policy ought to take account of the observations of the last two sections and avoid making unjust policies. What about government employees who do not make policy but are instructed to help enforce policies, some of which are unjust? Police officers, for example, are asked to arrest drug users and sellers. Judges are asked to sentence them. Soldiers are asked to fight in aggressive wars. What should these government employees do?

The police officer should refuse to arrest drug offenders. If he sees someone using drugs, he should leave that person alone or perhaps stop to give the user tips on how to avoid being seen by police officers. To arrest the drug user would be to initiate an unjustified act of coercion. The state has no right to commit unjust acts of coercion nor to order such acts to be committed, so it cannot confer on its employees a moral entitlement to perform such acts.

Of course, it is not as though police officers simply decide on their own to coerce drug users; they are required to do so as part of their job. If they refuse to enforce unjust laws, this fact will in all probability become known, and they will be reprimanded or fired. But this provides no excuse for violating the rights of others. Imagine that I have hired a chauffeur to drive me around town. Periodically, I ask my driver to perform unjustified acts of coercion. One day, for example, we see some children playing on the sidewalk. I tell the driver to stop and beat up one of the children for my entertainment. I warn the reluctant driver that if he does not follow my orders, I will fire him. So the driver proceeds to beat the child. As he does so, he regretfully tells the child, 'I am just doing my job. I don't make the rules.'

In this case, I have acted wrongly by ordering the child to be beaten. But the driver has clearly also acted wrongly by following this command. Perhaps I am *more* blameworthy than the driver, but this does not change the fact that the driver should refuse such commands, even if it results in his losing his job.

Some would deny that the driver is really just doing his job, because his job is to drive the car, not to beat up children. This is a red herring; it does not matter whether beating up children is part of his job description. Suppose that my original Help Wanted ad had read, 'Wanted: Person with clean driving record and strong muscles to drive car and beat innocent children.' My inclusion of the 'beat innocent children' clause in the job description does not afford the driver any ethical justification for beating up the child. The only ethical difference it might make is that it might render it wrong for the driver to have accepted the job in the first place. Having accepted the job, he still has no justification for beating up innocent children.

Similarly, it does not matter whether the job of a police officer includes the enforcement of unjust laws; this does not create any justification for enforcing unjust laws. The only difference it might make is that it might render it wrong to be a police officer in the first place.

Some would object that if all police officers took my arguments to heart, then all would either quit or get themselves fired, which would be much worse for society than having police who enforce both just and unjust laws. But surely, long before all police officers had resigned or been fired, the government would accede to the need for reform and repeal the unjust laws that were causing it to lose its police force, or at least allow the police to refrain from enforcing those laws. Thus, if all police were to adopt the view I have advanced, society would in fact be much better off.

For similar reasons, a judge in a case involving the violation of an unjust law should do his best to secure the minimum possible punishment. The judge should order the defendant released if feasible – that is, if this will not simply result in the defendant's being arrested again and brought before a more punitive judge. If a judge finds himself conducting a trial for something that ought not to be illegal and for which it would be unjust to punish the defendant, then the judge should do everything in his power to bias the outcome in favor of the defendant. If the judge winds up having to sentence the defendant, he should order the smallest sentence possible. If a judge finds himself routinely required, by the demands of his job, to participate in injustice, he should probably resign in search of a more just profession.

A soldier should likewise refuse to fight in an unjust war. Not to put too fine a point on it, to fight in an unjust war is to participate in murder. In joining the military, one volunteers to fight in whatever wars one's country may enter into. Therefore, if one cannot be assured that one's nation will not enter any unjust war, one should refrain from joining the military; if one is already in the military, one should resign as soon as possible.

Similar recommendations apply to all other government employees who are called upon to implement unjust policies. They should do their best to undermine those policies or, if that is not feasible, refuse to serve.

These recommendations are hardly ever followed. Government employees almost always enforce whatever policies, just or unjust, they are ordered to enforce. One reason is that they mistakenly believe in political authority; they believe that the state has the right to coercively impose these policies, even when the policies are in themselves wrong. They consider themselves permitted, perhaps even obligated, to help to enforce those policies in accordance with their job requirements. How does this affect our evaluation of their behavior?

We can distinguish the evaluation of an individual's *character* from the evaluation of the individual's *actions*. Often one of these evaluations is much more positive or negative than the other, particularly when the agent is ignorant of important facts about his behavior. Soldiers who fight in an unjust war, for example, are typically much better people and are typically much less blameworthy than private murderers. This is compatible with the fact that there are very strong objective reasons for refusing to serve in an unjust war, reasons about as strong as the reasons for refusing to participate in a private conspiracy to commit murder. As a rule, the fact that government employees believe themselves to be acting rightly makes them less blameworthy than they would otherwise be. It does not render them completely blameless; they may still be blameworthy if, as is probably the case, they have not exercised sufficient effort to find out where their true moral duty lies. In any case, government employees' ignorance of their ethical duty does not alter the appropriate assessment of what they really ought to do. It does not alter the fact that they have no right to enforce unjust laws.

7.4 Implications for private citizens

7.4.1 In praise of disobedients

If there is no authority, then disobedience to governmental edicts is justified far more often than is generally recognized.

Suppose that Sam has been issuing demands to his neighbors that he has no right to make, backed up by threats of punishment. A gang of followers helps him to forcibly impose punishments that they have no right to impose. Sam issues demands as to what his neighbors may eat, the terms of the contracts they may make with each other, which of them may provide medical care to others, how much money they must pay Sam's gang, and so on. He also issues some morally justified commands (though his issuing them is ethically redundant): he demands that no one murder, steal, and so on. Now imagine that you are one of Sam's neighbors. You wish to ingest a certain herb with psychoactive properties, but you are aware of Sam's demand, backed up by a threat of physical force from Sam's gang, that you not do so.

It seems clear that you have no ethical reason not to eat the herb, though you may of course have a strong prudential reason, arising from fear of Sam's gang, to avoid the herb. If anything, you have an ethical reason *to* eat the herb, as a way of standing up to Sam's bullying. To submit to a bully's demands is at best *excusable*. To defy Sam privately would be perfectly acceptable; to defy Sam publicly would be a praiseworthy act of courage.

Similarly, there is no question of its being wrong to defy unjust laws. The only ethical question is whether defiance is obligatory or supererogatory. In view of the severity and credibility of the threats commonly issued by the state to lawbreakers, I believe that in most cases, defiance of unjust laws is supererogatory. In some cases, defiance is foolhardy, as it would be foolhardy, when a mugger points a gun at you, to refuse to hand over your wallet. But it is not ethically wrong.

7.4.2 On accepting punishment

On some contemporary accounts, those who engage in civil disobedience must do so publicly and must accept the punishment that the state prescribes.[31] These accounts, however, are drawn against the backdrop of an assumed political authority. If there is no political authority, are there still reasons for submitting to legal punishment for acts of justified disobedience?

To disobey a law publicly is to disobey it in such a way and under such circumstances that one's action will become widely known (among those who follow such affairs), and it will be known that the action broke the law. In many cases, it will be possible to disobey a law publicly in this sense without revealing one's identity. (Imagine peace activists painting graffiti on a military factory in the middle of the night, then sneaking away.) When feasible, this form of disobedience affords obvious advantages: one may avoid suffering unpleasant punishments and remain free to perform further acts of disobedience in the future, while still communicating rejection of the unjust law.

Sometimes it is said that those who engage in civil disobedience should accept punishment for their actions to prove their sincerity and

---

[31] King (1991, 74) saw himself as expressing respect for law by practicing his civil disobedience openly and with a willingness to accept the legally prescribed punishments. Rawls (1999, section 55) seeks to build these conditions into the definition of 'civil disobedience'. Here I consider disobedience to unjustified state commands, including both what Rawls labels 'civil disobedience' and what he labels 'conscientious refusal' (1999, section 56).

seriousness to others.[32] For instance, some hold that in case of a draft, conscientious objectors should voluntarily go to prison – rather than, for example, escaping to another country – to prove that their objection to going to war is principled and unselfish.

There are a number of salient objections to this thinking. First, the requirement to accept punishment is excessively demanding. No doubt there is some value in communicating one's sincerity, moral seriousness, or other admirable traits to others. But one is not typically *obligated* to communicate this sort of information to others, even when the costs of doing so are minimal. For instance, suppose that I recently found a wallet, and I went out of my way to return it to its owner. I am not then morally obligated to relate this episode to other people, just to communicate my honesty and virtuousness, even if I can do so at no cost. Still less would I be obligated to communicate this information if doing so would require my spending some months or years in prison. It is unclear why the case should be different for acts of civil disobedience. If I have broken the law, I should no doubt prefer that others know that I had virtuous motives for doing so. But I am not obligated to communicate this information, even if I could do so for free, still less if doing so requires my spending months or years in prison.

One might argue that this case is different, because in disobeying the state, I might lead others to disobey other laws, including laws that should be obeyed, if others fail to understand the moral reasons behind my disobedience. This suggestion is contrived and implausible; it is in most cases highly unlikely that my act of disobedience will cause other people to disobey some unrelated law. In addition, it is typically not obligatory for a person to undertake extremely large sacrifices, such as spending time in jail, to prevent other people from irrationally choosing to do wrong.

Second, voluntarily accepting the state's punishment for an act of disobedience may (either instead of or in addition to communicating one's moral seriousness) communicate false and destructive ideas – most notably, that the state has the right to punish people for disobeying unjust laws. If a law is unjust, then the enforcement of that law through punishment of those who disobey is also unjust. Why, then, should one facilitate this injustice by submitting oneself for punishment? For example, suppose one's government is engaged in an unjust war, for which it has instituted a draft. In such a case, no one is obligated to participate in the war; if anything, citizens are obligated to refuse to

---

[32] Rawls 1999, 322.

participate. Now in addition to the injustice of the war itself, there will also be the injustice of the state's punishing those who virtuously refuse to participate in that war. And just as no one is obligated to facilitate the war itself, no one is obligated to facilitate or cooperate with the unjust punishing of those who refuse to participate in the war.

Consider an analogy. A homophobic gang in your neighborhood is beating up homosexuals.[33] If you are gay, should you present yourself at the gang's headquarters and announce your sexual orientation so that they may beat you? Obviously not. Among other things, to submit to a beating would wrongly communicate that you have done something that deserves punishment and that the gang has the right to punish you. Even if you believe that by submitting to a beating you would increase the probability that public outrage would eventually lead to a change in the gang's behavior, you still would not be obliged to submit to a beating.

I conclude that in most cases, those who disobey unjust laws are both ethically permitted and well advised to conceal their identity or otherwise evade punishment by the state.

7.4.3   On violent resistance

If there is a central premise of this book, it is the moral seriousness of coercion. But the resort to physical force is not always wrong. It is often justified for purposes of self-defense or defense of innocent third parties. It is not implausible, therefore, that violent resistance may often be justified in response to unjust coercion by the state.

To assess this thought, let us begin with some general principles governing the defensive use of force:

i) The use of force is justified only when necessary to prevent some serious wrong. That is, there must be no alternatives available that would prevent the wrong without using comparable levels of force, committing some other equally serious prima facie wrong, or demanding unreasonable sacrifices of the agent.

ii) The use of force must have a reasonable chance, on the agent's evidence, of preventing the wrong from occurring. Unless this condition is satisfied, the use of force will not count as a *defensive*

---

[33] Though beatings are rarely prescribed by the state, there have been a number of laws with similar motivations and effects to the actions of this hypothetical gang. Until a 2003 Supreme Court Case (*Lawrence v. Texas*, 539 U.S. 558), sodomy was outlawed in a number of U.S. states. Many other countries still have such laws (see www.glapn.org/sodomylaws/world/world.htm), which seem to be aimed at harming homosexuals.

measure. (It may instead count as a retaliatory measure; however, the conditions for justified retaliatory force are beyond the scope of this discussion.)

iii) The expected harm caused by the use of force may not be out of proportion to the expected harm averted. For example, it is not permissible to kill another person merely to prevent that person from stealing your stereo. It would, however, be permissible to kill a person if necessary to prevent that person from seriously injuring you.

iv) It is usually not permissible to harm innocent third parties in the course of defensive violence. Such harm to innocent third parties can sometimes be justified, but this will generally require expected benefits much greater than the expected harms.

Historically, there are two main forms of armed resistance to the state: terrorism and (attempted) revolution. In developed modern societies, attempted armed revolution is unlikely to be justified, for three reasons. First, there are usually nonviolent options available, which have shown surprising success in some cases, such as the well-known cases of Gandhi and Martin Luther King Jr. Second, the probability of successful revolution in most modern, developed societies is very close to zero. Third, in the case of attempted revolution, harm to innocent third parties is likely to be very great.

Terrorist attacks are no more likely to be justified. The same three points apply: nonviolent methods are typically available, terrorist methods are ineffective, and expected harms to innocent parties are excessive. A 2006 study examining 28 terrorist groups found that, using generous criteria of success, these groups achieved their policy objectives only 7 percent of the time. Later studies using larger samples have found success rates under 5 percent, and in many cases the terrorists' political goals were actually set back.[34] Why is terrorism so ineffectual? When terrorists attack civilians, populations tend to increase their support for right-wing political candidates proposing aggressive responses. These hard-liners are not frightened by terrorism, nor should they be; they are extremely unlikely to be personally victimized by terrorism, and in fact their political careers are strongly advanced by terrorism and the opportunity it provides them for aggressive posturing.[35] All of these points are illustrated by the infamous terrorist attacks of 11 September 2001

---

[34] Abrahms 2006; 2011, 587–8.

[35] Abrahms 2011, 589. Abrahms notes that attacks on military targets are more effective and account for most of the successes terrorists have had.

in the United States, which prompted the U.S. government to vastly increase its military presence in the Middle East, killing hundreds of thousands of Muslims. While this response was irrational and reprehensible, it was also predictable.

As a rule, therefore, terrorist attacks are morally wrong. The question of when one may harm innocent third parties in the course of bringing an end to oppression and injustice is a matter for debate. But surely one may not harm innocent third parties for the sake of ineffectual or counterproductive gestures.

7.4.4 In defense of jury nullification

Most readers will at some point be required to serve on a jury in a criminal trial. Many of these trials will be for crimes that genuinely deserve to be punished. But many others will be for the violation of unjust laws, such as the laws mentioned in Section 7.1. It is therefore of great practical interest what a juror should do in the latter sort of case.

When the law is unjust, the juror should vote to acquit, regardless of the evidence. Briefly, the argument is this: in general, it is wrong to knowingly cause unjust harm to another human being. To convict the defendant for violating an unjust law will, as a rule, result in his suffering significant, unjust harm at the hands of the state. Therefore, it is prima facie wrong to convict such a defendant.

Two objections must be considered. To begin with, it might be argued that a juror who votes for conviction would not be culpable for the defendant's suffering, because the juror did not make the unjust law nor is the juror himself directly imposing the punishment. Assuming that the prosecutor proves his case, the jury member who votes to convict is merely correctly reporting the fact that the defendant performed a certain action. What officials of the state do with that information is up to them; the juror is not telling them to punish the defendant (even though he knows that they will do so). A related objection is that one has a duty to tell the truth. To vote for an acquittal, in a case where the evidence shows that the defendant did in fact violate the unjust law, would be dishonest. It would be tantamount to a false assertion that the defendant was not shown to have violated that law.[36]

---

[36] This argument depends on the assumption that a jury verdict is an assessment solely of whether the defendant performed the actions ascribed to him. Duane (1996) contends instead that a jury verdict is an assessment of the justice or appropriateness of punishing the defendant.

Both objections may be addressed by the following analogy. You are walking down the street with one of your more flamboyantly dressed friends. You run into a gang of hoodlums. The leader of the gang asks you whether your friend is gay. You are convinced that these are gay bashers and that if you either answer 'yes' or refuse to answer, they will beat up your friend. The two of you have the best chance of being left unharmed if you answer 'no'. You know, however, that your friend is in fact gay. Thus, by answering 'no', you would be *lying*. Should you, therefore, either refuse to answer or answer 'yes'?

None but a fanatical Kantian would say so. Granted, lying is *usually* wrong, but not when the person to whom you are lying is someone who would use a truthful answer as a pretext for bringing serious and unjust harm upon another human being. If you should tell the hoodlums the truth, will you later be able to patch things up with your friend, as you visit him in the hospital, by reminding him that you didn't make the hoodlums hate gays to begin with nor did you personally pound on your friend with your own fists? Could you plead that all you did was report on a factual matter and that what the hoodlums did with that information was up to them?

Jurors in most courts are instructed that they must render a verdict based upon the evidence and that they must not choose to nullify the law. They may even be asked to take an oath to this effect, where refusal to do so results in dismissal from jury service. This does not alter the juror's true moral duty. Suppose that, in the above scenario, the homophobic gang leader asks you to *promise* to tell the truth about your friend. Suppose he also instructs you, with a great air of confidence and solemnity, that you *must* tell him the truth and that you have no right to lie because you disagree with his gay-bashing predilections. *Then* would you be obligated to tell him the truth? Again, no. Homophobic hoodlums do not have a right to know who is and is not gay. You should promise to tell the truth and then immediately lie.

In the United States, jurors who vote to acquit a defendant on the grounds that the law is unjust are subject to no punishment, and their verdicts cannot be overturned. Thus, despite what they may be told, jurors certainly *can* nullify laws, in the relevant senses of 'can'. The aversion to lying and promise breaking (if that is what jury nullification involves) is a trivial consideration next to the importance of preventing a person from suffering severe and unjust harms.

7.5   Objections in support of rule-worship

7.5.1   May everyone do as they wish?

People have their own opinions as to exactly which laws are just. It might therefore be thought that the philosophical view I have advanced affords carte blanche for individuals simply to do whatever they want, citing idiosyncratic interpretations of justice in their defense.

This would of course be a mistake. My philosophical position does not imply that individuals may break whatever laws they *want* to break. Suppose that Sally wants to steal money from her company so that she can live at others' expense. Sally therefore dishonestly claims to find the laws governing property 'unjust', and she uses this to rationalize her behavior. In this case, Sally's behavior is wrong. Her mere *assertion* that the property laws are unjust does nothing, ethically, to excuse her.

Suppose that Mary is also stealing money from her company. Mary, however, sincerely believes that the laws governing property are unjust, for she has been taken in by a misguided political ideology that rejects private property. In this case, is Mary's behavior right? No, it is not. Mary is mistaken in thinking that the property laws are unjust, so she is also mistaken in taking her own behavior to be ethically permissible. Depending on how understandable her error is, Mary may be less blameworthy than Sally, but her *action* is just as wrong. Thus, for example, it would be appropriate for third parties to use coercion to stop Mary from taking more money and to compel her to compensate her employer.

This is consistent with everything I have said earlier in this chapter. If a law *is unjust*, one may break it. But it is not the case that if one merely *believes* a law to be unjust, one may break it; it depends upon whether one's belief is correct.

There are many cases in which we cannot tell whether a law is just or unjust; justice is a difficult subject. What ought we to do then? In cases where we do not know whether the law is just, we will simply *not know* whether it is permissible to break that law. I can say nothing here that will cause readers to be able to know in all cases what is just or what they ought to do. My only advice for such situations is that one do further research on the topic (perhaps in the ethical and political philosophy literature) and then exercise one's best judgment.

To some, this view will be unsatisfying. A more satisfying view would be one that provides a simple, more or less mechanical rule for what to do in all cases. For instance, if we could say, 'When in doubt, always obey the law', many would find this a more satisfying position than the position that we sometimes cannot tell whether we should obey the law or not.

But satisfyingly simple and convenient rules are not therefore correct. In particular, there is no reason to think that whenever there is doubt as to the justice of a law, it is better to obey than to disobey that law. Suppose a soldier has been ordered by his government to fight in a war. The soldier is unsure whether this order is just, because he is unsure whether the war itself is just. Nothing in this description of the case enables us to infer that it would be right or good for the soldier to fight in the war. If he fights, he may be participating in mass murder. We do not know enough to say whether this is the case. The crucial information we would need, before we could advise the soldier as to what he ought to do, is a piece of moral information: we need to know whether the war is just. The fact that this knowledge may be difficult or even impossible to obtain does not prevent it from being the relevant and necessary knowledge for addressing the question at hand, nor does it enable some other, more easily knowable fact to settle the question. It simply is the human condition that our ethical questions frequently have no easy answers.

7.5.2   Process versus substance

In an early article defending the Fair Play Account of political obligation, John Rawls takes as his central question, 'How is it possible that a person, in accordance with his own conception of justice, should find himself bound by the acts of another to obey an unjust law ... ?' And he answers: 'To explain this ... we require two hypotheses: that among the very limited number of procedures that would stand any chance of being established, none would make my decision decisive ... ;and that all such procedures would determine social conditions that I judge to be better than anarchy.'[37]

My reading of that passage is that Rawls is assuming (1) that we must rely on some *procedural* criterion for deciding which laws are legitimate or ought to be obeyed, and (2) that an individual who disobeys a law on the grounds that the law is unjust is applying the following procedural rule: that a law is to be rejected if it conflicts with *that individual's* sense of justice. He finds the latter rule inadequate and inferior to democratic procedures. Therefore, Rawls believes, if a law has been made according

---

[37] Rawls 1964, 11–12. The context also contains some social contract imagery that I find unhelpful.

to democratic procedures, an individual should not disobey that law on the grounds that (he believes) the law is unjust.

But Rawls does not justify these assumptions; he does not explain why grounds for obeying or disobeying particular laws must be procedural. Instead, a law may be accepted or rejected on substantive grounds. When I say that the drug laws may be violated because they are unjust, I am not saying that the drug laws were made according to the wrong procedure. I am saying they are *substantively* unjust; they violate a substantive moral right, the right to control one's own body, that individuals possess regardless of the decisions of the state. This would be true regardless of how the law was made (except, of course, in the unlikely event of unanimous consent to the law, which would render it no longer a rights violation). I am not proposing a procedure according to which my personal opinion is decisive; if I did not exist or if I had sanctioned the drug laws, they would still be unjust. If I objected to some law that is actually just – for instance, if I objected to the murder statutes – my objection would not convert the just law into an unjust one. In other words: when I object to the drug laws, my *grounds* for objection are not simply *that I object*. My ground for objection is the right of self-ownership, the right of individuals to control their own bodies. Rawls's argument has nothing to say about whether *this* is a legitimate ground for rejecting, and hence disobeying, a law.

Why might it be thought that we must rely on procedural rules rather than substantive moral principles? Perhaps because it is thought that we do not *know* what is substantively morally correct, whereas we do know what a desirable procedure is. If this is the reasoning behind Rawls's proceduralist assumption, it is doubly mistaken. First, it is mistaken because it is false that in general we do not know what is substantively morally correct. *Sometimes* we do not know what is substantively just. But often we do know. I do not know, for example, whether a ban on abortion would be unjust. But I know that the Jim Crow laws were unjust. When we know that a law is unjust, our opposition to it can and should be based on *the fact that it is unjust*, not on the fact that it conflicts with our personal opinions or preferences.

Second, if it were true that we never knew what was substantively just, then we also would not know what was procedurally just. There is no reason to think that knowledge of just procedures would somehow evade the reach of a moral skepticism strong enough to rule out all knowledge of just outcomes. If, for example, we cannot know that laws that treat citizens grossly unequally on the basis of morally irrelevant characteristics are unjust, then why would we know that lawmaking *procedures* that fail to give citizens an equal voice are unjust?

7.5.3 Undermining social order?

Imagine that the views I have defended become widespread and, in particular, that the notion of political authority is widely rejected. Citizens thus feel free to violate any laws they find ethically objectionable whenever they can evade punishment. Government agents refuse to enforce laws they find ethically objectionable. Juries refuse to convict defendants under statutes that the juries find objectionable. Wouldn't this render our legal system too chaotic and unpredictable? Might social order not collapse entirely?

The suggestion of the preceding paragraph is simply that it may be very harmful to propagate the views advanced in this book, so much so that perhaps I should not have published the book. That is compatible with the possibility that everything I say is actually true.

The dire warnings about the collapse of social order, however, are ill taken. The views I advance are more likely to be socially beneficial than harmful. We have imagined citizens violating laws they find unjust, police refusing to enforce laws they find unjust, and juries refusing to convict under laws they find unjust – all because a general skepticism of authority has taken hold of society. In addition, we must assume that lawmakers themselves have absorbed the same philosophy of skepticism about political authority. In this case, there would be far fewer laws – and far fewer unjust laws in particular. Most of the laws that *would have* occasioned widespread civil disobedience would not exist, because legislators would not make them or would have repealed them during the period in which skepticism about authority was taking hold of society.

But suppose a particular law survives that some people consider unjust. If the number who find the law unjust is very small, there is no difficulty. For instance, suppose a tiny number of people consider the laws against theft unjust. Since the overwhelming majority of society considers those laws just, there would still be enough police officers, judges, and jurors willing to enforce the antitheft laws. The government would only encounter a problem when a large portion of society considers some law unjust. For instance, a significant number of people presently consider the drug laws unjust. If it were widely accepted that one should not help to enforce an unjust law, then some police officers would refuse to arrest drug offenders. Some judges would refuse to sentence them. And *many* juries would refuse to convict them. Trials under the drug laws and other controversial statutes would repeatedly result in hung juries. Once this pattern became clear, the state would probably give up trying to enforce such laws.

Is this the social disaster we should worry about? On the contrary, this would be a *much better* situation than the status quo. When the justice of a law is controversial, it is better to err on the side of freedom than on the side of restriction. Perhaps some just laws would, unfortunately, go unenforced. But the reduction in the number of people wrongly punished under unjust laws would more than compensate for this disadvantage. It is widely held that it is better for ten guilty people to go free than for one innocent person to be punished. If this is true, then it is also better for ten people to fail to be convicted under just laws than for one person to be convicted under an unjust law. Our present system, however, errs very much in the opposite direction: even when the moral status of a law is in doubt, police officers, judges, and juries almost always enforce the law without question.

On a realistic note, the picture of ordinary people as perched on the verge of disorder, waiting for an excuse to run rampant in disregard of law and order, flies in the face of everything we know about the psychology of authority (see Chapter 6). Evidence such as the Milgram experiments, the Holocaust, and the My Lai Massacre leave little doubt that the average human being is far more likely to commit heinous crimes in the name of obedience to authority than he is to rashly disobey justified commands of an authority figure. Literally millions have died because of the widespread disposition to obey unjust commands. So even if my skepticism about authority goes too far, it will more likely serve as a valuable corrective to our excessive tendency to obey rather than posing a danger of destroying social order.

7.5.4   The consequences of the doctrine of content-independence

I have argued that the state has the right to make and enforce only ethically correct laws. Some think that this asks too much of the state; any government run by fallible human beings will sometimes make mistakes, including moral mistakes.[38] If the agents of the state are thought to have no leeway, no entitlement to make mistakes, then they

---

[38] Estlund 2008, 157–8; Christiano 2008, 239–40; Klosko 2005, 116.

may be paralyzed into inaction by the fear of doing wrong. One might therefore think that the state should be accorded at least some leeway in the form of a content-independent entitlement to make rules, as long as its rules are not *too* unreasonable.

Parallel reasoning could be applied to private agents. It is also unrealistic, for example, to expect a large private corporation to be perfect; any such corporation will sometimes make mistakes, including moral mistakes. But no one thinks this means that we must ascribe to large corporations a moral entitlement to periodically perform unjust or wrongful actions just as long as they are not too unreasonable. We recognize that a large corporation will sometimes do wrong, but we do not acquiesce in those wrongs. We condemn them when they happen and demand that the corporation make amends. In the same way, we should not acquiesce in wrongdoing by the state, however predictable it may be; we should condemn it when it happens and demand that the state make amends. This attitude will not make it impossible to maintain a state, any more than the analogous attitude toward corporations makes it impossible to maintain a corporation.

What are the likely social consequences of the belief in content-independent authority? Christiano tells us that 'the democratic assembly has a right to do wrong, within certain limitations.' Rawls observes, 'It is, of course, a familiar situation…that a person finds himself morally obligated to obey an unjust law.'[39] Does this idea increase or decrease the state's likelihood of achieving the social aims for the sake of which the state is supposed to be needed?

Consider an analogy. You have hired a gardener to take care of the plants in your yard. You want him to care for all the plants, and you want him not to do anything else, such as entering the house and stealing your jewelry. Which of the following two instructions should you give the gardener?

A You must take care of all the plants. You must not enter the house and steal jewelry.

B Ideally, you should take care of all the plants, but you have some leeway; you are entitled to periodically damage or neglect a few of them. It would also be best if you did not enter the house and steal jewelry. But you may do that occasionally, as long as it doesn't get out of hand.

---

[39] Christiano 2008, 250; Rawls 1964, 5. By 'the democratic assembly', Christiano means the legislature in a representative democracy.

Rawls, Christiano, and other defenders of content-independent political authority are in effect giving the gardener instruction (B). I would tell the gardener (A). Which is really the socially dangerous philosophy?

7.6 A modest libertarian foundation

Libertarianism is a minimal government (or, in extreme cases, no government) philosophy, according to which the government should do no more than protect the rights of individuals.[40] Essentially, libertarians advocate the political conclusions defended in this chapter. But this position is very controversial in political philosophy. Many readers will wonder if we are really forced to it. Surely, to arrive at these radical conclusions, I must have made some extreme and highly controversial assumptions along the way, assumptions that most readers should feel free to reject?

Libertarian authors have indeed frequently relied upon controversial assumptions. Ayn Rand, for example, thought that capitalism could only be defended by appeal to ethical egoism, the theory that the right action for anyone in any circumstance is always the most selfish action.[41] Robert Nozick is widely read as basing his libertarianism on an absolutist conception of individual rights, according to which an individual's property rights and rights to be free from coercion can never be outweighed by any social consequences.[42] Jan Narveson relies on a metaethical theory according to which the correct moral principles are determined by a hypothetical social contract.[43] Because of the controversial nature of these ethical or metaethical theories, most readers find the libertarian arguments based on them easy to reject.

I have appealed to nothing so controversial in my own reasoning. I reject the foundations for libertarianism mentioned in the preceding paragraph. I reject egoism, since I believe that individuals have substantial obligations to take into account the interests of others. I reject ethical absolutism, since I believe an individual's rights may be overridden by

---

[40] Terminological note: capitalistic anarchism counts as an extreme form of libertarianism.

[41] Rand 1964, 33; 1967, 195–6, 200–1.

[42] Nozick 1974, 28–35. Nagel (1995, 148) reads Nozick as an absolutist, though in fact Nozick (1974, 30n) expresses some doubt about absolutism.

[43] Narveson 1988, chapters 12–14.

sufficiently important needs of others. And I reject all forms of social contract theory, for reasons discussed in Chapters 2 and 3.

The foundation of my libertarianism is much more modest: common sense morality. At first glance, it may seem paradoxical that such radical political conclusions could stem from anything labeled 'common sense'. I do not, of course, lay claim to common sense political views. I claim that revisionary *political* views emerge out of common sense *moral* views. As I see it, libertarian political philosophy rests on three broad ideas:

i) A *nonaggression principle* in interpersonal ethics. Roughly, this is the idea that individuals should not attack, kill, steal from, or defraud one another and, in general, that individuals should not coerce one another, apart from a few special circumstances.

ii) A recognition of *the coercive nature of government.* When the state promulgates a law, the law is generally backed up by a threat of punishment, which is supported by credible threats of physical force directed against those who would disobey the state.

iii) A *skepticism of political authority.* The upshot of this skepticism is, roughly, that the state may not do what it would be wrong for any nongovernmental person or organization to do.

The main positive ethical assumption of libertarianism, the nonaggression principle, is the most difficult to precisely articulate. In truth, it is a complex collection of principles, including prohibitions on theft, assault, murder, and so on. I cannot completely articulate this set of principles. Fortunately, it is not the locus of disagreement between libertarians and partisans of other political ideologies, for the 'nonaggression principle', as I use the term, is simply the collection of prohibitions on mistreating others that are accepted in common sense morality. Almost no one, regardless of political ideology, considers theft, assault, murder, and so on morally acceptable. We do not need a complete list of these prohibitions, since we have been able to construct the arguments of this book by relying on intuitions about specific cases. I have made no particularly strong assumptions about these ethical prohibitions. I do not, for example, assume that theft is *never* permissible. I simply assume that it is not permissible under normal circumstances, as dictated by common sense morality.

The second principle, that of the coercive nature of government, is equally difficult to dispute. The coercive nature of government is commonly forgotten or ignored in political discourse, in which the justification for coercion is seldom discussed. But virtually no one actually *denies* that the state regularly relies upon coercion.

It is the notion of *authority* that forms the true locus of dispute between libertarianism and other political philosophies. Libertarians are skeptical about authority, whereas most accept the state's authority in more or less the terms in which the state claims it. This is what enables most to endorse governmental behavior that would otherwise appear to violate individual rights: nonlibertarians assume that most of the moral constraints that apply to other agents do not apply to the state.

I have therefore focused on defending skepticism about authority by addressing the most interesting and important theories of authority. In defending this skepticism, I have, again, relied upon no particularly controversial ethical assumptions. I have considered the factors that are said to confer authority on the state and found that in each case, either those factors are not actually present (as in the case of consent-based accounts of authority) or those factors simply do not suffice to confer the sort of authority claimed by the state. The latter point is established by the fact that a nongovernmental agent to whom those factors applied would generally not be ascribed anything like political authority. I have suggested that the best explanation for the inclination to ascribe authority to the state lies in a collection of nonrational biases that would operate whether or not there were any legitimate authorities. Most people never pause to question the notion of political authority, but once it is examined, the idea of a group of people with a special right to command everyone else fairly dissolves.

These three ideas – the nonaggression principle, the coercive nature of government, and skepticism about authority – together call for a libertarian political philosophy. Most government actions violate the nonaggression principle – that is, they are actions of a sort that would be condemned by common sense morality if they were performed by any nongovernmental agent. In particular, the government generally deploys coercion in circumstances and for reasons that would by no means be considered adequate to justify coercion on the part of a private individual or organization. Therefore, unless we accord the state some special exemption from ordinary moral constraints, we must condemn most government actions. The actions that remain are just the ones that libertarians accept.

How might one avoid the libertarian conclusion? Only by rejecting one of the three core principles I have identified. It is extremely unpromising to question the coercive nature of government, and I doubt that any theorist will wish to take that tack. Some theorists will question common sense morality. I have not undertaken a general defense of common sense morality in this book, and I shall not do so now. Every book must begin somewhere, and beginning with such assumptions as that under normal conditions one may not rob, kill, or attack other people seems reasonable enough. This is about the least controversial, least dubious starting point for a book of political philosophy that I have seen, and I think few readers will feel happy about rejecting it.

The least implausible way of resisting libertarianism remains that of resisting the libertarian's skepticism about authority. I have addressed what strike me as the most interesting, influential, or promising accounts of political authority – the traditional social contract theory, the hypothetical social contract theory, the appeal to democratic processes, and appeals to fairness and good consequences. But I cannot address every possible account of authority, and a fair number of thinkers may react to my performance by proposing alternative accounts of authority.

I suspect, however, that the general strategy I have relied upon will be able to be extended to such alternative accounts. A theory of authority will cite some feature of the state as the source of its authority. My strategy begins by imagining a private agent who possesses that feature. Of course, this will not be possible if the feature in question entails statehood – but so far, the features that have been alleged as the source of the state's political authority have not entailed statehood (no one, for example, has proposed that authority is conferred simply by the property of *being a state*). For instance, the property of being something that would be agreed to by all reasonable people, the property of being actually accepted by the majority of society, and the property of producing very good consequences are all properties that a nongovernmental organization or the policies of such an organization could possess. As I say, then, we imagine a nongovernmental agent with the relevant feature. We then realize that intuitively we would not ascribe to that agent anything like a comprehensive, content-independent, supreme entitlement to coerce obedience from other people. And so we conclude that the proposed feature fails as a ground of political authority.

Part II
Society without Authority

8
Evaluating Social Theories

In the chapters to follow, I ask the reader to consider a broad theory of how society ought to be organized. Before explaining this theory and the arguments in its support, it may be helpful to discuss how theories of this kind ought to be evaluated.

8.1 General observations on the rational evaluation of social theories

8.1.1 Rational evaluation is comparative

We often decide whether to adopt a course of action by asking simply whether the action is good or bad. But the more appropriate question is whether the action is *better* or *worse* than the alternatives.[1]

Suppose that while driving my car, I see a dog in the street. I have the option of running over the dog. Should I do it? The answer depends upon what my alternatives are. If I also have the option of stopping the car and waiting for the dog to cross, then I should not hit the dog. But what if my brakes have failed, and I cannot stop the car? What if, furthermore, there is a child playing on the sidewalk to my right and an oncoming car in the lane to my left? My only options are to hit the child, hit the oncoming car, or hit the dog. In

---

[1] I state the point this way for simplicity of expression; I do not intend, however, to presuppose consequentialism. For cases in which nonconsequentialist duties apply, what matters is whether an action does a better job of satisfying one's prima facie duties than the available alternatives (see Ross 1988, chapter 2). For instance, whether I should break a promise depends upon whether my available alternatives would violate duties more stringent than the duty to keep that promise.

that case, I should hit the dog. This option is not good, but it is better than the alternatives.

The same point applies to the evaluation of social theories, where the relevant question is not whether some social structure would be good or bad simply but whether it would be better or worse than the alternatives; that is, the other social structures that we could adopt. This point may be obvious, but it bears stressing, because it is easy to forget in practice; we often criticize or defend political proposals without considering what the alternatives are.

A corollary is that our standard for evaluating social theories ought not to be one of perfection. We ought not, that is, to reject a proposed social structure because under it, some people will suffer from some social problems. Perfection is not one of the available options for human societies. We ought to reject a social system if and only if we can identify a superior alternative.

8.1.2   Rational evaluation is comprehensive

When evaluating a social system, we must consider all of the advantages and disadvantages of that system. We should not allow our evaluation to be unduly influenced by any single social issue.

Imagine a social activist, whom I shall call 'Mom', whose favorite social issue is drunk driving. She attends rallies against drunk driving, quotes statistics about the problem to her friends, and writes letters to her congressman and the local newspapers urging tougher laws to combat drunk driving. Mom knows that there are many other serious social problems; nevertheless, none call forth from her the same passion. This sort of phenomenon, I trust, is familiar enough; every social issue has its Moms. Suppose, furthermore, that Mom becomes convinced that anarchy, while it may adequately address every other problem, cannot address the problem of drunk driving nearly as well as some governmental system. As a result, Mom finds herself unable to accept anarchism.

The story of Mom is meant to illustrate a psychological point: we have emotional attachments to specific social issues which are often disproportionate to the objective significance of those issues, and these emotional attachments can bias our evaluation of social theories. Thinkers must become aware of this problem to guard against it. We must recognize the possibility that the system that is overall best for society may not solve all problems and may not solve the problems to which we feel the greatest psychological commitment.

8.1.3 Varieties of government and anarchy

Suppose that an anarchist, seeking to show the superiority of anarchy over government, takes the Soviet Union under communism as an illustration of the nature of government. Under Soviet communism, tens of millions of innocent people were killed by the government – some for disagreeing with the government, most simply for belonging to the wrong social class.[2] The rest were forced to live for decades under oppression and poverty. Anarchy will be better than that.

Few observers would have difficulty spotting the fallacy in this reasoning: those who defend government do not typically defend *any and all* forms of government. They need not defend, for example, communist dictatorship; they need defend only *some* feasible form of government. Thus, in comparing government with anarchy, we should examine the *best* feasible form of government. It does not matter if we also have available some terrible form of government that we would never want to adopt (unless, having decided to have a government, we lack control of what form of government we get). Hereafter, I shall assume without argument that the best form of government is representative democracy.

The same point applies to the other term of the comparison: anarchist theorists need not defend any and all nongovernmental conditions; they need defend only some feasible nongovernmental social structure. It does not matter if, in addition, there are terrible forms of anarchy that we would never want (unless, again, we lack control of which form of anarchy we get).

Anarchist thinkers differ over what the best nongovernmental system would be, particularly whether it would have a socialistic or a capitalistic economy.[3] I shall not enter that debate here. I shall simply assume capitalism as the better alternative. This is not because socialist forms of anarchism are not worth considering but simply because the comparison of two social systems, representative democracy and capitalistic anarchy, will prove complex enough to occupy us for the remainder of this book without the addition of further alternatives.

---

[2] Courtois et al. 1999, part 1.
[3] See Caplan n.d. for discussion of varieties of anarchism. For defenses of socialist anarchism, see Bakunin 1972; Kropotkin 2002.

8.1.4   Against status quo bias

Most human beings evince a marked tendency to view the present arrangements in their own society, whatever they may be, as right and good (see Section 6.4). This bias explains how people from extremely different cultures can each regard their own cultures' practices as the best.

One potential form of status quo bias is the practice of assigning a heavy burden of proof to anyone who proposes a new social system very different from the present system. We might hold that the reformer must *prove* the superiority of a new system and that any doubt about the relative merits of the new system and the old system redounds to the benefit of the old. Such a burden of proof may prove crushing for two reasons. First, the complexity and unpredictability of human societies renders it difficult or impossible to *prove* nearly anything of interest in social theory.[4] Intractable differences of opinion about the social consequences of policies, institutions, and social events are commonplace. Therefore, adopting a presumption in favor of the status quo might easily prove the decisive move blocking the acceptance of nearly any social change.

Second, the comprehensive comparison of broad social systems is extremely complex. A great many social issues and problems are affected by the overall structure of society – war, poverty, inflation, drunk driving, pollution, racism, drug abuse, school shootings, fossil fuel dependence, health care, abortion, animal rights, capital punishment, human cloning, education, euthanasia, teen pregnancy, gang violence, and so on. No single work could address every important social issue – and if one did, few would have the patience to read it through. Suppose, then, that we adopt the habit of assuming, for each social issue, that the status quo represents the best way of dealing with that issue until proven otherwise. This would, again, give the status quo an essentially insurmountable lead over any radical alternative. Even if a reformer succeeds in arguing painstakingly that the status quo fails on several important issues, there will always remain many more issues on which the status quo triumphs by default in virtue of our not having had time to thoroughly examine them.

What would be wrong with granting the status quo an enormous dialectical advantage over radical alternatives? The problem is not

---

[4] See Tetlock 2005 on the difficulty of political prediction; but see also Caplan 2007a for a qualified defense of political experts.

merely one of dialectical 'unfairness'. The problem is that such a methodology is very likely to lock us into an inferior social system. There is no reason to assume that one's own society happens to be arranged in the best way. Therefore, it is desirable to find a methodology in social theory that gives alternative social structures a reasonable chance of being chosen.

In the following chapters, I address what seem to me the most obvious and serious concerns about anarchism. I cannot address how every important social issue would be dealt with in an anarchist society. If, however, I can show that the problems that initially appear most likely to occasion decisive refutations of anarchism can in fact be well handled by an anarchist society, then the burden of proof will be shifted to the critics of anarchism.

8.2   A Simplified conception of human nature

Any attempt to work out the consequences of a broad social system must rely upon some beliefs about human nature. Here, I describe my most important general assumptions about human nature.

8.2.1   Humans are approximately rational

Human beings typically choose actions on the basis of their *beliefs* and their *goals*. A person is 'instrumentally rational' when he chooses the action that, based on his present beliefs, would appear to do the best job of realizing his goals, whatever those goals may be. In ordinary life, we rightly take it for granted that human beings are approximately, though not perfectly, instrumentally rational.

Consider a simple illustration. You see a small girl climbing a tree while calling out 'Snowball'. You notice that she is moving towards a white cat perched in the tree. How would you interpret the girl's behavior? Barring unusual conditions, the most natural interpretation would be that the girl is attempting to retrieve the cat from the tree. This interpretation takes (approximate) instrumental rationality for granted: it ascribes to the girl a goal, getting the cat out of the tree, such that her behavior makes sense as a way of pursuing that goal. Without an assumption of basic instrumental rationality, there would be no limit to the possible interpretations. If she is irrational, the girl might just as well be climbing the tree to get *away* from the cat. Or to slake her thirst. Or to depose the president of Egypt. In normal contexts, we would say that such 'explanations' make no sense – and the explanations don't make sense because they fail to make sense *of* the agent's behavior.

Nearly any ordinary intentional action could just as easily be used to illustrate the idea. Driving to the store, putting gas in your car, buying a jar of applesauce, asking for a raise, lying down in bed, going to the dentist, cooking a meal, picking up a telephone – any of these actions can be explained by reference to (i) a goal that can be plausibly ascribed to the agent, (ii) a host of accurate and reasonable beliefs on the agent's part about the world and about the consequences of one's actions, and (iii) the assumption of instrumental rationality on the part of the agent.

There are exceptions to the general rule of instrumental rationality. Psychologists have documented many specific failures of rationality, too numerous to list here.[5] In addition, there are some general conditions that render various failures of rationality more likely: human beings are most likely to make mistakes when facing unfamiliar, complex situations or situations in which abstract reasoning is required to work out the right choice. They are also likely to make errors in decisions that are unimportant to them, where they do not care to devote sufficient thought to identify the best option.

The assumption of instrumental rationality is most likely to hold good when people are facing simple, familiar situations in which the best option is easy to work out. It is also very likely to hold for managers of businesses in competitive industries. Businesses that are managed irrationally will tend to underperform rationally managed businesses. The latter will thus expand while the former shrink, until the market is dominated by relatively rational businesses.

8.2.2   Humans are aware of their environment

Human beings tend to possess a great deal of accurate and practically relevant information about their environments and about the potential consequences of their actions. They usually do not ignore useful information or adopt wildly inaccurate beliefs about matters relevant to decision making. This is a variation of what philosophers call 'the principle of charity'.[6] The same sort of examples that illustrate basic

---

[5] For a sampling, see Tversky and Kahnemann 1986 on framing effects; Arkes and Blumer 1985 on the influence of sunk costs; Tversky 1969 on intransitive preferences; and the various papers in Kahneman et al. 1982 and Gilovich et al. 2002.

[6] Philosophers often understand the principle of charity as the principle that, in interpreting others, one must ascribe mostly true beliefs to them (Davidson 1990, 129–30). In my view, the more fundamental principle is that one must ascribe mostly *rational* beliefs to others (see Huemer 2005, 159–61). However, under normal conditions, rational beliefs are generally true, so the

instrumental rationality can also be used to illustrate this principle of charity.

Consider again the girl climbing the tree. To understand her behavior, we must assume that the agent possesses a host of sensible beliefs about herself and her environment – that the cat is in the tree, that the tree is a solid object, that physical objects tend to fall downward when unsupported, that climbing the tree will bring her close to the cat, that her hand will not pass through the cat, and so on. In ordinary life, we would not pause over all these beliefs, but all of them are implicated in the girl's apparent plan to retrieve the cat by climbing the tree – if she were ignorant of any of these facts, she could not make that plan. Again, this is not an unusual example. Any of a great variety of ordinary actions could as easily be used to illustrate the point.

There are a number of exceptions. People tend to be ignorant of complicated, abstract truths about unfamiliar subjects. They tend to ignore information that they find uninteresting and that does not help them to achieve their goals. And if some information is costly to gather, either in monetary terms or in terms of time and effort, then relatively few people will possess that information.

On the other hand, when information is easily and cheaply acquired, easy to understand, and relevant to achieving our goals, then we will generally have that information. It is particularly likely that managers of businesses in competitive industries will possess accurate information relevant to managing their businesses, since the businesses whose managers remain ignorant of such information will tend to under-perform the businesses whose managers are well informed, allowing the latter businesses over time to dominate the industry.

8.2.3 Humans are selfish but not sociopathic

I am extremely selfish. I recently bought a winter jacket for myself at a cost of around $200. I already had some sweaters, shirts, and other jackets; I simply wanted a better jacket than any I already had. So I satisfied a fairly trivial desire with this expenditure. Had I donated it to a charity group working to combat world poverty, this same money might have saved another person's life.[7]

---

two principles of charity yield similar results. The idea discussed in the text goes beyond this, ascribing a reasonable level of practical knowledge to most human beings.

[7] Some charities claim to save one life per $100 donated (http://www.again-stmalaria.com/OneChild.aspx); however, Give Well provides an estimate of $2000 per life saved (http://givewell.org/international/top-charities/AMF).

This suggests that I value my own welfare perhaps thousands of times more highly than I value the welfare of strangers elsewhere in the world. Yet as disturbing as this may sound, it does not indicate some sort of sociopathic disorder on my part. It does not even indicate an abnormal level of selfishness. The average American gives even less to charity than I do, while a third of American households give nothing at all.[8] Most human beings, when given the chance to give money to others, will choose to keep the money for themselves, particularly if no one is watching.[9]

For another illustration, imagine that you were to learn that you are going to die tomorrow. Though it may be impossible to imagine accurately how you would feel, it is a safe guess that you would be quite upset. Now I will tell you something you probably did not know: based on recent worldwide mortality statistics, there are about 156,000 human beings who *will in fact* die tomorrow.[10] How do you feel now? You may find this information disturbing. But if you are like most people, you are far less upset at this news than you would be by the news that you yourself were about to die. This suggests, again, that your concern for yourself is perhaps thousands of times stronger than your concern for most other people.

Nevertheless, there are many exceptions to the rule of human selfishness. Many people voluntarily donate money to charity, albeit far less than they could afford.[11] Most are prepared to make great sacrifices for family, friends, lovers, or others to whom they are close. And a few people, such as Albert Schweitzer or Mother Theresa, virtually devote their lives to helping others.[12]

---

[8] National Philanthropic Trust 2011.

[9] In one experiment, Hoffman et al. (1994) gave subjects a chance to play 'the dictator game', in which a subject has the unilateral power to divide a sum of money between himself and another subject. In a carefully anonymized version, over 60 percent of dictator subjects chose to give $0 to the other subject. However, Hoffman et al. note that in nonanonymous variations, subjects are somewhat more generous.

[10] See United Nations 2009, table DB5_F1, http://esa.un.org/unpd/wpp2008/ xls_2008/DB05_Mortality_IndicatorsByAge/WPP2008_DB5_F1_DEATHS_ BY_AGE_BOTH_SEXES.XLS.

[11] The National Philanthropic Trust (2011) reports that charitable donations amounted to 2.1 percent of American GDP in 2009.

[12] Some people resist these sorts of examples, claiming that somehow all these kinds of behavior are really, deep down, selfish. See Rachels 2003, chapter 5, for a standard refutation of this claim.

Perhaps the largest and most pervasive exception to the rule of selfishness concerns the perceived negative rights of others: an ordinary human being may or may not sacrifice $200 to save the life of a stranger in a foreign land, but nearly everyone would be appalled at the thought of *killing* a stranger for $200. Admittedly, a small number would be happy to kill another person for $200 – sociopaths lack the respect for social norms and the capacities for empathy, guilt, fear, and horror that prevent most human beings from injuring each other under normal circumstances. Fortunately, however, sociopaths comprise only about 2 percent of the population.[13] The remaining 98 percent of human beings are concerned with social norms, are capable of empathy, and possess a rich array of emotions.

Thus, while ordinary human beings are willing to make very little positive effort to aid others with whom they lack close relationships, they tend also to be reluctant to directly attack other human beings or to positively violate generally accepted social norms in other ways, even when they stand to gain by doing so.

8.2.4 On behalf of simplification

The foregoing is a very simplified account of human nature. There are myriad variations among individuals and innumerable human motivations that I have not touched upon. Why is it useful to consider such a simplified picture of humanity?

First, note that the account identifies causal factors in human behavior that are both *real* and *large*. This is one requirement for a useful idealization.[14] We human beings really are moved by self-interest, and we really do tend to take actions likely to get us what we want. I have not mentioned every exception to these rules, but I have tried to mention the most important and well-established exceptions.

Second, the principles about human nature listed in the previous subsections are banal and driven by commonsense observations rather than any partisan ideology. In this way, they are unlike the Marxists' contention, for example, that human beings are strongly motivated by

---

[13] American Psychiatric Association 1994, 648. See Hare 1993 for an illuminating, if chilling, portrait of the psychopathic personality.

[14] Friedman (1953) argues that a model need not be at all close to reality; it need only have correct empirical predictions. It is possible for a theory that is very far from the truth to have very accurate predictions (as in the case of Ptolemaic astronomy). However, *pace* Friedman, I believe this is unlikely to occur for theories of human nature.

class interests.[15] The latter claim is highly controversial and accepted only by those with a particular ideology. This point is very important, because clashing ideologies are the greatest obstacle to progress in social theory.

Third, my simplified account of human nature enables us to derive many qualitative predictions about the effects of social systems relatively straightforwardly, with little need for judgment calls. There is a well-developed and compelling body of theory, comprising economics and game theory, that works out the consequences of the assumption of rational egoism. Those familiar with the theory can generally agree upon a large range of predictions, regardless of their initial moral, religious, or political leanings.[16] This is important, again, for making progress in social theory. The simpler a theory's assumptions are, and the more straightforward its predictions, the less room there is for human bias and irrationality to manipulate the theory. Due to the enormous role that bias plays in political discourse,[17] this is among the most important virtues that a theory in this area can have.

8.2.5   A historical application

The simplified account of human nature I have sketched makes useful predictions about certain social systems. Take the case of a social theory proposing that all citizens should work for the benefit of society, while receiving equal pay. A simple theoretical prediction is that, in such a system, productivity will decline. Individuals have a high degree of control over their own productivity, and greater productivity usually demands greater effort. Since most people are rationally selfish, they will not exert great effort to be productive unless they expect to receive personal benefits from doing so. So if all are paid equally, and if there are no other rewards or punishments attached to quality and quantity of work, then people will not be very productive.

This prediction is in fact correct. The twentieth century's experiments with social systems in this vicinity are well-known, so I shall not

---

[15] Marx and Engels 1978, 218.

[16] It is not possible to convey the power of modern economic theory in a short space. For an excellent introduction to microeconomics, see David Friedman's (1990) textbook, available at http://www.daviddfriedman.com/Academic/Price_Thy_ToC.html.

[17] See Huemer 'Why People Are Irrational about Politics' (n.d.) and Caplan 2007b.

dwell on them.[18] An interesting but little-known illustration is provided by America's first experiment with communism, which took place at Jamestown, the first permanent English settlement in America.[19] When the colony was established in 1607, its founding charter stipulated that each colonist would be entitled to an equal share of the colony's product, regardless of how much that individual personally produced. The result: the colonists did little work, and little food was produced. Of the 104 founding colonists, two-thirds died in the first year – partly due to unclean water but mostly due to starvation. More colonists arrived from England, so that in 1609 there were 500 colonists. Of those, only 60 survived the winter of 1609–10.[20] In 1611, England sent a new governor, Sir Thomas Dale, who found the skeletal colonists bowling in the streets instead of working. Their main source of food was wild plants and animals, which they gathered secretly at night so as to evade the obligation to share with their neighbors. Dale later converted the colony to a system based on private property, granting every colonist a three-acre plot to tend for his own individual benefit. The result was a dramatic increase in production. According to Captain John Smith's contemporaneous history,

> When our people were fed out of the common store and labored jointly together, glad was he [who] could slip from his labor or slumber over his task, he care not how; nay, the most honest among them would hardly take so much true pains in a week as now for themselves they will do in a day…so that we reaped not so much

---

[18] It is also unclear how equal communist societies in the twentieth century actually were. Vinokur and Ofer (1987, 193) estimate the Gini coefficient for the Soviet Union in 1973 at 0.31. For the United States, the Gini coefficient was approximately 0.38. The Gini coefficient is a standard measure of inequality, where 0 represents perfect equality, and 1 represents the most extreme possible inequality (that is, one person's receiving all the income). The Jamestown experience discussed in the text represents a much purer communism.

[19] The account in the text is based on Schmidtz 2008, Contoski 2010, Wadhwa 2005, and Smith 1986. Quotations from Smith are from the *Generall Historie of Virginia, New England, and the Summer Iles*, book 4, originally published by Captain John Smith in 1624. Smith was one of the colony leaders from 1607 until 1609, when he returned to England.

[20] According to Smith (1986, 232–3), the natives cut off trade at this time and attacked the colony. Nevertheless, Smith attributes the disastrous winter, which he calls 'the starving time', to 'want of providence, industry, and government, and not the barrenness of the country, as is generally supposed'.

corn from the labors of thirty, as now three or four do provide for themselves.[21]

One lesson from this episode is that, simple as the account of human nature I have advanced is, it can yield very useful predictions. If the company that created the Jamestown charter had known a little economics, hundreds of lives might have been spared. Another lesson is that the impact of human selfishness depends greatly on the social system in which people are embedded: in one kind of system, selfishness may have disastrous consequences, while in another, it promotes prosperity.

8.3   Utopianism and realism

8.3.1   The principle of realism

When proposed political and social arrangements are criticized, it is usually for being either harmful or unjust. But sometimes a vision of society is both perfectly just and highly beneficial, and yet we reject it on the grounds that the idea is too unrealistic, or 'utopian'.[22]

Consider, for example, a position that we might call 'utopian socialism'. The utopian socialist holds that everyone should be paid equally, regardless of productivity. In the last section, we saw that arrangements of this kind can lead to underproduction, putting things mildly. The utopian socialist addresses this problem by simply proposing that we all henceforth agree to behave selflessly. If we all voluntarily work our hardest for the good of society, then there will be no problem. Granted, this has not happened in the past; nevertheless, says the utopian socialist, it is what *ought* to happen.

Intuitively, this idea is defective as a political and social philosophy, regardless of whether the society it depicts is just or desirable, because the idea is too unrealistic. It seems to call for an alteration in a robust aspect of human nature, without proposing a plausible mechanism for bringing this about.

Many believe that anarchism, too, falls to the charge of excessive utopianism. These critics accuse anarchists of relying upon unrealistically optimistic assumptions about human nature.[23] How can we avoid this objection?

---

[21] Smith 1986, 247. I have modernized the spelling and punctuation. Smith is here slightly paraphrasing the words of colony secretary Hamor (1614, 17).

[22] See Cowen 2007a for discussion.

[23] Heywood 1992, 198; Wolff 1996, 33–4.

8.3.2 Prescription for a realistic anarchism

To avoid excessive utopianism, we should respect the following constraints:

i) We may not assume unrealistic levels of altruistic motivation. In examining the advantages and disadvantages of the system, we must assume that the anarchist society will be populated by people with relatively normal levels of selfishness, and we must accept the consequences of that selfishness within the particular social structure.

ii) We may not assume perfect rationality or knowledge. Our defense of anarchism must be consistent with the fact that people periodically make mistakes.

iii) We may not assume psychological uniformity. We must recognize the fact that human beings have a variety of motivations and character traits; for example, that some individuals are unusually aggressive or reckless.

iv) We may not simply assume persistence of the system over time. Rather, we must be able to *argue* that, once adopted, the system would be able to resist forces that might be thought to undermine it.

v) We may not assume simultaneous, worldwide adoption of the system, since there is no plausible way in which that could come about. We must imagine that (perhaps as a transitional stage) some limited region or group becomes anarchist in a world otherwise dominated by states.

On the other hand, it is worth noting two things that do *not* render a social theory overly utopian:

i) If a theory 'cannot' be implemented simply in the sense that people cannot be convinced to implement it, this does not render the theory too utopian.

As an analogy, suppose it is proposed to me that I should donate $200 to charity this month. I reply: 'No, that is not realistic, because I refuse to do it.' Intuitively, I have not articulated a valid objection to my donating $200, however intransigent my refusal may be. Similarly, the refusal of most members of society to take anarchism seriously, let alone to attempt to implement it, does not create a valid objection to anarchism. Of course, if most people have some *reason* for rejecting the theory, that reason might be cited as an objection to the theory. Anarchism is to be evaluated by supposing, perhaps improbably, that the system is adopted and considering from there whether a desirable and just state of affairs would result.

ii) To be sufficiently realistic, a model for society need not be feasible or desirable under *all* social conditions. It need only be argued that there are some conditions, likely to be realized now or in the future, under which the model would succeed.

In subsequent chapters, then, I shall attempt to characterize a kind of anarchist society that would be stable and livable under some realistic conditions, despite the existence of criminals, dissidents, ordinary human selfishness, and foreign governments.

8.3.3 Against utopian statism

It is widely recognized that anarchists face a significant challenge of avoiding utopianism. It is widely recognized, as well, that some nonanarchist theories, such as certain forms of socialism, face charges of utopianism. What is less well recognized is that even very conventional, moderate political theories can be utopian.

For example, the theory of liberal democracy might be too utopian. It would not be excessively utopian simply to advocate that we maintain current institutions, functioning exactly as they now do. But few thinkers adopt this position. Most believe that some degree of reform is called for – for example, that the democratic process should be less influenced by special-interest groups. The more one knows about how government actually functions, the less likely it is that one can sincerely assert that it operates as it should. This opens up the possibility that the changes we would like to see in democratic states are overly utopian. Advocates of liberal democracy face the same strictures against utopianism as advocates of more radical positions, such as anarchism or socialism.

It may seem strange to suggest that a mainstream, liberal democratic position might turn out to be too utopian, while some radical anarchist alternative might be sufficiently realistic. But the distinction between utopianism and realism is not a matter either of how far a proposal is from the status quo or of how far it is from the mainstream of political thought. The distinction between utopianism and realism chiefly concerns, roughly, whether a political or social idea requires violations of human nature. A mainstream political view might turn out to require such violations, while some radical alternative does not. It is perfectly possible for a small change to be unfeasible, while some much larger change is feasible.

One common form of utopianism consists of confusing the way individuals and organizations are 'supposed to' behave with the way they will behave. When social systems are evaluated, it does not matter how a system is supposed to work; what matters is how it can be expected to work under realistic assumptions about human nature. For example, we can say that the function of government is to protect the rights of its citizens, but nothing follows from this about what government will actually do. In the absence of an effective mechanism for inducing government agents to efficiently dispatch their stated functions, we cannot assume that citizens will receive appropriate protection. The point here is not that government will not protect us; the point is that whether government is an effective mechanism for protecting individual rights, promoting social welfare, or promoting any other aim needs to be established by argument and evidence, not taken for granted simply because of the stated purpose of government.

A related form of utopianism consists of suspending general assumptions about human nature when considering agents of the state. Defenders of government are often keen to point out the harms that might result from the widespread greed and selfishness of mankind in the absence of a government able to restrain our worst excesses. Yet they seldom pause to consider what might result from the very same greed and selfishness in the *presence* of government, on the assumption that government agents are equally prone to those very failings. It is not that statists have some account of why government employees are more virtuous than average people. Nor do they have some plan for *making* that be the case. Rather, it seems simply to have never occurred to most statists to apply realistic assumptions about human nature to the government itself. The state is treated as if it stood above the empirical human world, transcending not only the moral constraints but also the psychological forces that apply to individual human beings.

Any social system, whether it be anarchist or statist, must be judged by how it would perform when inhabited by real people, such as we find in the actual world. It does not matter if anarchy would work well in a world in which all individuals were selfless and always respected each other's rights. By the same token, it does not matter if government would work well in a world in which all government agents were selfless and always respected the rights of individuals.

9
The Logic of Predation

The direct use of physical force is so poor a solution to the problem of limited resources that it is commonly employed only by small children and great nations.

– David Friedman[1]

9.1 The Hobbesian argument for government

In the seventeenth century, Thomas Hobbes articulated one of the most influential accounts of the need for government.[2] Hobbes begins with the assumption that human beings are motivated entirely by self-interest and that they are of approximately equal mental and physical abilities, such that every individual may pose a serious threat to any other individual. Now imagine such beings living in the 'state of nature'; that is, a state without government or laws. These people would come into frequent conflict with one another, for three reasons. First, people would attack each other to steal each other's resources; Hobbes calls this 'competition'. Second, people would attack each other preemptively – that is, one may decide to kill or permanently injure another person, simply to prevent the other person from being able to injure oneself in the future; Hobbes calls this 'diffidence'. Third, people would fight for 'glory' – that is, one may attack another person to force the other person to express respect for oneself. For these reasons, Hobbes believed that the state of nature would be a state of perpetual war of everyone against everyone. There would be no industry, trade,

---

[1] Friedman 1989, 4.
[2] Hobbes 1996, especially chapters 13–17.

or culture. Everyone would live in constant fear of violent death, and their lives would be 'solitary, poor, nasty, brutish, and short'.[3]

The solution, in Hobbes's view, was for everyone to agree to establish a government and to grant that government absolute power. The government would then be able to protect individuals from each other. Nor, in Hobbes's view, should the people fear injury at the hands of the state itself. The rulers will naturally want the people to survive and prosper, because that will make the rulers themselves more wealthy and powerful.

Why should the state be granted absolute power rather than only limited, well-defined powers? Hobbes's answer is twofold: first, there is no need to limit the state's power, because excessive state power has not caused any significant problems. Second, it is not possible to limit the state's power unless there is some other, even more powerful agent who can exercise control over the state.[4]

The essence of the Hobbesian argument for government can be separated from some of Hobbes's more extreme claims. One need not hold that human beings are entirely selfish to agree with Hobbes that the state of nature would be riven with conflict; serious conflict might arise if people are largely, even if not entirely, selfish. Nor need one follow Hobbes in embracing totalitarianism; perhaps there are better, less absolute forms of government.

The Hobbesian argument for government is essentially a game-theoretic one. It relies on two main contentions: first, that when power is distributed roughly equally among individuals, it is prudent for individuals to attack each other frequently; second, that when power is distributed extremely unequally, concentrated almost entirely in the hands of a single person or organization, it is prudent, both for the powerful agent and for everyone else, to cooperate peacefully.

Though few today embrace either Hobbes's radical egoism or his totalitarianism, many accept his basic argument in favor of government. It is commonly held that the more pessimistic one is about human nature, the more absolute the form of government one should endorse – so that Hobbes, with the most cynical view of human nature, naturally endorses totalitarian government. In contrast, it is often thought, anarchists must hold radically optimistic views about human nature.[5] All

---

[3] Hobbes 1996, chapter 13, 89.
[4] Hobbes 1996, chapter 20, 144–5.
[5] Heywood 1992, 198; Adams 2001, 133–5; Wolff 1996, 33–4.

this, as I shall presently argue, is precisely backwards, as is Hobbes's analysis both of the state of nature and of government.

9.2 Predation in the state of nature

9.2.1 Game-theoretic considerations

Imagine that you and your neighbor Abel live in the state of nature. You are trying to decide whether it would be a good idea to attack Abel. Abel happens to have some tasty apples. The prospect of getting some food without having to work for it would be one potential advantage of attacking him. On the other hand, there is the disadvantage that the attack may lead to your being seriously injured or killed. There are three main reasons for this:

a) Abel will almost certainly attempt to defend himself. Being, as Hobbes says, of roughly equal mental and physical abilities to your-self, Abel would have a substantial chance of seriously injuring or killing you in the ensuing combat.

   Perhaps you might hope to catch Abel by surprise and thus kill him before he has a chance to kill you. It is unlikely, however, that you could devise a plan of this kind that would be without signif-icant risk to yourself. Plans often go wrong, and one who makes a habit of plotting the deaths of others will most likely slip up before long and end up dead himself.

   You might hope that Abel, being anxious to avoid injury, would flee from your attack rather than fight back. But Abel is not likely to simply let your theft pass. If he allows your theft to pass without retaliation, he invites both you and any other predators who learn of the event to attack and rob him in the future. If Abel flees the scene, therefore, it will most likely be only to plot his revenge at a more opportune moment.[6]

b) One or more of Abel's family members or friends may decide to avenge his death. One reason for this would be that they are angry about your psychopathic murder (*pace* Hobbes, people care about

---

[6] Friedman (1994) offers a more elaborate game-theoretic argument for rights-respecting behavior for rational egoists in a state of nature. Briefly, Friedman argues that agents in the state of nature face a coordination problem: no one wants war, but to avoid war, they must agree upon a set of rules for peaceful coexistence. Mutual respect for rights offers a Schelling point that solves this coordination problem.

their family and friends). Another reason is that they may wish to send a message to other potential predators: our family may not be attacked with impunity. Abel's avengers may attack you at a time and place of their choosing, and there may be more than one of them. Therefore, again, it is likely that you will be seriously injured or killed.

c) Recall that, on Hobbes's view, one of the three main sources of violence in the state of nature is preemptive attack (due to 'diffidence'). People interested in preemptive attacks are most likely to target those who pose the greatest threat. And those who have already engaged in unprovoked attacks against their neighbors are likely to be perceived as the greatest threats. So by attacking Abel, you mark yourself out for attack by diffident neighbors.

For these reasons, the risks of attacking your neighbors will normally greatly outweigh the potential benefits. Only if you were in danger of starvation and had no safe options for seeking food might it be prudent to attempt to rob Abel. You would naturally take precautions to avoid ever being in that situation.

What if, instead of attacking Abel on your own, you band together with a few like-minded predators to rob Abel and divide his property among yourselves? In this case, you are much less likely to be killed in the course of committing the crime. Nevertheless, this plan is fraught with danger. If you leave Abel alive, he may decide to take his revenge later, when you are alone. If necessary, he may bring his own gang to help. If you kill Abel, his family or friends may decide to avenge him. In either case, diffident other neighbors may decide that you are a threat that needs to be eliminated, and nothing prevents them from banding together just as you and your fellow thieves have done. Finally, there is the disadvantage that in order to carry out this plan, you must associate with a gang of thieves and (possibly) murderers. People of this sort are not known for their trustworthiness, so there is a fair chance that one or more of the others will at some point attempt to cheat you and/or kill you.

So far, I have been appealing to your rational self-interest. But as noted in the previous chapter, human beings are only approximately rational and only approximately egoistic. Does this alter our conclusions?

No, it does not. First, note that the kinds of cases in which we typically observe failures of rationality do not affect the foregoing reasoning. The reasoning for avoiding predatory behavior in the state of nature is not too complex, unfamiliar, or abstract for an ordinary person to follow. Nor is it hindered by any of the heuristics and biases that psychologists have discovered; it does not matter, for example, if a person regularly falls prey to the conjunction fallacy, ignores base rates, and attempts to recover sunk costs.[7] None of those cognitive failings prevent one from grasping the straightforward argument against predation in the state of nature: if you attack your neighbors, your neighbors may attack you in turn.

Nor do any of the exceptions to the rule of human selfishness speak against our conclusion. *Pace* Hobbes, most human beings are not sociopaths. Most care about others, particularly their family and friends. Most have both strong moral objections and strong negative feelings about violence and theft. These facts could only strengthen the conclusion of this section. When both prudence and morality point in the same direction, almost everyone will choose that course. In a later chapter (Chapter 10), I will discuss institutions designed to deal with the few imprudent individuals who commit aggression despite the foolishness of doing so.

The general game-theoretic principle is this: *Equality of power breeds respect.* No rational person wishes to enter violent conflict with others who are of equal strength to himself. The chances of losing the conflict are too great. Even the nominal victor is likely to end up worse off than before the conflict, because the damage caused by fighting is almost always greater than the value of the resources that are in dispute. For these reasons, rational individuals fight only defensive battles.

9.2.2 Social conditions affecting the prevalence of violence

The broad game-theoretic considerations canvassed in the preceding subsection help to explain why most normal adults never partake of physical combat. However, interpersonal violence was much more common in earlier centuries than it is today.[8] Why? Were our ancestors less rational than we? Did they face different circumstances, such that the preceding game-theoretic arguments somehow did not apply to them?

---

[7] The conjunction fallacy involves judging 'A and B' more probable than 'A'; see Tversky and Kahneman 2002. The base rate fallacy involves ignoring information about the frequency of a trait in a population; see Tversky and Kahneman 1982. The mistake about sunk costs involves choosing an inferior option because one has previously paid for it; see Arkes and Blumer 1985. All of these are well-established examples of human irrationality.

[8] See Pinker 2011, esp. chapter 3.

At least three broad social factors may help to explain the decline in violence. One is a matter of social values. Members of modern, Western societies harbor *far* more liberal beliefs and attitudes, particularly on the subject of violence, than those that have held sway in most cultures for most of human history.[9] Historically, physical combat was often seen as honorable, whereas we today generally view it as horrible. Civilized eyes look back with horror at such practices as gladiatorial combat, public beheadings, and medieval torture chambers. And one need only peruse traditional religious texts to be shocked at the range of crimes for which earlier generations of humans considered death or dismemberment to be appropriate punishments.[10]

A second important factor is economics. The game-theoretic argument for peaceful coexistence presupposes that the goods one needs for survival are available through peaceful means. In primitive societies, however, conditions of life-threatening scarcity were far more common than they are today; thus, people had less to lose by engaging in theft and violence. As human beings become more prosperous, the notion of fighting over resources becomes increasingly irrational.

The third factor is weapons technology. The argument of the preceding subsection assumes that individuals pose approximately equal physical threats to one another, such that violent conflict between two individuals poses grave risks to both. But in earlier centuries, the capacity to defend oneself depended upon strength and skill with a sword or similar weapon, neither of which was evenly distributed among the population. Today, effective self-defense is available through modern firearms, requiring minimal strength and skill and only modest economic means. It was in view of this change that in the nineteenth century the popular Colt revolver came to be called 'the Equalizer'.

The main reasons for expecting the state of nature to be a state of peace do not apply with equal force in all social conditions. In a society with very scarce resources, limited weapons technology, and complacent attitudes toward violence, we should expect violent conflict to be much more common than in one characterized by prosperity, advanced technology, and a liberal culture.

---

[9] Mueller 2004; Pinker 2011.

[10] The Bible prescribes execution for adultery (Leviticus 20:10), homosexuality (Leviticus 20:13), premarital sex (Deuteronomy 22:20–1), working on the Sabbath (Exodus 35:2), and cursing one's parents (Leviticus 20:9). The Koran prescribes dismemberment for thieves (Sura 5.38) and death for those who oppose Islam (Sura 5.33, 9.5, 9.29–31).

A Hobbesian might argue that, if one begins with a primitive society in a state of nature, constant violent conflict will prevent the society from ever evolving into an advanced, prosperous society, unless the society first establishes a government. Be that as it may, once one has an advanced, prosperous, liberal society, the continuing need for government is far from clear, regardless of what role government may have played in bringing about that state of society. Game-theoretic arguments do not establish such a need. To defend a need for government, one would have to posit a high degree of irrationality and imprudence.

9.2.3   Interstate violence

It is natural to wonder whether the above analysis can be applied to nation-states as well as to individuals. Should we expect states to get along with each other peacefully, at least when they are of roughly equal power?

The answer is no. States are not individuals, and their behavior cannot be correctly explained in the same way as that of individuals – for example, by citing their beliefs and desires. States have no beliefs or desires of their own. The behavior of a state must be explained in terms of the choices of the individuals who have decision-making power within the state.

A state's decision as to whether to go to war differs in crucial ways from that of an individual deciding whether to enter physical combat with another individual. Most notably, the individual would bear the personal risk of injury or death should the other party prove difficult to subdue. But leaders who decide to take their country to war almost never *personally* bear the risks of injury or death that result from that war. In deciding to invade Iraq in 2003, for example, President Bush did not need to weigh the risk that *he* would be killed in the conflict. Thus, the main prudential argument that leads us to expect individuals to choose peaceful coexistence with other individuals does not apply to states.

Of course, no leader wishes to enter a conflict that his nation will lose. But when the costs of defeat are more along the lines of a loss of face rather than personal injury or death, leaders can be expected to evince far greater risk acceptance than an individual who decides whether to personally initiate mortal combat with another individual. For the same reason, it is not clear a priori that rough equality of power between two states will deter their leaders from initiating hostilities in the same way that we would expect it to deter private individuals. Indeed, scholarship in international relations has found that pairs of nations of comparable power are actually *more* likely to go to war than pairs with a large power difference.[11]

We will return to the question of the causes of war in Chapter 12, below. For now, the important point is that one should not assume that individual-level analyses of cooperation and conflict can be transferred to the level of government.

9.3   Predation in a totalitarian state

We have seen that, in the state of nature, there were three fears holding you back from attacking and robbing Abel: first, that Abel may resist your aggression with force; second, that Abel's family or friends may avenge him; third, that apprehensive neighbors may see you as a threat needing to be neutralized. But now imagine that you have just been granted the power of government, which, in Hobbes's view, is as absolute as any human power can be.[12] Now all three reasons for respecting Abel's rights have been removed. If you decide to steal Abel's food, he will have no effective means of resistance. If you kill Abel, his family and friends will have no effective means of vengeance. And however much they may recognize you as a threat, diffident neighbors will have no effective means of trying to neutralize that threat. There is no longer anything to hold you back from whatever you might wish to do to your hapless neighbors. As a rational egoist, therefore, you will certainly want to consider stealing most of Abel's resources, then forcing him to keep working to produce more for you to steal.

What about endeavoring, through good governance, to ensure that your society is as prosperous as possible? This will give you more to steal. As Hobbes proclaims, the stronger and more prosperous the people are, the stronger and more prosperous the ruler will be.[13]

While this is one reason for working to ensure a productive society, there are other reasons why you may not wish to bother. To begin with, if the society over which you rule is reasonably large, it should be possible to extort sufficient spoils from the population to keep yourself in comfort even if the people are destitute. Kim Jong-il, communist dictator of North Korea, amassed over $4 billion while millions of his subjects starved and his country's per capita GDP languished at

---

[11] Bremer 1992, 326, 334–8.
[12] Hobbes 1996, 121–7, 144–5, 148.
[13] Hobbes 1996, chapter 19, 131.

just under one-fifth of the world average.[14] Granted, Kim might have accumulated even more wealth had his country had a more productive economic system. But wealth has diminishing marginal utility: after one gathers the first four billion dollars, most of one's needs have been satisfied, and the next billion makes relatively little difference to one's overall well-being. It is not worth going to any great trouble or giving up anything else that one cares about to collect more money. And good governance is often a difficult thing to achieve. It often requires wisdom, careful reasoning, and long hours of research. To identify the best policies, one must work tirelessly at remaining objective, gathering more evidence to test one's assumptions, and so on. All of this is intellectually and emotionally demanding. It is much easier to proclaim simple, ill-thought-out precepts and follow them dogmatically regardless of the evidence.

What about actually injuring or killing Abel? It might be thought that, once you possess absolute power, you will have no reason to attack Abel, since he is no longer a threat to you. Indeed, your subjects are the source of your power, so you should want to keep as many of them as possible, as long as they remain cooperative. If Abel is prudent, he will submit to all your demands, and despite the loss of most of his food and other goods, he will thereby remain alive.

Again, this is too optimistic. First, given the existence of a powerful government, the people who are most likely to wind up in control of that government are those who (a) have the greatest drive for power, (b) have the skills needed for seizing it (for example, the ability to intimidate or manipulate others), and (c) are unperturbed by moral compunctions about doing what is required to seize power. These individuals are not in the game for the money. They are in it for the pleasure of exercising power. The way one feels the exercise of power is, all too often, by abusing those under one's power while observing their helplessness to resist. This is among the lessons of the Stanford Prison Experiment, as discussed earlier (Section 6.7). Particularly if the ruler perceives some act of defiance on the part of subjects – for example, a subject criticizes the government in some way – the ruler is likely to feel a desire to demonstrate his power by crushing the subject. The motive would be precisely that passion for 'glory' that Hobbes considers among the causes of conflict in the state of nature.

---

[14] On Kim Jong-il's assets, see Arlow 2010. On North Korean famine, see Macartney 2010. For GDP statistics, see U.S. Central Intelligence Agency 2011.

Second, a great many people harbor hostility toward certain groups in their society – for instance, the members of a certain race, religion, or social class; or the people who adhere, or fail to adhere, to certain political doctrines. If the ruler happens to have some such prejudice, he may well feel it worth losing a few million subjects to indulge his hatred for that group.

The game-theoretic principle is this: *Concentration of power breeds abuse*. When one group of people holds great power over another group, the strong will typically use their power to abuse or exploit the weak for their own aggrandizement.

All this, tragically, is much more than armchair theorizing. It is also the horrifying lesson of history. Everyone knows that close to six million Jews were executed in Nazi Germany in the middle of the last century because the ruler hated Jews. Fewer people realize that that was only the tip of the iceberg of twentieth-century mass murder. The total number of people killed by their *own* governments in the twentieth century has been estimated at *123 million*.[15] These victims, in general, were killed for belonging to the wrong groups, whether it be the wrong race, the wrong class, or the wrong ideology. The murderous regimes did not stop at the thought that their crimes against humanity would cost them a great deal of tax revenues, for they were not primarily seeking money. They were moved partly by hatred, partly by the love of power, and partly by the drive to remake the world in accordance with their ideologies. The number of people killed by their own governments in the twentieth century was more than four and a half times greater than the number killed by nongovernmental murderers[16] – which raises the question of whether a strong government should be counted more a source of security or a source of danger.

---

[15] Rummel 1998, 355. If we add people murdered by foreign governments, including through intentional targeting of civilians during wartime (but not including the killing of combatants), the total rises to 163 million. Almost all these murders were committed by authoritarian and totalitarian regimes. White (2010) estimates the total number of twentieth-century deaths by war and oppression at 203 million.

[16] About 520,000 people were murdered (privately) worldwide in the year 2000 (Holguin 2002), giving a murder rate of 8.54 per 100,000 population per year. If we take this as representative of the century as a whole, there were about 26.5 million private murders in the twentieth century. (For population estimates throughout the century, see U.S. Census Bureau 2011a; 2011c. I have used interpolation to estimate populations for years not shown in the tables.) Comparing this to Rummel's statistic, we have a ratio of 4.6 governmental murders for every private murder. Including wartime murders of foreign

Hobbes was right to highlight human selfishness, though he overstates the point. He was right also to recognize the essential equality of the state of nature and the inequality created by government. But the political implications of these facts are the opposite of what Hobbes claimed. Equality of power breeds respect and peaceful cooperation; vast inequality breeds contempt and abuse. The more cynical one is about human nature, the more important it is to avoid great differences of power.

9.4   Predation under democracy

Fortunately, totalitarianism is not the only form of government. There are several ways of trying to limit the power of government and prevent its abuse: choosing leaders by popular election, dividing the government into separate branches, writing a constitution that defines and delimits the government's powers. All of these mechanisms provide some advantage. Nevertheless, they do not work exactly as advertised, and they do not fully solve our problems.

9.4.1   The tyranny of the majority

According to one simple argument for democracy, people generally know their interests and will vote on the basis of those interests when given the chance. Therefore, the leaders in a democratic state will be those who best serve the interests of the most people.

Perhaps the simplest problem with this system is that the majority may choose to abuse a minority. If the majority of people have even a slight preference for some policy, however noxious or unjust it may be to the minority, the majority can implement their preference through the state. This explains, for example, why gay marriage is not permitted in most of the United States. It explains the Jim Crow laws prior to the civil rights movement. And it explains how the Nazis could become the largest party in the Reichstag by 1932, despite their evident hatred of various groups of people.

9.4.2   The fate of nonvoters

A similar problem is that the government may disregard the interests of those who lack the vote. Typically, this includes convicted felons,

---

civilians, the ratio is 6.2. However, these ratios may be inaccurate, since they use the 2000 private murder rate to estimate private murders over the twentieth century.

children, and, most importantly, foreigners. This last category of people may be affected by the government's immigration policy, international trade policy, military policy, and other forms of foreign policy. The interests of foreigners are often ignored or severely discounted in these areas. In setting immigration policy, national governments discount the interests of potential immigrants. In setting trade policy, they discount the interests of producers and consumers in other countries. In deciding whether to go to war, they discount the interests of the foreign citizens who will be killed.

In America's most recent war with Iraq, for example, estimates of the number of Iraqi citizens killed vary from about one hundred thousand to over one million.[17] The war had an enormous impact on the Iraqi people, much more so than the American people. And yet the Iraqi people had no say in the decision to invade, which was made entirely by representatives of the American people. Any advocate of democracy must surely recognize this as a serious problem. This problem results from the extreme inequalities of power made possible by the institution of government. In this case, the U.S. government had sufficiently greater power than either the Iraqi people or the Iraqi government that the U.S. government had no need to consider the opinions of Iraqis.

9.4.3 Voter ignorance and irrationality

One might assume that a democratic state will at least serve the interests of the majority of voters. Yet even this need not be true.

To see why, first consider the amount of practical power you wield by virtue of your ability to vote. For simplicity, assume that you are voting in an election with exactly two candidates. You as an individual are in a position to determine the outcome of the election if and only if the outcome turns on a single vote – that is, without your vote, the two candidates' vote totals would have differed by no more than one. If the totals would have been tied, then you can cast the tie-breaking vote; if one candidate would have won by a single vote, you can cause the election instead to be tied. In all other cases, your vote makes no difference to the outcome. If the candidates' vote totals differ by two or more, then the winning candidate would have won regardless of how you voted. But given the circumstances voters are actually in and can expect to

---

[17] See Gamel 2009 for the low estimate. For the high estimate, see Opinion Research Business 2008.

be in for the foreseeable future, the probability of a national election turning on a single vote is negligible. So for all practical purposes, each voter knows in every election that his vote will make no difference whatsoever.

It is true that *the voters as a whole* have a great deal of power, in that they determine who holds the reins of government. But that is not our concern now. Our concern at the moment is how it is rational for you, as an individual, to behave. From the standpoint of rational choice, it is irrelevant what others can do; what is relevant is what you can do. You cannot make everyone else, or even a majority, vote in a particular way; you can control only your own vote. And this gives you approximately zero power over election outcomes.

Now assume that you are a rational egoist. Should you vote for the candidate who best serves your own interests? At first glance, since your vote will have no effect on what policies you get, it simply does not matter whether you vote for a candidate who serves your own interests, a candidate who serves the interests of society, or a candidate who is so terrible that he serves no one's interests. But this is not exactly right. There is a minuscule but nonzero chance – perhaps one in ten million[18] – that an election will turn on a single vote, so as long as it costs you nothing to vote for the candidate who best serves your interests, you might as well do so. Is this tenuous motivation enough to make democracy work?

The problem is that it *does* cost you something to vote for the candidate who best serves your interests. To know which candidate best

---

[18] The one-in-ten-million estimate is arrived at as follows. In recent years, U.S. presidential elections have turned on fewer than ten million votes (Mount 2010). Suppose, as an approximation, that it is certain that the two major candidates' vote totals will differ by ten million or fewer. And suppose that we assign an equal probability to each possible vote total within that range. Then each possibility, including the possibility that the totals differ by zero (that is, the election is tied), has a one-in-ten-million probability.This method might overestimate the odds, since it is not 100 percent certain that the vote totals will fall in the specified range. However, if we suppose that it is only, say, 80 percent certain that the totals differ by less than 10 million, then we get a lower bound for the probability of a tied election of 0.8/10,000,000, or one in 12.5 million. On the other hand, this may be an underestimate of the odds, because vote totals closer to equal are more likely than ones that are less equal; in a more precise approach, we would assign a bell-shaped probability distribution, with the peak closer to the middle.All things considered, the one-in-ten-million estimate is of the right order of magnitude for present conditions in the United States. This suffices for the present argument.

serves your interests, you must first gather detailed information about all the available candidates. If they have served in public office, you will need to look up their voting records. Then you will need to look up a large sample of the bills or other proposals on which they voted. You will need to attempt to understand these bills. To assess in each case whether the proposals would have served your interests, you will need to research an array of complex economic and social issues. You may need to take some courses in economics to figure out the effects of some of these policies. Since human beings tend to be affected by strong biases with regard to political issues, you will need to make a special effort to identify and overcome your biases. All of this would require enormous time and effort. The probability that this effort will be rewarded with some actual effect on election outcomes is minuscule. Thus, it does not make sense to do what is necessary to vote consistently in your own interests.[19]

Accordingly, many surveys have found strikingly low levels of public political knowledge. Caplan summarizes some of these results:

> About half of Americans do not know that each state has two senators, and three-quarters do not know the length of their terms. About 70 percent can say which party controls the House, and 60 percent which party controls the Senate. Over half cannot name their congressman, and 40 percent cannot name either of their senators. Slightly *lower* percentages know their representatives' party affiliations. Furthermore, these low knowledge levels have been stable since the dawn of polling, and international comparisons reveal Americans' overall political knowledge to be no more than moderately below average.[20]

What sort of things *do* Americans know about politics? Delli Carpini and Keeter give the flavor of public political knowledge:

> The most commonly known fact about George [H. W.] Bush's opinions while he was president was that he hated broccoli. During the 1992 presidential campaign 89 percent of the public knew that Vice President Quayle was feuding with the television character Murphy Brown, but only 19 percent could characterize Bill Clinton's record on the environment. Also during that campaign, 86 percent of

---

[19] For similar arguments, see Schumpeter 1950, 261–2; Downs 1957, 244–5; Caplan 2007b.

[20] Caplan 2007b, 8, emphasis in original.

the public knew that the Bushes' dog was named Millie, yet only 15 percent knew that both presidential candidates supported the death penalty. Judge Wapner (host of the television series 'The People's Court') was identified by more people than were Chief Justices Burger or Rehnquist.[21]

Now imagine that you are an elected official in a democratic state. You know the foregoing facts. You know that most of your constituents do not know your name and that only on very rare occasions will more than a negligible portion of the electorate know how you voted on a question before the legislature. The only activities of yours likely to make the news are sex scandals, should you be reckless enough to be caught in one. You may therefore do virtually anything you wish (with the exception of causing sex scandals), with little fear of incurring disfavor with the public. You may cast votes on the basis of whims. You need not read the bills you vote on, and you need do no research to determine the best policies. You may grant favors to your friends and campaign contributors. On the off chance that someone questions you about any of your special-interest legislation, you can supply specious economic arguments explaining why the legislation is really in the public interest. It won't matter that your arguments are fallacious, because the public knows next to nothing of economics – it isn't in their interests to learn economics, any more than it is in yours.

Sadly, this is more than idle theorizing; it explains the consistent experience of any modern observer of government. It is not possible here to examine the myriad actions of any contemporary government that bear this out. Here I simply select one example to illustrate what I mean.

As of mid-2012, the most recent farm bill in the United States was the Food, Conservation, and Energy Act of 2008.[22] Among other things, this law continues the federal government's established policy of farm subsidies, which total over $12 billion per year, most of which goes to large commercial farms.[23] This benefits a small number of mostly wealthy people at the expense of the rest of the country. The $12 billion, spread over 311 million Americans, comes to just under

---

[21] Delli Carpini and Keeter 1996, 101.
[22] Public Law 110–246, available at http://www.ers.usda.gov/farmbill/2008/ (accessed 8 March 2011).
[23] U.S. Department of Agriculture 2011.

$40 per person. Of course, without researching this particular law, you would not know these figures; but let us suppose you know that, in general, if you did enough research, you could find various laws of this kind that cost you amounts of money in this neighborhood. In each case, you could attempt to influence the legislation, with a chance of success of perhaps one in a million.

It is not in your interests to research the provisions of the latest farm bill and how your representative voted on it to secure a one-in-a-million chance of saving yourself something on the order of $40. The exact numbers are immaterial. Even if the law cost you much more money – say, $400 per year – and your chances of altering the law were much better – say, one in a thousand – it still would not be in your interests to do anything about it.

On the other hand, the businesses that receive the government's largesse have reason to pay close attention. Each of them stands to gain millions or billions of dollars, and they have millions of dollars to spend in the attempt to influence the legislative process. Accordingly, agribusiness spent $80 million on lobbying in the year leading up to the passage of the farm bill.[24]

The farm bill was also criticized for its contribution to the world food crisis. World food prices have risen dramatically in recent years, leading to hunger and food riots. According to a World Bank study, the increased use of biofuels in developed nations was responsible for a 75 percent rise in food prices between 2002 and 2008.[25] The 2008 U.S. farm bill came under fire for exacerbating the problem through increased support for biofuels.[26] This problem, however, mainly concerns people in developing nations, who have even less chance of influencing U.S. policy than the average American.

I stress here that there is nothing special about farm policy. This is how modern democracy works. Concentrated, well-organized special-interest groups use the apparatus of the state to extract profit at the expense of the majority of their own society, often in addition to hapless victims in other countries. Farm policy is just one of many illustrations.[27]

---

[24] Etter and Hitt 2008.
[25] Chakrabortty 2008.
[26] Lawson-Remer 2008.
[27] For an economic account of the phenomenon, see Downs 1957, 254–6. For further examples, see Friedman 1989, 39–45; Green 1973; and especially Carney 2006.

9.4.4   Activism: a utopian solution

Some say that the solution to the problems with democracy is for the public to be more active, to watch what their representatives are doing and pressure them to do what is best for society.[28] We should write letters to our representatives, organize demonstrations, and so on.

This is a utopian solution. It is utopian because it requires changes in human nature without proposing a realistic mechanism to bring about those changes. The democratic failures that I have described are not a mysterious accident, nor are they the product of a few bad actors. They result from the operation of normal human selfishness within the incentive structure of a democratic state. It is not in individual citizens' interests to keep tabs on their elected representatives. The behavior of citizens and elected representatives will not change unless either the incentive structure changes or people become much less selfish than they are.

I do not mean that social activism cannot solve any problems. Major political advances have been brought about by popular social movements, as in the case of the abolitionist movement, the women's suffrage movement, the Indian movement for independence from Britain, and so on. Occasionally, popular social movements arise to combat large and simple injustices, particularly when these involve glaring inequalities between the treatment of different groups.

What I find utopian is the suggestion that popular activism might be the solution to the constant, everyday malfeasance of government, that people might be called forth to set aside their own interests and concerns and summon the time and energy to actively monitor the thousands of activities of the government as a permanent way of life.[29] Some human beings may enjoy monitoring the daily activities of their government, but for the vast majority, it is a mind-numbing chore. This chore would consume every spare moment of one's life, if one were to take seriously one's alleged obligation to oversee the state. The 2008 farm bill I have been discussing comprises 663 pages of legalese. Just knowing what the bill contains is a feat in itself, but tracing the effects

---

[28] Nader 1973.

[29] An alternative would be to monitor a small, random sample of government activities but to punish each discovered infraction very severely. To work, this strategy would probably require very severe penalties, such as prison time, for even minor lapses. Though this might occur in a society populated by economists, no other society would consider, for example, sending a legislator to prison for failing to read a bill before voting on it.

of its hundreds of sections would require a background expertise in such areas as economics, agriculture, energy use, and international relations that would probably require years of study to acquire. And that bill was just one of the *over ten thousand* bills introduced into Congress that year.[30] The most conscientious activist could only monitor a minuscule fraction of his government's activities, even if doing so was his sole occupation.

Conceivably, the activists could divide up the work. We could each choose one of a thousand different areas in which to monitor government activities. But this is not realistic. On those rare occasions when social movements inspire large segments of the public to become involved in politics, it is because some large, glaring injustice stirs our passions. But no one will become passionate about monitoring a thousandth of the daily activities of government. To propose that the general public voluntarily sacrifice large portions of their lives to the task of studying such tedious matters as the provisions of the latest farm bill, all so that each can have a microscopic chance of improving a microscopic fraction of government policies, is at least as utopian as proposing that we all simply agree henceforth to work selflessly for the good of society.

9.4.5 The news media: the sleeping watchdog

Instead of our having to monitor the everyday activities of government officials, we might in effect delegate that responsibility to the news media, which could assign people full time to watching the government. Journalists would warn the public when the government was doing anything particularly bad, at which point voters would take appropriate action. If the mechanism worked well, so that wayward politicians were reliably punished, only occasional warnings would be needed.

Without further explanation of what might maintain this happy state of affairs, however, this solution to the problems of democracy is overly utopian. It does not matter if we say that this is the media's 'job' or what the media is supposed to do. What matters is the incentive structure. Is it in the interests of media companies to play the role of alert watchdog?

There are three reasons why it is not. First, monitoring the tens of thousands of government activities is a difficult, expensive, and time-consuming task. When reporting on government activities, it is

---

[30] Harper 2008.

easier to accept government officials' own statements as one's source of information rather than attempt to confirm or refute them. It is easier to run opinion pieces and reports on simple, entertaining items such as celebrity gossip than to prepare detailed reports on complex social issues.

Second, the government is the most powerful organization in society; it possesses an enormous and irresistible apparatus of coercion, and reports critical of government officials are likely to anger the government. At a minimum, government officials will refuse to give interviews or information to journalists who establish a reputation for criticizing the government. In more serious cases, the government deploys force directly against journalists or their sources.

A famous case in point is that of Daniel Ellsberg, who in 1971 leaked a classified Pentagon study revealing that the government knew the Vietnam War was an unwinnable quagmire. The government brought twelve felony counts against Ellsberg (ultimately dismissed), and President Nixon ordered illegal wiretaps and a break-in at the office of Ellsberg's psychiatrist in an effort to find information to discredit Ellsberg.[31]

A more recent case is that of Wikileaks, which published thousands of government documents in 2010, most of which concerned the wars in Afghanistan and Iraq, including videos showing U.S. troops killing civilians. The uniform reaction from American politicians on both the left and the right was one of outrage at both Wikileaks and its sources. Vice President Biden called Wikileaks founder Julian Assange a terrorist and promised that the Justice Department would be looking for ways to prosecute him. Former Arkansas governor and sometime presidential candidate Mike Huckabee called Wikileaks' source a traitor and called for his execution. As of this writing (mid-2012), Wikileaks' source for the Iraq documents, U.S. military intelligence analyst Bradley Manning, is being prosecuted by the military under numerous charges, including 'aiding the enemy', a capital offence (though the government will not seek the death penalty).[32]

These cases show that not everyone is easily intimidated. But they also show that journalists and their sources have rational cause for fear should they publish information embarrassing to the government.

---

[31] Kernis 2011. Ellsberg is the subject of the popular documentary *The Most Dangerous Man in America*.

[32] For the famous 'Collateral Murder' video released by Wikileaks, see Wikileaks 2010. For Biden's remarks, see Mandel 2010. On Huckabee, see Wing 2010. On the charges against Manning, see CBS News 2011.

The third and most important reason why it is not in the media's interests to act as an alert watchdog is the demands of the consumer. Newspapers, magazines, television stations, and radio stations depend upon the interest of their audience; it does not matter how diligent and courageous their reporters are if the public does not want to tune in. For the reasons discussed above, average citizens are not willing to expend significant time, money, or effort learning about the government. Suppose, for example, that one television station is running a story about the upcoming farm bill. The story discusses some of the features of this bill, its impact on the budget, its wider effect on the economy, and so on. Academic economists and agricultural experts are interviewed. Meanwhile, another station runs a gossip piece about popular entertainer Lindsay Lohan, who has just gotten into trouble again. Which station gets more viewers?

Farm policy is boring. Lindsay Lohan's misadventures are titillating. Farm policy is complicated and hard to understand. Lohan is simple and easy to understand. The story about farm policy has graphs and statistics. The story about Lohan has pictures of Lohan.

Some people may prefer hearing about farm policy. But the majority of media outlets cater to the majority of people. A few small outlets cater to intellectuals, but this is not enough to stop most government misuse of power; the impact of the tiny minority of people who enjoy reading statistics about farm policy will be swamped by the much larger group of people who don't know of the existence of farm policy and wouldn't care even if they knew.

9.4.6 The miracle of aggregation

According to a recent theory in the literature on democracy, it does not matter if most voters are ignorant, since a small minority of informed voters are enough to swing an election.[33] To see how this might be so, assume that we have an election between two candidates, Superior and Inferior, with Superior being the objectively better candidate. There are millions of voters, 90 percent of whom are completely ignorant; when they enter the voting booth, they vote completely at random. The remaining 10 percent are well informed and invariably vote for the better candidate. Who wins the election?

Superior wins, with near 100 percent probability. Since the uninformed voters vote randomly, they split about evenly, half for Inferior

---

[33] See Converse (1990, 377–83), who coined the phrase 'miracle of aggregation'. See Caplan 2007b, chapter 1, for criticism of the theory.

and half for Superior. The informed voters, however, all vote for Superior. Superior thus beats Inferior, 55 to 45 percent. If this model were correct, we could have very low levels of average voter knowledge yet still achieve results as good as those of a fully informed electorate.

The weak link in the argument is the assumption that ignorant voters vote randomly, as if by a coin flip. People who lack relevant information are more likely to vote on the basis of *biases* rather than flipping a coin. They might decide to vote for the candidate who is better looking or more likable, the candidate who ran more television ads, or the candidate whose name sounds most familiar. They might automatically vote for the Democrat or automatically vote for the incumbent.[34] It doesn't matter exactly what the basis is; the point is simply that there is likely to be *something* about a candidate that causes people to vote for him, even if that feature is mostly irrelevant to the candidate's objective qualifications to hold the office. Whatever that factor or cluster of factors is, it may well swamp the support or opposition of the informed voters.

For illustration, suppose that, as before, 10 percent of the electorate are well informed and always choose the better candidate. But this time, suppose that only 70 percent of voters vote by flipping a coin. The remaining 20 percent always vote for the more *charismatic* candidate. Who wins?

The more charismatic candidate wins, with near 100 percent probability. If Superior happens to be more charismatic, then he wins with 65 percent of the vote (half of the coin-flipping voters, plus all of the charisma-driven voters, plus all of the informed voters). But if Inferior happens to be more charismatic, then he wins with 55 percent of the vote (half of the coin flippers plus all of the charisma voters). As long as there are more charisma voters than well-informed voters, charisma determines the outcome, regardless of what the well-informed voters think. The general point is that the less rational and informed the

---

[34] Using statistical analysis, Bartels (1996) found that poorly informed people tend to vote for incumbents and Democrats more often than people who are more informed but otherwise similar in age, race, social class, and so on. He concludes that public ignorance produces a five-percentage-point advantage for incumbents in U.S. presidential elections, and a two-percentage-point advantage for Democrats. These advantages are probably larger for congressional elections, where public knowledge is lower than in the case of presidential elections. This is consistent with the fact that incumbents are reelected about 95 percent of the time in the House of Representatives and 88 percent of the time in the Senate (Center for Responsive Politics 2011).

electorate is, the more likely it is that irrelevant factors will outweigh the small influence of the quality of candidates' policy positions.[35]

9.4.7 The rewards of failure

On 11 September 2001, America suffered the most devastating terrorist attack in history. Four airplanes were hijacked and destroyed, the Pentagon was attacked, and the World Trade Center was destroyed, resulting in close to three thousand fatalities. This was many times worse than any other terrorist attack ever suffered by the U.S. or any other country.

What were the consequences for the United States government? First, the president's approval rating underwent an immediate and enormous jump, from about 55 percent to almost 90 percent. Over the following seven years, it dropped steadily, finally ending below 30 percent in 2008.[36] Though this remains a matter for speculation, it is plausible that George W. Bush would not have been reelected in 2004 if not for the terrorist attack.

On the face of it, this is paradoxical. If there was anyone whose job it was to protect Americans from this sort of attack, it would be the executive branch of the U.S. government. As the head of that branch, George W. Bush might have been expected to come under criticism. As an analogy, imagine that you have hired a company to provide security for your building. You have just learned that last night, vandals broke into the building and destroyed thousands of dollars' worth of equipment. Someone now asks you what you think of the job that your security company is doing. What do you say? 'Best security company ever!'?

Why did Americans so enthusiastically approve of Bush after the attacks? Partly, it was because they felt that it was patriotic to support the president, and that is partly because people tend to confuse the country with the government and the government with the government's officeholders.

---

[35] Essentially the same problem vitiates attempts to use the law of large numbers to defend democracy. The argument is that even if each voter is only slightly more likely to vote for the better candidate than to vote for the worse candidate, when there are millions of voters, it is overwhelmingly probable that most will vote for the better candidate (Wittman 1995, 16; Page and Shapiro 1993, 41). This assumes that voter errors are random and uncorrelated, an assumption that is falsified by the existence of common biasing influences, such as candidate charisma, campaign funding, and so on.

[36] Ruggles 2008; *Wall Street Journal* 2011.

My aim in raising this example is not to blame the government for 9/11. My aim is to examine the incentives applying to the government. What happens when the government fails to achieve its purposes? Often, the result is that the government is more rewarded than punished. In the present case, Bush reaped the highest approval ratings of his career, along with the opportunity to expand executive power in ways that otherwise would have met with much greater resistance.[37]

Similar things are true of other parts of government. Suppose that a city suffers from a crime wave. What will be the effects on the police department? It is much more likely that the police department will receive greater funding to combat the problem than that their funding will be cut. Or suppose that a society suffers from a severe increase in poverty. If the government has no agencies designed to combat poverty, one or more will probably be established. If some already exist, they will most likely receive greater funding rather than less. Few public figures would have the temerity to argue that the poverty programs should be cut because there is too much poverty. The general lesson is that if some part of the government fails in its function, it will most likely be given greater funding and power. Of course, the *purpose* of this is not to reward failure; the thinking would be that more money and power will enable the agency to solve the problem. But the *effect* is that government grows when social problems grow, and thus it is not in the government's interest to solve society's problems.

My claim is not that government agents actually try to fail. I do not think, for example, that the Bush administration actually wanted 9/11 to occur. My claim is twofold: first, that government agencies simply do not try as hard as they could to succeed at their assigned tasks, because they do not suffer from the negative consequences of failure. Second, that unsuccessful government programs tend to persist and grow, with the result that over a period of decades the government will come to be dominated by such programs.

Of course, other anecdotes could be told about government officials' losing their jobs because of some prominent failure. My claim is not that failure is always rewarded; my claim is that failure tends to be rewarded in a large range of cases, leading to serious problems in democratic states. If a government official is guilty of some simple and demonstrable malfeasance, with large and well-publicized negative consequences, then that official will probably lose his job. If a government

---

[37] I have in mind in particular the Patriot Act (public law 107–56, text available at http://frwebgate.access.gpo.gov/cgi-bin/getdoc.cgi?dbname=107_cong_public_laws&docid=f:publ056.107.pdf; accessed 29 March 2011).

agency that is felt to be dispensable – for example, NASA or the NEH – fails in *simple* and *well-publicized* ways, then that agency's funding will likely be cut, and the agency might even be eliminated. But suppose that some essential part of the government – say, the court system or law enforcement – fails chronically in ways that are complicated, difficult to understand, and not readily traceable to specific actions by a small number of individuals. Then that part of the government will more likely be rewarded than punished. People will feel that eliminating the dysfunctional agency or branch is not a feasible option, and since there are no specific individuals to blame, none will lose their jobs over it. The members of that part of the government will blame inadequate funding, and ill-informed voters are likely to find that explanation more understandable than the complicated truth. Thus, over time, the kinds of failures we should expect to see accumulating are *low-profile* and *systemic* failures in *essential* government services.

9.4.8 Constitutional limits

Perhaps the failures of government can be mitigated through a written constitution strictly limiting the state's functions. The fewer things the government is responsible for, the easier it will be for the people to monitor its activities, and thus the more responsive the government will be.[38]

We cannot simply assume, however, that if a constitution exists it will be followed. Without a realistic mechanism to induce compliance, it is overly utopian to assume that a government will restrain its activities simply because a document directs it to do so. As an analogy, imagine that I propose to solve the problem of predation by writing on a piece of paper, 'No one should attack or rob other people.' Without some sort of enforcement mechanism, this would be inadequate. What will cause self-interested human beings to obey the directives written on that paper? The central question about constitutions is the same. Who will enforce the constitution? No other organization has the power to coerce the government. Therefore, we will have to rely upon the government to enforce constitutional restrictions *against itself*.[39] Why is this more realistic than the parallel proposal that ordinary criminals be left to arrest and punish themselves?

---

[38] See Somin (1998), though he does not discuss by what mechanism the government should be limited.

[39] Compare Hamilton et al., no. 51, 163: '[Y]ou must first enable the government to control the governed; and in the next place oblige it to control itself.'

Perhaps one branch of the government can be tasked with enforcing the constitution against the other branches. The courts, for example, may invalidate a law when they find it to be unconstitutional. But what mechanism induces the courts to faithfully discharge this duty? What stops them from nullifying laws that are constitutional but that they simply disagree with or putting their imprimatur on laws that are in fact unconstitutional? As always, when we hire one group of people to watch over others, the question arises, 'Who will watch the watchers?'[40]

Constitutional limits have in fact been tried. How well have they worked? I focus again on the experience of the United States. Some aspects of the U.S. Constitution have been followed closely, particularly those describing institutional structures. The government is divided into executive, legislative, and judicial branches, just as the Constitution prescribes; the legislature is divided into a Senate and a House of Representatives; and so on. However, with respect to the extent of government power, constitutional restrictions are routinely and unapologetically flouted. It is worth devoting a few pages to this case study.

The Ninth and Tenth Amendments to the Constitution make clear that the powers of the government are to be limited to what are listed in the document itself, whereas the rights of the people are open-ended and not limited to what has been listed:

> *Amendment 9*: The enumeration in the Constitution, of certain rights, shall not be construed to deny or disparage others retained by the people.
>
> *Amendment 10*: The powers not delegated to the United States by the Constitution, nor prohibited by it to the States, are reserved to the States respectively, or to the people.

The Ninth Amendment may be difficult to apply – it refers to rights that are not enumerated, but how is one to know what these rights include? The Tenth Amendment, however, is clear. The federal government is not permitted to do anything other than the things that the Constitution grants it the power to do. All else is unconstitutional. This much is uncontroversial; even the government has never denied it.

---

[40] This phrase derives from the Roman poet Juvenal (1967, Satire VI, 140), writing in the first or second century. In the original context, the meaning was that it is no use hiring guards to ensure your wife's fidelity, since the guards cannot be trusted. Plato (1974, 73, 403e) uses a similar phrase, where he has Glaucon state that 'it would be absurd for the guardian to need a guardian.'

What, then, does the Constitution grant the government the power to do? Of most relevance is Article I, section 8, which delineates the powers of the legislature:

Section 8

The Congress shall have Power To lay and collect Taxes, Duties, Imposts and Excises, to pay the Debts and provide for the common Defence and general Welfare of the United States; but all Duties, Imposts and Excises shall be uniform throughout the United States;

To borrow money on the credit of the United States;

To regulate Commerce with foreign Nations, and among the several States, and with the Indian Tribes;

To establish an uniform Rule of Naturalization, and uniform Laws on the subject of Bankruptcies throughout the United States;

To coin Money, regulate the Value thereof, and of foreign Coin, and fix the Standard of Weights and Measures;

To provide for the Punishment of counterfeiting the Securities and current Coin of the United States;

To establish Post Offices and Post Roads;

To promote the Progress of Science and useful Arts, by securing for limited Times to Authors and Inventors the exclusive Right to their respective Writings and Discoveries;

To constitute Tribunals inferior to the supreme Court;

To define and punish Piracies and Felonies committed on the high Seas, and Offenses against the Law of Nations;

To declare War, grant Letters of Marque and Reprisal, and make Rules concerning Captures on Land and Water;

To raise and support Armies, but no Appropriation of Money to that Use shall be for a longer Term than two Years;

To provide and maintain a Navy;

To make Rules for the Government and Regulation of the land and naval Forces;

To provide for calling forth the Militia to execute the Laws of the Union, suppress Insurrections and repel Invasions;

To provide for organizing, arming, and disciplining, the Militia, and for governing such Part of them as may be employed in the Service of the United States, reserving to the States respectively, the Appointment of the Officers, and the Authority of training the Militia according to the discipline prescribed by Congress;

To exercise exclusive Legislation in all Cases whatsoever, over such District (not exceeding ten Miles square) as may, by Cession of particular States, and the acceptance of Congress, become the Seat of the Government of the United States, and to exercise like Authority over all Places purchased by the Consent of the Legislature of the State in which the Same shall be, for the Erection of Forts, Magazines, Arsenals, dock-Yards, and other needful Buildings; And

To make all Laws which shall be necessary and proper for carrying into Execution the foregoing Powers, and all other Powers vested by this Constitution in the Government of the United States, or in any Department or Officer thereof.

That is the entire section, and the entire list of legislative powers. The constitutional authority for every federal law must be found in that list.

The list includes authority to establish a post office, a military, and a system of federal courts, all of which the country has. But which clause in that list authorizes the establishment of a CIA, an Environmental Protection Agency, or a Department of Health and Human Services? Which clause authorizes the federal government to control the wages employers may pay, what drugs people may ingest, or how fast people may drive? Why may the federal government subsidize agribusiness, give loans to college students, and send people into space? None of these things even remotely appears to be included, explicitly or implicitly, in the list of congressional powers. Nor do myriad other present-day government activities. Any randomly chosen U.S. federal law, program, or agency today is almost certain to be clearly unconstitutional.

Why has the Supreme Court not struck down all these laws? Here is the official story: appearances to the contrary notwithstanding, they are all really authorized by the Constitution. A typical illustration of the logic is provided by the case of *Wickard v. Filburn*, decided in 1942.[41] The Roosevelt administration had successfully sponsored a law designed to increase the price of wheat by restricting the amount of wheat that farmers could grow. Roscoe Filburn was a farmer growing wheat entirely for use in feeding livestock on his own farm. Filburn exceeded the amount allowed by the law and was fined by the Department of Agriculture. Filburn then sued in federal court to prevent the enforcement of the law against him, arguing that there was no constitutional authority for the federal government to control how much wheat he grew on his farm. The Supreme Court unanimously upheld the law, claiming that it was authorized by the third clause in Article I, section 8,

---

[41] 317 U.S. 111 (1942).

which grants Congress the power 'To regulate Commerce with foreign Nations, and among the several States, and with the Indian Tribes.' The court reasoned that because Filburn grew wheat to feed his livestock, he would therefore buy less wheat from other farmers. If many farmers were to do this, it would significantly lower the price of wheat. This, in turn, would have an effect on commerce in wheat, some of which crosses state borders. Therefore, by fining Filburn for growing too much wheat, the federal government was simply exercising its constitutional power to regulate interstate commerce.

It is hard to believe that any unbiased observer competent in the English language would read the phrase 'regulate commerce [...] among the several states' in this way. Here is the unofficial but more truthful account of events: At the beginning of his presidency in the early 1930s, Franklin Delano Roosevelt's New Deal programs were repeatedly and decisively struck down for exceeding the powers granted by the Constitution.[42] President Roosevelt sought to circumvent these decisions by proposing the Judicial Procedures Reform Bill of 1937, which would have given him the power to appoint six new justices to the Supreme Court, bringing the total to fifteen. Had the plan gone through, Roosevelt would have selected only candidates who would support the New Deal. However, shortly after Roosevelt proposed this plan, the court switched direction and began to approve of Roosevelt's programs (though only by a narrow margin);[43] FDR thus abandoned his 'court-packing' plan. Over the next few years, several judges retired and were replaced by Roosevelt appointees anyway, with the result that by the time of the Wickard case, eight of the nine Supreme Court justices owed their tenure to Franklin Roosevelt.[44] These judges were determined to approve of Roosevelt's agenda, no matter what the Constitution said. They therefore invented rationalizations for reversing earlier court opinions.

On this account, the problem lay not in any ambiguity or unclarity in the Constitution, such as might have been remedied by a more judicious choice of words at the time the document was written. There

---

[42] See *Carter v. Carter Coal Co.*, 298 U.S. 238 (1936); *A. L. A. Schechter Poultry Corp. v. United States*, 295 U. S. 495 (1935); *Louisville Joint Stock Land Bank v. Radford*, 295 U.S. 555 (1935).

[43] See *NLRB v. Jones & Laughlin Steel Corp.*, 301 U. S. 1 (1937); *West Coast Hotel Co. v. Parrish*, 300 U.S. 379 (1937).

[44] Harlan Stone, Hugo Black, Stanley Reed, Felix Frankfurter, William Douglas, Frank Murphy, James Byrnes, and Robert Jackson. The exception was Owen Roberts, a Hoover appointee. See U.S. Supreme Court 2011.

was no misunderstanding; the judges simply chose not to enforce the Constitution. The particular content of the opinion penned by Justice Jackson in the Wickard case is essentially irrelevant. It functions as a very thin veil to disguise the intentional expunction of the constitutional limits on the power of Congress – but if that veil had not been available, there would have been another one. If the commerce clause did not exist, the court would have devised another rationalization. Perhaps they would have claimed that the New Deal law fell under the fifth clause, permitting Congress 'To coin Money, regulate the Value thereof, and of foreign Coin, and fix the Standard of Weights and Measures.' The restriction on wheat production had an effect on wheat prices; in that sense, it affected the value of money (the lower prices are, the more valuable a given quantity of money is). So perhaps Congress was only exercising its power to regulate the value of money.

Many today might argue that it was a good thing that the Court chose to overrule the Constitution, because the document as written was overly restrictive. Think of how many wonderful federal programs would not exist today if we had to stick to a natural reading of the words in the Constitution! But regardless of what one thinks of these programs, the American experience should give pause to any democrat who would place his faith in the power of constitutions to limit governmental power. Even if the New Deal programs were good policy, they should still, in theory, have required a constitutional amendment before they could be enacted. The fact that they did not and that so many other clearly unconstitutional laws are routinely passed without apology bears witness to the fundamental problem facing a constitutional regime. The constitution is a law, and laws require enforcement. But once we establish a supreme authority, there is no one to enforce the law against that authority.

9.4.9 Of checks, balances, and the separation of powers

Americans are taught that they live under a system of 'checks and balances', whereby the executive, judicial, and legislative branches of government each restrain the others from abusing their power. This idea derives from Montesquieu, who influenced the framers of the American Constitution.[45] Thus, the judiciary has the power to strike down unconstitutional laws, thereby serving as a check on the power of the legislature. The executive branch has the power to appoint judges,

---

[45] Montesquieu 1748, 11.4, 11.6; Hamilton et al. 1952, nos. 47–51; Jefferson 1782, 214–15.

which the legislature must approve; thus, the executive and legislative branches act to ensure the integrity of the judiciary. The legislature has the power to impeach the president, and the legislature may thus check the power of the executive branch. And so on. No branch of government is supreme, and each has important powers over the others.

This theory is missing one crucial element. That is an account of why each branch of government should be expected to use its powers to prevent the other branches from abusing their powers rather than, say, to assist the other branches in abusing their powers or to prevent the other branches from carrying out their legitimate functions. Again, it does not matter what our theory labels as the proper function of government officials. What matters is the incentive structure. Do the three branches of government each have an interest in ensuring that the other branches function properly without overstepping their constitutionally prescribed bounds?

Perhaps the theory is that the three branches are to some degree in competition with each other, such that no branch wishes to see the others become too powerful.[46] Neither Montesquieu nor the American founders, however, clearly explain why this should be thought to be the case. The legislature makes laws, the judiciary interprets the laws and determines when they have been violated, and the executive enforces the laws. Now suppose that the legislature passes laws that extend beyond the matters that the Constitution authorizes it to regulate. By this I mean, not laws that infringe upon the powers of the other branches of government, but laws that infringe upon the liberties of the people. In what way would this render the executive or judicial branches worse off? If anything, the latter two branches should be expected to expand. The more laws there are to enforce, the larger the executive branch will have to be. Likewise, the more restrictive the legal regime is, the more cases the courts will have to try and thus the larger the judiciary will have to be. If each branch wants to be larger and more powerful, there is some reason to think they should make common cause. There is, at any rate, no obvious reason to think they should each try to prevent the others from infringing upon the freedoms of the people.

Nor is there any reason to think that the powers each branch of government has over the others can be used only for good and not for ill. Take the power of the executive branch to appoint judges. The president *could* use this power to ensure the integrity of the judiciary. Or he

---

[46] This seems to be suggested in no. 51 of the *Federalist Papers* (Hamilton et al. 1952, 162–4).

could use it to ensure a *lack* of integrity – for example, to ensure that only judges who share his ideology and are prepared to advance that ideology without regard to the Constitution are appointed. The realistic pessimism with which the American founders viewed human nature should have led them to see the latter possibility as far more likely than the former.

All of this is borne out by experience. At least since the time of the New Deal, Presidents have routinely appointed judges according to ideology, and both the executive and judicial branches of government have been complicit in the expansion of legislative power. The various unconstitutional federal agencies and programs are by now so entrenched that it is extraordinarily unlikely that any judge would at this point vote to start enforcing the Tenth Amendment. Any individual suspected of harboring attitudes sympathetic to such a move would have no chance of being appointed by any president nor of being confirmed by the Senate.

9.5   Conclusion

We human beings are selfish social animals. We live together, and yet we each care much more about ourselves than about the vast majority of others. As a result, we face the fundamental social problem of predation: how are things to be arranged so that human beings do not continually exploit and abuse each other?

The standard solution in social philosophy begins by proposing a radical inequality: a single institution with power over all other individuals and organizations. For Hobbes, the solution ends there. For democratic theorists, a series of fetters must next be attached to the central authority in the effort to restrain it from exploiting and abusing the rest of society. The mechanisms of restraint include popular elections, a free press, constitutional limits, and the separation of powers.

Despite their limitations, these mechanisms have proved valuable. They produce a form of government markedly less abusive than the typical totalitarian government. Democratic societies rarely suffer acute, easily preventable disasters, and they almost never murder large numbers of their own people. Some of the more blatant governmental misdeeds are reported in the popular press, so that the worst sort of excesses are deterred. Judges have been sympathetic to at least some constitutional restrictions on government and have therefore chosen to enforce them. Freedom of speech, freedom of the press, and freedom of religion are usually fairly well preserved in constitutional democracies.

Thus, if one is confined to the design of a state-based social system, the traditional mechanisms of restraint are by no means to be scorned. My aim, however, has been to argue that these mechanisms cannot satisfy all the hopes that democratic theorists have pinned on them. The ballot box is of limited utility in ensuring responsive government, since it is not in the interests of individual voters to make more than token efforts at rational and informed voting. The complexity of modern government makes it impossible for even the most dedicated citizen to stay informed about more than a vanishingly small fraction of the state's activities. The news media are of limited utility, since it is not in their interests to report on the great majority of governmental errors and turpitudes. Constitutions are of limited use, since one must rely upon the government to enforce the constitution against itself, and it is rarely in the government's interests to do so faithfully. Finally, the separation of powers is of limited utility, since the separate branches of government stand to gain more by making common cause in extending government power than by vigilantly restraining each other's power. As a result, even democratic governments have grown to enormous proportions in modern times and developed into tools for small, well-organized interest groups to exploit the rest of society.

To make further headway on the problem of social predation, we must confront its underlying cause. Predatory behavior does not occur merely because human beings are selfish. It occurs because human beings are selfish *and* some human beings are much more powerful than others. Powerful, selfish people use their positions to exploit and abuse those much weaker than themselves. The standard solutions to the problem of human predation all start by cementing the very condition most likely to cause predatory behavior – the concentration of power – and only then do they try to steer away from its natural consequences. The alternative is to begin with an extreme decentralization of coercive power. How such a system works will be discussed in more detail presently.

10

Individual Security in a Stateless Society

10.1 A nonstate system of justice

10.1.1 Protection agencies

In any realistic human society, even an anarchist one, at least some individuals will commit aggression against others. The inhabitants of the anarchic society would most likely wish to develop systematic institutions for the provision of security, including a collection of protection agencies or security companies whose function would be to protect individuals from aggression against their persons and property and to apprehend aggressors after the fact.[1] These agencies, in brief, would serve the function that police serve in governmental systems.

In the absence of government, protection agencies would arise for the same reason that most businesses arise in a free market; namely, that there is a need which people are willing to pay to have satisfied. The agencies would charge money for their services, just as private security companies presently charge for their services.

Who would pay the security agencies? Individuals might hire their own security company, or neighborhood homeowners' associations might hire security for their neighborhoods, or owners of apartment buildings or businesses might hire security for their buildings, or some combination of these might occur.

Why does the anarchist not stipulate the details of nonstate security arrangements? Because the functioning of the system is determined by the individuals occupying it; therefore, the answers to questions about

---

[1] This proposal derives from Rothbard (1978, chapter 12) and Friedman (1989, chapter 29).

how the system would work must take the form of speculative predictions rather than stipulations (the same is true of any untried institution, though this fact is little recognized). The details of security arrangements would be determined by market forces and individual choices. If, for example, customers strongly preferred to patronize businesses that provided their own security, then most businesses would hire their own security.

What services would protection agencies provide? This, too, would depend upon customer demand. In some cases, they might provide armed patrols. In other cases, they might provide security cameras and alarm systems. After a crime was committed, they might provide detectives and armed 'police' to apprehend the criminals. Once apprehended, the criminals would be compelled to pay compensation for their crimes.

What would protection agencies do in the event that an accused criminal maintained his innocence? In that case, some institution serving the function of a court system would be needed.

10.1.2 Arbitration firms

In an anarchic society, just as in government-based societies, people would sometimes have disputes. One important kind of dispute occurs when a person is accused of a crime which he denies committing. Another type occurs when people disagree over whether a particular type of conduct ought to be tolerated; for instance, I may think my neighbor is playing his music too loud, while he thinks the volume is just fine. A third type concerns the terms of business relationships, including disputes about the interpretation of contracts. In each of these cases, the disagreeing parties need an institution functioning like a court to resolve their dispute.

In the absence of a state, this need would be supplied by private arbitration firms. Arbitration by a neutral third party is the best way to resolve most disputes, since it generally provides a good chance of delivering a reasonably fair resolution, and the costs of achieving this resolution are almost always far less for both parties than the costs of attempting a resolution through violence. For these reasons, almost all individuals would want their disputes to be resolved through arbitration.

Who would hire the arbitrators? Perhaps the parties to a dispute would agree on an arbitrator and split the cost between them. Or perhaps their security agencies would select the arbitrator. Suppose Jon accuses Sally of stealing his cat. He informs his security agency of the theft and asks them to retrieve the cat. But Sally notifies *her* security agency that

Jon is attempting to steal her cat and asks them to defend the cat. If Jon and Sally patronize the same security agency, this agency may hire an arbitration company to determine to whom the cat belongs, so that the agency may decide whose claim to enforce. If Jon and Sally patronize different agencies, the two agencies will jointly select an arbitration company, with the understanding that both will accept the verdict of the arbitrator.

These are the basic institutions of a well-ordered anarchist society. In such a society, the most fundamental functions commonly ascribed to the state are not eliminated but privatized. A great many questions naturally arise about such a system. In the remainder of this chapter, I address the most important questions about private protection agencies. Questions concerning arbitration firms will be taken up in the following chapter.

10.2   Is it anarchy?

The system just sketched is commonly referred to as 'anarcho-capitalism', 'free market anarchism', or 'libertarian anarchism'. One might ask, however, whether the system truly qualifies as a form of anarchy rather than, say, a system of competing governments.[2]

Semantic questions about the use of 'government' and 'anarchy' are of no great importance. However, the system differs in two crucial respects from all presently existing governmental systems, and it is these differences that lead me to call the system a form of anarchy.

The first difference is one of *voluntariness versus coerciveness.* Governments force everyone to accept their services; as we have seen (Chapters 2 and 3), the social contract is a myth. Protection agencies, by contrast, are chosen by customers, who make actual, literal contracts with them.

The second difference is one of *competition versus monopoly.* Governments hold geographical monopolies on protection and dispute-resolution services,[3] and changing one's government tends to be very difficult and costly, so governments feel little competitive

---

[2] Rand (1964, 112–13) refers to the system as 'competing governments' but then argues that it is really a form of anarchism; she appears to be under the misapprehension that the advocates of anarcho-capitalism themselves called the system 'competing governments'.

[3] Compare Weber's well-known definition of government: 'The state is a human community that (successfully) claims the *monopoly of the legitimate use of physical force* within a given territory' (1946, 78; emphasis in original).

pressure. In the anarchist system, protection agencies and arbitration companies are in constant competition with each other. If one were dissatisfied with one's protection agency, one could switch to another agency at little cost without moving to another country. These two differences are the fundamental source of all the advantages claimed for anarcho-capitalism over traditional government. The voluntariness of the anarcho-capitalist scheme makes it more just than a coercive system, and both traits make the anarcho-capitalist system less abusive and more responsive to people's needs than coercive, monopolistic systems.

10.3 Conflict between protectors

Competing security agencies might seem to have significant motives for direct physical confrontation with one another. Since they are in direct economic competition, one agency might wish to attack another in the hopes of putting the other agency out of business. Or in the event of a dispute between customers of different agencies, security agencies might go to war to defend their respective clients' interests rather than allowing the dispute to be resolved by arbitration. For these reasons, some argue that an anarchist society would be riven with interagency wars.[4]

10.3.1 The costs of violence

As discussed earlier (Section 9.2), violent conflict tends to be very dangerous for both parties; rational individuals therefore seek to avoid provoking such conflicts and prefer peaceful methods of dispute resolution, such as third-party arbitration, whenever available.

But in spite of the prudential and moral arguments against engaging in avoidable violent confrontations, such confrontations periodically break out among ordinary individuals. Why does this occur? In essence, the reason is that in the general population, there are a wide variety of attitudes and motivations, and among all this variety there are some individuals with unusually high degrees of physical confidence, unusually low concern for their own physical safety, and unusually low capacity for impulse control – a collection of traits often referred to as 'recklessness'.[5]

---

[4] This objection appears in Wellman (2005, 15–16) and Rand (1964, 113). Friedman (1989, 115–16) responds.

[5] The theory that violent conflict is due to aggressive personalities rather than, say, to rational self-interest is evidenced by the fact that such conflict is an almost exclusively male phenomenon.

Business managers, however, are considerably more uniform than the general population. They tend to share two traits in particular: a strong desire to generate profits for their businesses, and a reasonable awareness of the effective means of doing so. Individuals who lack these traits are unlikely to emerge at the head of a business, and if they do, the market is likely either to remove them from that position (as where a company's board of directors replaces its CEO) or to remove the company from the marketplace (as in bankruptcy). Thus, business managers are even less likely to behave in clearly profit-destroying ways than ordinary individuals are to behave in ways that clearly endanger their own physical safety.

But war is, putting it mildly, expensive. If a pair of agencies go to war with one another, both agencies, including the one that ultimately emerges the victor, will most likely suffer enormous damage to their property and their employees. It is highly improbable that a dispute between two clients would be worth this kind of expense. If at the same time there are other agencies in the region that have not been involved in any wars, the latter agencies will have a powerful economic advantage. In a competitive marketplace, agencies that find peaceful methods of resolving disputes will outperform those that fight unnecessary battles. Because this is easily predictable, each agency should be willing to resolve any dispute peacefully, provided that the other party is likewise willing.

10.3.2   Opposition to murder

Employees of a security agency have their own individual wills, distinct from the goals of the agency. If management decided to attack another agency solely to put a competitor out of business, widespread desertion is the most probable result. There are two reasons for this. First, most human beings are opposed to undertaking very large risks to their own lives for the sake of maximizing profits for their boss. Combat with another security agency would be much more dangerous than the normal work of apprehending common criminals, since the other agency would be better armed, organized, and trained than typical criminals.

Second, most people in contemporary societies are strongly opposed to murdering other members of their society.[6] This 'problem' has long been recognized by military experts whose concern is convincing

---

[6] Grossman (1995, 1–39) provides an overview of the empirical evidence for this.

soldiers to kill as many of the enemy as possible. On the basis of interviews with World War II soldiers, General S. L. A. Marshall famously concluded that no more than one-quarter of American soldiers actually fired their weapons in a typical battle.[7] Lieutenant Colonel Dave Grossman relates numerous cases in which the casualty rate during a battle was far lower than could plausibly be reconciled with the assumption of a genuine effort by each side to kill the other. In one striking incident, a Nicaraguan Contra unit was ordered by its commander to massacre the passengers on a civilian river launch. When the time came to open fire, every bullet miraculously sailed over the heads of the civilians. As one soldier explained, 'Nicaraguan peasants are mean bastards, and tough soldiers. But they're not murderers.'[8]

This is not to deny that some human beings are murderers; it is only to say that the overwhelming majority of human beings are strongly opposed to murder. A small percentage of people are willing to murder; however, these individuals are not generally desirable employees, and thus it is unlikely that a protection agency would wish to staff itself with such people.

What about the finding of the Milgram experiment (Section 6.2), in which people proved willing to electrocute a helpless victim when so ordered by a scientist? The fear of defying authority can overcome people's resistance to murder. Though business managers have much less of an aura of authority than government officials, might a security agency manager nevertheless be able to exploit this flaw in human nature to induce employees to kill members of rival agencies?

Perhaps one could, though it is worth noting a few other features of Milgram's experiment. First, the gradual escalation of the experimenter's demands, starting from a seemingly legitimate scientific experiment, was a crucial feature of the design. If Stanley Milgram had simply handed a pistol to his subjects as they walked in the door and told them to shoot another subject, he would not have succeeded. But perhaps a clever security agency manager, versed in psychology, could similarly manipulate circumstances.

---

[7] Marshall 1978, chapter 5. Others have questioned Marshall's statistics, which are probably guesswork (Chambers 2003), but the overall picture remains unaltered (Grossman 1995, 333, n. 1). Commenting on the problem faced by military leaders, Grossman (1995, 251) remarks, 'A firing rate of 15 to 20 percent among soldiers is like having a literacy rate of 15 to 20 percent among proofreaders.'

[8] Dr. John, quoted in Grossman 1995, 14–15.

Second, Milgram's subjects were not in any personal danger from the person they were supposedly electrocuting. If the 'learner' in the experiment had the ability to shock the teacher back, it is doubtful how far the teacher would have continued with the experiment. A warlike company manager would need to convince employees not only to murder but to risk being killed in turn.

Third, though most of Milgram's subjects obeyed, they did so with great reluctance, exhibiting signs of extreme stress. Even if a warlike agency managed to get employees to commit murder, the employees would be extremely unhappy, and the agency would probably soon lose most of its employees. During the 1960s, American war protesters displayed posters and bumper stickers with the slogan, 'What if they gave a war and nobody came?'[9] In the unlikely event that a protection agency declared war against another agency, residents of the anarchist society might finally have the chance to observe the answer to this question.

10.3.3   Conflict between governments

We have just seen why war between security agencies is unlikely. If, on the other hand, we rely upon government for our protection, is there any account of why war between states would be unlikely? A statist might offer two reasons for considering interstate war a smaller threat than interagency war:

i) Since governments possess territorial monopolies, citizens of different states come into conflict less often than the customers of different protection agencies would.

ii) There is less competition among governments than there is among protection agencies. The large costs of moving from one country to another, including the barriers that governments themselves often place in the way, enable a government to extract monopoly profits from its populace with little fear of losing 'customers' to a rival government. Therefore, a government has less cause to wish to eliminate rival governments than a protection agency has to wish to eliminate rival agencies.

---

[9] The phrase seems to derive from Sandburg (1990, 43; originally published 1936). The original phrase is 'Sometime they'll give a war and nobody will come.'

These are valid considerations. On the other hand, there seem to be several reasons for expecting the problem of intergovernmental warfare to be more serious than that of interagency warfare:

i) Business leaders tend to be driven chiefly by the profit motive. Government leaders are more likely to be driven by ideology or the desire for power. Because of the enormous costs of armed conflict, the latter motivations are much more likely motives for armed conflict than the desire for financial gain.

ii) Due to their monopolistic positions, governments can afford to make extremely large and costly errors without fear of being supplanted. For example, the estimated combined cost of the U.S. wars in Iraq and Afghanistan is $2.4 trillion,[10] and yet the U.S. government need fear no loss of market share as a result of this dubious investment. If each American could choose between a government that carried on these wars and one that did not and if each individual were guaranteed to actually get what he chose, then even the most ardent hawks might find themselves thinking twice about the price tag. Fortunately for the government, individuals have no such choice.

iii) Governments have better propagandistic tools at their disposal than private businesses. Since most people believe in political authority, the state can claim that citizens are morally obligated to go to war, whether they support the war or not. The state may portray combat under its command as 'fighting for one's country', which is generally seen as noble and honorable. A private business seeking to increase profits by killing competitors would have a harder sell.

iv) Human beings are far more willing to kill those who are perceived as very different from themselves, especially foreigners, than to kill ordinary members of their own society.[11] Consequently, it is easier to convince people to go to war against another country than it would be to convince people to attack employees of another company.

---

[10] Reuters 2007a, reporting a Congressional Budget Office estimate of total costs through the year 2017. The estimated cost for Iraq alone is $1.9 trillion. Stiglitz and Bilmes (2008), however, put the cost for both wars at at least $3 trillion.

[11] Zimbardo 2007, 307–13; Grossman 1995, 156–70.

v) Modern military training employs techniques of intensive psychological conditioning and desensitization to overcome soldiers' humane instincts. The U.S. military adopted techniques of this kind in response to Marshall's findings concerning the low rate of firing by World War II soldiers. As a result, the rate of fire reportedly increased from under 25 per cent in World War II to 55 per cent in the Korean War and close to 90 per cent in the Vietnam War.[12] Employees of a security company, however, are less likely to submit to military-style conditioning, since they would not see the need of combat with other security agencies to begin with.

vi) Due to its pervasive control over the society from which its soldiers are drawn, the state can and does apply powerful sanctions to soldiers who refuse to fight or citizens who refuse to be drafted. Under a governmental system, those who refuse to fight at their government's command must flee the country to avoid imprisonment or execution;[13] under an anarchist system, those who refuse to fight at their employer's command must merely find another job.

vii) Because of their monopolistic position and their ability to collect nonvoluntary payments from the populace, governments tend to have far greater resources than nongovernmental organizations, enabling them to accumulate vast arsenals even during peacetime. For example, as of this writing, the U.S. government maintains ten Nimitz-class aircraft carriers, which cost $4.5 billion apiece plus $240 million per year for maintenance[14] while generating zero revenue. As a result, when war breaks out between governments, it is far more destructive than any kind of conflict involving any other agents. The death toll from war in the twentieth century is estimated in the neighborhood of 140 million,[15] and the problem may yet prove the cause of the extinction of the human species.

Taking all of these observations into account, then, it appears that warfare is a greater concern with governments than with protection agencies.

---

[12] Marshall 1978, 9; Grossman 1995, 249–61.

[13] The U.S. Uniform Code of Military Justice, Article 85, allows for any penalty up to and including death for desertion during wartime (www.ucmj.us).

[14] U.S. Navy 2009; Birkler et al. 1998, 75.

[15] Leitenberg 2006, 9. Most of these are civilian deaths; military deaths were close to 36 million (Clodfelter 2002, 6).

10.4 Protection for criminals

I have described a system of private agencies devoted to protecting individuals from crime; that is, from theft, physical aggression, and other rights violations. But why should there not be agencies devoted to protecting criminals from their victims' attempts to secure justice? What asymmetry between criminals and peaceful cooperators makes it more feasible, profitable, or otherwise attractive for an agency to protect ordinary people than to protect criminals?

10.4.1 The profitability of enforcing rights

There are at least three important asymmetries that favor the protection of noncriminal persons over criminals. First, far more people wish to be protected against crime than wish to be protected in committing crimes. Almost no one desires to be a crime victim, while only a few desire to be criminals. Second, the harms suffered by victims of crime are typically far greater than the benefits enjoyed by those who commit crimes. Ordinary people would therefore be willing to pay more to avoid being victimized than criminals would be willing to pay for the chance to victimize others. In virtue of these first two conditions, there is far more money to be made in the business of protection *against* criminals than in the business of protection *for* criminals. Given that the two 'products' exclude each other – if one product is effectively supplied in the marketplace, then the other necessarily is not – it is the less profitable one that will fail to be supplied. If a rogue protection agency decides to buck the trend by supporting criminals, it will find itself locked in perpetual and hopeless conflict with far more profitable and numerous protection agencies financed by noncriminal customers.

The third asymmetry is that criminals choose to commit crimes, whereas crime victims do not choose to be victimized. Criminals, in other words, intentionally engage in behavior guaranteed to bring them into conflict with others. From the standpoint of a protection agency, this is an unattractive feature in a client, since the more conflicts there are in which the agency is called upon to protect clients, the higher the agency's costs will be. Ordinary, noncriminal clients are aligned with the agency's goals in this respect: they do not wish to be involved in conflicts any more than the agency wishes them to be. Criminal clients are a very different story. Offering protection for criminals is analogous to offering fire insurance for arsonists.

10.4.2 Criminal protection by governments

What about the analogous problem for governments: are there forces that prevent a government from acting to protect criminals?

Governments commonly act to protect society against those who violate others' rights, such as common murderers, thieves, rapists, and so on. On the other hand, during the slavery era, government protected slave owners from their slaves rather than the other way around. Before the civil rights movement in the United States, government enforced racial segregation. And today, democratic governments function as tools for special-interest groups to steal from the rest of society.[16]

These examples show that both patterns are possible: government can protect people's rights, and it can also protect rights violators. The question is whether the unjust pattern of protecting rights violators would be more common for a protection agency than for a government. Governments and protection agencies are both human organizations, staffed by agents with human motivations. To assume that governments are altruistically motivated while protection agencies are selfishly motivated is to apply a double standard designed to skew the evaluation in favor of government.

If we avoid such double standards, it is hard to see why governments should be thought less prone to protect rights violators than private agencies would be. One could argue that democratic governments must respond to the desires of voters, most of whom are opposed to crime. But one could equally well argue that protection agencies must respond to the desires of consumers, most of whom are opposed to crime, and there are reasons for expecting the market mechanism to be more responsive than the democratic mechanism (see Sections 10.7 and 9.4).

10.5 Justice for sale

Some object to free market provision of protective services on the grounds that justice should not be bought and sold. On the surface, this objection skirts uncomfortably close to a bare denial of the anarcho-capitalist position. To avoid begging the question, the objector must articulate a specific reason why protection and dispute resolution services should not be bought and sold. Two initially plausible reasons might be offered.

---

[16] For discussion, see Section 9.4.3.

10.5.1 Preexisting entitlement

One argument is that people should not have to pay for justice, because everyone is entitled to justice to begin with. Just as I should not have to pay for my own car (again) once I already own it, I should not have to pay for anything else to which I am already entitled.

In one sense, this is correct – no one should have to pay for justice. But what the objection points to is, not a flaw in the anarcho-capitalist system, but a flaw in human nature, for the necessity of paying for justice is created, not by the anarcho-capitalist system, but simply by the fact that criminals exist, and that fact has its roots in the perennial infirmities of human nature. In an idealistic, utopian sense, we can say that everyone should simply voluntarily respect each other's rights so that no one need ever pay for protection.

Given, however, that some people do not in fact respect others' rights, the best solution is for some members of society to provide protection to others. This costs money, and there are at least two reasons why the protectors cannot be asked simply to shoulder the costs themselves. First, there is the practical argument that few people are willing to expend their time and resources, to say nothing of the physical risks undertaken by security providers, without receiving some personal benefit in return. If we decide that it is wrong to charge money for a vital service such as rights protection, whereas one can charge whatever one likes for inessential goods such as Twinkies and cell phones, then we will build a society with plenty of Twinkies, cell phones, and rights violations.

Second, those who provide protective services are *justly entitled* to ask for compensation for their time, their material expenses, and the physical risks they undertake, at least as much as anyone else who provides services of value to others. It would be unjust to demand that they bear all these burdens while their beneficiaries, those whom they protect, may simply proceed with their own self-serving occupations, bearing none of the costs of their own defense. If anything, the vital importance of the protection of rights entitles those who provide this service to ask for greater rewards than those who provide less essential goods and services.

10.5.2 Basing law on justice

Another reason for thinking that protection from crime should not be subject to market forces is that this is incompatible with the laws' being determined, as they ought to be, by what is morally right and just.

Again, there is something obviously correct in this thought: human beings *should* respect moral principles, and they *should* design social rules to promote justice and ethical behavior. But this is no objection to anarcho-capitalism. In adverting to self-interest to explain how security agencies in an anarchist society would behave, I am not *advocating* selfishness; I am *recognizing* it as an aspect of human nature which exists regardless of what social system we occupy. One can design social institutions on the assumption that people are unselfish, but this will not cause people to be unselfish; it will simply cause those institutions to fail.

This is not to say that people are *entirely* selfish. Insofar as human beings are moved by ideals of justice and morality, these motives would only strengthen the rights-protecting institutions of the anarchic society. The ethically proper job of a protection agency is to protect the rights of its customers, and in the case of disagreement, to enforce the decisions of an arbitrator. The proper job of an arbitrator is to find the fairest, wisest, and most just resolutions possible of the disputes placed before him. The faithful discharge of these duties is not precluded by the fact that the agencies and the arbitrators have self-interested reasons to do these things.

10.5.3   Buying justice from government

The preceding objections in any case cannot favor government over anarchy, because government is subject to the very same objections. In a government-dominated system, people must pay for justice, just as surely as in an anarchist system. It is not as though courts and police forces can somehow operate without cost if only they are monopolistic and coercive. If anything, the monopolistic and coercive aspects of government justice systems make them more expensive than a competitive, voluntaristic system. The difference is simply that in governmental systems, payments are collected coercively under the name of 'taxation', and provision of the service is not guaranteed even if you pay.[17] Presumably, these differences do not render the system more just.

Likewise, the laws enforced by a government are no more determined by justice and morality than those enforced by private protection agencies and arbitration firms. In a representative democracy, the laws are

---

[17] U.S. courts have repeatedly ruled that police and other government agents are not obligated to protect individual citizens. See *Warren v. District of Columbia* (444 A.2d. 1, D.C. Ct. of Ap., 1981); *Hartzler v. City of San Jose*, 46 Cal.App. 3d 6 (1975); *DeShaney v. Winnebago County Department of Social Services*, 489 U.S. 189 (1989).

determined by the decisions of elected officials and the bureaucrats they appoint. Election outcomes, in turn, are affected by such factors as charisma, physical attractiveness, campaign funding, name recognition, the skill and ruthlessness of campaign managers, and voter prejudices.

Some say that politicians and bureaucrats are *supposed* to serve impartial ethical values, whereas business managers are only supposed to generate profits for their business. What does this mean? *Who* supposes that public officials are motivated in this way, and what difference does such supposition make? One argument is that because there is a general socially accepted norm to the effect that public officials should serve justice, public officials will themselves feel more inclined to behave in that way than they would in the absence of such a norm. In contrast, since no such norm is generally accepted in the case of businesses, business managers will feel little sense of obligation to serve justice.

There are two natural replies to this argument. The first is to question the relative importance of moral motivation, emphasizing instead the practical value of aligning agents' self-interest with the requirements of justice. Granted, the ideal system is one in which people serve justice for the right reasons. But for the reasons explained in Chapter 9, government is unlikely to be that system. If one must choose between a system in which people serve self-interest in the name of justice and one in which people serve justice in the name of self-interest, surely we must prefer the latter. To prefer a system that hands people the tools to exploit others for selfish ends while assuring them that they are *supposed* to serve justice, over a system that makes justice profitable and allows people to choose their course, would be to repose a utopian faith in the power of supposition.

The second reply is that there is no reason why the members of an anarchy may not embrace equally idealistic norms as those of a democratic society. Just as citizens of a democratic state believe that public officials should promote justice, the members of an anarchy may hold that protection agencies and arbitration firms should promote justice. However much efficacy that kind of social norm has in policing human behavior, the anarchist may harness it just as well as the statist.

10.6 Security for the poor

Another concern is that security agencies, driven by the profit motive, will cater solely to the rich, leaving the poor defenseless against criminals.

10.6.1 Do businesses serve the poor?

Unfortunately, there are no actual societies with a free market in security. We can, however, examine societies with relatively free markets in a variety of other goods and services. In such societies, for how many of these other goods and services is it true that suppliers cater solely to the rich, providing no products suitable for middle- and lower-income customers? Is clothing manufactured solely for the wealthy, leaving the poor to wander the streets naked? Do supermarkets stock only caviar and Dom Pérignon? Which chain is larger: Walmart or Bloomingdale's? Admittedly, there are some products, such as yachts and Learjets, that have yet to appear in affordable models for the average consumer, yet the overwhelming majority of industries are dominated by production for lower- and middle-income consumers. The main explanation is volume: for most products, there are many more consumers seeking a cheap product than consumers seeking an expensive product.

The wealthy, of course, tend to receive higher quality products than the poor, from food to clothing to automobiles (that is the point of being wealthy). Under anarchy, they would no doubt receive higher-quality protection as well. Is there an injustice in this?

In one sense, yes: as a result of imperfect protection, some poor people will become victims of crime. This is unjust, in the sense that it is unjust that anyone ever suffers from crime. The injustice inherent in crime, however, points to a flaw in human nature rather than in the anarchist system. Some people will suffer from crime under any feasible social system. The question is whether anarchy faces a *greater* problem or a greater injustice than governmental systems.

One might think that anarchy will suffer from a further injustice beyond simply the existence of crime; namely, the inequality in the distribution of crime, the fact that the poor are subject to greater risks of crime than the wealthy. In my view, this is not an additional injustice over and above the fact that people suffer from crime. In other words, given a fixed quantity of crime, as measured perhaps by the number and seriousness of rights violations occurring in a society, I do not believe that it matters, ethically, how the crime is distributed across economic classes. Questions in this vicinity, however, are beyond the scope of this book.[18]

---

[18] On egalitarianism, see my 2003 and forthcoming.

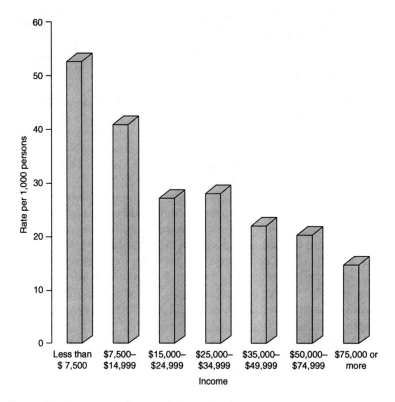

Figure 10.1 Frequency of crime victimization by income

10.6.2 How well does government protect the poor?

Even if inequality in the distribution of crime is an independent injustice, this does not obviously favor government over anarchy, since large inequalities in the distribution of crime occur in all state-based societies as well, where the wealthy are much better protected than the poor. To take a contemporary example, Americans with incomes below $7500 per year are three and a half times more likely to suffer personal crimes than those with incomes over $75,000 (see Figure 10.1), despite that the wealthy might initially seem a more attractive target for most crimes.[19] Though this is not the only possible explanation, it is plausible to hold that this inequality is at least partly due to inadequate protection offered by the state to the poor. Whether an anarchist system

---

[19] U.S. Department of Justice 2010a, table 14.

would have more or less inequality in the distribution of crime remains a matter for speculation.

10.7   The quality of protection

How well would private protection agencies protect their clients, in comparison with police under the status quo? This comparison is difficult to make since we cannot observe an anarchist society. The best we can do is to examine the effectiveness of government police and then make theoretical predictions about the anarchist alternative on the basis of the incentive structures.

The status quo leaves considerable room for improvement. We do not know how many people are deterred from a life of crime by the prospect of being punished by the state, but we have a fair idea of how often those who turn to a life of crime are in fact punished. According to FBI statistics, only about half of all reported violent crimes and a fifth of reported property crimes are solved by law enforcement agencies (see Figure 10.2).[20] These figures actually give an *over*estimate of the effectiveness of government law enforcement since they do not account for unreported crimes.

On a theoretical level, it is not difficult to understand why government police might be less effective than private protection agencies. If a protection agency provides poor protection or charges excessive fees, it must fear loss of customers to rival agencies. But if the police provide poor protection at a high price, they need have no fear of losing market share or going out of business. Since they have monopolized the industry, the customers have nowhere else to turn, and since their revenue derives from taxation, the customers cannot decide to fire their protectors and fend for themselves. These enviable features of the state's position enable it to survive indefinitely almost irrespective of its performance. Indeed, the poor performance of police is more likely to bring them financial rewards than to bring financial losses, since rising crime rates tend to cause increases in law enforcement budgets

---

[20] U.S. Federal Bureau of Investigation 2010, table 25. The statistics in the text and figure refer to the percentage of offenses 'cleared by arrest or extraordinary means'. This requires law enforcement officers to have located a suspect whom they had sufficient evidence to charge and to have either arrested and turned over the suspect to the courts for prosecution or been prevented from doing so by circumstances outside their control, such as the death of the suspect or refusal of extradition.

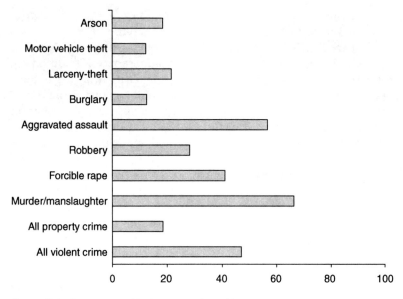

Figure 10.2 Percentage of U.S. crimes cleared by arrest

rather than cuts (compare Section 9.4.7). Private protection agencies, lacking these advantages, would have no recourse but to provide sufficient protection to their customers at a reasonable price.

10.8 Organized crime

Private protection agencies might be able to deal with the common criminal, but how would they deal with *organized* crime? Do we not need a central authority to combat this problem?

Government has extensive programs for fighting organized crime; they focus almost entirely on direct enforcement efforts – that is, efforts to arrest and prosecute criminals, particularly the criminal leadership. But doubts have been raised about the effectiveness of this approach.[21] Evidence of the effect of these enforcement efforts on overall crime levels is lacking, and it may well be that the roles occupied by jailed crime bosses are simply filled by other criminals, resulting in negligible benefits to society in terms of total crime.[22]

---

[21] Paoli and Fijnaut 2006, 326; Levi and Maguire 2004.
[22] Levi and Maguire 2004, 401, 404–5.

A plausible alternative approach would be to attempt to deny organized crime its most important sources of revenue. Criminal organizations are chiefly focused on collecting money, which they do mostly through the provision of illegal goods and services. Traditionally, organized crime has generated revenue for itself through gambling operations, prostitution, and (during the Prohibition era in the United States) the illegal sale of alcohol. By far the main source of revenue for organized crime today appears to be the illicit drug trade, which is estimated to generate between $500 billion and $900 billion in sales worldwide per year.[23]

Why have criminal organizations focused on these industries? Why sell gambling services, sexual services, and drugs rather than, say, shoes and chocolates? There is no controversy about the answer to this: it is because gambling (in some forms), prostitution, and narcotic drugs are illegal. Al Capone made his fortune selling alcohol, not when it was legal, but during the era of Prohibition. Today, organized criminals make their fortune selling marijuana and cocaine rather than penicillin and Prozac. The reason is that criminals have no advantages in the provision of ordinary goods and services; their only special asset is their willingness and skill in defying the law. Unlike ordinary businesspeople, criminal individuals are willing to risk imprisonment for the sake of money; they are willing to forgo all social respectability; and they are willing to engage in bribery, threats, and violence to pursue their business. These are the traits needed to supply a good that is illegal. By prohibiting certain drugs, we grant control of the recreational drug industry to people with those characteristics. If these same drugs were legalized, the criminals now making fortunes from their sale would no longer be able to do so because they would no longer have any economic advantage in that industry. This is the lesson of Capone and Prohibition.

Thus, a powerful strategy for crippling organized crime would be to legalize drugs, gambling, and prostitution. I do not claim that this would eliminate all organized crime. It would, however, strike a blow to organized crime more devastating than anything the state could hope to do by way of wiretaps, sting operations, and indictments. The vast majority of organized crime's revenue stream would dry up virtually overnight, forcing most of its members to seek other employment.

In an anarchist society, it is highly probable that drugs, gambling, and prostitution would all be legal. The essential difference between

---

[23] Finckenauer 2009, 308.

these 'crimes' and more paradigmatic crimes such as murder, robbery, and rape is that the latter crimes have victims, whereas gambling, drug use, and prostitution have no victims – or at any rate, no victims who are likely to complain.[24] In the anarcho-capitalist society, rights are enforced by the victim of a rights violation bringing a complaint against the rights violator through his protection agency and relying upon a private arbitrator to judge the validity of the complaint. There is no effective mechanism for prohibiting victimless crimes, because there is no legislature to write the statutes and no public prosecutor to enforce them.

What if a large number of people were so strongly opposed to prostitution that they were willing to pay their protection agencies to 'protect' them from living in a society in which other people buy and sell sexual services? And what if arbitrators in this society agreed that anyone complaining about someone else's trade in sexual services had in fact been wronged (perhaps through being offended) and was entitled to compensation by either the prostitute or the prostitute's client? In theory, a society of this kind could end up with antilibertarian prohibitions on prostitution; however, this is an improbable scenario, since few people in fact think that a contract to purchase sexual services victimizes any person who merely finds out about it and doesn't like it, and few are in fact willing to pay as much to prevent other people from engaging in prostitution as prostitutes and their clients are willing to pay to be left alone. Similar observations apply to other victimless crimes, such as gambling and recreational drug use.

This does not eliminate all possible revenue sources for organized crime; criminals could still collect money, for example, through extortion and fraud. Nevertheless, denied their largest sources of revenue, criminal organizations would be much weaker in an anarchist society than they are today and would probably play a very small role.

10.9 Protection or extortion?

Rather than providing protection in exchange for agreed-upon fees, it might seem that it would be more profitable for a 'protection' agency

---

[24] Some claim that illegal drug use victimizes the drug user's family, spouse, or coworkers (Wilson 1990, 24). However, these alleged crime victims are unlikely to bring a court case against the drug user and unlikely to prevail in a complaint against either user or supplier.

simply to rob people without bothering about protecting them. Why wouldn't protection agencies evolve into mere extortion agencies?

10.9.1   The discipline of competition

Interagency competition is the main force restraining abusive practices by protection agencies. Customers would subscribe to the agency that they expected to serve them best at the lowest cost, without robbing, abusing, or enslaving them.

Imagine two protection agencies operating in the same city, Tannahelp Inc. and Murbard Ltd.[25] Tannahelp is a legitimate agency that enters into voluntary agreements with its customers, providing protection in exchange for a fee. Murbard is a rogue agency that extorts money from people while providing little of value in return. Almost anyone would prefer Tannahelp, and therefore, if individuals could freely choose their protection agency, Murbard would quickly go out of business. If Murbard tried to force people to join it instead of Tannahelp, people would appeal to Tannahelp for protection.

We saw above the incentives that oppose violent conflict between agencies. Tannahelp might therefore attempt to resolve the dispute with Murbard through third-party arbitration. Murbard could accept the offer of arbitration, in which case any fair judge would rule against it; it could abandon its extortionist plan, or it could prepare for war.

There are four reasons why Murbard would be more likely to either back down or be destroyed than Tannahelp. First, Tannahelp would be perceived as more legitimate than Murbard by the rest of society. Tannahelp would therefore have a much better chance of convincing employees to fight on its behalf than Murbard, though it might be that neither agency would succeed and that employees on both sides would desert rather than fight.

Second, Tannahelp would have the support of all the customers over whom the agencies were fighting. The customers would therefore be likely to attempt to assist their favored agency and hinder the extortionist agency.

Third, Tannahelp would have more reason to fight than the criminal agency. If Tannahelp allows some of its would-be customers to be enslaved to a criminal agency, it establishes a precedent that will likely ultimately lead to its own demise. Murbard, on the other hand, could at any time desist from its extortionist plans and decide to run

---

[25] These names are taken from Friedman (1989, 116–17), apparently based on modifications of the names of prominent libertarian authors.

a legitimate business protecting people from criminals. We have seen earlier the reasons why violent conflict would be very harmful for both agencies. Since both agencies are aware of this and both also know that it is Murbard that can better afford to back down, that is what will most likely occur.[26]

Fourth, the rest of society, including the other protection agencies in the area, would side with Tannahelp. This is partly due to common sense ethical beliefs – almost everyone considers extortion to be unjust – and partly due to self-preservation – if Murbard triumphs against Tannahelp, Murbard will probably next move on to the customers of other agencies. Other agencies are thus likely to assist Tannahelp enough to ensure its victory, even if they allow Tannahelp to do most of the work.

The preceding scenario supposes that Murbard starts out as an extortionist agency and tries to steal customers of other agencies or to force unaffiliated customers to join Murbard. What if Murbard starts out as a legitimate agency, acquiring customers through voluntary agreements, and only later evolves into an extortionist agency that prohibits existing customers from leaving?

In this case, it seems less likely that Tannahelp would fight a war to free Murbard's existing customers. Nevertheless, there are three factors that would limit the damage potential of this type of scenario. First, any such transition is unlikely to occur suddenly and without warning. Because the sorts of people who tend to be attracted to legitimate, service-providing businesses are different from those who are attracted to mafia-like crime rings, the transition from the former to the latter would most likely involve a change of personnel, both at the management level and at the level of average workers. Perhaps a criminally minded person somehow gets into a management position, where he starts making changes, expelling existing personnel and hiring friends and family members with criminal leanings. While this transition was taking place, customers who did not like the direction in which the company was moving would leave the company in favor of competing agencies. The resulting drop in company profits would probably cause the company to stop what it was doing. If not, most of the customers would probably have left by the time the process was complete.

Second, the most credible version of the scenario would have the extortionist agency controlling one or more small geographical areas, such as individual neighborhoods whose homeowners' associations

---

[26] See also David Friedman's (1994) argument that rational egoists in a state of nature avoid conflict through mutual respect for rights.

had originally signed on with the agency voluntarily. If, however, the agency's behavior was sufficiently egregious, customers would prefer to leave the neighborhood rather than continue being subject to extortion. Assuming that there were many other protection agencies in the society serving otherwise similar neighborhoods, it would be extremely difficult for Murbard to keep its victims from leaving.

A similar observation could be made about governments: if one country's government is sufficiently tyrannical, corrupt, or otherwise objectionable, citizens may leave the country. Note, however, that the mechanism of exit is more effective on the neighborhood level than it is on the national level. Individuals who flee their native country are generally forced to leave behind their culture, their jobs, and their family and friends. In contrast, those who merely relocate to a different neighborhood within the same society can generally retain their culture, job, family, and friends. Furthermore, other nations typically impose severe barriers to immigration, whereas other neighborhoods within the same society generally do not. As a result, a national government can be much more abusive before it loses most of its citizens than can an organization limited to a single neighborhood.

Finally, even if Murbard holds onto some of its original customers, it is unlikely to acquire any new customers. As a result, Murbard's customer base will slowly dwindle, while other agencies that better serve their customers expand. This is likely to serve as an example to companies considering making the transition to extortion rings in the future.

10.9.2   Extortion by government

Now consider the analogous problem for governmental systems: why shouldn't the government extort money from people without protecting them? All governments in fact extort money, though the practice is usually termed 'taxation' rather than 'extortion'. Few statists even contemplate ending this practice. How, then, might government be thought superior to anarchy in this area?

Perhaps one might think that government takes less of our money than private protectors would charge or that government provides better service than private protectors would provide. But it is difficult to see why this would be so. Imagine that a private protection agency somehow acquired a monopoly in a large geographical area and began to extract payments from the population by force. Few would contend that, once this state of affairs transpired, prices would drop and service would improve. Surely the opposite would occur. But that is precisely the position of societies with government-based protection.

Perhaps it is the democratic process that is supposed to induce government to control costs and maintain high-quality service: if the government does a poor job, people will vote for different politicians. The question then becomes whether this mechanism is more or less effective than the mechanism of free market competition. One shortcoming of the democratic mechanism is that the choices tend to be very limited. In some democratic societies, elections regularly offer only two choices; for example, the Democrats and the Republicans in the United States. Even systems of proportional representation rarely give voters the range of options present in typical free markets.

But the more important shortcoming is that, in the democratic system, when one chooses one politician over another, one does not thereby get what one chooses; one gets what the majority chooses. Therefore, there is little incentive to expend effort on rational or informed voting (see Section 9.4.3).

10.10 Monopolization

Some believe that a free market anarchist system would evolve into a state, as one protection agency monopolized the industry.

In the present system, nearly all monopolies and monopoly-like conditions are created by government intervention, usually prompted by special-interest groups seeking rents.[27] To endorse the objection from monopolization, therefore, we need some reason to believe that the protection industry would differ from most other industries in some way that would render it particularly prone to monopolization in the absence of state intervention.

10.10.1 The size advantage in combat

Robert Nozick contends that the protection industry would succumb to natural monopoly because the value of a company's service is determined by the relative power of that company in comparison with other companies.[28] Nozick imagines agencies doing battle to resolve disputes between customers. If one agency is more powerful than another, the more powerful agency will triumph. Recognizing that it is better to be protected by the stronger agency, the customers of weaker agencies will migrate to stronger agencies, making the latter even stronger. Since this sort of process tends to amplify initial differences in power, the natural

---

[27] See Brozen 1968; Friedman 1989, chapters 6–7; Green 1973.
[28] Nozick 1974, 15–17.

end result is that one agency holds all the power; that is, a monopoly of the industry. Nozick goes on to explain how this dominant protection agency might develop into a full-fledged government.[29]

If the task for which one hires a protection agency were that of fighting other agencies, then Nozick's analysis would be correct. But one does not hire a protection agency to fight other agencies, nor would agencies provide that service (Section 10.3). One hires a protection agency to prevent criminals from victimizing one or to track down criminals after the fact. In this task, one's protection agency must have the power to apprehend criminals, but it need not have the power to defeat other protection agencies, given that other agencies are not in the business of protecting criminals (Section 10.4).

Nozick considers the possibility of agencies relying on third-party arbitration, which he assumes would occur only if two agencies were of approximately equal strength. *Pace* Nozick, the peaceful arbitration solution does not depend upon the assumption that agencies are of approximately equal strength nor that combat between them results in stalemate. It depends only upon the assumption that physical combat between agencies is *more costly* than arbitration, an assumption that is virtually guaranteed to hold in almost any conflict.

Nozick assumes that arbitration would lead to 'one unified federal judicial system' to which all would be subject.[30] He then proceeds, in his subsequent reasoning about the emergence of a state, to speak of the activities of 'the dominant protective association', leaving the reader perhaps to assume that a unified judicial system is equivalent to a dominant protection agency. He does not explain why the arbitration industry would be controlled by a monopoly nor why a monopoly of arbitration would be equivalent to a monopolistic protection agency.

10.10.2   Determining efficient size of firms

Under some conditions, a monopoly can develop naturally in a free market. If the most efficient size for a firm in a particular industry is so large that there is room for only one such firm in the marketplace, then the conditions are ripe for a natural monopoly.[31]

Large firms often benefit from economies of scale. For example, in the automobile industry, the lowest per-unit production costs are achieved by operating a type of factory that is capable of producing tens

---

[29] Nozick 1974, chapter 5.
[30] Nozick 1974, 16.
[31] See Friedman 1990, 264.

or hundreds of thousands of cars per year. Because there is a large *fixed cost* for building such a factory – a cost that must be borne to produce any cars at all but that does not increase as one builds more cars up to the maximum capacity of the factory – it is most economically efficient to use the factory to full capacity once built. Any firm trying to sell less than many thousands of cars per year is thus at a competitive disadvantage to larger firms – it will be forced to charge higher prices for its cars. Economies of scale, however, operate only up to a certain point – there is no greater efficiency involved in operating ten automobile factories than in operating one.

On the other hand, large firms also suffer from *dis*economies of scale. Factors that tend to make a larger firm less efficient include bureaucratic insularity, alienation on the part of employees, increased costs of communication within the organization, and increased risk of duplication of effort within the organization.[32]

Because economies of scale cease to apply after a certain point and diseconomies of scale begin to apply at a certain point, there is a limit to how large an efficient firm can be (see Figure 10.3). This limit varies with the industry. In the automobile industry, the most efficient firms are very large because of the nature of automobile factories, which cost hundreds of millions of dollars. In industries with lower fixed costs, the most efficient firms will be smaller.

What about the protection industry? The fixed costs for a protection agency are minimal. The business owner must have sufficient funds to hire a few employees and equip them with weapons and tools for enforcement and investigation. No expensive factory, large land area, or large reserve of capital is required. There are no obvious significant economies of scale. It therefore appears that there is no economic pressure towards the formation of large firms in this industry, and the industry will most likely contain a very large number of small and medium-sized firms. Large firms would be at a disadvantage, as they

---

[32] See Canbäck et al. 2006 for theoretical and empirical discussion of economies of scale, diseconomies of scale, and the determination of efficient size for firms in an industry. As Canbäck et al. point out, there often are firms of a variety of sizes in an industry, suggesting that there is a significant range of sizes over which average per-unit costs of production remain approximately constant. See Carson 2008, chapters 5–9, for further discussion of the inefficiency of large firms. Carson (chapter 3) argues that government intervention has facilitated the survival of firms that are much larger than the most efficient size.

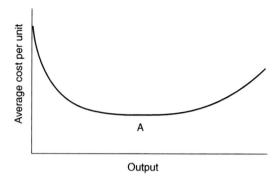

Figure 10.3 Average cost curve for a firm in an industry with both economies and diseconomies of scale. Point A represents the most efficient size (the output level with lowest average cost)

would suffer from the usual diseconomies of scale without reaping significant compensatory economies of scale.

10.10.3 Government monopoly

As in the case of the previous objections, the threat of monopoly poses a more serious objection to government than to anarchy. We need not present arguments to show that a government may develop into a monopoly, because a government, by definition, already is a monopoly. Whatever ills are to be feared from the monopolization of industries, why should we not fear precisely those ills from government? The fact that an organization is labeled a 'government' rather than a 'business' will hardly render its actions beneficent if the actual incentive structure it faces is the same as that of a monopolistic business.

What is the problem with monopolies? Economic theory teaches that a monopoly will restrict output to socially suboptimal levels while raising prices to levels that maximize its own profits but lower the total utility of society. If, for example, a company held a monopoly on shoe production, there would be too few shoes, and they would be too expensive.[33]

That is the problem with a rationally self-interested monopolist. But matters are worse than this, because we cannot even assume that a monopolist will be rational. Competition makes firms act as something

---

[33] Friedman 1990, 248–55, 466–8.

approximating rational profit maximizers by eliminating those who do not behave in that way. In the absence of competitive pressures, a firm has much more leeway. Optimists may observe that an organization with a robust monopoly can survive while magnanimously sacrificing profits for the good of society, if it happens to be so inclined. But it can also survive while clinging to inefficient production methods and resisting innovation; rewarding well-connected but incompetent people; wasting money on half-baked, ideologically motivated plans; ignoring evidence of customer dissatisfaction; and so on. To assume that monopoly privilege will be used only for good would seem to be an exercise in wishful thinking. Almost everyone accepts this in the case of nongovernmental monopolies; nothing essential changes when the label 'government' is applied to a monopolistic protection agency.

10.11 Collusion and cartelization

Apart from monopoly, there is a second anticompetitive practice that may increase the profits of firms in a given industry. This is the practice of forming a cartel, an association of firms that agree among themselves to hold prices at an artificially high level or otherwise cooperate to promote their mutual interests. As Adam Smith warned, 'People of the same trade seldom meet together, even for merriment and diversion, but the conversation ends in a conspiracy against the public, or in some contrivance to raise prices.'[34] Some critics argue that the protection industry would fall under the dominance of a consortium of this kind, leading to results similar to those of an industry monopoly.

10.11.1 The traditional problem for cartels

Most cartels have difficulty enforcing their policies. Suppose that the competitive market price for widgets is $100 per widget. The leaders in the widget industry, however, in a recent backroom meeting, have agreed that $200 is a much nicer price. One small firm, Sally's Widgets, demurs. While the cartel firms charge $200, Sally decides to charge only $150 per widget.[35] What happens?

---

[34] Smith 1979, 145. Smith goes on to argue that one cannot prohibit such meetings without unduly infringing on freedom but that one should not make regulations that actually induce businesspeople to meet together.

[35] In theory, assuming perfect information and identical widgets, Sally could maximize her profit by charging $199 per widget. But in reality, a larger

At these prices, nearly all customers prefer a Sally widget over a cartel widget. Once a struggling small firm, Sally's Widgets suddenly can't expand fast enough for all the new customers approaching it. The cartel, tired of losing business, eventually abandons its scheme and competes with Sally on price but not before Sally's Widgets has enjoyed its greatest-ever boom in sales at the expense of the industry leaders. The incident stands as a lesson to players in other industries, where the smaller firms struggling to get established dream that, one day, the leaders in their industry, too, will devise a harebrained price-fixing scheme.

10.11.2   Cartelization by threat of force

Some industries may differ materially from the famously competitive widget industry. In those industries in which a firm's success depends upon its good relations with other firms, anticompetitive collusion may be more feasible because the large firms in the industry can effectively punish those who reject cartel policies. Tyler Cowen and Daniel Sutter suggest that this may be true in the protection industry because the success of a protection agency depends upon its ability to peacefully resolve disputes with other agencies.[36] Cowen and Sutter imagine the protection agencies in a given area forming a single multilateral agreement detailing the procedures for resolving disputes involving customers of different agencies. Having tackled that problem, the agencies might next agree to fix prices at artificially high levels and to refuse to cooperate with any new firms that may subsequently enter the market.

The agreement on procedures for arbitrating disputes would be self-enforcing, in the sense that firms choosing to violate it would be sabotaging themselves (Section 10.3). But who would enforce the anti-competitive agreements to fix prices and exclude new agencies? Cowen and Sutter imagine that the cartel excludes new entrants to the industry by refusing to accept arbitration with them; cartel members resolve any disputes with nonmembers through violence.[37] The same mechanism is used to enforce the price-fixing agreement: if any member company is found to have set prices too low, the remaining members expel the price-cutting agency and henceforth treat it like any other

---

price difference might be needed to convince consumers to switch brands. A
$50 price difference creates a powerful argument for switching while leaving
Sally a very comfortable profit margin.

[36] Cowen 2007b; Cowen and Sutter 2007.
[37] Cowen and Sutter 2007, 318.

outsider, refusing arbitration in any future disputes with the ostracized agency.[38]

Although this seems to be a possible mechanism for taking over the industry, I do not find it very plausible that the mechanism would be employed. Suppose that agency A, which is a member of the cartel, has a dispute with agency B, which is not a member. A is supposed to be prepared to go to war with B rather than resolve the dispute peacefully. We have already seen that there are powerful motives for protection agencies to avoid violent confrontations, chiefly because (a) violent conflict is extremely costly and (b) most people have antimurder values. Therefore, for A to engage in armed conflict with B, A would have to be willing to sacrifice its own interests for the sake of maintaining the cartel.[39] Since the motivation for joining the cartel to begin with was one of economic self-interest, it is not plausible that A would make such a sacrifice.

Perhaps A might be moved to fight for the cartel by a further threat made by other cartel members: if A resolves its dispute with B peacefully, then *other* cartel members will henceforth go to war against A whenever they have a dispute with A. And what would motivate the other cartel members to do this? Well, the fact that if they don't, other members will go to war against *them*, and so on. This thinking, however, strikes me as a regress of increasing implausibility. If it was implausible that A would go to war against B for not being a member of the cartel, it is still less plausible that another agency, C, would go to war against A for not going to war against B for not being a member of the cartel. If A wishes to avoid armed conflict, its best bet would be to avoid the immediately looming conflict with B, perhaps doing its best to conceal its agreement with B from the other cartel members, and worry about possible future conflicts with other agencies later.

10.11.3 Cartelization through denial of extended protection

George Klosko proposes a different mechanism for cartelization of the protection industry.[40] He imagines a collection of gated communities,

---

[38] Cowen (2007b, 272–3) also suggests that nonmembers might be refused such advantages as extradition of criminals and access to databases for tracking down criminals. Because these are relatively minor sanctions, I focus on the coercive enforcement mechanism.

[39] As Caplan and Stringham (2007, 299–302) put it, the cartel agencies face a prisoner's dilemma with each other, in which it pays each to renege on the agreement to punish outsider agencies.

[40] Klosko 2005, 30–3.

each served by a private security agency. Customers would desire 'extended protection'; that is, one would wish to be protected not only in one's own neighborhood but also when one left the neighborhood to go to work, visit friends, shop, and so on. To satisfy this demand, protection agencies would need to work together, developing common procedures and agreeing to protect each other's customers. But once the agencies had formed a consortium to provide extended protection, the consortium could easily evolve into a cartel designed to raise prices, limit competition, and so on. The cartel would limit competition by denying extended protection to the customers of nonmember agencies. Since almost everyone desires extended protection, nonmember agencies would be effectively excluded from the market. The cartel would enforce its policies internally by threatening to expel members who violate cartel policies.

How might this result be avoided? Let us begin by imagining a competitive, noncartelized protection industry, and consider whether extended protection is likely to be provided without the development of an industry cartel. Suppose, as Klosko does, that security agencies are hired by associations of property owners to protect particular areas (whether gated or not). This may include both residential and commercial areas.

Now suppose that a homeowners' association is deciding whom to hire for neighborhood security. Agency A offers to protect residents, and only residents, from crime occurring in the neighborhood. If one of their security guards witnesses a crime, he will first try somehow to check whether the victim is a resident or a visitor. If the victim appears to be a visitor, the guard will allow the crime to proceed. Agency B, on the other hand, offers to combat all crime in the neighborhood, whoever the victim may be. There are two evident reasons why A's offer will be rejected: first, homeowners are likely to perceive the idea of verifying the identity of a victim before acting to stop a crime as both impractical and immoral; second, most people would like to be able to have visitors to their neighborhood and would like those visitors to be safe while in the neighborhood. Agency B will therefore win the contract.

A similar point applies even more clearly to owners of commercial property. It takes no great altruism for a business owner to recognize that he had better provide a safe environment not just for himself but also for his customers and employees. If people other than the owner are frequently attacked or robbed while on company premises, it may be difficult to run the business. Therefore, businesses will pay protection agencies to protect everyone on their premises.

Thus, extended protection is provided with no need for industry-wide collusion. Each protection agency, acting independently, simply provides what its customers desire. If several agencies decide to form a consortium and announce that henceforth, they will only protect customers of member agencies, every agency in the consortium will quickly lose nearly all of its contracts.[41]

10.12 HOA versus government

I have imagined local homeowners' associations and associations of property owners generally hiring agencies to provide security in particular neighborhoods or business districts. Why would such associations exist in an anarchic society, and why do they not qualify as governments?

The developer of a housing complex creates a homeowners' association, which residents are required to join as a condition of buying a unit in that complex, with the understanding that membership in the association is attached to the property so that all subsequent owners are subject to the same condition. The developer creates this institution because it increases the value of the property; most potential buyers are willing to pay more for a unit in the complex knowing that everyone in the complex will be a member of the association than they would if there were no association or if only some residents were to be members of it.[42] This is because an association to which all belong can provide important goods, such as a set of uniform policies for residents or (particularly in an anarchist society) arrangements to prevent crime within the development. HOAs have spread rapidly in the United States since 1960 and now cover 55 million people.[43] In an anarchist society, they would probably be even more widespread.

Since HOAs can make rules for residents, which may be enforced through the HOA's security agency, it might be thought that an HOA amounts to a kind of government, albeit a very small, localized government, so that the system here envisioned is not anarchy after all.[44]

---

[41] Klosko (2005, 31) also suggests that agencies must join together 'to regularize their standards and procedures'. I have not addressed this in the text because I find it unclear what Klosko has in mind or why he makes this assumption.

[42] Agan and Tabarrok (2005), examining five zip codes in northern Virginia, found that HOAs increased home values by an average of about 5.4 percent, or $14,000.

[43] Agan and Tabarrok 2005, 14.

[44] Agan and Tabarrok (2005) refer to HOAs as 'private governments'.

On the semantic question of whether an HOA qualifies as a small government, it is worth noting that these entities actually exist at present and some even hire their own security guards, yet they are not generally considered to be governments. It might be suggested that they would qualify as 'governments' but for the existence of other bodies with power over them; namely, the entities actually called 'governments'. This semantic question, however, is of no great import, and I am not concerned to dispute the position of one who wishes to describe my proposal as one of very small, decentralized government rather than anarchy. What is important, however, is to see how an HOA differs from the institutions traditionally called 'governments'. It seems to me that there are at least three important differences.

The first is that because of its small size, residents have a much greater chance of influencing the policies of their HOA than they have of influencing the policies of a national, provincial, or even a typical city government. For this reason, members are more likely to vote in a relatively rational and informed way in HOA elections, and HOAs are more likely to be responsive to their members' needs and desires than a national government.

Second, more apropos of the central themes of this book, an HOA has the consent of its members through an actual, literal contract, in contrast to the merely hypothetical or mythological social contract offered by traditional governments. This gives them a moral legitimacy that no traditional government can claim.

Third, competition among housing developments with different HOAs is much more meaningful than competition among traditional governments. Individuals who are dissatisfied with their HOA can sell their interest and relocate to another housing development. The costs of relocation are not trivial, but nor are they enormous. By contrast, the difficulties of relocating to an entirely new country are much greater, if one is even allowed to relocate at all.

As a result of these factors, competitive pressure between governments is close to nonexistent, and governments can therefore afford to be much less responsive to their citizens than a typical HOA is to its members.

10.13   Conclusion

All social systems are imperfect. In every society, people sometimes suffer from crime and injustice. In an anarchist society, this would remain true. The test of anarchism as a political ideal is whether it can *reduce* the quantity of injustice suffered relative to the best alternative system, which I take to be representative democracy. I have argued that a particular sort of anarchist system, one that employs a free market for the provision of security, holds the promise of a safer, more efficient, and more just society.

The radical nature of this proposal usually calls forth strong resistance: it is said that justice should not be for sale; that the agencies will be at constant war with one another; that they will serve criminals instead of their victims; that they will serve only the rich; that they won't be able to protect us as well as the government; that they will turn into extortion agencies; that a monopoly or cartel will evolve to exploit the customers. These objections fairly flood forth when students, professors, and educated laypeople are first introduced to the idea of nonstate protective services. But if we examine the proposal more carefully and at greater length, we see that none of these objections are well founded. Anarchists have well-reasoned accounts, grounded in economic theory and realistic premises about human psychology, of how an anarchist society would avoid each of the disasters that critics fear.

Most of the objections raised against anarchy in fact apply more clearly and forcefully to government. This fact is often overlooked because, when confronted with radical ideas, we tend to look only for objections to the new ideas rather than for objections to the status quo. For example, the most common objection to anarchism, the objection that protection agencies would go to war with one another, overlooks both the extreme costliness of combat and the strong opposition that most people feel to murdering other people. The very real threat of war between governments appears a much more serious concern than conflict between private security agencies.

Similarly, the common objection that the security industry will be monopolized lacks foundation. Once we abandon the notion of security agencies doing battle with one another, economic features of the industry, particularly the minimal fixed costs for a security company, should lead us to predict a great number of small firms rather than a single enormous firm. On the other hand, a governmental system is monopolistic by definition and should therefore be expected to suffer from the usual problems of monopolies.

The central advantages of the free market anarchist system over a governmental system are twofold: first, the anarchist system rests on voluntary cooperation and is therefore more just than a system that relies on coercion. Second, the anarchist system incorporates meaningful competition among providers of security, leading to higher quality and lower costs. As a result of these features of the system, individuals living in a free market anarchy could expect to enjoy greater freedom and greater security at a lower cost than those subject to the traditional system of coercive monopolization of the security industry.

11
Criminal Justice and Dispute Resolution

Libertarian anarchists envision a system in which disputes between individuals are resolved peacefully through the mediation of wise and fair-minded private arbitrators. Is this wishful thinking? In the present chapter, I review several questions and objections concerning this picture of justice in the anarchist society.

11.1 The integrity of arbitrators

What mechanism will keep arbitrators honest and impartial? We can best address this question by first considering in more detail what makes arbitration a viable dispute resolution mechanism to begin with. If two parties have a dispute that they cannot resolve by direct discussion with one another, they may nevertheless be able to agree upon a general *procedure* for resolving their dispute. This depends upon a contingent but robust fact about human beings in a wide range of cultures: that appeal to a neutral third party is widely perceived as a fair and reasonable dispute resolution mechanism.

But how is it that two parties who disagree about some practical matter are able to agree upon a third party to resolve the dispute? Why isn't the first dispute simply replaced with a second dispute about whom to appeal to to resolve the first dispute? Again, this depends upon a contingent but robust fact about human normative perceptions: people tend to agree to a large extent on who constitutes an impartial judge.

But why would both parties to a dispute seek an impartial judge instead of each insisting on a judge biased in his own favor, such as a personal friend or family member? The reason is that they are attempting to reach a peaceful resolution of the original dispute. The fundamental idea behind arbitration as a strategy for reaching such a resolution is that the parties seek something that they can agree upon that might be used to generate a solution to the original dispute. Given that goal, it makes sense for both parties to choose an arbitrator who is generally viewed in their society as fair. They should not each propose an arbitrator obviously biased in their own favor, since that would not be a viable strategy for generating the needed point of agreement. Of course, if the two parties do *not* both desire a peaceful resolution of their dispute, then they may simply fight it out; there is no need to propose a biased or corrupt arbitrator in that case.

Based on this understanding of the logic of arbitration as a solution to conflict, an arbitrator has one critical asset: his reputation for honesty, impartiality, and wisdom. That reputation is the central determinant of the perceived quality of his product, and only if he jealously guards that asset can he expect that contentious parties, frequently unable to agree upon anything else, will be able to agree upon him as the person to resolve their disputes. If an arbitrator acquires a reputation for corruption, bias, or capricious decision making, his business will quickly disintegrate. An arbitration company, therefore, would need to be careful in its choice of arbiters, knowing that a corrupt judge could ruin the business.

In many cases, it may be that no matter how a dispute is resolved, one party or the other will regard the decision as unfair after the fact. The best that an arbitrator can do in such a case is to render a decision that will be perceived as fair by most third party observers. It is the perception of such observers that will determine how well the arbitrator's reputation is maintained and thus how much business he can expect to attract in the future. Admittedly, public perception is an imperfect guide to justice, as the public might misunderstand a case or have incorrect values. Nevertheless, the reputational mechanism provides incentives for arbitrators to uphold justice at least approximately in most cases.

In the present system, by contrast, mechanisms for insuring the integrity of judges are much weaker. Judges' decisions are reviewed only by other judges, with the exception of Supreme Court members, whose decisions are reviewed by no one. If the judicial system acquires a reputation for unfairness, inefficiency, and so on, its members can nevertheless retain their positions without fear of being supplanted by the competition.

11.2   Corporate manipulation

Why won't corporations manipulate the system by requiring employees or customers to sign an agreement to have all disputes settled by an

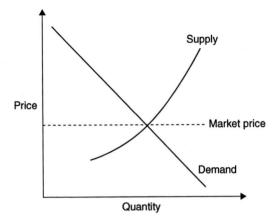

Figure 11.1 A standard price theory diagram shows the competitive market price of a good at the intersection of the supply curve, as determined by marginal costs of production, and the demand curve, as determined by marginal utility of consumption

arbitrator biased in the company's favor, such as an arbitrator in the permanent employ of the corporation itself?

Here is a more fundamental question: why don't businesses make unlimited demands on employees and customers? Why not require customers to give the company all the money they have? Why not require employees to work for free? These arrangements would certainly be more favorable to the company than the sort of arrangements businesses actually offer.

To understand why businesses do not behave in these ways, we should first consider how market prices are determined. For any given business, there is some optimum level at which the business should set its prices to maximize its profit. If it sets prices below that level, the company will lower its total profits due to lower profit per unit. If it sets its prices above that level, the company will lower its total profits due to lower volume of product sold. A precise account of the optimum price level is given in standard price theory, where this price is said to lie at the intersection of supply and demand curves (see Figure 11.1).[1] For our purposes, the important point is simply that market forces determine an optimal price level such that the company does worse for itself if it exceeds that level.

---

[1] See Friedman 1990 for an accessible account of the standard theory.

Now the plan of making unreasonable legal demands is essentially equivalent to a plan to increase the price of one's product. Suppose that Sally's widget business requires all customers to agree that, in case of any dispute arising in connection with the sale of a Sally widget, including complaints regarding product quality or safety, the customer will accept binding arbitration by Sally's nine-year-old daughter, Susan. Sally's Widgets is then in effect adding to the price of Sally's widgets: in addition to the $150 that one must pay for a widget, the customer must also accept the risk of having a dispute with the company resolved by the owner's daughter. Clients might consider this undesirable.[2] They might even take the policy as a signal that the company intends to cheat its customers. For this reason, if $150 was the market price for widgets, then Sally's addition of the unreasonable stipulation in regard to the resolution of disputes with her company will have the effect of placing the real price of her product above the market level and thus lowering Sally's total profit.

What if the market price for widgets is $200 and Sally charges only $150, leaving Sally some leeway to make additional demands on customers? Even in this case, insisting that all disputes should be resolved via Susan is not Sally's best option for taking advantage of that leeway. The reason is that customers are likely to place a greater negative value on Sally's dispute resolution procedure than the positive value that Sally places on it, because customers tend to place negative value on perceived unfairness *in addition* to the potential monetary costs of unfair procedures. Instead, Sally's best (profit-maximizing) option is simply to raise her price by $50.

The same principles apply to employer-employee relationships. There is an optimal wage for an employer to pay such that, if the employer pays more than that, he lowers his total profits due to increased labor costs, but if he pays less, he lowers his total profits due to difficulty in attracting desirable employees. Any provision in an employment contract that employees regard as unfair or simply disadvantageous amounts to an extra cost of accepting a job with this employer or, equivalently, a decline in the rewards of the job. A provision that would naturally be taken as signaling an intention to cheat one's employees would normally lower the attractiveness of any job too much to be worth

---

[2] For a different perspective, see Caplan (2010), who suggests that most customers would be unconcerned by such a clause, since they do not expect ever to sue the company.

inserting. If an employer feels that he is giving too much to employees, it would make more sense for him simply to offer lower wages.

Empirically, businesses in free market economies rarely take unreasonable positions in disputes with customers. The following is not an uncommon sort of consumer experience: I buy a product from the local Target, take it home, cut off the packaging, and then decide that I don't like it. I go back to the store and ask for my money back. 'Is there anything wrong with it?' the cashier asks. 'Nope', I say, 'I just decided I don't like it. So take it back.' My position in this dispute, if one can call it that, is utterly capricious. I voluntarily bought the product, I know that they can't resell it after I have opened it, and I have no real complaint about the product. The product is not defective, nor was it misrepresented either by the manufacturer or by the store. I have no argument for why they should take it back. Yet in my experience, the company has never refused a return.

This evidence about the behavior of businesses is of course anecdotal, and certainly others could relate anecdotes of unsatisfactory experiences. Nevertheless, I do not think it an unfair illustration of the overall tendency of the market: consumers are much more likely to take unreasonable positions – and prevail – than the businesses they patronize.

11.3 Refusing arbitration

We have discussed the reasons for accepting arbitration as a mechanism of dispute resolution. But what if, in a particular case, you have strong reason to believe that any reputable arbitrator will find against you? This could be true for any of a number of reasons, including that you have in fact violated someone else's rights and are attempting to get away with it; that you are out of step with the values of the majority of your society, so that what you consider acceptable behavior a typical arbitrator will not; or that there is a large amount of misleading evidence that indicates that you are guilty of some crime of which you are in fact innocent. In any of these cases, it may seem that you would be best advised to reject arbitration.

But even in these cases, you will probably be forced to accept arbitration. If you reject the option of having your dispute arbitrated, your security agency will probably draw the reasonable inference that you are in the wrong according to prevailing norms, since the most likely explanation for your rejection of arbitration is that you expect any reputable arbitrator to decide against you. For the same reasons that protection agencies will not defend criminals (Section 10.4), they will not defend people who reject arbitration as a means of dispute resolution. Security agencies will anticipate this eventuality, writing provisions into their contracts specifying the procedures that customers must accept for resolving disputes and absolving the company of the responsibility to protect clients who violate these procedures.

In some cases, this system would generate unjust or ethically objectionable results, as in the case where strong evidence points to the guilt of someone who is in fact innocent, or where the values of the majority of society are wrong. But the anarchist system nevertheless does as well as could reasonably be asked. In any functioning justice system, whether government-based or market-based, if powerful but misleading evidence points to someone's guilt, then that person will be treated as guilty. Only the unattainable standard of absolutely conclusive proof of guilt could eliminate the possibility of misleading evidence leading to punishment of the innocent.

Likewise, every social system generates unethical outcomes if the people who make decisions in that system have incorrect ethical beliefs and values. Under anarchy, unethical outcomes result if most members of society have incorrect values, which will be reflected in the decisions of arbitrators seeking to cultivate a good reputation with the public. In a government-based system, unethical outcomes result if legislators, judges, or other public officials have incorrect values. This is not less likely to be true than that the majority of society's members have incorrect values.

11.4   Why obey arbitrators?

In the event that you have a dispute with another member of an anarchist society, why should you not agree to try arbitration to resolve the dispute, hoping that the arbitrator will side with you, and then simply ignore the arbitrator's decision if it goes against you?

This sort of behavior, if anything, would be even less tolerated by the rest of society than a refusal to accept arbitration to begin with. For the same reasons that security agencies would not agree to defend criminals, you could expect your security agency to leave you to fend for yourself if you violated an arbitration decision.

Beyond that, arbitration companies could maintain lists of individuals who had violated an arbitration agreement. There might be criminal-record-reporting agencies, functioning analogously to credit-reporting agencies, providing reports of past criminal activity for a nominal fee. Given knowledge of your past violation of an arbitration agreement, it would not be rational for others in the future to enter into business relationships in which you might attempt to cheat them and then refuse to pay compensation. It might therefore become very difficult to find a job, get a credit card, take a bank loan, rent an apartment, and so on.

11.5 The source of law

In the status quo, the decisions of judges and juries are based largely on laws written by legislators or bureaucrats working for regulatory agencies. Since the anarcho-capitalist society contains neither legislators nor regulators, on what basis could arbitrators make their decisions?

There would be two sources of law in the anarchic society. First, property owners or local associations of property owners could specify the body of law to govern interactions occurring on their property. Provided that all who entered the property were given fair notice of the legal code in effect there, arbitrators would most likely honor the owner's choice of law. Legal scholars might develop suggested standardized legal codes, with business owners, landlords, or homeowners' associations choosing which of several widely used legal codes should hold sway on their land. Consumers with strong objections to a particular legal code would avoid patronizing businesses that adopted that code. In choosing a home, individuals would weigh the advantages of the legal code subscribed to by the local homeowners' association.

The other major source of law would be the arbitrators themselves. When the solution to a particular dispute was not determined by any law of the kind described in the foregoing paragraph, the judge would look to similar cases for guidance, attempting to apply the same principles in the present case that had generally been used to decide cases of this kind in the past. If the case before him had novel features, the judge would exercise his own judgment to devise a resolution that seemed fair and in keeping with the generally accepted values of his society. He would then write an explanation for his decision, which would be added to the body of precedent for other judges to consult in future cases. It makes sense for arbitrators to follow this tradition, since it usually results in decisions that most observers regard as fair, and it preserves the sort of consistency that most observers value in a legal system.

This bottom-up approach to generating law has three key advantages over the top-down approach of law created by a legislature. First, judge-made law is more closely tied to the problems that ordinary people encounter and their actual circumstances, because it is made by individuals with regular experience in resolving interpersonal disputes – the problems that give rise to the need for law in the first place – and it is made only in the context of deciding such disputes. Second, judge-made law is more flexible than statutory law. No rule of conduct that human beings devise can foresee all possible future contingencies. In a common-law system, when a court encounters a case of a kind not previously considered, it can decide that case in the manner that seems most fair rather than being forced by earlier oversights to render unjust rulings. Third, the common-law system makes far smaller cognitive demands on the individual lawmaker. A legislature faces the nearly impossible task of anticipating every issue that might occur in every area of human conduct and writing rules valid for all circumstances. A judge in a common-law system faces at any given time only the task of understanding the case now before him and deciding how *that case* should be resolved; at no time need a judge or anyone else attempt to anticipate every possible type of problem.

We know that this is a viable way of developing an extremely sophisticated and subtle system of law, because this is in actual fact the source of the common law that now holds sway (alongside statutory and regulatory law) in Great Britain and several other countries influenced by Great Britain, such as the United States, Canada, Australia, and New Zealand. In these countries, most of contract law and tort law is judge-made common law. Most of the criminal law was also common law prior to the twentieth century. In the anarchist society, given the absence of statutory and regulatory law, common law would play an even greater role than it does in these countries today.[3]

11.6   Punishment and restitution

Existing government-based criminal justice systems rely on imprisonment of criminals as a response to crime. It is thought that society as a whole benefits from this practice because it keeps criminals off the streets for a time and deters others from entering a life of crime. The victims of a particular crime, however, generally receive nothing in the way of compensation, and the rest of society is forced to pay for criminals' upkeep during their terms of imprisonment.

---

[3] See Barnett 1998 for a more thorough account of nongovernmental legal systems.

The anarcho-capitalist justice system would most likely focus on restitution rather than punishment. That is, criminals would be forced to pay compensation to their victims. This system would be preferred over punishment-based systems because it is better for the crime victims and it does not require anyone to pay for the criminals' upkeep. The required compensation would most likely include compensation for the inconvenience and lost time suffered by the victim in attempting to secure justice, as well as reasonable costs incurred by the victim's protection agency in identifying, apprehending, and prosecuting the criminal. As a result, a thief, for example, would have to pay back significantly more than the value of what he stole. This would provide a deterrent to crime.

What if the victim of a crime was dead (whether killed by the criminal or killed by other causes after the crime) and thus unable to collect compensation? In this case, the victim's family or friends might collect the owed compensation. Alternately, individuals might, in advance, authorize their protection agencies to collect compensation on their behalf in the event that they were unable to receive compensation for a crime. The compensation that a crime victim is owed can be thought of as property of the victim, which he therefore has the right to give, sell, or bequeath to someone else. Granting one's protection agency the right to collect compensation in the event that one is murdered might serve to deter potential murderers.

11.7 Uncompensable crimes

What would happen if a criminal lacked the funds to compensate his victims? One possibility is that the criminal would be remanded to a private prison where he would be required to work off his debt.

But what if the criminal could not work off his debt? Imagine, say, a criminal con artist who has defrauded his victims of $20 million, almost all of which has been spent. The criminal has no realistic hope of ever paying his victims back. What would be done with this criminal? One possibility is that the criminal might be housed indefinitely in a prison-labor facility, to pay as much of his debt as possible. Or the victims might settle for some partial repayment, such as the criminal could realistically make within his lifetime. It would be up to the arbitrator in the case, in consultation with the victims, to decide upon the most appropriate remedy. In any case, the information as to what the criminal had done would most likely be made publicly available and possibly sent to criminal-record-reporting agencies so that future landlords, employers, and so on could be on guard.

In some cases, however, a criminal's behavior is so heinous that not only is it impossible for him to compensate his victims but the criminal can never be safely released. Imagine, for example, that a protection agency has taken Ted Bundy into custody. Bundy protests his innocence, but the arbitration company finds him responsible for at least thirty murders. Bundy will never compensate his victims, and if he is ever released, he will kill again. There would seem to be two options: he can be imprisoned indefinitely (probably in a forced-labor facility), or he can be executed. Again, it would be up to the arbitrator in the case to determine the best course of action. As in the case of the real Ted Bundy, execution appears a likely possibility.

11.8   Excess restitution

The victim of a crime is justly entitled to collect full compensation for the crime; that is, sufficient compensation to return him to the welfare level he would have enjoyed if the crime had not occurred. But what if a particular court regularly awarded excess compensation – say, twice what the victim was justly entitled to and twice what other courts generally awarded for a given crime? Wouldn't the excess compensation court be favored by victims? And since almost everyone considers himself more likely to become a crime victim than to become a criminal, almost everyone would want any future disputes of theirs to be resolved by such a court. Taking account of this, protection agencies would agree to use courts that provide excess compensation. Soon, almost all criminal cases would be tried in courts of this kind. Criminals could protest at the injustice, but their voices would be little heeded, since protection agencies and arbitration firms would be more keen to satisfy the overwhelming majority of law-abiding customers than to satisfy the criminals.

What is problematic about this result? The obvious problem is that this situation is an injustice, albeit one over which we may find it difficult to rouse much indignation – it is an injustice to the criminals. But Paul Birch argues that the problem would go deeper than this, undermining the entire anarcho-capitalist system.[4] Once the practice of awarding excess compensation started, firms would compete to offer higher and higher awards to victims, perhaps ten times, twenty times,

---

[4] Birch 1998.

or even fifty times the amount to which the crime victim was justly entitled. These excessive awards would create powerful deterrents to crime, resulting in a dramatic drop in the crime rate. While this may sound like a happy result, it would put increasing financial pressure on arbitration firms. As the crime rate dropped, arbitration firms would continue to raise their compensation awards in the effort to collect a larger share of the dwindling market. This would only cause the market to shrink further. Eventually, either all firms would go out of business, in which case society would devolve into a state of chaos, or the last firm able to hold out would acquire a monopoly on the industry, whereupon it would evolve into a state.

There are several reasons why the foregoing scenario is unlikely to transpire:

i) The argument unrealistically assumes that actual and potential crime victims favor unlimited compensation. This assumption may be driven by a conception of human beings as *homo economicus*, pure profit maximizers: since higher compensation equals higher profit, crime victims will favor unlimited increases in compensation. Normal human beings, however, do not see criminal victimization as an opportunity to get rich; that sort of thinking is generally reserved for scam artists. Most normal people wish to avoid being crime victims, if possible, and to secure justice in the event that they are victimized.

A more plausible concern is that crime victims will be motivated by vengefulness, rather than profit seeking, to push for excessive sanctions on their malefactors. Surprisingly, this concern is undermined by empirical evidence: surveys of attitudes toward criminal sentencing have found that crime victims in fact harbor attitudes no more punitive than those of the average member of the population.[5]

ii) Birch imagines arbitration companies advertising that they award excessive compensation – announcing, for example, that they award each victim compensation equal to ten times the loss the victim has suffered. This is very close to a court's explicitly announcing that it is unjust. It is difficult to imagine this occurring. For reasons discussed earlier, arbitration companies would carefully select their judges and guard their reputations for fairness, impartiality, and

---

[5] Walker and Hough 1988, 10; Hough and Moxon 1988, 137, 143–6.

wisdom. The sort of people who would wind up as judges would be unlikely to explicitly and intentionally promote injustice for the sake of profit maximization.

A more realistic concern is that arbitration companies would be *biased* in favor of victims rather than explicitly embracing injustice. They would almost certainly claim to be administering justice, but their perceptions of what justice demands might be slanted in favor of victims; for instance, they might tend to perceive most crimes as more damaging than they really are. It is plausible that arbitration companies could hire judges with such slanted perceptions without unduly tainting their reputation for integrity. I therefore think it plausible that in an anarcho-capitalist society, criminals would often suffer somewhat more than they deserved.

This is a possible problem with the system, but it is not a terrible problem. Moreover, it is plausible that overpunishment occurs also in governmental systems, and it is not obvious that governmental systems deliver more just punishments than those that would emerge from an anarcho-capitalist system.

iii) Apart from their concern for the rights of criminals, which admittedly is limited, there is another reason for ordinary individuals to oppose absurdly excessive compensation for crimes: in any realistic criminal justice system, innocent people are sometimes convicted. Most people find this prospect troubling even in the abstract and perhaps more so when they reflect that they themselves or someone they are close to may one day be among the wrongly convicted. The problem cannot be eliminated without entirely dispensing with the criminal justice system; however, most people would find the problem much less troubling if the penalties for crimes were reasonable than if they were absurdly excessive. This would lead most people in the anarchist system, just as in the present system, to support some degree of restraint on the part of judges in the process of assigning compensation awards.

iv) Excessive compensation awards tend to be more difficult or expensive to collect. If, for example, the compensation for the theft of a video-game cartridge was $100,000, this might prove difficult to enforce. If a shoplifter could expect to be imprisoned for life in a compulsory labor facility if caught, then shoplifters might be willing to kill to escape or to fight to the death rather than surrendering. Knowing this, security agencies would have a reason to favor reasonable compensation awards.

v) A criminal who is wronged by a clearly excessive compensation award would seem to have a valid complaint against the court that made the unjust award. There is no obvious reason why he could not file a lawsuit against that court in a different court. If all the courts had the same excessive standards for compensation, then the criminal's suit would fail. But if the courts generally started out with approximately just standards and one court decided to seek a larger market share by offering excessive compensation awards, then that court would suffer for its indiscretion as other courts found its judgments unjust and awarded compensation to those who had been wronged by the court. Thus, if the system starts out in a generally just position, it will be stable.

vi) Even extreme increases in the penalties for crime would not eliminate all crime. This is because some criminals, unfortunately, are highly resistant to deterrence. They recklessly ignore the future or blithely assume that they won't get caught.[6] Thus, a market for private courts would continue to exist even in a regime of absurdly high compensation awards.

vii) Even if excessive compensation awards resulted in a dramatic drop in crime rates, this would not cause all or nearly all arbitration firms to go bankrupt. However much crime might drop, honest disputes among ordinary people would continue to arise, and they would still need to be adjudicated by arbitration firms. If crime suffered a precipitous drop, arbitration companies would experience a decline in revenues and would need to scale back operations to the point that the market would support. But this would not lead all of them to go bankrupt, nor would it cause the industry to be monopolized.

Consider an analogy. As automobiles became more practical in the early twentieth century, the demand for horses suffered a drastic drop. But the entire industry did not collapse, nor was it monopolized – there remains more than one horse breeder in the world today. The industry simply shrank to the size that could be supported by the new levels of demand. Likewise, if we should be so blessed as to find ourselves worrying about unduly low crime levels, the arbitration industry will shrink so that it includes only the number of courts needed to satisfy however much demand remains.

---

[6] Banfield 1977.

11.9   The quality of law and justice under a central authority

To better assess the merits of a nongovernmental justice system, we must first consider some of the flaws of the present system.

11.9.1   Wrongful convictions

One disturbing aspect of the present system is the rate at which the innocent are punished. Michigan law professor Samuel Gross studied cases in which convicts were exonerated in the United States between 1989 and 2003.[7] He found 340 such cases, including 205 murder cases, 121 rape cases, and 14 cases involving other crimes. Prosecutors and police often refuse to accept that they arrested and prosecuted an innocent person, even after proof of the person's innocence has been uncovered.[8] On average, these defendants suffered eleven years of wrongful imprisonment before finally being officially exonerated.

Why were murder and rape so overrepresented among the crimes of which defendants were exonerated? The main reason for the dramatic overrepresentation of rape cases lies in the development of DNA testing in the late 1980s and thereafter, which led to the reexamination of a number of rape cases in which semen samples had fortunately been preserved. Application of the new techniques revealed that many convictions prior to the advent of reliable DNA testing were erroneous. The main reason for the overrepresentation of murder cases seems to lie in the much greater scrutiny that such cases receive as compared to less serious cases, especially when the death penalty is involved.[9]

Omitted from Gross's statistics are cases of mass exonerations due to the exposure of large-scale police corruption. One such case involved the CRASH ('Community Resources against Street Hoodlums') program of the Los Angeles Police Department. In 1999, Officer Rafael Perez revealed that he and other officers in the program had routinely lied in arrest reports, shot unarmed suspects and innocent bystanders, planted guns on suspects after shooting them, fabricated evidence, and framed innocent defendants. In the wake of these

---

[7] Gross et al. 2005.

[8] Gross et al. 2005, 525–6.

[9] Gross et al. 2005, 531–2, 535–6. Gross et al. (532–3) point out that there may also be more pressure to convict someone in capital cases, leading to more mistakes. However, there may also be greater care exerted by defense attorneys, judges, and juries in cases where extremely severe punishments are at issue.

revelations, over 100 defendants had their convictions vacated in 1999 and 2000.[10]

Why were the defendants in Gross's sample wrongly convicted? Most cases involved witness misidentification. Many involved perjury by police, forensic scientists testifying for the government, the real criminal, jailhouse snitches, or others who stood to gain by providing false testimony. In 15 percent of the cases, the defendants, under the stress of high-pressure police interrogations, actually confessed to crimes they had not committed. Most of those 15 percent were under the age of 18, mentally retarded, or mentally ill.

Since the defendants in these cases were ultimately exonerated, may we rest easy that the system works and that justice is served? There are two reasons for rejecting such complacency: first, there are the eleven years that these defendants, on average, were forced to spend in what may be the worst conditions that any significant segment of society must live under. Second, and more importantly, there are the implications for the number of people who continue to be unjustly imprisoned.

There are no reliable estimates of the frequency of wrongful convictions, due to the inherent elusiveness of such cases. Though it is reasonably clear that all or nearly all of Gross's 340 cases were indeed wrongful convictions, we have no way of knowing how many additional erroneous convictions went undiscovered during the same time period. The 74 death row inmates who were exonerated constituted about 2 percent of the death row population.[11] This suggests that if we applied the same level of scrutiny to all cases that we apply to death penalty cases, we might find a 2 percent false positive rate in these other cases as well.

But we have no idea how many death penalty cases there were in which erroneous convictions went undiscovered. The wrongful convictions in Gross' sample were due mainly to witness error, perjury, and false confessions. But when a witness misidentifies a suspect, a witness lies on the stand, or the police extort a false confession, in how many of such cases can we assume that proof of the defendant's innocence, elusive at the time of trial, will later luckily appear and rescue him from prison? Proof of innocence is not generally very easy to come by, and the authorities, having closed the case, will not be looking for any such evidence. The defendant himself will have difficulty uncovering such

---

[10] Gross et al. 2005, 533–4.
[11] Gross et al. 2005, 532, n. 21.

evidence from his position in prison. For these reasons, it would seem overly optimistic to assume that in the majority of wrongful convictions (even in death penalty cases), proof of innocence is later discovered. It therefore seems probable that the actual false conviction rate is much greater than the 2 percent exoneration rate that Gross found among death penalty cases.

Could anything be done to improve the system, or are these mistaken convictions simply the price of criminal justice? Several measures have been suggested to improve the reliability of the system: reducing the use of high-pressure interrogation techniques, particularly for underage or mentally disabled suspects; having witnesses questioned by officers who do not know the details of the investigation and therefore cannot influence the witnesses; showing witnesses one suspect at a time rather than a group of suspects all at once; and instructing juries on the limitations of eyewitness evidence. Despite studies indicating that these measures would reduce the risk of wrongful convictions, American police and courts have generally not adopted them.[12]

11.9.2   Oversupply of law

Under a legal system based on a central authority with legislative powers, a great deal more law is provided than under a pure common-law system. Some see that as an advantage – perhaps we need a strong network of regulations to protect us against the failures of laissez-faire capitalism. Nevertheless, it is worth considering whether a governmental system might provide too much law.

As an exercise, try to imagine an ideal legal system. Before reading on, try to estimate how many pages worth of laws that system would contain. There are many difficulties with making such an estimate; nevertheless, attempting at least a vague, order-of-magnitude estimate before finding out how much law actually exists may help to forestall the tendency to rationalize the status quo.

Most citizens in modern states, whether they would describe themselves as supporting a strong regulatory regime or not, have little idea of how much regulation they actually have. In the United States, the rules promulgated by regulatory agencies of the national government are recorded in the Code of Federal Regulations (this does not include statutes passed directly by Congress, nor does it include state or local laws). Over the last half century, the quantity of these regulations has

---

[12] Duke 2006.

ballooned from about 23,000 pages to about 150,000 pages (see table below).

Year	Length of CFR (pages)[13]
1960	22,877
1970	54,834
1980	102,195
1998	134,723
2010	152,456

These statistics cannot capture qualitative information about the content of these regulations, and of course there is no prospect of reviewing any significant fraction of these regulations here (or anywhere). Nevertheless, I suggest that these numbers might prompt even the strongest ideological supporter of regulation to consider whether dedicated lawmaking bodies might have a tendency to provide a greater than optimal quantity of regulation. The reader unfamiliar with regulation is invited to peruse the CFR at random to obtain a qualitative sense of the regulatory regime. One may, for example, chance upon a paragraph describing the spacing of spark plug gaps, another prescribing the use of the expression 'all day protection' in antiperspirant labels, another describing the signing of documents related to excise taxes on structured settlement factoring transactions, and so on.[14]

What is objectionable about such overprovision of law? The first objection is that it represents an excessive reliance on coercion. Each of these regulations is a command backed up by a threat of force issued by the state against its citizens. While some of these threats may be justified, those that are not constitute a violation of the rights of all those who are thereby coerced.

Second, a surplus of laws can have large economic costs. Ronald Coase, Nobel laureate and former editor of the *Journal of Law and Economics*, reports that his journal published a series of empirical studies of the

---

[13] Figures for 1970 and 1998 are from Longley n.d. Figures for 1960 and 1980 are from Crews 2011, 15. The figure for 2010 is computed from the edition of the CFR available from the Government Printing Office, http://www.gpo.gov/fdsys/; I have omitted the 'Finding Aids' at the end of each volume from the total page count for 2010.

[14] 40 CFR, Appendix I to subpart V of part 85 (H)(1)(b); 21 CFR 350.50(b)(3); 26 CFR 157.6061.

effects of a wide variety of regulations, in which it turned out that every regulation studied had overall negative effects on society.[15] The Small Business Administration of the U.S. government has estimated the annual cost of federal regulations to the U.S. economy at $1.75 trillion, a burden that they find falls disproportionately on small businesses.[16]

Third, an excessive quantity of law, as well as an excessively complex and technical body of law, renders it unreasonable to demand that citizens know, understand, and follow all laws. To threaten to punish citizens for violation of rules that, in the light of the extreme cognitive burdens, they could not reasonably be expected to know or understand, is a form of injustice. These cognitive burdens at some point defeat the primary purpose of establishing written laws to begin with – namely, that the law should be accessible to all who are expected to follow it.

One solution to the last problem is for citizens to hire experts to advise them in any area in which the law is complex and difficult to follow. This, however, leads us to the next problem with the currently accepted system of justice.

11.9.3 The price of justice

For most citizens of modern states, the costs of government justice in both time and money are prohibitive. The typical civil dispute requires anywhere from several months to a few years to resolve through governmental channels.[17] In 2009, the average American law firm billed $284 per hour, with a typical divorce costing between $15,000 and $30,000. To the average American, with an annual income of $39,000, any use of the government's justice system represents an overwhelming financial burden.[18]

Why are legal services so expensive? One reason is the oversupply of law mentioned above. The complexity, technicality, and sheer length of the laws and legal procedures forces individuals to pay experts to handle any legal procedure, and it forces those experts to expend a great deal of labor on each case. Another reason can be found in the restrictions on the supply of legal services, which by law may only be purchased from government-approved sources (lawyers who have been

---

[15] Hazlett 1997, 43.

[16] Crain and Crain 2010.

[17] In the United States, delays vary from about six months to about three years, with an average of eleven months (Dakolias 1999, 18).

[18] On average lawyer fees, see California Attorney's Fees 2011, quoting a survey by Incisive Legal Intelligence. On the price of divorce, see Hoffman 2006. On average incomes, see U.S. Census Bureau 2011b, 443, table 678.

admitted to the bar, generally after a lengthy and very expensive law school education).[19]

These costs are troubling for at least three salient reasons. First, the high cost of legal services means that only the wealthy can afford justice. Middle- and low-income individuals cannot afford to seek justice or must take justice into their own hands when they believe they have been wronged. In criminal cases, low-income defendants may receive inadequate legal representation due to heavy case loads on public defenders.

Second, even defendants who win their cases, whether the cases be civil or criminal, may be financially ruined. This acts as a kind of unjust punishment imposed on all defendants, whether they are guilty of wrongdoing or not.

Third, large businesses may be able to afford the legal fees necessary to ensure compliance with complex bureaucratic regulations, while the same costs may prove prohibitive for small businesses. As a result, the present legal regime tends to promote concentration of industries in the hands of large corporations, even if those corporations are in themselves less efficient than smaller firms.

11.9.4 The failure of imprisonment

Today's governments rely on imprisonment as a response to serious crimes. Imprisonment serves two main functions: first, it protects society from convicted criminals for a limited time by separating the criminals from the rest of society. Second, it punishes the criminals by forcing them to live in highly undesirable conditions. The suffering on the part of the criminals may be valued intrinsically as a form of retributive justice or it may be valued instrumentally as a means of deterring future criminal behavior.

Existing jails and prisons, however, suffer from a number of very serious problems. In the United States, these facilities are regularly extremely overcrowded, and inmates live in danger of gang violence, rape by other prisoners, beatings by guards and other prisoners, and other forms of abuse. The rate of such violence and abuse is unknown, but anecdotal reports are numerous.[20] In recent years, the use of solitary confinement has become increasingly common, a practice that leads

---

[19] The price of law school often exceeds $100,000. Only seven U.S. states allow individuals to take the bar exam without attending law school (Macdonald 2003).

[20] Commission on Safety and Abuse in America's Prisons 2006, 11–12, 24. A U.S. Department of Justice survey found that 4.4 percent of prison inmates and

to mental deterioration on the part of the prisoner and higher rates of recidivism once the convict is released.[21]

Under these conditions, incarceration could hardly be expected to rehabilitate criminals. Accordingly, two-thirds of criminals are rearrested within three years of being released from prison.[22] This statistic must be assumed to underestimate the true rate of recidivism, given the low rate at which law enforcement solves crimes (Section 10.7); thus, the great majority of criminals return to a life of crime shortly after their release. Some observers have argued that incarceration not only fails to rehabilitate criminals but actually renders them more dangerous when released than they were when they entered. This may be true, for example, because inmates make new criminal contacts and learn new criminal skills and ideas from other inmates while in prison, because they absorb antisocial values from the other inmates, and because inmates become more angry and resentful as a result of the abuse they suffer while in prison. Some have gone so far as to suggest that incarceration may cause more crime than it prevents.[23]

These problems are not inevitable in a criminal justice system; critics have offered numerous potential reforms that would seem likely to significantly reduce these problems. Some rehabilitation programs have been found to reduce recidivism rates by up to 30 percent. Policymakers simply have not chosen to adopt these reforms.[24]

11.9.5   Reform or anarchy?

The problems listed in the preceding subsections are only the most prominent of those afflicting the present government-based system of justice. A sanguine observer, however, while acknowledging the seriousness of the problems, might take them to show merely that the justice system ought to be substantially reformed while still remaining in the hands of government.

Indeed, there are a number of measures that would greatly mitigate the problems listed above, and we cannot rule out the possibility that government officials will one day begin a serious reform of the

---

3.1 percent of jail inmates suffered some form of sexual abuse in the preceding year (Beck et al. 2010); however, such incidents may be underreported.

[21] Commission on Safety and Abuse in America's Prisons 2006, 14–15.

[22] Commission on Safety and Abuse in America's Prisons 2006, 106.

[23] Pritikin 2008.

[24] Pritikin 2008, 1092; Commission on Safety and Abuse in America's Prisons 2006, 12, 28, 108.

prison and court systems. Nevertheless, it is no mere accident that problems of the sort we have been discussing are found to persist in government-based justice systems. Coercive monopolies have a systematic tendency to foster a variety of problems, and they tend to be slow to recognize and address their own shortcomings.

The reasons are familiar. Because government collects its revenues in the form of taxes which citizens have no choice but to pay, government programs can survive financially even with extreme levels of consumer dissatisfaction. More importantly, because government is monopolistic, citizens have nowhere else to turn if they find its services inefficient, of low quality, or abusive. Most of the problems with America's justice system are obvious and have been well known for a very long time. National and state governments have done little to address these problems, not because the problems are difficult or impossible to address, but because the government suffers no negative consequences as a result of its failure to address them.

Consider the problem of wrongful convictions. In a competitive system, a local homeowner's association could choose from among many protection agencies, arbitration firms, and bodies of law to apply to its neighborhood and could alter its choice if and when it became dissatisfied with the security and justice arrangements. Furthermore, residents dissatisfied with their HOA's decisions could relocate at relatively little cost. Since no one wants to be wrongly convicted, a protection agency that used unreliable methods of investigation or an arbitration firm that used unreliable methods of assessing guilt or innocence would have to worry about being supplanted by competitors who offered services with less risk of wrongful convictions. Similar points apply to the problem of oversupply of law and excessive costs of legal services.

What about the problems associated with incarceration of criminals? These would be greatly reduced by a justice system that focused on restitution rather than punishment. In such a system, the hundreds of thousands of people presently incarcerated for victimless crimes, chiefly drug-related offenses, would be free. Only individuals who had harmed another person and were otherwise unwilling or unable to pay the required compensation to the victim would be held captive in prison-labor facilities. These facilities' focus on productive work would diminish the risk of in-prison violence as well as recidivism.

It is theoretically possible for a government to reform itself – to eliminate all victimless crime statutes, shift its focus from punishment to restitution, and so on. But when we look around and see that no government has in fact done so and when we notice that this kind of unresponsiveness to problems has a systemic explanation rooted in the basic incentive structure of government, conversion to an alternative system begins to seem like a more rational and less utopian solution than that of reforming the present system. There will always be room for improvement in any justice system. In governmental systems, reform will tend to be slow and difficult to implement. By contrast, businesses in a competitive industry tend to move quickly to improve their products or reduce their costs when the opportunity presents itself.

11.10   Conclusion

There are two main systems by which a society may provide for the resolution of disputes and the remedying of rights violations. The first is the coercive, monopolistic system, in which a single organization assumes exclusive authority for making laws, resolving disputes, and punishing criminals. Large and well-known problems tend to occur in systems of this kind, including frequent erroneous convictions, excessive and excessively complex legal restrictions, high monetary costs, long delays, overcrowded prisons, abuse of prisoners, and high rates of recidivism. Governments on the whole have done little to address these problems, despite the identification by social scientists and other experts of numerous steps that could be taken to greatly improve the system. This neglectfulness on the part of government can be traced to the defining characteristics of this approach to justice; namely, its coercive and monopolistic character. Because the governmental system is funded through compulsory taxation, courts, prisons, and other elements of the justice system can continue to collect as much revenue as the government wishes to allocate, regardless of consumer satisfaction. Because the government holds an effective monopoly on the provision of justice, these organizations need not fear replacement by competitors, regardless of their performance.

The alternative is a market-based system of justice, in which arbitration companies compete with one another in the resolution of disputes. When one individual violated the rights of another, an arbitrator would decide upon the compensation to be paid by the criminal to the victim. In cases in which a criminal had no other means of making payment, the criminal would be housed in a private prison, where he would be required to work off his debt. Individual property owners or associations of property owners, such as homeowners' associations, would choose the body of law to apply to interactions occurring on their property. Any issues not resolved by such laws would be dealt with through a form of law devised by the arbitrators, similar to the British common law in the actual world.

To attract customers, arbitrators in the free market justice system would seek to maintain a reputation for fairness, consistency, impartiality, and wisdom. Security companies would most likely require their customers to resolve any disputes through reputable third-party arbitrators and would refuse to defend customers who either rejected arbitration or violated the arbitrator's decision after submitting a dispute to arbitration.

In this system, arbitrators might evince a bias in favor of crime victims and against criminals, so that criminals might be forced to pay somewhat higher amounts in compensation for their crimes than justice truly demanded. However, it is far from clear that this problem would be more severe than the overpunishment that occurs in government-based systems, which focus on incarceration of criminals in oppressive and dangerous conditions. The problem of excess compensation awards would likely be a relatively modest and tolerable problem in comparison with the problems of the status quo.

12
War and Societal Defense

12.1 The problem of societal defense

Ideally, all human beings would live without nation-states or national armies, so that there would be no need for national defense. But this happy state of affairs could not be expected to come about all at once; we must assume a transitional period in which an anarchic society coexists with state-dominated societies. Could the two kinds of society coexist, or would the one inevitably overtake the other?

A natural assumption is that if a country has a more powerful military than its neighbors or than all of its potential enemies, then the country will be secure, whereas if it has a much weaker military or no military at all, then it will be insecure. From this standpoint, an anarchist society seems to face an obvious problem. Modern military forces are both extremely powerful and extremely expensive. A single aircraft carrier, for example, costs about $4.5 billion up front, plus $240 million per year for maintenance.[1] In 2010, the United States spent nearly $700 billion on the military. For comparison, the most profitable U.S. company in that year, Exxon Mobil, had profits of $19 billion.[2] Admittedly, the United States is an outlier, with 43 percent of the entire world's military expenditures.[3] Nevertheless, most countries spend hundreds of millions or billions of dollars on their military forces every year. It is difficult to imagine any nongovernmental organization competing with a government in this arena – partly because no other sort of organization has the kind of resources at its disposal

---

[1] U.S. Navy 2009; Birkler et al. 1998, 75.
[2] CNN Money 2012.
[3] Stockholm International Peace Research Institute 2012.

that a government can command and partly because military defense is a public good whose provision, in the absence of some coercive mechanism, would seemingly require altruistic sacrifice on the part of those who pay for it. As a result, it seems unlikely that an anarchic society could maintain anything like the military forces typical of modern governments. For these reasons, members of an anarchic society could not hope to defeat a governmental army in open combat, nor could they hope, as governments often do, to wage an aggressive war against another country.

But the focus on relative military power may be misdirected, for two reasons. First, the requirements for effective defense may be more modest than the requirements for effective aggression, and the military expenditures of most modern governments may be far greater than defense requires. Second, as in the case of interpersonal relations, the strategy of avoiding armed conflict may prove more important than that of attempting to win armed conflicts.

My aim in what follows will not be to show that an anarchic society could survive in any and all political climates. My aim will be to show that an anarchic society could survive in some realistic conditions, conditions that obtain in some parts of the world or could reasonably be expected to obtain in the future. It is to be expected that there will also be many other realistic conditions under which an anarchist system would not survive.

12.2   Nongovernmental defense

12.2.1   Guerrilla warfare

The above characterization of the problem of defense suggests that successful defense requires military power comparable to or greater than one's opponent. Yet guerrilla fighters have given the lie to this alleged requirement for military victory in several twentieth-century conflicts during which advanced military forces have been defeated by far weaker opponents.

The paradigm case is that of Vietnam, which expelled the French colonialists in 1954. The United States then assumed responsibility for combating the spread of communism by supporting the anticommunist, authoritarian government of South Vietnam in its contest against the communist government of North Vietnam and the communist insurgents in South Vietnam. American involvement began with military advisors but escalated into direct warfare in the mid to late 1960s, when hundreds of thousands of American troops were committed to fighting the Vietcong insurgents in the south.[4] In terms of military and economic resources, the United States was far superior to the Vietcong, and yet for year after year, American forces proved unable to subdue their opponents, until the United States finally in effect acknowledged defeat and withdrew all forces from the country in 1973. The most powerful nation in the world had been defeated by the rebels of a small Third World nation. The defeat was due partly to the inherent difficulty of countering guerrilla warfare tactics and partly to the fact that the Vietnamese were far more deeply committed than the Americans to controlling the fate of Vietnam.[5]

This was no isolated episode; several twentieth-century conflicts provided similar lessons. Great Britain governed the island of Ireland until 1919, when Irish nationalists declared independence and began a guerrilla campaign against the British. For the next two years, the British fought an unsuccessful war against the rebels, culminating in the treaty that established the Irish Free State in 1922.[6]

The French ruled Algeria before 1954, when Algerian nationalists began a guerrilla war for independence, which continued for several years. Despite some military successes, the French ultimately lacked the rebels' degree of commitment, and French President Charles de Gaulle agreed to submit the question of independence to popular votes in 1961 and 1962, resulting in Algerian independence in 1962.[7]

In 1979, the Soviet Union sent military forces to Afghanistan to defend the communist government there against the mujahideen guerrillas. Over the next nine years, the Soviets were unable to prevail against the mujahideen. The Soviets gave up and withdrew in 1988. The Afghan government subsequently fell to the rebels in 1992.[8]

In each of these cases, the rebels were fighting in defense of their homeland against what they saw as foreign aggressors. In the cases of Vietnam and Afghanistan, the guerrillas also had support from foreign governments. But even taking account of that support, the guerrillas were far weaker than their opponents by traditional measures in each of these conflicts. The United States, France, Great Britain, and the Soviet Union were four of the most powerful nations in all of world history. Therefore, if they could be defeated by guerrillas fighting in defense of

---

[4] Twenty-Fifth Aviation Battalion n.d.
[5] For an account of the Vietnam conflict, see Herring 2002.
[6] For an account of the Irish war of independence, see Hopkinson 2002.
[7] For an account of the Algerian revolt, see Horne 1987.
[8] For an account of the Soviet-Afghani conflict, see Maley 2009.

their homeland, then any nation contemplating a war of conquest in modern times must anticipate enormous difficulties in controlling the occupied territory. This is all the more true in territories, such as most of the present-day United States, where a large percentage of average citizens are armed to begin with.[9]

12.2.2 The difficulty of conquering an ungoverned territory

In one respect, conquering an anarchic society would be more difficult than conquering a nation-state. To conquer a territory that is already governed, the aggressor must convince the existing government to surrender, which can generally be done either by attacking fixed government military assets or by killing enough members of the population. Once the government surrenders, the apparatus of that very government may be co-opted to control the society on behalf of its new rulers.

By contrast, the task of taking control of an ungoverned society is more complex. In the absence of any central authority structure, the society must be conquered one neighborhood at a time. To control each neighborhood, the aggressor will need either to station troops in the neighborhood or to hire the equivalent of police from the local population. Either option is likely to be expensive, and in either case, those charged with enforcing the conquerors' will are likely to be frequent targets of guerrilla attacks. In addition, if the conquering state wishes ultimately to govern the conquered people, it will need to set up all the apparatus of government.

A determined and wealthy aggressor *could* nevertheless establish government over an initially ungoverned society. But the task of doing so is likely to be more expensive and time-consuming than that of taking over some society that already has a government but a weak military. Since there are many societies satisfying the latter description, an anarchist society is not likely to be the most attractive target for an expansionist regime.

12.2.3 Nonviolent resistance

A priori, it might seem that force can only be countered with greater force. Since governments command greater coercive power than any other agents, it might then seem that the only effective defense against

---

[9] An estimated 47 percent of American households own firearms (Saad 2011), and the nation contains over 200 million private guns, nearly one-third of the world's total gun supply (Reuters 2007b).

a government is another government. Yet several historical episodes over the last century have revealed the surprising effectiveness of nonviolent methods of resistance to tyranny and injustice, demonstrating that even when injustice is coercively imposed, violence is not the only, and perhaps not even the most effective solution.

The best-known case is that of the Indian struggle for independence from Britain, led by Mohandas Gandhi. Gandhi's tactics included hunger strikes; marches and demonstrations; boycotts of British goods, schools, and courts; civil disobedience, including refusal to pay taxes; labor strikes; and social ostracism of those Indians collaborating with the British. While Indian independence was a long time coming, it was eventually won with a minimum of bloodshed (relative to the cases discussed in Section 12.2.1), thanks in large measure to the efforts of the Mahatma. This is so despite the fact that the British, at least at the start, showed considerably greater willingness to resort to violence than did the followers of Gandhi.[10]

Another well-known case is that of the American civil rights movement of the 1950s and 1960s. Under the leadership of Martin Luther King Jr. and others, the movement relied upon such nonviolent tactics as sit-ins, boycotts, and protest marches. Civil rights activists often faced violence at the hands of local police, the Ku Klux Klan, and other opponents of racial integration. Thousands of activists were arrested, many were beaten, and several civil rights leaders, including Dr. King, were murdered. In spite of this, the movement remained predominantly nonviolent, and the movement ultimately triumphed over its more violent opponents, seeing the passage of major civil rights legislation in the mid-1960s, along with dramatic changes in American culture and society.[11]

Towards the end of the twentieth century, a number of nations, including the Soviet 'republics' and the satellite countries of eastern Europe, achieved independence from the Soviet Union through predominantly nonviolent means (with the exception of Romania, where the transition was more violent than in the other nations). The process began in Poland in 1980, when workers formed a nationwide labor union known as Solidarity. Solidarity quickly became a tool for advocating political and economic reform. The government tried to squash Solidarity by outlawing the union and arresting thousands of its members, but the movement persisted. Eventually the government gave

---

[10] For an account of the Indian independence movement, see Sarkar 1988.
[11] For an account of the American civil rights movement, see Williams 1987.

up trying to eliminate Solidarity. The union persistently wielded the nonviolent tool of the labor strike to attempt to force reform. In 1989, the government finally bowed to the pressure and entered negotiations with representatives of Solidarity, during which the government agreed to allow free elections in which Solidarity candidates could run against some of the communist candidates. Though polls predicted victory for the communists, in the event the communist party suffered a crushing defeat, losing every single seat that was contested in the legislature. Further defeats were to come, freeing Poland from communist rule.[12]

In August 1991, hard-line communists in the Soviet Union, seeking to halt the tide of reform initiated by President Gorbachev, took Gorbachev prisoner and launched a coup d'état. Boris Yeltsin, then president of Russia, faced down the coup leaders in Moscow with the help of tens of thousands of civilian protesters who gathered around him at the Russian White House. The coup failed, due in part to dedicated civilian support for Yeltsin, in part to divided opinion among the military, and in part to the refusal of Soviet special forces to carry out orders to attack the White House. Shortly after the failed coup, though Gorbachev had nominally been restored to power, the Soviet Union fell apart, as the member states (those which had not already done so) declared independence. All of this took place, surprisingly, with a minimum of bloodshed. In the case of Estonia, independence was achieved with no bloodshed at all.[13]

More recently, longtime Egyptian president Hosni Mubarak was expelled from office as a result of a predominantly peaceful protest movement. For 30 years, Mubarak headed a corrupt and dictatorial regime in Egypt, until protesters, angered by recent police brutality and emboldened by the Tunisian revolution of 2010–11, took to the streets in early 2011 to demand their ruler's resignation. The protests were so widespread that Mubarak soon stepped down, many other members of his government either resigned or were dismissed, and most other demands of protesters were met. Parliamentary elections were held beginning in November, with the presidential election scheduled for 2012. As of this writing, Egypt's future remains uncertain; nevertheless,

---

[12] For an account of the Polish struggle, see Mason 1996, 26–9, 51–4; Sanford 2002, 50–5; BBC News 1999.

[13] See Coleman 1996, chapter 16, for a brief account of the August coup and the collapse of the Soviet Union. On the refusal of Soviet special forces to attack the White House, see Ebon 1994, 7–9. On the case of Estonia, see Tusty and Tusty 2006.

the sudden collapse of an administration that had lasted 30 years is a testament to the power of nonviolent resistance.

Prima facie, historical episodes such as these may seem puzzling. How can a national government, with massive stockpiles of armaments and tens or hundreds of thousands of troops, be defeated by unarmed, peaceful civilians?

The explanation lies in the nature of government power. Chairman Mao Tse-tung is often quoted as saying that 'political power grows from the barrel of a gun.'[14] But this is only part of the truth. Political power comes fundamentally from the people over whom it is exercised. Though governments wield enormous coercive power, they do not possess sufficient resources to directly apply physical force to all or most members of a society. They must be selective, applying their violence to a relatively small number of lawbreakers and relying upon the great majority of the population to fall in line, whether out of fear or out of belief in the government's authority. Most people must obey most of the government's commands; at a minimum, they must work to provide material goods to the government's leaders, soldiers, and employees if a government is to persist.

When an injustice is sufficiently large and obvious, there often arise large numbers of protesters who are willing to defy the state, despite the threat of repression. In response, tyrannical governments usually resort to violence. Yet this violence often backfires by legitimizing the protesters and delegitimizing the state in the eyes of previously uninvolved agents. This can have the effect of expanding rather than suppressing the resistance. Eventually, the state may lose the source of its power, the cooperation of the majority of citizens.[15] In the case of a government attempting to control a foreign territory, it would become necessary to send enormous domestic resources to the foreign territory in the attempt to maintain control, thereby defeating one of the main purposes of seeking foreign territory to begin with, that of profiting through the extraction of foreign resources.

This is not to encourage a Pollyannaish optimism about nonviolent action. Nonviolent resistance has achieved some dramatic successes, but it has also often failed, as in the case of the small pockets of nonviolent resistance to the Nazis in Germany or the 1989 protests in China. The same is true of all forms of resistance: violent resistance also often fails, and even violent resistance by a government (that is, war) often fails to

---

[14]   Mao 1972, 61.
[15]   This account is loosely derived from Sharp 1990, chs. 2–3.

achieve its aims. What the historical episodes I have mentioned show is that the idea of combating a coercive government through nonviolent means is not merely a naive ideal. Indeed, this form of resistance is often more effective and almost always far less costly than violent resistance.

12.2.4 Conclusions

None of the historical cases mentioned in this section features an anarchic society resisting a hostile foreign state. This is mainly because there have been very few anarchic societies and none following the anarcho-capitalist model. Nevertheless, as we have seen, there have been many cases of successful resistance on the part of citizens to governments, including governments imposed by foreign states. The decolonization movement of the twentieth century shows that it is particularly difficult for a foreign state to keep control of a territory in modern times. There is no obvious reason why members of an anarchic society could not resist foreign aggressors equally effectively as members of actual societies have in fact resisted foreign powers and domestic tyrants in the recent past.

There is no guarantee of success; an anarchy might be taken over by a foreign government. But this is also true of governed societies – indeed, societies of every known type of government have been taken over by foreign governments. No one argues that this shows government to be unworkable. The fact that the same fate could befall an anarchy therefore does not show anarchy to be unworkable. Anarchy would be unworkable if there were no plausible means of defense, but the evidence is that this is not so; a society would not be left without plausible means of resistance merely by virtue of lacking a governmental military.

12.3 Avoiding conflict

In the last section, I discussed ways of resisting a foreign power, given that one's society has been taken over or is under attack. But this is not the best way for a society to maintain its freedom. The best way for a society to maintain its freedom is to avoid violent conflict to begin with.

To assess the prospects for avoiding intersocietal violent conflict, we must first identify the most likely causes for conflicts of this kind. The best way to identify the likely causes of war in the future is to examine what has generally caused war in the past. It is conceivable that anarchist societies might become involved in war for different reasons from those that have led government-controlled societies to war; however, the best evidence we have concerning why a society, whether anarchist or statist, might become involved in warfare nevertheless lies in the historical record of actual warfare. We shall therefore begin with that record.

Most theorists who have considered the causes of war have tried to identify some single most important factor. The truth, however, is probably more complex: a variety of factors contribute to the risk of war, with no single factor predominating across all cases.[16] Here I review some of the most important of these factors.

12.3.1 Natural human aggression

Some believe that human beings are naturally aggressive and that this natural aggression explains the human propensity for warfare. The natural aggressiveness of mankind is sometimes supported by arguments from ethology or evolutionary psychology.[17]

An extreme form of this thesis (perhaps not actually held by any prominent thinker)[18] would be that frequent warfare is *inevitable* because of the aggression inherent in human nature. This thesis is clearly false. Anthropologist Douglas Fry lists over 70 societies that do not make war, mainly primitive tribes.[19] Among modern nation-states, Switzerland has not fought another country since the famous principle of Swiss neutrality was formally established in 1815. Their last war was a civil war in 1847; it lasted 25 days and claimed fewer than 100 lives.[20] Generations of Swiss have never known war, despite being surrounded by warring parties during both world wars. Liechtenstein disbanded its army in 1868 and has likewise remained at peace ever since. Vatican City has never been at war. Costa Rica abolished its military in 1948 and has been at peace since then. And despite all the violence of the twentieth century, the world as a whole has experienced a marked long-term

---

[16] See Sobek 2009, 2–3; Cashman and Robinson 2007, 3–4.

[17] Lorenz 1966, 42–3, chapter 13; Wilson 2000, 254–5.

[18] Robert Sapolsky (in Fry 2007, foreword, x) attributes the thesis to Lorenz (1966). However, Lorenz concludes his book with a discussion of ways of avoiding war (1966, chapter 14), going so far as to predict that one day, love and friendship will embrace all of humanity (298–9).

[19] Fry 2007, 17, 237–8.

[20] Remak 1993, 14, 157. The principle of Swiss neutrality was put in writing in the 1815 Treaty of Paris, following the defeat of Napoléon Bonaparte, who had previously taken over Switzerland.

downward trend in violent interstate conflicts, suggesting that further declines in the rate of war making are possible.[21]

A more moderate thesis is that human nature contains a *propensity* for aggression which sometimes erupts in warfare, perhaps when certain environmental triggers occur.[22] This thesis seems sufficiently weak and vague that few could object to it (indeed, the general thesis may simply follow from the observation that there are wars, along with other trivial background facts), although there is room for differing opinions as to how difficult it is for human beings to resist killing each other.

This moderate thesis, however, is of little use for present purposes. Our aim is to determine whether and how a society may avoid war. If human nature contains a propensity for aggression, but this propensity erupts in warfare only under certain conditions, then we must examine the other theories of the causes of war to determine what these conditions are, since this would seem to be the key to avoiding war (short of embarking on a program of genetic engineering to eliminate our aggressive tendencies).

12.3.2 Land and resources

One reason states go to war is for the purpose of seizing one another's resources and territory.[23] World War II was initiated by Adolf Hitler's invasion of Poland, motivated by a desire to control more territory (*Lebensraum*, as Hitler put it). India and Pakistan have fought over control of the territory of Kashmir ever since India and Pakistan gained their independence in 1947.[24] The Iran-Iraq war was fought partly over control of the Shatt al-Arab river, which forms Iraq's main access to the Persian Gulf and is therefore of great economic value to Iraq. Iraq also attempted to take over Khuzestan, the oil-rich Iranian province bordering the Shatt al-Arab.[25] Iraq's later invasion of Kuwait in 1990 was even more clearly economically motivated, prompted in part by Iraq's complaints over Kuwaiti violation of OPEC oil quotas and in part by the sheer value of the oil-rich land of Kuwait.[26]

If a predatory desire for others' land and resources is the main cause of war, then the avoidance of war might appear nearly impossible,

---

[21] Cashman and Robinson 2007, 1; Gat 2006, 591; Pinker 2011.
[22] Gat (2006, 39–41) takes this position.
[23] Gat (2006, 61–7, 409–14) takes this as the central underlying cause of war.
[24] Cashman and Robinson 2007, 205, 216–23.
[25] Cashman and Robinson 2007, 271–3.
[26] Karsh 2002, 89–92.

regardless of whether one has a nation-state or an anarchic society. While an anarchic society cannot initiate a predatory war, its land and resources may cause it to become a victim of such wars.

This pessimistic conclusion, however, is premature. Not all regions of the globe are equally prone to land- and resource-centered conflicts. Conflicts over resources occur in areas with unusually high concentrations of especially valuable resources, such as the oil-rich areas of the Middle East. Modern conflicts over territory usually occur in one of a limited number of specific regions of long-standing territorial dispute, particularly areas with a history of what might be seen as unjust occupation, areas in which borders were drawn by foreign powers, and areas containing large and mutually hostile religious or ethnic subpopulations. Thus, for example, Khuzestan province contains both Arab and Persian subpopulations, and the Shatt al-Arab was long disputed between Iraq and Iran.[27] India and Pakistan's long-standing tensions, which have periodically erupted in war, trace back to 1947, when the British agreed to leave the region. In the process, the British created the states of India and Pakistan but failed to settle the alignment of Kashmir, which was left to choose which (if either) of the two countries it would join. Kashmir has a majority Muslim population in addition to a substantial minority Hindu population. Also in 1947, the United Nations adopted a plan to partition Palestine, then a British-occupied territory with large Jewish and Arab subpopulations, into a new Jewish state and an Arab state. This decision led to the creation of Israel and initiated the notorious Arab-Israeli conflict, which has periodically erupted in violence ever since 1948.

These observations enable us to make some predictions regarding the stability of any future anarchist society. If such a society were created by nations foreign to the region in which it was located, if it contained large and mutually hostile ethnic or religious groups, and if it were created in an area with a long history of conflict, then the anarchist society would probably prove unstable. Nearby states would likely turn the anarchist homeland into a battlefield. The same holds true for any sort of society, whether anarchist or statist.

In light of such considerations, anarchy is practically viable only under certain conditions, conditions that obtain in some but not all

---

[27] A 1975 treaty had set the border between the two countries at the middle of the river. However, Saddam Hussein, feeling that Iraq had been coerced into accepting this treaty, desired a return to the terms of an earlier, 1937 treaty, which had set the border at the eastern bank of the river.

of the world. The first successful anarchist societies will need to be (i) founded by indigenous movements rather than imposed by foreign nations, (ii) located in regions with relatively peaceful histories, and (iii) occupied by people with minimal racial and religious tensions. Under such conditions, the anarchists would have a strong chance of avoiding both civil war and war with neighboring states.

12.3.3 Conflict spirals and intergovernmental disputes

Rarely if ever has war broken out because of a dispute between the *peoples* of two nations, nor between the government of one nation and the people of another. The usual case is that war breaks out as a result of a dispute between the *governments* of two or more nations. Studies in international relations have found that the largest determinant of hostile behavior by one state towards another is the hostile behavior of the second state towards the first.[28] A frequent pattern is the conflict spiral: one state performs an action that another state perceives as hostile. The second state responds with a hostile action of its own. The first state retaliates with another hostile act. This series of actions and reactions creates a spiral of escalating tensions. At each stage, there is a strong risk that the level of hostility will increase, either because of increasing anger on the part of leaders or because of differing perceptions, particularly where one party perceives its own action as less hostile than the other party perceives it to be. The interaction thus has a risk of escalating until it reaches the highest level of hostility, that of outright war.

Not all wars have arisen out of interstate disputes; sometimes a country wages a purely aggressive war in which the prior behavior of the other country's government is irrelevant. However, this is very rare. Nearly any war, especially in modern times, can be used to illustrate the idea of intergovernmental dispute as a cause of war. World War I began as a result of the assassination of Archduke Franz Ferdinand of Austria. Though the assassination was not officially supported by the Serbian government, the Austrian government believed (correctly) that some Serbian government officials were involved in the conspiracy. The Austro-Serbian conflict became the seed for the wider war. Germany, Russia, France, and Britain were each drawn into the conflict through their alliances with other participants in the conflict. The process involved some fast-moving conflict spirals in which, among other

---

[28] Cashman 1993, 165–72; Choucri and North 1975, 248–9, 254.

things, one nation's military mobilization was taken as a sign of hostile intentions, leading other nations to mobilize their militaries.[29]

The Iran-Iraq war, though partly a war over territory, was also prompted by earlier hostile interactions between the two nations' governments. Up until 1969, Iraq had ownership of the Shatt al-Arab river, until Iran unilaterally decided to move the border between the two nations from the river's eastern bank to the middle of the river. Iraq accepted the change to avoid war with what was then a much more powerful neighbor. When Khomeini took power in Iran in 1979, he began calling upon Shiite Muslims in Iraq to overthrow their government, just as Khomeini himself had done in Iran. This touched off a conflict spiral involving efforts by both governments to foment rebellion in one another's countries, ultimately leading to the Iraqi invasion of 1980.[30]

Even World War II, the paradigm of a war of conquest initiated by a predatory state, was also partly caused by the previous behavior of other states. It is widely recognized that the seeds of the war were planted 20 years earlier, when the Treaty of Versailles was signed in 1919.[31] The punitive and humiliating conditions of the treaty, including the enormous war reparations that it required Germany to pay to the victors of the First World War, occasioned widespread and powerful resentment in Germany, helping to pave the way for the rise of a demagogue who promised a restoration of German pride. Even British observers at the time of the signing found the treaty outrageously unfair to Germany. John Maynard Keynes summed up his opinion of the Versailles Treaty thus:

> The policy of reducing Germany to servitude for a generation, of degrading the lives of millions of human beings, and of depriving a whole nation of happiness should be abhorrent and detestable, – abhorrent and detestable, even if it were possible, even if it enriched ourselves, even if it did not sow the decay of the whole civilized life of Europe.[32]

I am not suggesting here that in starting World War II, Hitler was simply seeking revenge for Versailles; Hitler himself was motivated more by a

---

[29] Cashman and Robinson 2007, 55–68.
[30] Cashman and Robinson 2007, 271–3, 288–92.
[31] Parker 1997, 2; Miller 2001, 20; Lindemann 2010, 68–70.
[32] Keynes 1920, 225. British opinion at the time was largely in agreement with Keynes (Henig 1995, 50–2).

megalomaniacal drive to control more territory, as well as a hatred of other races. I am suggesting, however, that German resentment over Versailles enabled Hitler to rise to power.

How can we avoid the kinds of disputes between governments that lead to war? Here is one possibility: we could eliminate our government. An anarchist society would be incapable of having the sort of disputes or hostile interactions that have most often led to war because it would lack the agents who carry on those interactions. Even if some private individuals in the anarchic society were to take hostile stances toward a foreign government, this would be very unlikely to lead to war, as foreign governments rightly feel far less threatened by hostile individuals than they do by hostile governments. If I as a private individual call upon dissidents in Iraq to overthrow the government, Iraq will not invade my country. If I declare that my goal is to see the Russian government crushed, that I refuse to trade with Russians, and that I refuse to speak to the Russian government, this is far less likely to lead to war (or any reaction at all from the Russian government) than the same actions undertaken by the U.S. government.

This is not to say that war involving an anarchist society is unthinkable. It is simply to say that an anarchic society is less likely to become involved in conflict than a state-dominated society. While the state proudly declares itself our one great protector against a hostile world, it is that very protector above all that makes the world hostile to begin with.

12.3.4 Power relations

Nations often vie for the position of the dominant power in their region or in the world. Changes in relative power relations among the most powerful nations in a region are particularly dangerous. When the dominant country's power is on the decline, and another nation's power is on the rise, the rising power may attempt to seize the dominant position by initiating war with the dominant nation.[33] Alternately, the dominant nation may decide that it must attack the rising power before the latter becomes too powerful, to prevent the latter nation from seizing the dominant position.[34]

World War I has been interpreted by different observers as an example of each of these patterns. On the first interpretation, Britain was the dominant power in Europe, Germany the rising power, and Germany

---

[33] Organski 1968, 371.
[34] Copeland 2000, 4–5.

started the war to challenge British dominance.[35] On the second interpretation, Germany was the dominant power in continental Europe, Russia was the rising power, and Germany started a war with Russia before the Russians could become too powerful.[36] Admittedly, it was Austria's invasion of Serbia that most directly initiated World War I; Austria, however, acted with the encouragement and promised military support of Germany, without which it would have feared to proceed, and German officials at the time expected a war with Russia to result.[37]

Similar interpretations have been offered of World War II; once again, Germany started the war, either to challenge British dominance[38] or to preempt the rise of Russia.[39]

The Iran-Iraq war of the 1980s again illustrates the danger of shifting power relations. Initially, Iran was far more powerful than Iraq. This is why, when Iran unilaterally readjusted the border between the two nations in 1969, Iraq acceded to the arrangement rather than going to war. But by 1980 Iraq's power had grown, while Iran's had declined, bringing the two nations to rough parity. It was then that Saddam Hussein felt he could afford a war with Iran. One of the factors motivating the war was probably Saddam Hussein's desire to position Iraq as the leader of the Arab world and the dominant power in the region.[40]

Again, one response to the problem is to eliminate government. The sort of dominance that nation-states contend for is largely a matter of military power; that is why nations have thought to either establish or retain dominance through military victory. By abolishing its government, a society would remove itself from contention for the dominant position in this sense, for two reasons: first, because the society would possess no standing military forces; second, because the society would possess no central authority and hence would not behave as a unitary agent. There would be only a large number of distinct individuals, businesses, private clubs, and so on; none of these is likely to be perceived as a contender for dominance alongside nation-states. Because wars for dominance are normally fought between the dominant nation-state and a challenger, there would be no reason for an anarchic society to be involved in a war for dominance.

---

[35] Organski 1968, 356–9.
[36] Copeland 2000, 56–117.
[37] Cashman and Robinson 2007, 30–6, 57. Copeland's (2000, 79–117) evidence shows how German officials manipulated Austria, Russia, and France into war.
[38] Organski 1968, 357–8.
[39] Copeland 2000, 118–45.
[40] Cashman and Robinson 2007, 278–81.

12.3.5 The liberal democratic peace

Among the most important modern developments in the theory of international relations is the rise of the *democratic peace* thesis. Scholars have observed that although dictatorships often fight other dictatorships and democracies often fight dictatorships, democracies almost never fight other democracies.[41] Kant predicted this phenomenon on theoretical grounds in a 1795 essay, arguing that wars tend to be costly to the people of the nations engaged in warfare, and thus voters will tend to favor the sort of leader who avoids aggressive war. Dictatorships are much more liable to fight aggressive wars because dictators do not personally bear most of the costs of war.[42]

The theoretical argument is open to challenge. Since most voters realize that their individual votes have no actual impact on their nation's policies, they may vote ignorantly or irrationally, and they may support hawkish leaders for emotional reasons.[43] Some have also challenged the empirical evidence for democratic peace, citing a number of alleged exceptions to the rule: the War of 1812 between the United States and Britain; World War I, during which democratic Germany fought France and Britain; World War II, during which democratic Finland joined the Axis powers; the Indo-Pakistani wars of 1947 and 1999; and so on.

In spite of these criticisms, there is clearly an important phenomenon in the neighborhood of a 'democratic peace'. While war between democracies is not unheard of, it remains the case that, for whatever reason, there are far fewer wars between democracies than one would expect purely from the general rate of war fighting in the world.[44] Moreover, there is a large and growing group of nations for which war between any two of their number is, intuitively, almost unthinkable. No one seriously contemplates war between the United States and Canada or between Australia and New Zealand or between England and France. Despite the many wars that plagued the region in past centuries, no one today is worried about war in western Europe.

There is room for debate about why these nations are peacefully inclined towards each other. Some say it is because they are democratic. Others attribute the peace to a broader political liberalism.[45] Others

---

[41] See Babst's (1972) seminal statement. See Gleditsch 1992 for a brief literature review.
[42] Kant 1957, 12–13.
[43] See Section 9.4.3. Gat (2006, 582–3) observes that bellicose masses in many societies have driven their leaders to war.
[44] Bremer 1992, 316, 328–30, 334–6; Russett and Oneal 2001, 108–11.
[45] Doyle 2010a; 2010b.

cite the pacifying effects of free trade, which creates interdependencies between businesses in different nations and makes war between nations more expensive to both sides.[46] Others appeal to the effects of economic development; as societies reach a certain level of economic development, it becomes easier and more efficient to acquire resources through trade rather than combat.[47] Members of affluent societies have less to gain and more to lose by fighting.[48] Finally, some point to a large-scale shift in the moral values accepted in many societies, a shift in which war has come to be seen as hideous and immoral rather than glorious and honorable.[49]

These explanations need not be seen as competing; these factors may work in tandem to promote peace, and some may explain or reinforce others. Whatever the relative importance of the various factors, there is a certain type of society that appears highly unlikely to fight wars with other societies of the same type. This type of society is generally liberal, democratic, and economically developed and has low barriers to trade and modern, pacific values. Because of the variety of factors to which the peace may be ascribed, 'democratic peace' may be a misnomer; nevertheless, I shall, for the sake of brevity, continue to employ that name. By the same token, I shall continue to refer to these peacefully inclined (towards each other) societies as 'liberal democracies', although this may be a mischaracterization of the relevant category.

The preceding observations suggest a plausible set of conditions under which an anarchist society would avoid war. First, the society should be located in a region surrounded by strong liberal democracies. This would render it highly improbable that the society would be attacked by nonliberal nations. Wars between distant nations are rare in general,[50] and in this case an invader would have to cross through one of the liberal democratic states. Second, the society should share the characteristics of liberal democracies apart from those that inherently require government. It should be affluent; it should share broadly liberal, peace-loving values; and it should possess numerous and strong commercial relations with its neighbors. Third, the society must be established with the consent – or at least without the opposition – of

---

[46] Domke 1988, chapter 5.
[47] Gartzke 2010.
[48] Gat 2006, 587–97.
[49] Mueller 2004, 1–2, 32–40; Pinker 2011, chapter 4.
[50] Bremer 1992, 312–13, 327, 334–6.

the surrounding liberal states. Under these conditions, the society is very unlikely to suffer attack by foreign states.

Are these conditions realistic? The first condition is certainly realistic: large regions of the globe are controlled by liberal democracies, these regimes generally appear highly stable, and ever more of the globe has come under the control of liberal democracies over the past two centuries. So there are many suitable regions, and many more will exist in the future.

The second condition is also realistic, though not inevitable, provided that anarcho-capitalism is workable in other respects. Of course, if anarchy degenerates into universal fighting and pillaging, then the anarchist society would not be affluent and would not maintain strong commercial ties with its neighbors. The arguments of previous chapters regarding the internal peacefulness and stability of the anarcho-capitalist order are thus important also to establishing the potential for peaceful relations between an anarchist society and its neighbors. If those arguments are correct and if an anarchist society were started by initially affluent, liberal, peace-loving people, then the society would continue to share those traits.

It is the third condition that would be the most difficult to realize. Since every habitable portion of the earth's surface is presently controlled by states, the anarchist society would seemingly have to be founded within the territory of some state. This seems unlikely at present, mainly because almost no one believes in anarchism. Indeed, very few have even heard of the form of anarchism discussed in this book. This suggests that anarchism will not be adopted any time soon. Nevertheless, I maintain that, in the event that it were adopted, it would be a successful social system. If the only obstacle to its success is that people refuse to try it, then I think this is no obstacle to holding that it is the correct social system.

12.3.6 If you desire war, prepare for war

I have argued that an anarchist society could be relatively free of the factors that typically cause states to become involved in war. But what if there were some feature unique to anarchist societies that would cause them to become involved in war? This feature would not have appeared in any of the historical studies of the causes of war.

There is one obvious difference between anarchies and states that seems relevant: almost all states maintain standing armies, whereas an anarchist society would presumably have no standing army. Would this make the anarchist society more prone to war?

Some thinkers in the field of international relations (often tendentiously dubbed 'realists') take power relations among states, especially the presence or absence of deterrence, to be the main determinants of war and peace. It is often said that if one desires peace, one must prepare for war.[51] These thinkers might argue that an anarchist society would be unable to deter aggressors and would therefore soon be attacked.

Other thinkers maintain an almost opposite position, that military preparations make war more likely rather than less. One reason is that leaders who believe their nation well prepared for war or who see themselves as commanders of great military forces may behave more aggressively in interstate interactions, thus provoking more aggressive responses from others. A second problem is that the maintenance of a standing army creates a permanent class in society with an economic interest in war – the military, arms manufacturers, and others who do business with the military – and this 'war lobby' may promote suspicion of foreign nations and support hawkish leaders who are more likely to initiate or escalate conflicts. A third problem is that, despite the popularity of the adage 'if you desire peace, prepare for war', those in foreign countries are less likely to take your war preparations as evidence of peaceful desires than as evidence of hostile intentions. The suspicion and hostility engendered in foreign nations will increase the likelihood of conflict spirals leading to war.[52]

Conservatives and liberals will differ with one another over which theoretical argument is more plausible. Fortunately, we need not rely only on gut feelings; we can turn to empirical evidence. The deterrence argument would lead us to expect two things: first, that more militarized states (roughly, states that expend more resources on the military per capita) are less likely to be involved in war. The safest condition should be that in which both members of a pair of states are highly militarized, since in that case both sides could anticipate enormous harms from war. In contrast, if neither state is highly militarized, the consequences of war are relatively low, and neither side will face a strong deterrent.

Second, states that are nearly equal in power should be less likely to go to war with one another than states that are very unequal in power. When two states are nearly equal in power, both stand to suffer serious losses from war, and thus both will face a strong deterrent, whereas when

---

[51] The saying, 'Si vis pacem, para bellum', derives from the fourth-century Roman writer Vegetius (2001, 63).

[52] Bremer (1992, 318) discusses these arguments.

one state is much more powerful than the other, the more powerful state will face little deterrent. We cannot be absolutely confident of either of these predictions. Perhaps states that are already more likely to go to war are also, for that reason, more likely to make preparations for war. And perhaps powerful states refrain from attacking their weaker neighbors because their weaker neighbors simply accede to all the demands of the powerful states. These possibilities would interfere with the predictions I have suggested. Nevertheless, it seems that, on balance, the finding of an inverse correlation between militarism and war would be taken by most observers as at least some evidence in favor of the theory that military preparation deters war, as would the finding of an inverse relationship between equality of power and war. Conversely, then, positive correlations in each of these cases would undermine the theory that military preparation deters war.

Political scientist Stuart Bremer analyzed data on all wars between 1816 and 1965. Among other things, he found that militarization either had no effect on or slightly increased the probability of war. He also found that states were most likely to go to war when they were roughly equal in power and least likely to go to war when there was a large power difference. Both of these factors – relative power and militarization – were less important than the factors of democracy and economic development, suggesting that the emphasis of the 'realists' is misplaced.[53]

Another way of testing the theory that military deterrence is necessary for a society to be secure against foreign invasion is to examine cases of societies that have little or no military forces. The deterrence theory would predict that any such society would quickly be taken over by another country, just as an anarchist society allegedly would be.

At present, there are at least fifteen countries without military forces, including Andorra, Costa Rica, the Federated States of Micronesia, Grenada, Kiribati, Liechtenstein, the Marshall Islands, Nauru, Palau, Saint Lucia, Saint Vincent and the Grenadines, Samoa, the Solomon Islands, Tuvalu, and Vatican City.[54] Most of these nations have

---

[53] Bremer 1992, 326, 334–8. Bremer notes that, after controlling for other factors, the effect of militarization is minimal.

[54] U.S. Central Intelligence Agency 2011. Wikipedia lists an additional five nations with 'no standing army but...limited military forces': Haiti, Iceland, Mauritius, Monaco, and Panama (http://en.wikipedia.org/wiki/List_of_countries_without_armed_forces; accessed 28 September 2011), all of which the CIA lists as having 'no regular military forces'.

nonetheless remained at peace for decades. The largest of these nations is Costa Rica, whose last war was a civil war in 1948. The following year, the country adopted a constitution banning the military. Costa Rica has been at peace ever since.[55]

Advocates of the need for deterrence might seek to explain away these cases in either of two ways. First, each of these nations maintains a national police force, and perhaps it is this police force that deters invaders. Given that none of these police forces could be expected to defeat a traditional army, their military deterrence value is open to question. But if they provide sufficient deterrence against invasion, then the private security agencies and ordinary armed citizens in an anarchist society should provide a comparable deterrent as well.

Second, if any of these nations were invaded, some other state might come to its defense. In many but not all cases, these demilitarized countries have understandings with more powerful nations whereby the more powerful nations are responsible for their defense. Even without any agreement, there is a good chance that some other nation would intervene to stop a hostile invasion. The United States, for example, has a history of intervention in many parts of the world, including an invasion of Grenada in 1983 in which U.S. forces overthrew a Marxist military coup and restored democratic government.[56] If, therefore, Grenada were invaded by a foreign nation, it seems likely that the U.S. would intervene again. The same holds true for other small nations in the region, such as Costa Rica, Saint Lucia, and Saint Vincent and the Grenadines. Similarly, in the (highly improbable) event that some other nation attacked Vatican City, the Italian military would undoubtedly intervene; Andorra could probably count on French or Spanish protection; Nauru would probably be defended by Australia.

This raises some theoretical questions. Why would the larger nation defend the small, demilitarized nation in these cases? Why, for example, would the United States defend Grenada? Grenada has no means of compelling the U.S. to come to its aid, nor can Grenada afford to pay the U.S. for the service (nor would the U.S. ask it to do so). One reason seems to be that the United States sees itself as the police officer of the Caribbean (and, to a lesser extent, of the world). American leaders can afford to act in a manner consistent with this image because American voters are generally comfortable with this image of their nation's role, provided that U.S. military interventions

---

[55] U.S. Department of State 2011.
[56] U.S. Central Intelligence Agency 2011.

are not too long or costly. Another factor is that the U.S. government would not wish to see another, aggressive government gain influence in the region. When the United States invaded Grenada in 1983, it was partly to stop the island from being controlled by communists friendly to Cuba's Fidel Castro.

A second theoretical question is even sharper for 'realists': what protects Grenada *from the United States?* Why has the U.S. not taken over the island and run it as a colony? Those who seek to explain international relations in terms of power relations and who emphasize deterrence as a necessary condition for security must have difficulty accounting for the continued enjoyment of peace and independence by Grenada and other defenseless nations.

Here is one plausible (nonrealist) explanation. If American leaders were to launch a hostile takeover of Grenada, the action would immediately receive extremely negative publicity. Grenada would be widely perceived (correctly) as a harmless and defenseless nation, and the invasion would therefore be extremely unpopular among American voters. U.S. politicians, though perhaps happy to ignore the desires of the populace when no one is watching (which is almost always), typically fear to defy voter opinion in high-profile cases, particularly when there is as little to gain as there would be in this case. Any military invasion is bound to be high profile, so leaders will be reluctant to attack nations that are seen as harmless.

It is not only among the handful of literally defenseless nations in the world that one finds cases of security without military deterrence. There are in addition many nations with military forces *much weaker* than those of neighboring countries. For example, the U.S. military maintains approximately 1.4 million active-duty personnel, while the Canadian forces number 68,000.[57] No realistic *military* considerations prevent the United States from taking Canada over. Considering the number of nation pairs in the world for which one nation is much more powerful than the other and contrasting this with the very small number that are actually at war, one must begin to doubt the importance of deterrence in explaining how peace is maintained.

Returning to the question of anarchy, statists will be quick to argue that the security of the demilitarized nations under discussion depends upon the power and benevolent intentions of other states, which must protect the weak nations. Therefore, the security of a society really

---

[57] U.S. Department of Defense 2010; Canadian Department of National Defence 2011.

depends upon government, albeit not necessarily that society's *own* government.

Be that as it may, the question of interest was whether an anarchic society can hope to be secure against foreign aggression. If a society may be safe because of the character of other nations' governments, then it appears that the society need not have a government of its own, and an anarchic society can therefore be secure. An anarchic society could depend upon the strength and benevolent intentions of nearby liberal democracies, in the same way that many existing states presently do.

Even if a few secure anarchic societies could be established, one might still wonder whether the system could possibly serve as an ideal for the world as a whole. This question will be taken up in Chapter 13.

12.4   Avoiding Terrorism

Since 2001, Americans have been preoccupied with the threat of terrorism, and this concern has led to a significant expansion in the powers of the central government. It might be thought that government is needed to protect people from this threat.

12.4.1   The terrorist threat

Between 1968 and 2009 (the years for which data were available), terrorist attacks claimed a total of about 3200 lives within the United States (almost all on 11 September 2001) and 64,000 lives worldwide.[58] During the same time period, nonterrorist murderers within the United States took 802,000 lives.[59] The total number of American deaths from all causes during that time period was close to 91 million.[60] Thus, in the United States, terrorism accounted for approximately 0.4 percent of murders and 0.004 percent of all deaths. These figures initially make it difficult to see terrorism as among the most serious threats facing either the United States or the world.

The only way in which one could see terrorism as a serious threat, therefore, is if one suspects that future terrorism will be many times worse than past terrorism. This might be true if terrorists gained control

---

[58] All data on terrorist fatalities is from the RAND Corporation (2011).

[59] Disaster Center 2011a. I focus on American deaths here because reliable U.S. statistics are more readily available than worldwide statistics.

[60] Disaster Center 2011b. Death totals for years not shown in the table were estimated based upon death totals in nearby years.

of nuclear or biological weapons. There is no reliable way of estimating the odds of such an occurrence; however, some experts on the subject have given alarming assessments. In 2005, U.S. Senator Richard Lugar surveyed 85 nonproliferation and national security experts from around the world on their assessments of the risk of terrorism involving weapons of mass destruction (WMD). On average, respondents considered a terrorist nuclear attack somewhere in the world within the following ten years to be 29 percent likely and a major biological attack 33 percent likely.[61] In 2008, the U.S. government's Commission on the Prevention of WMD Proliferation and Terrorism deemed it more likely than not that a WMD terrorist attack would occur somewhere in the world by the year 2013, with a biological attack being more likely than a nuclear attack.[62]

These assessments should be taken with a grain of salt, as national security experts may have a bias toward overstating threats to national security. Those who are most predisposed toward concern about national security threats are most likely to become national security experts. Many of these experts work for governments, which tend to profit from public perception of serious national security threats. Most importantly, the assessments mentioned in the previous paragraph are subjective guesses, assessments of the sort that is least reliable and most easily influenced by bias.[63] This unreliability is perhaps reflected in the fact that expert assessments of the probability of WMD terrorism cover the whole range from 0 to 100 percent.[64] Experts who provide detailed consideration of the various ways in which a terrorist plot might fail

---

[61] Lugar 2005, 14, 19.

[62] Commission on the Prevention of WMD Proliferation and Terrorism 2008, xv. For similarly dire warnings, see Allison 2004, 15; Bunn 2006.

[63] The usual method of assessing the probability of an event involves observing its frequency in a large number of trials. In the present case, no instances of the event have been observed. Another approach is to observe the frequency of near misses – cases in which the event *almost* occurred. There are no known cases in which terrorists came very close to a successful major WMD attack; however, there have been numerous cases in which terrorist plots to distribute toxic agents have been foiled, and others in which unauthorized individuals or groups have been caught with samples of highly enriched uranium (Cordesman 2005, 22–4). The most reliable way of assessing probabilities may be to establish a betting market (see, e.g., www.intrade.com). The U.S. government has considered establishing a terrorism betting market but rejected the proposal for emotional reasons (CNN 2003).

[64] Lugar 2005, 14, 19.

tend to see the risks as much smaller than indicated in the previous paragraph.[65]

While there is no agreement on even the approximate likelihood of a terrorist WMD attack, there is general agreement that such an attack would have extremely serious consequences, beginning with possibly hundreds of thousands of deaths.[66] In the worst scenarios entertained by experts, the fatalities would be equivalent to a few decades' worth of ordinary murders in the United States. While this is not an existential threat to American society or any other, it remains a serious concern.

12.4.2   The roots of terrorism

Why do terrorist attacks occur? There are two broad views about the motivations of most terrorists. The first is the 'clash of civilizations' picture, expressed eloquently by U.S. President George W. Bush in 2001:

> They hate what they see right here in this chamber: a democratically elected government. [...] They hate our freedoms: our freedom of religion, our freedom of speech, our freedom to vote and assemble and disagree with each other. [...] These terrorists kill not merely to end lives, but to disrupt and end a way of life. [...] This is civilization's fight. This is the fight of all who believe in progress and pluralism, tolerance and freedom.[67]

On this view, terrorists are moved by fundamentally evil goals, and America is targeted because of its most notable virtues. No change in government policy, short of conversion to Islamic theocracy, could be expected to have any significant impact on terrorist motivations.

Another view attributes anti-American sentiment to specific U.S. foreign policies, particularly in the Middle East. Among these policies are the U.S.-sponsored sanctions against Iraq following the first Persian Gulf war; U.S. support for Israel in what some describe as the oppression

---

[65] See Levi 2007. Though Levi declines to offer a numerical assessment of the risk of nuclear terrorism, the impression he leaves is far less alarming than that left by the previous authors. Nevertheless, Levi counsels strongly in favor of strengthening defenses against nuclear terrorism.

[66] Levi (2007, 38) mentions the possibility of 100,000 deaths due to a terrorist nuclear attack on New York; Allison (2004, 4) mentions the possibility of half a million immediate deaths from the same event, plus hundreds of thousands more in the ensuing hours.

[67] Bush 2001.

of the Palestinians; the continuing presence of U.S. troops in Muslim countries, particularly on the Arabian Peninsula since the first Gulf war; the recent invasions and occupations of Afghanistan and Iraq, with the consequent deaths of hundreds of thousands of citizens of those countries; and the abuse of prisoners at Abu Ghraib and elsewhere. Each of these actions, it is argued, contributes to a tide of resentment towards America, particularly in Muslim countries, thereby enabling terrorist groups to recruit additional members.[68]

Which of these basic conceptions is more accurate? The evidence weighs heavily in favor of the 'foreign policy retaliation' theory. To begin with, the actual statements of bin Laden and other terrorist leaders in calling for jihad against America cite particular American foreign policies as justification, chiefly the presence of U.S. troops in 'the land of the two Holy Places' (the Arabian peninsula), U.S. support for Israel, and the U.S. war and economic sanctions against Iraq.[69] They do not cite America's liberal democratic values, nor do they target liberal democracies with no Middle East involvement. Presumably, these terrorist leaders would be in a better position to know their own motivations than American government officials or other distant observers, and it would be in their interests to reveal those motivations if they hope to coerce nations to accede to their desires. In contrast, the assessments of government officials may suffer from a bias in the direction of discounting the responsibility of the government itself for terrorist sentiments, particularly if officials have no intention of changing the policies that may have led to those sentiments.

Experts who study terrorist motivations come to similar conclusions. Anthropologist Scott Atran has spent years studying terrorists in a number of countries around the world, entering their communities and interviewing terrorists. Atran found recent terrorists to be driven by moral outrage at the violence performed by Americans against Muslims in Iraq, Afghanistan, and elsewhere. He found that jihadis are not moved by hatred for freedom and democracy, as Bush stated, nor are they 'nihilists', as Barack Obama has stated.[70] They see themselves as

---

[68] See, for example, Hornberger 2006.

[69] bin Laden 1996; bin Laden et al. 1998.

[70] See Obama 2004, x: 'Nor do I pretend to understand the stark nihilism that drove the terrorists that day and that drives their brethren still. My powers of empathy, my ability to reach into another's heart, cannot penetrate the blank stares of those who would murder innocents with abstract, serene satisfaction.'

courageous heroes standing up against an enormous oppressor. As one Hamas politburo member put it, 'George Washington was fighting the strongest military in the world, beyond all reason. That's what we're doing. Exactly.'[71]

Robert Pape and James Feldman studied all 2200 suicide-terrorist attacks that occurred around the world between 1980 and 2009. They found that these attacks were not chiefly motivated by religious differences. Instead, almost all the attacks were motivated by a desire to end foreign military occupation of a territory that the terrorists prized. This was the one constant across both secular and religious terrorist groups and across all countries, from the West Bank to Sri Lanka to Lebanon to Chechnya.[72] This includes the 9/11/2001 terrorist attacks that prompted horrified Americans to ask, 'Why do they hate us?' Here are the words of three of the 9/11 hijackers:

> Abu al-Jaraah al-Ghamidi: What is happening in Muslim countries today? Blatant occupation about which there is no doubt. ... There is no duty more obligatory after faith than to repel him.
> Abu Mus'ab Walid al-Shehri: [R]epelling the Americans occupying the land of the Two Sanctuaries ... is the most obligatory of obligations.
> Hamza al-Ghamdi: And I say to America: if it wants its armies and people to be safe, then it must withdraw all of its forces from the Muslim lands and depart from all our countries.[73]

It should go without saying that the effort to understand the motivations of terrorists does not entail sympathy for terrorists, nor does it involve any attempt to shift the moral blame for terrorist actions away from the terrorists themselves. An accurate understanding of terrorist motivations, free of self-serving biases, is simply the first step in understanding how to avoid terrorist attacks in the future.

12.4.3   Violent and nonviolent solutions

How should the problem of terrorism be addressed? Most governments focus on the enforcement strategy: tracking down and capturing or killing as many terrorists as possible. It is hoped that this will incapacitate

---

[71] Atran 2010, 347. See Atran 2010, 53–4, 55–6, 114–15, 290, on terrorist motivations. Atran (2010, 4–5, 42–3) contests Bush's and Obama's remarks.
[72] Pape and Feldman 2010, 9–10.
[73] From the 9/11 martyr videos, quoted in Pape and Feldman 2010, 23.

most of the people who would otherwise commit terrorist acts, in addition to deterring others who might consider becoming terrorists. Many terrorists have been captured or killed, and this has presumably directly prevented many terrorist attacks that would otherwise have occurred.

At the same time, there are reasons for apprehension about the general strategy. It is impossible to capture *all* terrorists, and even capturing a large percentage of them may prove difficult and demand large sacrifices, both in material terms and in terms of civil liberties. Enforcement will likely become ever more difficult in the future, for as society advances economically and technologically, ever more people will have access to tools capable of wreaking great destruction. Governments may resort to increasingly draconian methods of enforcement. Yet these methods may themselves create further resentment, pushing more people to become terrorists; this is most likely if those methods include torture or other prisoner abuse. If the government also continues the policies that led to terrorist sentiment to begin with, new terrorist recruits may continue to appear on a regular basis, perpetuating a constant state of conflict. According to a Gallup survey, 7 percent of the world's 1.6 billion Muslims considered the 9/11 attacks completely justified, while 37 percent considered the attacks either completely, largely, or somewhat justified.[74] With such a large number of people harboring some sympathy for terrorism, it seems that an effective strategy must focus more on reducing that tide of outrage rather than on deploying ever more violence to destroy the enemy. When faced with opponents who are drawn from a community containing tens or hundreds of millions of outraged people, a purely combative strategy is most likely to produce an endless cycle of bloodshed that will prove tragic for both sides.

The ideal approach to terrorism would be to somehow act so that no one, or at most very few people, the sort of anger that would motivate them to commit terrorist attacks to begin with. If terrorist attacks are motivated by sheer evil or by hatred of freedom, then this will not be feasible. But if, as I have argued, terrorism is retaliation for specific government policies, then the problem could be solved through the elimination of those policies.

An anarchist society would be much safer from terrorism than a government-dominated society, for the anarchist society would have no mechanism for undertaking the sorts of actions that typically motivate terrorist attacks. The anarchists would not, for example, station

---

[74] On the poll results, see Atran 2010, 57–8; Satloff 2008. On the world Muslim population, see Pew Research Center 2009.

troops on foreign soil, impose economic embargoes on other countries, or invade other countries.

Of course, a nation with a government can practice a noninterventionist foreign policy and thereby avoid becoming a target of terrorism. Nevertheless, it should be borne in mind that the existence of a government creates an ongoing, nontrivial risk that the government will undertake policies that cause its own citizens to become targets for terrorist attacks. The self-image of government, almost by its very nature, is that of an agency that functions to combat threats to society through force. Thus, while it is not inevitable, it is natural that governments will react to perceived threats in an aggressive manner that perpetuates the cycle of violence. Democratic polities are more likely to support than to restrain the state once such a cycle begins. In a 2011 presidential debate, Republican candidate Rick Santorum received cheers from the audience for declaring that America was attacked in 2001 because of terrorist hatred for freedom, opportunity, and 'American exceptionalism'. Rival candidate Ron Paul responded by citing al Qaeda's actual statements as evidence that U.S. foreign policies were the motive for the attacks. Paul received catcalls from the audience for his observations.[75] This admittedly anecdotal evidence suggests that democratic polities tend to prefer candidates who blame threats on the sheer evil of the nation's enemies over candidates who truthfully attribute enemy hostility to earlier government policies. This bodes ill for the prospects of resolving conflicts without terrible bloodshed.

12.5   The dangers of 'national security'

12.5.1   The risk of unjust aggression

Suppose I develop a plan to render my home secure from burglars and other trespassers: I will plant land mines in my front yard. Clearly, it would be barbarous to discuss this proposal purely in terms of how well it promoted the security of my own home. I would be ethically bound to consider as well such questions as what will happen if neighborhood children stray onto my lawn – even if they are not my children.

Similarly, any society is ethically bound to consider how its national security apparatus affects not only its own security but also the security of other peoples around the world. This question is particularly pointed for Americans, whose 'defense' apparatus includes over 700 military

---

[75] CNN 2011; video clip, http://www.youtube.com/watch?v=V9RaV44a0EE; accessed 11 February 2012.

bases in 39 foreign countries[76] and has recently been involved in the Middle Eastern conflicts mentioned above. But it is not only Americans who have cause for moral concern about their governments' actions; 27 countries sent troops to join the war in Iraq, including over 10,000 British troops.[77]

One might wonder whether the recent aggressiveness of the American and allied governments is a historical accident or whether there is something in the nature of government that encourages such results. The answer is that while such aggression is far from inevitable, it remains a nontrivial risk for any society that maintains a government in a geopolitical environment anything like the one that currently exists. As long as there remain many undemocratic countries in the world, democratic countries are at risk of going to war with undemocratic countries, particularly those that are perceived as alien by the populaces of the democratic nations. The national security apparatus itself creates a permanent interest in war. Governments, particularly their branches devoted to national security, tend to profit from a state of war, as do the contractors who sell goods and services to the military. At a minimum, therefore, one could expect these interests to have a keen perception of the arguments in favor of war at any given juncture and a relatively duller perception of the arguments for peace.

But it is not only military contractors and members of the government's national security apparatus who are liable to support war. Many ordinary citizens, whether out of a misguided sense of patriotism, out of a desire to project a manly self-image, or out of ignorance and misunderstanding, may support aggressive wars. While such cognitive and character flaws are present in any large population, it is only in a government-controlled society that they are likely to lead to large-scale violence, for only in a government-controlled society is there a standing apparatus that enables such individuals to bring about large-scale violence at minimal cost to themselves, simply through showing up at the polls and voting in hawkish politicians. Even if, for example, a majority of Americans desired a war with Iran, hardly any would consider actually taking up arms and, as private individuals, flying to Iran to attack. It is only through a governmental apparatus that their hostility is likely to lead to mass violence.

---

[76] Perry 2008. Militarybases.com reports that U.S. forces are deployed in over 135 countries worldwide (http://militarybases.com/; accessed 18 October 2011).

[77] BBC News 2003.

As in the case of the land mines on the front lawn, then, we have a strong *moral* reason for eliminating our government; namely, the threat that it poses to innocent people elsewhere in the world.

12.5.2   The risk of global disaster

The human species is not immortal. In all probability, it will one day become extinct. We may hope that this day will come far in the future, perhaps millions of years hence. But we should fear that it will come much sooner, perhaps within only hundreds of years.

Our species has survived for 200,000 years so far. But this is no cause for complacency; during most of that time, we possessed no technology plausibly capable of extinguishing ourselves. Since the end of World War II, we do. A nuclear war between the United States and the Soviet Union might have extinguished the species and in any case would certainly have been a catastrophe the likes of which humanity has never seen.

The United States and the Soviet Union managed to avoid such a war for the crucial four and a half decades from the end of World War II until the collapse of the Soviet Union. One might regard this as a testament to the efficacy of deterrence and the capacity of national leaders to act rationally when the stakes were high enough. But again, we have little cause for complacency. The U.S. and the Soviet Union came closer to war than many realize. During the Cuban Missile Crisis of 1962, President Kennedy thought that the odds of a nuclear war were about one in three.[78] At one point during the crisis, American naval ships were dropping depth charges on a Soviet submarine in an effort to force it to surface. Unknown to the Americans, the sub was armed with a nuclear torpedo. The captain wanted to fire the torpedo, but Vasily Arkhipov, second in command, managed to convince the captain to hold off and surface the sub instead.[79]

This incident illustrates the fragility of the barriers to war between rival nation-states, even when the opposing nations are each aware that any war would be catastrophic. Had Vasily Arkhipov agreed with his captain or had a more hawkish individual been on the submarine in place of Arkhipov, the torpedo would have been fired, and in all likelihood a global nuclear war would have ensued, with hundreds of millions, perhaps billions, of casualties.

---

[78]   Blanton 1997, 93.
[79]   Dobbs 2008, 302–3, 317.

This incident should give us pause. If the world came that close to nuclear war in 1962, it could do so again. The superficial circumstances would be different. The date might be decades or centuries in the future. The nations involved might be different. In place of nuclear weapons, the armies of that day might be armed with some even more fearsome weapons not yet invented. As long as armies inhabit a technologically advanced world, there will be weapons of mass destruction. And as long as weapons of mass destruction exist, there remains a chance that they will be used – if not under the explicit orders of a national leader, then under the authority of a military commander in the field. Any use of such weapons, in turn, risks a rapid escalation into apocalyptic war.

How does this threat relate to the case for or against government? Government is the source of all presently existing weapons of mass destruction. The U.S. government invented nuclear weapons and remains the only organization ever to have used them in anger. A handful of national governments, particularly the U.S. and Soviet governments, are responsible for building all of the presently existing nuclear weapons. If history is any guide, the next weapons of mass destruction to be invented will almost certainly be invented by some national government (most likely the U.S. government, whose military budget, as of this writing, accounts for 40 percent of the entire world's military spending). Whatever this technology will be, it will probably pose an even greater threat to the survival of humanity than nuclear weapons. Thus, the apparatus we have devised for rendering ourselves secure against foreign aggression is itself the primary source of the greatest danger that the human species has ever faced.

12.6 Conclusion

Without the state's national security apparatus – its armies, intelligence agencies, and so on – how could a society hope to be safe from foreign threats, such as hostile foreign governments and terrorist organizations? There are several plausible answers to this.

First, a society could be defended against foreign invaders by guerrilla fighters. Several recent historical episodes suggest that native insurgents can pose an extremely serious problem even for the most advanced and powerful of armies seeking to occupy foreign lands.

Second, nonviolent popular resistance movements have often proven highly effective in convincing oppressive governments to give people their freedom.

Third, an ungoverned society is much less likely to become involved in violent conflicts to begin with than is a government-controlled society. The great majority of wars are caused by intergovernmental disputes, and all or nearly all terrorist acts are performed in retaliation for government policies.

Fourth, an anarchist society might be established under conditions that make war unlikely. Provided that

i) the society were established in a region otherwise dominated by liberal democracies,
ii) the society itself embraced liberal values,
iii) the society maintained strong social and economic relations with its neighbors,
iv) the society lacked large internal religious or ethnic tensions,
v) the society were not established in a region of long-standing territorial dispute,
vi) the society were established through an indigenous movement rather than being imposed by foreign powers, and
vii) the society were established with the consent of the state previously controlling the territory,

then an anarchist society would probably be stable and free from violent conflict with other nations. The first six of these conditions (in conjunction) are entirely realistic. Only the seventh seems unattainable in the near future, chiefly because very few people have accepted the theory defended in this book.

Finally, it is important to consider the danger that one's own national security apparatus poses to the rest of the world. As long as it exists, the state has a nontrivial risk of committing unjust violence against others, in the form of aggressive war, as well as a nontrivial risk of developing and using weapons of mass destruction, which threaten the survival of the human species. We are morally and prudentially obligated to minimize these risks.

13
From Democracy to Anarchy

Anarchy may be desirable in theory, but is it attainable? In this chapter, I argue that the eventual development of an anarcho-capitalist order, while not inevitable, is neither impossible nor exceedingly improbable.

13.1 Against presentist bias: the prospects for radical change

We may be tempted to conclude that the rise of an anarcho-capitalist world is exceedingly improbable or impossible simply on the grounds that anarcho-capitalism has never been realized and is very different from the status quo. I argue that we should resist this temptation. Three broad observations contribute to my optimism. First, many radical changes have occurred in human history, including major political and cultural changes. Second, the future will most likely see even more rapid change than the past. Third, some of the most important long-term social changes have been in a direction consistent with the eventual emergence of anarcho-capitalism.

To elaborate on the first observation: anatomically modern *homo sapiens* emerged 200,000 years ago. For the first 190,000 years, there was no civilization, and humans lived mainly as nomadic hunter-gatherers. Little changed during all that time. An alien observer would have long since given up on seeing anything interesting. But around 10,000 years ago, human beings began the radical shift from primitive society to civilization, which has by now encompassed nearly the entire species.

During most of the history of civilization, human society was organized in a manner that could best be described as tyranny – societies ruled by individual autocrats or small groups of aristocrats, with little

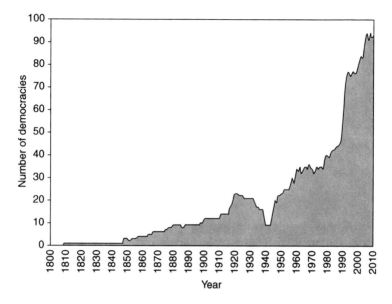

Figure 13.1   The number of democratic nations in the world, 1800–2010

regard for the rights or interests of the citizens. Democracy had been tried only sporadically and very imperfectly. But beginning around 200 years ago – after 9800 years of tyranny – human beings finally began a determined move toward democracy, a change that accelerated in the twentieth century and by now seems destined to encompass the entire earth (see Figure 13.1).[1]

Human beings are unusual among nature's products – they may do the same thing for thousands or hundreds of thousands of years and then rapidly shift to a radically new form of behavior. The rise of civilization and the shift from tyranny to democracy are both examples of radical changes in human social organization made possible by human intelligence. And many other dramatic social and political changes have occurred in recorded history: the abolition of slavery, the spread of women's suffrage, extreme declines in rates of violence, the rise and

---

[1] Center for Systemic Peace 2011. I count as democracies all countries with scores of 6 or higher on the polity2 variable in the Polity IV dataset. Note that the dataset includes only countries with populations of at least 500,000 and that data are sparse before 1900. Nevertheless, the trend toward democracy is dramatic and undeniable.

fall of communism, increasing globalization, and so on. It would be foolish to suppose that radical social change has stopped. If anything, the pace of social change appears to be accelerating. In the last 20 years, for example, democracy spread to about as many new countries as it had reached during the preceding 200 years. Both economic and technological development appears to be exponential. New information technologies and the increasing interconnectedness of the world appear to make possible more rapid social change than ever before.

We cannot now predict what human society will look like a century or more in the future, any more than our ancestors of centuries past could have predicted the shape of our society. What we do know is that the future will not look like the present. The radical changes of the past have been not only economic and technological but social and political as well. It would therefore be myopic to suppose that our current social and political institutions will remain immune from radical change. I am not predicting the inevitable rise of worldwide anarchy. I am, however, holding out anarchy as one possible outcome for humanity, given the chaotic nature of human history and the large uncertainty of the future.

Are there any specific reasons for considering this a plausible outcome? One sort of reason is that of the broad trends seen over human history, some of the most salient are consistent with a move in the direction of anarcho-capitalism. The most philosophically interesting trends are the trends in human values. It is difficult to overstate the degree of liberalization that humanity has seen over its history. Consider just a few examples.

- Today, some observers decry the brutality of the sport of boxing. In ancient Rome, however, the entertainment of the day was gladiatorial combat. Imagine a boxing official today proposing that boxers be given swords, the better to dismember each other with.
- Aristotle, one of history's greatest philosophers, wrote that some men are by nature suited to be slaves while others are naturally suited to be their masters, and he held it just to make war on those natural slaves who refuse to submit willingly.[2] Imagine a contemporary philosopher proposing that America start a war to capture slaves.
- In recent years, the George W. Bush administration incurred widespread and outraged criticism for authorizing the use of torture, in the form of waterboarding, forcing prisoners to stand in stress

---

[2] Aristotle 1941, *Politics*, 1255b4–12, 1255b37–9, 1256a22–6.

positions, and so on. But these milquetoast interrogation techniques would have been scoffed at by the torturers of the Middle Ages, whose punishments included cooking people alive; tearing a victim's body apart on the rack; suspending a person upside down and then sawing the victim in half lengthwise, starting from the groin; and so on.[3]

- In recent decades, many nations have abolished the death penalty, and those that retain it generally reserve it for the worst murderers. But in earlier times, death was meted out cavalierly, even for trivial offences such as sodomy, gossip, and working on the Sabbath.[4]

Broadly speaking, the evolution of values has been in the direction of greater respect for persons, a stronger presumption against violence and coercion, and a recognition of the equal moral status of all persons. This shift in values has driven the trend away from authoritarianism and towards liberal democracy. But these moral values are ultimately not consistent with government in any form. All governments are founded practically upon unjust coercion and philosophically on a claim by the state to a special moral status that sets it above all nongovernmental persons and groups. Equal respect for persons is not compatible with the doctrine of political authority.[5] It seems plausible, therefore, that as these trends in moral attitudes advance, the realization may one day dawn on humanity that in fact no one possesses political authority.

Some may reject my optimism, citing the great expansion in the powers of central governments in Western countries over the last century. Projecting this trend forwards, one might anticipate that in 100 years, if not much sooner, the entire world will be fully socialist.

A worldwide (state) socialist future is possible, just as a world anarchist future is possible. Some trends point towards consolidation of state power, while others point in the opposite direction. The collapse of communism at the end of the twentieth century marked an enormous move in the direction of freedom and away from government control. And as I have suggested, the move toward liberal democracy over the past 200 years likewise marked an enormous victory for individual liberty. Whether the world will ultimately settle on democratic socialism, anarchism, or some other social system depends in part on the outcome of philosophical debates that are presently in progress in our society.

---

[3] Pinker 2011, 129–33.
[4] Pinker 2011, 149–53. Compare Chapter 9, footnote 10.
[5] Compare Section 4.3.6.

13.2 Steps toward anarchy

If anarchy had to be achieved through a sudden abolition of all government, it would be a remote prospect. Such a rapidly achieved anarchy would also likely have disappointing results – if government were to suddenly disappear, without any prior development of such alternative institutions as private security and arbitration firms, chaos would likely ensue. Perhaps alternative institutions would arise spontaneously in due time, but it is also likely that the chaos would give rise to immediate demands for a new government. For these reasons, it is desirable to develop a gradualist model of the abolition of government in which alternative institutions grow at the same time that the government shrinks.

13.2.1 Outsourcing court duties

A first step toward anarchy is to diminish the role of government courts by outsourcing their work to private arbitrators. This process is already underway. Many readers hold credit cards whose agreements specify binding arbitration in the event of a dispute between the cardholder and the credit card company – a situation that in times past would have called for litigation in a government court. In recent years, commercial disputes are increasingly resolved through private arbitration. The VISA corporation provides arbitration for all disputes among its member banks.[6] In the United States, the practice of including arbitration clauses in employment contracts has spread dramatically since the 1970s, so that today an estimated 15 to 25 percent of employers use arbitration for the resolution of disputes with employees.[7] Courts generally recognize these clauses and thus refuse to overrule arbitrators' decisions (with a few exceptions);[8] private arbitrators thus form an effective substitute for government courts in a wide range of cases. It is easy to imagine this trend continuing until private arbitrators hear almost all disputes between parties to a contract.

---

[6] Caplan and Stringham 2008, 507–8.

[7] Ventrell-Monsees 2007. This estimate should be read with caution, as data on the subject are scarce.

[8] Batten 2011, 346. Exceptions include cases of fraud or corruption on the part of arbitrators and some cases in which arbitration decisions are contrary to specific public policies. On the public policy exception, see *United Paperworkers v. Misco, Inc.*, 484 U.S. 29 (1987) and *Eastern Associated Coal Corp. v. Mine Workers*, 531 U.S. 57 (2000).

Government could push the process further by declaring that its courts will no longer hear certain kinds of cases and referring these cases to arbitrators.[9] For example, a great burden would be lifted from the court system if all divorce cases had to be handled through private arbitrators (even without a prior agreement between the parties to that effect). The most controversial step would be to outsource the resolution of criminal cases. This step would be more plausible once we began to view criminal cases, not as disputes between the defendant and the state, but as disputes between the defendant and the crime victim. When viewed in this way, there is no reason why these cases, too, could not be handled through private arbitration.

Why would any government agree to promote its own eventual obsolescence by outsourcing one of its most central functions? One reason is that courts are severely overburdened and would welcome the lightening of their caseloads. Some state legislatures and courts in the United States already require certain disputes (particularly those involving automobile insurance claims) to be resolved by arbitration.[10] Another possible reason is public opinion. Should the public become sufficiently disenchanted with the government's court system, a democratic legislature might pass laws requiring the sort of changes described above.

13.2.2 Outsourcing police duties

Along with court duties, the government could outsource its policing duties. This process, too, is already underway. According to a recent report, there are now 20 million private security guards worldwide – about twice as many as the number of government police.[11] In America, private security guards number about 1 million, compared to 700,000 government police. In some cases, the government itself hires private security guards to protect public spaces, including the Liberty Bell in Philadelphia, the Statue of Liberty in New York, and the main bus terminal in Durham, North Carolina.[12] If this trend continues, we could one day see a situation in which all public spaces are protected by private security guards.

In many countries – the United States, the United Kingdom, Canada, Australia, and others – private citizens are legally authorized to make citizens' arrests. The conditions for a legal citizen's arrest, however,

---

[9] Caplan (2010) defends this proposal.
[10] Batten 2011, 345.
[11] UN News Centre 2011.
[12] Goldstein 2007.

tend to be much more restricted than the conditions under which government police may make an arrest. Legal authorization for citizens' arrests may be limited to certain kinds of crimes, and the arresting citizen may be required to personally witness the crime in progress. One could imagine a liberalization of such laws, permitting citizens' arrests for all crimes, including cases in which the suspect's guilt is established by investigation after the fact. Private security agencies could then take over not only patrol duties but duties of investigation and arrest of suspected criminals.

Care would need to be taken in making this transition. If a state or local government were to give up its monopoly on policing only to grant that monopoly to a private corporation, the private corporation could be expected to exhibit the same problems as government police, possibly even more problems. The keys to realizing the benefits of the free market are *voluntariness* and *competition*. Thus, in making the transition to private enforcement of laws, we must preserve a number of competing private security agencies, and small groups of citizens must choose their protectors. For instance, individual neighborhoods or apartment buildings should have the choice of which security agency would be responsible for security on their grounds.

Again, there are two reasons why governments might acquiesce in this social change. First, overburdened governments facing budget pressures might welcome the lightening of their policing duties. Second, an enlightened public may one day recognize the need for competition and voluntariness in traditionally governmental services and demand reforms from their representatives.

13.2.3 The end of standing armies

In early America, the idea of maintaining standing armies in peacetime was controversial, with several of the American founders warning against the dangers such armies posed to freedom.[13] Today, the debate has been resolved in favor of standing armies, with very little dissension.

But it is not obvious that we have resolved the issue either correctly or permanently. Future generations may prove ever more peace loving, continuing the trend of past centuries and millennia. As war becomes ever more despised, perhaps in a world dominated by liberal democracies, the idea of maintaining vast armies at all times, equipped with

---

[13] Hamner n.d.

city-destroying weapons, may come to seem increasingly foolish and primitive.

Some national governments are already in a position to drastically reduce their militaries without fear of endangering national security. The United States, for example, could cut its military budget by 83 percent and still remain the largest military spender in the world.[14] Such a change would probably require much greater public awareness of the facts about the military budget, as well as a greater disposition towards peace on the part of American citizens. If the nations with the world's largest militaries were to begin to draw down their forces, other nations, perceiving a reduced foreign threat, could also reduce their militaries. Two key facts would drive this process: first, a military is needed only to counter other nations' militaries; if no one had a military, no one would need a military.[15] Second, it requires more military power to invade a country than it does to defend a country. Therefore, if in each year, every country were to maintain only the military force needed for defense, the world level of military forces would continually ratchet downwards until ultimately no nation either had or needed a standing army.

Since one militaristic nation can stall it, this process is likely to be slow and may have to wait on the emergence of a worldwide culture of antimilitarism. Unfortunately, this means that the final solution to the problem of war (elimination of the entities that make war) may have to wait until the problem has been nearly eliminated through other means (the rise of democracy and increasing unpopularity of war).

13.2.4   The rest of the way

The above speculated changes would take the world to what we might call 'the subminimal state': a government or government-like entity that has given up what are often considered some of the core, or minimal, functions of the state – namely, the police, courts, and military.[16] The state thus arrived at, through gradual changes, is very close to anarchy. Indeed, some may consider the condition I have imagined to be already one of anarchy.

What remains is the abolition of the legislature. At present, the legislature is considered necessary to make the laws that police and courts

---

[14] Stockholm International Peace Research Institute 2012; statistics based on 2010 spending levels.

[15] Caplan (2009) stresses this point.

[16] This 'state' would be even more minimal than what Nozick (1974, 26) dubs the 'ultraminimal state'.

are to enforce. And a legislature is indeed necessary to make most of the kinds of laws that exist in modern nations, including moralistic laws, paternalistic laws, rent-seeking laws, and so on.[17] If, however, a society adopted a libertarian philosophy of law, which calls only for laws that prevent victimization of one individual or group by another, then judge-made common law should suffice. Once a society had replaced government courts with private arbitrators and government police with private security guards, assuming that these private mechanisms worked reasonably well, it would be possible to disband the legislature.

Exactly how this would come about is unclear. Would the legislature vote to disband itself? It is hard to imagine any politician supporting such a move. Would public demonstrators march on the capitol and pressure the obsolete politicians into resigning? Perhaps. One thing that seems very plausible, in any case, is that if the legislature no longer had the power, through police or armies, to coerce the rest of society, and the rest of society no longer wished to have a legislature, then the legislature would not long persist.

I have focused here on police, courts, the military, and the legislature because these are usually seen as the most basic and indispensible arms of government. Modern governments have many other tentacles reaching into all aspects of life, and I cannot discuss these here. Even with the aspects of government I have addressed, my account has been speculative and sketchy. No one can predict in detail what the future may hold. My aim, however, has been to show that the eventual emergence of anarchy from the present state of affairs is not implausible and could proceed in gradual steps.

13.3 The geographical spread of anarchy

Anarchy is unlikely to overtake the whole world simultaneously. It is unlikely even to overtake a single large country all at once. What is more likely is that a few small countries or small local governments will take the lead in starting or expanding the sort of experiments in the outsourcing of police and court functions described above. The smaller a government is, the less inertia that government will experience, and the more likely it is to consider radical proposals, especially those that involve giving up government power. Consider, for example, that the world's leaders in the abolition of standing armies are all small countries

---

[17] See Section 7.1.3.

(Costa Rica, Liechtenstein, and so on).[18] The current world leader in the liberalization of drug laws is another small country, Portugal.[19] The world leader in economic liberalization is a single city, Hong Kong. And according to one libertarian-oriented ranking, the freest country in the world is the small nation of Estonia.[20] Once someone takes the lead in reducing a particular sort of government power, it becomes more likely that other cities or countries will follow suit. In the global information age, this sort of spread of good political ideas is more likely than ever, because large numbers of people can see how policies elsewhere are working. Although the process took decades, the stark contrast between life in Marxist-communist regimes and life in the capitalist West ultimately undermined communism from within. As the living standards in democratic capitalist nations drew further and further ahead of those in communist countries, year after year, it became ever more difficult to believe communist ideology, until hardly anyone believed it any longer. A similar process could transpire in the future, between large-government societies and societies practicing something closer to anarcho-capitalism.

The entire process could take centuries. Even today, about half the world's nations continue to embrace autocratic forms of government, despite the overwhelming evidence of the superiority of democracy over authoritarianism. The evident superiority of democracy is not causally impotent – it explains why democracy has spread to half the world, starting from a situation two and a half centuries ago in which no nations were democratic. But some human societies are slower to change than others, so that many will continue a practice long after it is obvious to all that the practice is a terrible idea. Thus, if anarcho-capitalism arrives on the scene, it will probably do so at a time when most of the world lives under democratic government, while some of the world lives still under despotic government. Nations bordering

---

[18] See Section 12.3.6.

[19] Vastag (2009) discusses the benefits of Portugal's drug decriminalization program.

[20] State of World Liberty Project 2006. The ranking is based on a composite of four indexes of freedom: (1) the Fraser Institute/Cato Institute's '2005 Economic Freedom of the World', (2) the Heritage Foundation/*Wall Street Journal*'s '2006 Index of Economic Freedom', (3) Freedom House's '2005 Freedom in the World', and (4) Reporters without Borders' 'Press Freedom Index'. Hong Kong ranks first in economic freedom, while the top position for personal freedom is a four-way tie among the Bahamas, Luxembourg, Malta, and Barbados.

on despotic countries will be ill advised to abandon their governments until after their neighbors' despotic governments have finally fallen.

I have written as if the world's march toward democracy will continue, with all authoritarian governments ultimately destined to fall. This is not inevitable. Perhaps the progress of democratization will stall. Perhaps the world will fall into totalitarianism. But it is at least plausible to think not.

13.4   The importance of ideas

Historical events are often explained in terms of the interests of competing individuals and factions. Sometimes, nonrational emotions and biases are brought into the picture. But we should remember that human beings also possess intelligence and a basic ability to distinguish good ideas from bad ideas. This is the most important and fundamental reason for my optimism regarding the future of anarcho-capitalism. Let me make the reasoning explicit.

1. The theory of anarcho-capitalism is true and well justified.
2. If the theory of anarcho-capitalism is true and well justified, it will come to be generally accepted.
3. If the theory of anarcho-capitalism becomes generally accepted, anarcho-capitalism will be implemented.
4. Therefore, anarcho-capitalism will be implemented.

The first premise is supported by the rest of this book.

The second premise rests on the general tendency for correct ideas to win out in the long run. At any moment in history, it will be tempting to look around at all the people with bad ideas and conclude that humanity is too irrational and ignorant ever to grasp the important truths. But this is historical myopia. The most salient and important trend that stands out in any study of the intellectual history of the past 2000 years must surely be the gradual accretion of knowledge and the corresponding move from worse ideas to better ideas. The process is of course not monotonic – there are cases of stagnation and regression – but the undeniable difference between humanity's knowledge today and its knowledge 2000 years ago is staggering. In the short run, the forces of prejudice may outweigh those of rationality. But prejudices can be worn down over time, while the basic truth of a given idea remains intact over the centuries, exerting whatever force it has on the human mind.

Sometimes it is said that, unlike the sciences, fields such as philosophy, ethics, and politics have made little or no progress in the last 2000 years. While the natural sciences have made the most impressive intellectual progress, the dramatic progress that has occurred in philosophical, moral, and political matters can be missed only through a modern lens that filters out all those issues that we no longer consider worth discussing because we have already resolved them. Throughout most of human history, slavery was widely accepted as just. The mass slaughter of foreigners for purposes of capturing land and resources, forcing conformity to one's own religion, or exacting vengeance for perceived wrongs against one's ancestors was often viewed with approval, if not glorified. Alexander 'the Great' was so called because of his prowess at waging what nearly anyone today would unhesitatingly judge to be unjust and vicious wars. Judicial torture and execution for minor offences was widely accepted. 'Witches' were burned at the stake or drowned. Despotism was the standard form of government, under which people were granted no right to participate in the political process. Even when democracy was at last accepted in some countries, half the adult population was denied any rights of political participation because they were deemed inferior.

When people today say that there is little agreement in ethics and politics, they are ignoring all the issues mentioned in the preceding paragraph. For us, none of those issues is worth discussing, since the correct evaluation is intellectually trivial. 'Should we torture someone to extract a confession of witchcraft and then execute her for being a witch?' This question merits no more than a laugh. But practically speaking, these questions are far from trivial. Slow though it may have been in coming, the current consensus on all these questions represents an enormous advancement from terrible ideas to not-so-terrible ideas.

One might question how far the trend of moral progress will continue. The wrongness of slavery, torture, despotism, and the like is obvious, whereas the wrongness of government, if it is wrong, is more subtle. Perhaps human beings were smart enough, over the course of a few thousand years, to figure out the blindingly obvious moral issues but are not smart enough to figure out more subtle ones.

Perhaps. Then again, what is obvious may be relative to one's time. If a thinker of the stature of Aristotle could not see that slavery was unjust, we must question how objectively obvious it was. And on the other hand, future generations will likely find obvious some things that we have difficulty seeing today. 'Is there a special group of people with the right to use threats of violence to force everyone else to obey their commands, even when their commands are wrong?' Future generations may view the answer to that as too obvious to merit discussion.

My third premise was that, if anarcho-capitalism is generally accepted, it will be adopted. Notwithstanding the sketchy speculations offered in Sections 13.2 and 13.3, I do not know how this will come about. Nevertheless, I consider the premise highly probable. The image of a society continuing to maintain its government, year after year, generation after generation, when most people have long since reached the consensus that it is a bad idea, seems almost absurd. Human social practices are not so disconnected from our beliefs. If society reaches an anarchist consensus, someone will figure out how to get the politicians to go home.

We are a long way from that state of affairs today. Almost everyone believes that some form of government is practically necessary and ethically legitimate. The first step on the road to a nongovernmental society is therefore to change attitudes about government. Those who have been persuaded of anarchism need to make the case to the rest of their society. I hope this book will form part of a societal discourse that in due time accomplishes that task.

In an earlier chapter, I characterized as overly utopian the idea of remedying the flaws in democracy purely through citizen activism (Section 9.4.4). I argued that this would require too much sacrifice on the part of citizens. Why is the proposal of this chapter not similarly utopian? Why is it more realistic to expect that citizens convinced of the illegitimacy of government will work to abolish their government than it is to expect that citizens apprised of the flawed policies implemented by a democratic government will work to perfect their government's policies?

The answer is that acquiring awareness of the illegitimacy of government in general is much, much less cognitively demanding than acquiring sufficient awareness of the specific policy errors of a particular government to enable one to make rational plans to correct most of those errors. To realize that government is illegitimate, it suffices to accept the arguments in this book. But to identify most of the specific policy errors of one's government would require detailed familiarity with thousands of statutes and regulations; dozens of government agencies, boards, and commissions; and hundreds of political figures. One would have to update this knowledge continuously throughout one's life to take account of each new action of each arm of the government. It is much more realistic to hope that a consensus could be reached on a single philosophical principle, the rejection of authority, than to hope that a consensus could be reached on the specific flaws of most particular government policies.

13.5   Conclusion

13.5.1   The argument of Part I

The modern state claims a kind of authority that obliges all other agents to obey the state's commands and entitles the state to deploy violence and threats of violence to enforce those commands, independent of whether the commands are in themselves just, reasonable, or beneficial. The argument of the first half of this book is that that sort of authority, 'political authority', is an illusion. No state is legitimate, and no individual has political obligations. This leads to the conclusion that at minimum, the vast majority of government activities are unjust. Government agents should refuse to enforce unjust laws, and individuals should feel free to break such laws whenever they can safely do so.

The argument against political authority proceeded by examining the most important arguments *for* authority and finding each inadequate. The traditional social contract theory fails due to one salient fact: there is no actual contract. The most common theory of contemporary social contract enthusiasts – that an arrangement is rendered voluntary and contractual by the fact that one could have escaped its imposition through relocation to Antarctica – would draw scarcely more than a laugh in any other context.

The alternative of a purely hypothetical social contract fails for two reasons: first, there is no reason to think that all reasonable persons could agree, even in idealized circumstances, on even the most basic political theory. Second, a merely hypothetical contract is ethically irrelevant. However fair, reasonable, and impartial a contract might be, one is not typically thereby entitled to force others to accept it.

The democratic process fails to ground authority, as one typically does not acquire a right to coerce someone merely because those who want one to coerce the victim are more numerous than those who want one to refrain. The appeal to the ideal of deliberative democracy fails, because no actual state remotely resembles an ideal deliberative democracy, and in any case, no mere method of deliberation negates the rights of an individual. The appeal to the obligations to promote equality and to respect others' judgment fails for several reasons, including that these obligations are not strong enough to override individuals' rights, that they are not the sort of obligation that may typically be enforced through coercion, and that the idea of political legitimacy itself is a much clearer violation of the value of equality than the failure of individuals to obey democratically made laws.

The appeal to the good consequences of government fails to ground authority because an individual's obedience to the law has no impact on the state's ability to provide those benefits, and an agent's provision of large overall benefits does not confer on the agent an entitlement to coerce others to obey the agent's commands independent of the content of those commands. The appeal to fairness likewise cannot ground an obligation to obey harmful, unjust, or useless commands nor an ethical entitlement to deploy coercion in support of such commands.

A review of psychological and historical evidence concerning human attitudes to authority suggests two important lessons: first, most individuals have strong pro-authority biases that render their intuitions about authority untrustworthy. Second, institutions of authority are extremely dangerous, and the undermining of trust in authority is therefore highly socially beneficial.

13.5.2 The argument of Part II

Pace Hobbes, when diverse agents have roughly equal power, it is prudentially irrational for any agent to initiate conflict. In contrast, centralization of power invites exploitation and abuse by the powerful. The democratic process inhibits the worst government abuses, but it remains imperfect due to widespread ignorance and irrationality on the part of voters. Constitutional restrictions are often impotent, since there is none but the government to enforce the constitution. The separation of powers fails because the branches of government can best promote their interests through making common cause in expanding state power rather than protecting the rights of the people.

The contention of Part II of this book is that a superior alternative exists, in which governmental functions are privatized. Police duties may be taken over by private security guards, perhaps hired by small local property owners' associations. This system differs from governmental provision of security in that it relies on genuine contractual arrangements, and it incorporates meaningful competition among security providers. These differences would lead to higher quality, lower cost, and less potential for abuse than found in coercive monopolistic systems.

Resolution of disputes, including disputes about whether a given individual committed a crime and whether a given type of conduct ought to be tolerated, would be provided by private arbitrators.

Individuals and firms in an anarchic society would choose this method of resolving disputes because it is far less costly than resolution through violence. Law would be generated chiefly by the arbitrators themselves, in the manner in which the common law has developed in the actual world. The voluntariness and competitiveness of the system, again, would lead to higher quality, lower costs, and less abuse.

The elimination of government military forces need not leave a society insecure. Under certain favorable conditions, a society can be safe from invasion despite the lack of military deterrence. In the event of invasion, guerrilla warfare or nonviolent resistance can prove surprisingly effective at expelling foreign occupiers. In some ways, having a government makes a society more rather than less likely to be involved in war – for example, because one's government may provoke a conflict. A number of small countries have already successfully abolished their militaries without being conquered as a result. The maintenance of standing armies entails a nontrivial risk of those armies being used unjustly, as well as a risk of one's government inventing new weapons of mass destruction that threaten the human species.

13.5.3 The argument of this chapter

It is reasonable to believe that anarchy may come to the world in due time. The most plausible transitional model is one in which democratic societies move gradually toward anarcho-capitalism through progressive outsourcing of governmental functions to competing businesses. No obstacle but public opinion and inertia prevents government from turning over policing, dispute resolution, or even the conduct of criminal trials to private agents. Governmental armed forces could be drawn down and ultimately eliminated through an extended ratcheting-down process in which each country repeatedly cuts back its military forces to only those needed for defense. The process of eliminating government is likely to be spearheaded by small democratic countries or cities. Larger countries could be expected to follow suit only after the success of small-scale experiments was evident to most observers.

The most important determinant of whether this process will occur is intellectual: if anarcho-capitalism is a good idea, then it will probably ultimately be recognized as such. Once it is generally recognized as desirable, it will probably eventually be implemented. Abolishing the state is more realistic than reforming it, because abolition requires people to accept only a single philosophical idea – skepticism about authority – whereas reform requires people to familiarize themselves on an ongoing basis with the myriad flaws of specific policies.

This book is an effort to help push society along towards the needed skepticism of authority. It may seem that my position is extreme – as of course it is, relative to the current spectrum of opinion. But current mainstream attitudes are also extreme, relative to the spectrum of opinion of earlier centuries. The *average* citizen of a modern democracy, if transported back in time 500 years, would be the most wild-eyed, radical liberal on the planet – endorsing an undreamt-of equality for both sexes and all races; free expression for the most heinous of heretics, infidels, and atheists; a complete abolition of numerous standard forms of punishment; and a radical restructuring of all existing governments. By current standards, every government of 500 years ago was illegitimate.

We have not come to the end of history (*pace* Fukuyama). The evolution of values can proceed further in the direction it has moved over the past two millennia. It could proceed to an even greater distaste for the resort to physical force in human interactions, a fuller respect for human dignity, and a more consistent recognition of the moral equality of persons. Once we take these values sufficiently seriously, we cannot but be skeptical of authority.

My method of pushing readers along this path has been to appeal to implicit values that I think you share. I do not rely on an abstract, theoretical account of these values; I rely on the intuitive reactions we have to relatively specific scenarios. Nor do I rely on tentative or controversial intuitions; I rely on clear, mainstream intuitions. For example, the judgment that an employer who draws up a fair and reasonable employment contract would not thereupon be entitled to force potential employees to accept it (Section 3.3.3), is not particularly dubious or controversial. It is not something that only libertarian ideologues would agree to.

Consider now the antiwar argument offered by the Chinese philosopher Mozi in the 5th century B.C.:

> To kill one man is to be guilty of a capital crime, to kill ten men is to increase the guilt tenfold, to kill a hundred men is to increase it a hundredfold. This the rulers of the earth all recognize, and yet when it comes to the greatest crime – waging war on another state – they praise it! [...] If a man on seeing a little black were to say it is black, but on seeing a lot of black were to say it is white, it would be clear that such a man could not distinguish black and white. [...] So

those who recognize a small crime as such, but do not recognize the wickedness of the greatest crime of all [...] cannot distinguish right and wrong.[21]

Mozi's argumentative strategy is simple and compelling: he begins from an uncontroversial ethical prohibition, applies the same principle to a particular kind of government policy, and finds that the policy is morally unacceptable. It is in the spirit of Mozi that I question the institution of government as a whole. If one individual travels to another country to kill people, coercively extracts money from members of his own society, forces others to work for him, or imposes harmful, unjust, or useless demands on others through threats of kidnapping and imprisonment, the governments of the world all condemn that individual. Yet these same governments do not shy away from undertaking the same activities on a national scale. If we find Mozi's argument compelling, then it seems that we ought to find similarly compelling the argument that the great majority of government actions are ethically unacceptable.

---

[21] From the epigraph to Kurlansky 2006.

References

Abrahms, Max. 2006. 'Why Terrorism Does Not Work', *International Security* 31, 2: 42–78.

——. 2011. 'Does Terrorism Really Work? Evolution in the Conventional Wisdom since 9/11', *Defence and Peace Economics* 22: 583–94.

Acton, John. 1972. *Essays on Freedom and Power*, ed. Gertrude Himmelfarb. Gloucester, MA: Peter Smith.

Adams, Ian. 2001. *Political Ideology Today*, second edition. Manchester, UK: Manchester University Press.

Agan, Amanda, and Alexander Tabarrok. 2005. 'What Are Private Governments Worth?' *Regulation* 28, 3: 14–17.

Allison, Graham. 2004. *Nuclear Terrorism: The Ultimate Preventable Catastrophe*. New York: Henry Holt.

American Psychiatric Association. 1994. *Diagnostic and Statistical Manual of Mental Disorders*, fourth edition. Washington, DC: American Psychiatric Association.

Arendt, Hannah. 1964. *Eichmann in Jerusalem: A Report on the Banality of Evil*, revised and enlarged edition. New York: Viking Press.

Aristotle. 1941. *The Basic Works of Aristotle*, ed. Richard McKeon. New York: Random House.

Arkes, Hal, and Catherine Blumer. 1985. 'The Psychology of Sunk Cost', *Organizational Behavior and Human Decision Processes* 35: 124–40.

Arlow, Oliver. 2010. 'Kim Jong-il Keeps $4bn "Emergency Fund" in European Banks', *Sunday Telegraph*, March 14, www.telegraph.co.uk/news/worldnews /asia/northkorea/7442188/Kim-Jong-il-keeps-4bn-emergency-fund-in-Europe an-banks.html. Accessed March 4, 2011.

Aronson, Elliot. 1999. 'Dissonance, Hypocrisy, and the Self-Concept'. Pp. 103–26 in *Cognitive Dissonance: Progress on a Pivotal Theory in Social Psychology*, ed. Eddie Harmon-Jones and Judson Mills. Washington, DC: American Psychological Association.

Aronson, Elliot, and Judson Mills. 1959. 'The Effect of Severity of Initiation on Liking for a Group', *Journal of Abnormal and Social Psychology* 59: 177–81.

Aronson, Joshua, Geoffrey Cohen, and Paul R. Nail. 1999. 'Self-Affirmation Theory: An Update and Appraisal'. Pp. 127–47 in *Cognitive Dissonance: Progress on a Pivotal Theory in Social Psychology*, ed. Eddie Harmon-Jones and Judson Mills. Washington, DC: American Psychological Association.

Asch, Solomon E. 1956. 'Studies of Independence and Conformity: A Minority of One against a Unanimous Majority', *Psychological Monographs: General and Applied* 70, 9: 1–70.

Asch, Solomon E.. 1963. 'Effects of Group Pressure upon the Modification and Distortion of Judgments'. Pp. 177–90 in *Groups, Leadership and Men: Research in Human Relations*, ed. Harold Guetzkow. New York: Russell & Russell.

Atran, Scott. 2010. *Talking to the Enemy: Faith, Brotherhood, and the (Un)making of Terrorists*. New York: HarperCollins.

Babst, Dean V. 1972. 'A Force for Peace', *Industrial Research* 14, 4: 55–8.

Bakunin, Mikhail. 1972. *Bakunin on Anarchy*, ed. and tr. Sam Dolgoff. New York: Knopf.

Banfield, Edward C. 1977. 'Present-Orientedness and Crime'. Pp. 133–42 in *Assessing the Criminal: Restitution, Retribution, and the Legal Process*, ed. Randy E. Barnett and John Hagel III. Cambridge, MA: Ballinger.

Barnett, Randy E. 1998. *The Structure of Liberty: Justice and the Rule of Law*. Oxford: Clarendon.

Bartels, Larry M. 1996. 'Uninformed Voters: Information Effects in Presidential Elections', *American Journal of Political Science* 40: 194–230.

Batten, Donna, ed. 2011. 'Arbitration'. Pp. 344–8 in *Gale Encyclopedia of American Law*, third edition, vol. 1. Detroit, MI: Gale Cengage Learning.

BBC News. 1999. 'Pushing Back the Curtain: Poland', http://news.bbc.co.uk/hi/english/static/special_report/1999/09/99/iron_curtain/timelines/poland.stm. Accessed September 7, 2011.

———. 2003. 'Foreign Troops in Iraq', November 29, http://news.bbc.co.uk/2/hi/middle_east/3267451.stm. Accessed October 18, 2011.

Beck, Allen J., Paige M. Harrison, Marcus Berzofsky, Rachel Caspar, and Christopher Krebs. 2010. *Sexual Victimization in Prisons and Jails Reported by Inmates, 2008–09*, U.S. Department of Justice, Bureau of Justice Statistics, www.bjs.gov/content/pub/pdf/svpjri0809.pdf. Accessed January 30, 2012.

Bhagwati, Jagdish, François Bourguignon, Finn Kydland, Robert Mundell, Douglass North, Thomas Schelling, Vernon Smith, and Nancy Stokey. 2009. 'Expert Panel Ranking'. Pp. 657–79 in *Global Crises, Global Solutions*, second edition, ed. Bjørn Lomborg. Cambridge: Cambridge University Press.

bin Laden, Osama. 1996. *Declaration of War against the Americans Occupying the Land of the Two Holy Places*. English translation provided by PBS as 'Bin Laden's Fatwa', www.pbs.org/newshour/terrorism/international/fatwa_1996.html. Accessed October 13, 2011.

bin Laden, Osama, Ayman al-Zawahiri, Ahmed Refai Taha, Mir Hamzah, and Fazul Rahman. 1998. *Jihad against Jews and Crusaders*. English translation provided by the Federation of American Scientists, www.fas.org/irp/world/para/docs/980223-fatwa.htm. Accessed October 13, 2011.

Birch, Paul. 1998. 'A Fatal Instability in Anarcho-Capitalism? The Problem of What Happens to the Restitution Ratio', *Legal Notes* 27: 1–4, www.libertarian.co.uk/lapubs/legan/legan027.pdf. Accessed April 19, 2011.

Birkler, John, Michael Mattock, John Schank, Giles Smith, Fred Timson, James Chiesa, Bruce Woodyard, Malcolm MacKinnon, and Denis Rushworth. 1998. *The U.S. Aircraft Carrier Industrial Base: Force Structure, Cost, Schedule, and Technology Issues for CVN 77*. Santa Monica, CA: RAND.

Blake, Michael. 2002. 'Distributive Justice, State Coercion, and Autonomy', *Philosophy and Public Affairs* 30: 257–96.

Blanton, Thomas. 1997. 'Annals of Blinksmanship', *Wilson Quarterly* 21 (1997): 90–3, www.gwu.edu/~nsarchiv/nsa/cuba_mis_cri/annals.htm. Accessed January 22, 2012.

Borenstein, Seth. 2008. 'American Life Worth Less Today', *Huffington Post*, July 10, www.huffingtonpost.com/2008/07/10/american-life-worth-less_n_112030.html. Accessed August 12, 2010.

Brandt, Richard. 1964. 'The Concepts of Obligation and Duty', *Mind* 73: 374–93.

——. 1992. *Morality, Utilitarianism, and Rights*. Cambridge: Cambridge University Press.

Brehm, Jack W. 1956. 'Post-decision Changes in Desirability of Alternatives', *Journal of Abnormal and Social Psychology* 52: 384–9.

Bremer, Stuart A. 1992. 'Dangerous Dyads: Conditions Affecting the Likelihood of Interstate War, 1816–1965', *Journal of Conflict Resolution* 36: 309–41.

Brennan, Jason. 2011. 'The Right to a Competent Electorate', *Philosophical Quarterly* 61: 700–24.

Brook, Marisa. 2007. 'Sympathy for the Devil', *Damn Interesting*, www.damninteresting.com/sympathy-for-the-devil. Accessed July 20, 2010.

Brozen, Yale. 1968. 'Is Government the Source of Monopoly?' *Intercollegiate Review* 5, 2: 67–78.

Buchanan, Allen. 2002. 'Political Legitimacy and Democracy', *Ethics* 112: 689–719.

Bunn, Matthew. 2006. 'Confronting the Specter of Nuclear Terrorism', *Annals of the American Academy of Political and Social Science* 607: 103–20.

Bush, George W. 2001. Address before Congress, 21 September. Transcript, http://articles.cnn.com/2001–09–20/us/gen.bush.transcript_1_joint-session-national-anthem-citizens?_s=PM:US. Accessed October 13, 2011.

Bushman, Brad. 1988. 'The Effects of Apparel on Compliance: A Field Experiment with a Female Authority Figure', *Personality and Social Psychology Bulletin* 14: 459–67.

California Attorney' s Fees. 2011. *Reasonableness of Fees: Two Recent Incisive Legal Intelligence Studies Show Average Billing Rates for Small and Mid-Sized Firms and Internal Costs for In-House Counsel Departments*, February 13, www.calattorneysfees.com/2011/02/reasonableness-of-fees-two-recent-incisive-legal-intelligence-studies-show-average-billing-rates-for-small-and-mid-sized-fir.html. Accessed January 27, 2012.

Canadian Department of National Defence. 2011. *Recruiting and Retention in the Canadian Forces*, www.forces.gc.ca/site/news-nouvelles/news-nouvelles-eng.asp?id=3792. Accessed September 29, 2011.

Canbäck, Staffan, Phillip Samouel, and David Price. 2006. 'Do Diseconomies of Scale Impact Firm Size and Performance? A Theoretical and Empirical Overview', *Journal of Managerial Economics* 4, 1: 27–70, http://canback.com/publications.htm. Accessed April 20, 2011.

Caplan, Bryan. n.d. *Anarchist Theory FAQ*, version 5.2, http://econfaculty.gmu.edu/bcaplan/anarfaq.htm. Accessed April 24, 2011.

——. 2006. 'The Myth of the Rational Voter', *Cato Unbound*, www.cato-unbound.org/2006/11/06/bryan-caplan/the-myth-of-the-rational-voter/. Accessed March 25, 2010.

——. 2007a. 'Have the Experts Been Weighed, Measured, and Found Wanting?' *Critical Review* 19: 81–91.

——. 2007b. *The Myth of the Rational Voter*. Princeton, NJ: Princeton University Press.

——. 2009. *A Simple Proof that 'National Defense' Is Not a Public Good*, http://econlog.econlib.org/archives/2009/10/a_simple_proof.html. Accessed January 26, 2012.

——. 2010. 'Less than the Minimal State' (podcast), *Foundation for Economic Education*, http://castroller.com/Podcasts/FoundationForEconomic/1454459. Accessed January 26, 2012.

Caplan, Bryan, and Edward P. Stringham. 2007. 'Networks, Law, and the Paradox of Cooperation'. Pp. 295–314 in *Anarchy and the Law: The Political Economy of Choice*, ed. Edward P. Stringham. New Brunswick, NJ: Transaction.

———. 2008. 'Privatizing the Adjudication of Disputes', *Theoretical Inquiries in Law* 9: 503–28.

Carens, Joseph. 1987. 'Aliens and Citizens: The Case for Open Borders', *Review of Politics* 49: 251–73.

Carney, Timothy. 2006. *The Big Ripoff: How Big Business and Big Government Steal Your Money*. Hoboken, NJ: Wiley.

Carson, Kevin A. 2008. *Organization Theory: A Libertarian Perspective*. N.p.: Booksurge.

Cashman, Greg. 1993. *What Causes War? An Introduction to Theories of International Conflict*. New York: Lexington Books.

Cashman, Greg, and Leonard C. Robinson. 2007. *An Introduction to the Causes of War: Patterns of Interstate Conflict from World War I to Iraq*. Lanham, MD: Rowman & Littlefield.

CBS News. 2011. 'WikiLeaks: Bradley Manning Faces 22 New Charges', *CBS News*, 2 March, www.cbsnews.com/stories/2011/03/02/national/main20038464. shtml. Accessed March 10, 2011.

Center for Responsive Politics. 2011. *Reelection Rates over the Years*, www.opensecrets.org/bigpicture/reelect.php?cycle=2006. Accessed March 15, 2011.

Center for Systemic Peace. 2011. *Polity IV Annual Time-Series 1800–2010* (dataset from Polity IV project), www.systemicpeace.org/inscr/inscr.htm. Accessed January 24, 2012.

Chakrabortty, Aditya. 2008. 'Secret Report: Biofuel Caused Food Crisis', *The Guardian*, July 3, www.guardian.co.uk/environment/2008/jul/03/biofuels. renewableenergy. Accessed March 8, 2011.

Chambers, John Whiteclay. 2003. 'S. L. A. Marshall's Men against Fire: New Evidence Regarding Fire Ratios', *Parameters* 33, 3: 113–21.

Chomsky, Noam. 2005. *Chomsky on Anarchism*, ed. Barry Pateman. Edinburgh: AK Press.

Choucri, Nazli, and Robert C. North. 1975. *Nations in Conflict: National Growth and International Violence*. San Francisco, CA: W. H. Freeman.

Christiano, Thomas. 2004. 'The Authority of Democracy', *Journal of Political Philosophy* 12: 266–90.

Christiano, Thomas. 2008. *The Constitution of Equality: Democratic Authority and Its Limits*. Oxford: Oxford University Press.

Cialdini, Robert. 1993. *Influence: The Psychology of Persuasion*, revised edition. New York: William Morrow.

Clodfelter, Michael. 2002. *Warfare and Armed Conflicts: A Statistical Reference to Casualty and Other Figures, 1500–2000*, second edition. Jefferson, NC: McFarland.

CNN. 2003. *Amid Furor, Pentagon Kills Terrorism Futures Market*, July 30, www.cnn.com/2003/ALLPOLITICS/07/29/terror.market/index.html. Accessed March 28, 2012.

———. 2011. *Tea Party Republican Debate*, September 12. Transcript available at http://archives.cnn.com/TRANSCRIPTS/1109/12/se.06.html, accessed October 18, 2011. Video clip available at www.youtube.com/watch?v=V9RaV44a0EE, accessed October 18, 2011.

CNN Money. 2012. 'Fortune 500', http://money.cnn.com/magazines/fortune/fortune500/2010/full_list/. Accessed February 8, 2012.

Cohen, Gerald A. 1992. 'Incentives, Inequality, and Community'. Pp. 261–329 in *The Tanner Lectures on Human Values*, vol. 13. Salt Lake City, UT: University of Utah Press.

Cohen, Joshua. 2002. 'Deliberation and Democratic Legitimacy'. Pp. 87–106 in *Democracy*, ed. David Estlund. Malden, MA: Blackwell. Originally appeared in *The Good Polity*, 17–34, ed. Alan Hamlin and Phillip Petit. New York: Blackwell, 1989.

Coleman, Fred. 1996. *The Decline and Fall of the Soviet Empire: Forty Years that Shook the World, from Stalin to Yeltsin*. New York: Saint Martin's Press.

Commission on Safety and Abuse in America's Prisons. 2006. *Confronting Confinement*. New York: Vera Institute of Justice, 2006.

Commission on the Prevention of WMD Proliferation and Terrorism. 2008. *World at Risk: The Report of the Commission on the Prevention of WMD Proliferation and Terrorism*. New York: Random House.

Condorcet, Marquis de. 1994. *Condorcet: Foundations of Social Choice and Political Theory*, ed. and tr. Iain McLean and Fiona Hewitt. Aldershot, UK: Edward Elgar.

Contoski, Edmund. 2010. 'Obama Fails to Learn the Pilgrims' Lesson', Forces International, forces.org/Forces_Articles/article_viewer.php?id=690. Accessed August 26, 2012.

Converse, Philip E. 1990. 'Popular Representation and the Distribution of Information'. Pp. 369–88 in *Information and Democratic Processes*, ed. John A. Ferejohn and James H. Kuklinski. Urbana: University of Illinois Press.

Copeland, Dale C. 2000. *The Origins of Major War*. Ithaca, NY: Cornell University Press.

Cordesman, Anthony H. 2005. *The Challenge of Biological Terrorism*. Washington, DC: Center for Strategic and International Studies.

Courtois, Stéphane, Nicolas Werth, Jean-Louis Panné, Andrzej Paczkowski, Karel Bartošek, and Jean-Louis Margolin. 1999. *The Black Book of Communism*, tr. by Jonathan Murphy and Mark Kramer. Cambridge, MA: Harvard University Press.

Cowen, Tyler. 2002. 'Does the Welfare State Help the Poor?' *Social Philosophy and Policy* 19: 36–54.

——. 2007a. 'The Importance of Defining the Feasible Set', *Economics and Philosophy* 23: 1–14.

——. 2007b. 'Law as a Public Good: The Economics of Anarchy'. Pp. 268–83 in *Anarchy and the Law: The Political Economy of Choice*, ed. Edward P. Stringham. New Brunswick, NJ: Transaction.

Cowen, Tyler, and Daniel Sutter. 2007. 'Conflict, Cooperation and Competition in Anarchy'. Pp. 315–21 in *Anarchy and the Law: The Political Economy of Choice*, ed. Edward P. Stringham. New Brunswick, NJ: Transaction.

Crain, Nicole V., and Mark Crain. 2010. 'The Impact of Regulatory Costs on Small Firms', report for the U.S. Small Business Administration, September, http://archive.sba.gov/advo/research/rs371tot.pdf. Accessed April 15, 2011.

Crews, Clyde Wayne. 2011. *Ten Thousand Commandments: An Annual Snapshot of the Federal Regulatory State*. Washington, DC: Competitive Enterprise Institute, http://cei.org/10KC. Accessed May 3, 2011.

Dakolias, Maria. 1999. *Court Performance around the World: A Comparative Perspective*, World Bank Technical Paper no. 430. Washington, DC: World Bank.

Dancy, Jonathan. 1993. *Moral Reasons*. Oxford: Blackwell.

Davidson, Donald. 1990. 'A Coherence Theory of Truth and Knowledge'. Pp. 120–38 in *Reading Rorty*, ed. Alan Malachowski. Cambridge, MA: Basil Blackwell.

de Fabrique, Nathalie, Stephen Romano, Gregory Vecchi, and Vincent van Hasselt. 2007. 'Understanding Stockholm Syndrome', *FBI Law Enforcement Bulletin* 70, 7, www.fbi.gov/publications/leb/2007/july2007/july2007leb.htm. Accessed July 20, 2010.

DeLue, Steven M. 1989. *Political Obligation in a Liberal State*. Albany, NY: SUNY Press.

Delli Carpini, Michael, and Scott Keeter. 1996. *What Americans Know about Politics and Why It Matters*. New Haven, CT: Yale University Press.

Disaster Center. 2011a. *United States Crime Rates 1960–2010*, www.disastercenter.com/crime/uscrime.htm. Accessed October 2, 2011.

———. 2011b. *Number of Deaths, Death Rates, and Age-adjusted Death Rates, by Race and Sex: United States, 1940, 1950, 1960, 1970, and 1980–2006*, www.disastercenter.com/cdc/Table_1_2006.html. Accessed October 2, 2011.

Dobbs, Michael. 2008. *One Minute to Midnight: Kennedy, Khrushchev, and Castro on the Brink of Nuclear War*. New York: Knopf.

Domke, William K. 1988. *War and the Changing Global System*. New Haven, CT: Yale University Press.

Downs, Anthony. 1957. *An Economic Theory of Democracy*. Boston, MA: Addison-Wesley.

Doyle, Michael W. 2010a. 'Kant, Liberal Legacies, and Foreign Affairs'. Pp. 17–44 in *Democratic Peace in Theory and Practice*, ed. Steven W. Hook. Kent, OH: Kent State University Press. Originally published in *Philosophy and Public Affairs* 12 (1983): 205–35.

———. 2010b. 'Kant, Liberal Legacies, and Foreign Affairs, Part 2'. Pp. 115–41 in *Democratic Peace in Theory and Practice*, ed. Steven W. Hook. Kent, OH: Kent State University Press. Originally published in *Philosophy and Public Affairs* 12 (1983): 323–53.

Duane, James Joseph. 1996. 'Jury Nullification: The Top Secret Constitutional Right', *Litigation* 22, 4: 6–60.

Duke, Steven B. 2006. 'Eyewitness Testimony Doesn't Make It True', *Yale Law School*, www.law.yale.edu/news/2727.htm. Accessed April 26, 2011.

Dworkin, Ronald. 1989. 'The Original Position'. Pp. 16–53 in *Reading Rawls: Critical Studies on Rawls' A Theory of Justice*. Stanford, CA: Stanford University Press.

Ebon, Martin. 1994. *KGB: Death and Rebirth*. Westport, CT: Praeger.

Edmundson, William A. 1998. *Three Anarchical Fallacies: An Essay on Political Authority*. Cambridge: Cambridge University Press.

Estlund, David. 2008. *Democratic Authority: A Philosophical Framework*. Princeton, NJ: Princeton University Press.

Etter, Lauren, and Greg Hitt. 2008. 'Farm Lobby Beats Back Assault on Subsidies', *Wall Street Journal*, March 27, A1, http://online.wsj.com/article/SB12065764541996707.html. Accessed March 8, 2011.

Festinger, Leon, and James Carlsmith. 1959. 'Cognitive Consequences of Forced Compliance', *Journal of Abnormal and Social Psychology* 58: 203–10.

Finckenauer, James. 2009. 'Organized Crime'. pp. 304–24 in *The Oxford Handbook of Crime and Public Policy*. Oxford: Oxford University Press.

Fitzpatrick, Laura. 2009. 'A Brief History of Stockholm Syndrome', *Time*, August 31, 2009, www.time.com/time/nation/article/0,8599,1919757,00.html. Accessed July 20, 2010.

Foot, Philippa. 1967. 'The Problem of Abortion and the Doctrine of the Double Effect', *Oxford Review* 5: 5–15.

Freud, Anna. 1937. *The Ego and the Mechanisms of Defence*, tr. Cecil Baines. London: Hogarth.

Friedman, David. 1989. *The Machinery of Freedom*. LaSalle, IL: Open Court.

——. 1990. *Price Theory: An Intermediate Text*. Cincinnati, OH: Southwestern.

——. 1994. 'A Positive Account of Property Rights', *Social Philosophy and Policy* 11: 1–16.

Friedman, Milton. 1953. 'The Methodology of Positive Economics'. Pp. 3–43 in *Essays in Positive Economics*. Chicago: University of Chicago Press.

Fry, Douglas P. 2007. *Beyond War: The Human Potential for Peace*. Oxford: Oxford University Press.

Gamel, Kim. 2009. 'Secret Government Tally Has 87,215 Iraqis Dead since 2005', *Associated Press*, April 24, www.pantagraph.com/news/article_302ea350-d639-50e9-b5f1-b9b280acefe4.html. Accessed March 6, 2011.

Gartzke, Erik. 2010. 'The Common Origins of Democracy and Peace'. Pp. 61–78 in *Democratic Peace in Theory and Practice*, ed. Steven W. Hook. Kent, OH: Kent State University Press.

Gat, Azar. 2006. *War in Human Civilization*. Oxford: Oxford University Press.

Gaus, Gerald. 2003. *Contemporary Theories of Liberalism: Public Reason as a Post-Enlightenment Project*. London: Sage.

Gauthier, David. 1986. *Morals by Agreement*. Oxford: Clarendon Press.

Gilovich, Thomas, Dale Griffin, and Daniel Kahneman. 2002. *Heuristics and Biases: The Psychology of Intuitive Judgment*. Cambridge: Cambridge University Press.

Gleditsch, Nils P. 1992. 'Democracy and Peace', *Journal of Peace Research* 29: 369–76.

Goldstein, Amy. 2007. 'More Security Firms Getting Police Powers: Some See Benefits To Public Safety, But Others Are Wary', *San Francisco Chronicle*, Sunday, January 7, A3, www.sfgate.com/cgi-bin/article.cgi?f=/c/a/2007/01/07/MNGVENCASV1.DTL&ao=all. Accessed January 26, 2012.

Goodin, Robert. 1988. 'What Is So Special about Our Fellow Countrymen?' *Ethics* 98: 663–86.

Graham, Dee, Edna Rawlings, Kim Ihms, Diane Latimer, Janet Foliano, Alicia Thompson, Kelly Suttman, Mary Farrington, and Rachel Hacker. 1995. 'A Scale for Identifying "Stockholm Syndrome" Reactions in Young Dating Women: Factor Structure, Reliability and Validity', *Violence and Victims* 10: 3–22.

Graham, Dee, Edna Rawlings, and Roberta Rigsby. 1994. *Loving to Survive: Sexual Terror, Men's Violence, and Women's Lives*. New York: New York University Press.

Green, Leslie. 1988. *The Authority of the State*. Oxford: Clarendon Press.

Green, Mark J. (ed.). 1973. *The Monopoly Makers: Ralph Nader's Study Group Report on Regulation and Competition*. New York: Grossman.

Gross, Samuel R., Kristen Jacoby, Daniel J. Matheson, Nicholas Montgomery, and Sujata Patil. 2005. 'Exonerations in the United States 1989 through 2003', *Journal of Criminal Law and Criminology* 95: 523–60.

Grossman, Dave. 1995. *On Killing: The Psychological Cost of Learning to Kill in War and Society*. Boston: Little, Brown.

Habermas, Jürgen. 1975. *Legitimation Crisis*, tr. by Thomas McCarthy. Boston: Beacon Press.

——. 1979. *Communication and the Evolution of Society*, tr. by Thomas McCarthy. Boston: Beacon Press.

——. 2002. 'Deliberative Politics'. Pp. 107–25 in *Democracy*, ed. David Estlund. Malden, MA: Blackwell.

Hamilton, Alexander, James Madison, and John Jay. 1952. *The Federalist*, in *Great Books of the Western World*, vol. 43, ed. Robert Maynard Hutchins. Chicago: Encyclopaedia Britannica. *The Federalist* originally published 1787–8.

Hamner, Christopher. n.d. 'American Resistance to a Standing Army', Teaching History, http://teachinghistory.org/history-content/ask-a-historian/24671. Accessed January 26, 2012.

Hamor, Ralph. 1614. *A True Discourse of the Present Estate of Virginia and the Successe of the Affaires There Till the 18 of Iune*, http://memory.loc.gov/cgi-bin/query/r?ammem/lhbcb:@field(DOCID+@lit(lhbcb02778)). Accessed May 14 2012.

Hanson, Robin, and Tyler Cowen. 2004. 'Are Disagreements Honest?' unpublished ms., http://hanson.gmu.edu/deceive.pdf. Accessed January 29, 2012.

Hardin, Garrett. 1974. 'Lifeboat Ethics: The Case against Helping the Poor', *Psychology Today* 8, September: 38–126.

Hare, Robert D. 1993. *Without Conscience: The Disturbing World of the Psychopaths among Us*. New York: Simon & Schuster.

Harper, Jim. 2008. '10,000 Bills Introduced in Congress, While Government Management Goes Neglected', *WashingtonWatch.com Blog*, August 23, www.washingtonwatch.com/blog/2008/08/03/10000-bills-introduced-in-congress-while-government-management-goes-neglected/. Accessed March 8, 2011.

Harsanyi, John C. 1953. 'Cardinal Utility in Welfare Economics and in the Theory of Risk-Taking', *Journal of Political Economy* 61: 434–5.

——. 1955. 'Cardinal Welfare, Individualistic Ethics, and Interpersonal Comparisons of Utility', *Journal of Political Economy* 63: 309–21.

——. 1975. 'Can the Maximin Principle Serve as a Basis for Morality? A Critique of John Rawls's Theory', *American Political Science Review* 69: 594–606.

Hart, H. L. A. 1955. 'Are There Any Natural Rights?' *Philosophical Review* 64: 175–91.

——. 1958. 'Legal and Moral Obligation' in *Essays in Moral Philosophy*, ed. A. I. Melden. Seattle: University of Washington Press.

Hazlett, Thomas W. 1997. 'Looking for Results' (interview with Ronald Coase), *Reason* 28, 8: 40–6.

Henig, Ruth. 1995. *Versailles and After: 1919–1933*, second edition. London: Routledge.

Herring, George C. 2002. *America's Longest War: The United States and Vietnam, 1950–1975*, fourth edition. Boston: McGraw-Hill.

Heywood, Andrew. 1992. *Political Ideologies: An Introduction*. New York: Saint Martin's Press.

Hobbes, Thomas. 1996. *Leviathan*, ed. Richard Tuck. Cambridge: Cambridge University Press. Originally published 1651.

Hoffman, Elizabeth, Kevin McCabe, Keith Shachat, and Vernon Smith. 1994. 'Preferences, Property Rights, and Anonymity in Bargaining Games', *Games and Economic Behavior* 7: 346–80.

Hoffman, Leah. 2006. 'To Have and To Hold on To', *Forbes*, November 7, www.forbes.com/2006/11/07/divorce-costs-legal-biz-cx_lh_1107legaldivorce.html. Accessed May 3, 2011.

Holguin, Jaime. 2002. 'A Murder a Minute', *CBS News*, October 3, www.cbsnews.com/stories/2002/10/03/health/main524231.shtml. Accessed March 21, 2011.

Holmes, Stephen, and Cass Sunstein. 1999. *The Cost of Rights: Why Liberty Depends on Taxes*. New York: Norton.

Honoré, Tony. 1981. 'Must We Obey? Necessity as a Ground of Obligation', *Virginia Law Review* 67: 39–61.

Hopkinson, Michael. 2002. *The Irish War of Independence*. Montreal: McGill–Queen's University Press.

Hornberger, Jacob G. 2006. *Why Do They Hate Us?* www.fff.org/comment /com0608c.asp. Accessed October 13, 2011.

Horne, Alistair. 1987. *A Savage War of Peace: Algeria, 1954–1962*. New York: Penguin.

Horton, Sue, Harold Alderman, and Juan Rivera. 2009. 'Hunger and Malnutrition'. Pp. 305–33 in *Global Crises, Global Solutions*, second edition, ed. Bjørn Lomborg. Cambridge: Cambridge University Press.

Hough, Mike, and David Moxon. 1988. 'Dealing with Offenders: Popular Opinion and the Views of Victims in England and Wales'. Pp. 134–48 in *Public Attitudes to Sentencing: Surveys from Five Countries*, ed. Nigel Walker and Mike Hough. Aldershot, UK: Gower.

Huemer, Michael. n.d. 'Why People Are Irrational about Politics', http://spot.colorado.edu/~huemer/irrationality.htm.

——. 1996. 'Rawls's Problem of Stability', *Social Theory and Practice* 22: 375–95.

——. 2001. *Skepticism and the Veil of Perception*. Lanham, MD: Rowman and Littlefield.

——. 2003. 'Non-Egalitarianism', *Philosophical Studies* 114: 147–71.

——. 2005. *Ethical Intuitionism*. New York: Palgrave Macmillan.

——. 2007. 'Compassionate Phenomenal Conservatism', *Philosophy & Phenomenological Research* 74: 30–55.

——. 2010a. 'America's Unjust Drug War'. Pp. 354–67 in *The Ethical Life*, ed. Russ Shafer-Landau. New York: Oxford University Press. Rev. and reprinted from *The New Prohibition*, 133–44, ed. Bill Masters. Saint Louis, MO: Accurate Press.

——. 2010b. 'Is There a Right to Immigrate?' *Social Theory and Practice* 36: 429–61.

——. 2011. 'Epistemological Egoism and Agent-Centered Norms'. Pp. 17–33 in *Evidentialism and Its Critics*, ed. Trent Dougherty. Oxford: Oxford University Press.

——. Forthcoming. 'Against Equality and Priority', *Utilitas*.

Hume, David. [1777] 1987. 'Of the Original Contract'. Pp. 465–87 in *Essays, Moral, Political, and Literary*. Indianapolis: Liberty Fund.

——. [1739] 1992. *Treatise of Human Nature*. Buffalo, NY: Prometheus.

Hunt, Lester. 1999. 'Flourishing Egoism', *Social Philosophy and Policy* 16: 72–95.

Jefferson, Thomas. 1782. *Notes on the State of Virginia*. Paris.

Jencks, Christopher. 1992. *Rethinking Social Policy: Race, Poverty and the Underclass.* Cambridge, MA: Harvard University Press.

Julich, S. 2005. '"Stockholm Syndrome" and Child Sexual Abuse', *Journal of Child Sexual Abuse* 14: 107–29.

Juvenal, Decimus Junius. 1967. *The Sixteen Satires,* tr. Peter Green. Baltimore: Penguin.

Kahneman, Daniel, Paul Slovic, and Amos Tversky, eds. 1982. *Judgment under Uncertainty: Heuristics and Biases.* Cambridge: Cambridge University Press.

Kant, Immanuel. 1957. *Perpetual Peace,* ed. and tr. Lewis White Beck. Indianapolis: Bobbs-Merrill. Originally published 1795.

Karsh, Efraim. 2002. *The Iran-Iraq War 1980–1988.* Oxford: Osprey.

Kelman, Herbert, and V. Lee Hamilton. 1989. *Crimes of Obedience: Toward a Social Psychology of Authority and Responsibility.* New Haven, CT: Yale University Press.

Kernis, Jay. 2011. 'Daniel Ellsberg: All the Crimes Richard Nixon Committed against Me Are Now Legal', *CNN,* June 7, http://inthearena.blogs.cnn.com/2011/06/07/daniel-ellsberg-all-the-crimes-richard-nixon-committed-against-me-are-now-legal/. Accessed January 29, 2012.

Keynes, John Maynard. 1920. *The Economic Consequences of the Peace.* New York: Harcourt, Brace and Howe.

King, Martin Luther. 1991. 'Letter from Birmingham City Jail'. Pp. 68–84 in *Civil Disobedience in Focus,* ed. Hugo A. Bedau. London: Routledge.

Klosko, George. 1992. *The Principle of Fairness and Political Obligation.* Lanham, Md.: Rowman & Littlefield.

Klosko, George. 2005. *Political Obligations.* Oxford: Oxford University Press.

Kropotkin, Peter. 2002. *Anarchism: A Collection of Revolutionary Writings.* New York: Dover.

Kurlansky, Mark. 2006. *Nonviolence: Twenty-five Lessons from the History of a Dangerous Idea.* New York: Random House.

Ladenson, Robert. 1980. 'In Defense of a Hobbesian Conception of Law', *Philosophy and Public Affairs* 9: 134–59.

Lang, Daniel. 1973. 'A Reporter at Large: The Bank Drama', *New Yorker,* November 25, 56–126.

Lawson-Remer, Terra. 2008. 'The US Farm Bill and the Global Food Crisis', *Huffington Post,* May 30, www.commondreams.org/archive/2008/05/30/9317. Accessed March 8, 2011.

Leitenberg, Milton. 2006. *Deaths and Wars in Conflicts in the Twentieth Century,* third edition. Cornell University, Peace Studies Program, www.cissm.umd.edu/papers/files/deathswarsconflictsjune52006.pdf. Accessed April 20, 2011.

Lerner, Abba P. 1944. *The Economics of Control.* New York: Macmillan.

Levi, Michael A. 2007. *On Nuclear Terrorism.* Cambridge, MA: Harvard University Press.

Levi, Michael, and Mike Maguire. 2004. 'Reducing and Preventing Organised Crime: An Evidence-Based Critique', *Crime, Law and Social Change* 41: 397–469.

Lindberg, David C. 1992. *The Beginnings of Western Science: The European Scientific Tradition in Philosophical, Religious, and Institutional Context, 600 BC. to AD. 1450.* Chicago, IL: University of Chicago Press.

Lindemann, Thomas. 2010. *Causes of War: The Struggle for Recognition.* Colchester, UK: ECPR Press.

Locke, John. [1690] 1980. *Second Treatise of Government,* ed. C. B. Macpherson. Indianapolis: Hackett.

——. [1689] 1990. *A Letter concerning Toleration.* Buffalo, NY: Prometheus.

Longley, Robert. n.d. 'Federal Regulations: The Laws Behind the Acts of Congress', *About.com,* U.S. Government Info, http://usgovinfo.about.com/od /uscongress/a/fedregulations.htm. Accessed May 3, 2011.

Lorenz, Konrad. 1966. *On Aggression,* tr. Marjorie Kerr Wilson. New York: Harcourt, Brace & World.

Lugar, Richard G. 2005. 'The Lugar Survey on Proliferation Threats and Responses', http://lugar.senate.gov/nunnlugar/pdf/NPSurvey.pdf. Accessed October 13, 2011.

Macartney, Jane. 2010. 'North Koreans Fear the Country Is on the Verge of a New Famine', *Sunday Times,* March 20, www.timesonline.co.uk/tol/news /world/asia/article7069225.ece. Accessed March 4, 2011.

MacDonald, G. Jeffrey. 2003. 'The Self-Made Lawyer', *Christian Science Monitor,* June 3, www.csmonitor.com/2003/0603/p13s01-lecs.html. Accessed February 7, 2012.

MacIntyre, Alasdair. 1986. 'The Intelligibility of Action'. Pp. 63–80 in *Rationality, Relativism and the Human Sciences,* ed. J. Margolis, M. Krausz, and R. M. Burian. Dordrecht: Kluwer.

Mackie, John L. 1977. *Ethics: Inventing Right and Wrong.* New York: Penguin.

Maley, William. 2009. *The Afghanistan Wars,* second edition. New York: Palgrave Macmillan.

Mandel, Nina. 2010. 'Biden: Wikileaks' Julian Assange Closer to a "High-Tech Terrorist" Than Pentagon Papers', *New York Daily News,* December 19, http: //articles.nydailynews.com/2010–12–19/news/27084869_1_vice-president-joe -biden-world-leaders-accuser. Accessed March 10, 2011.

Mao Tse-tung. 1972. *Quotations from Chairman Mao Tsetung.* Peking: Foreign Languages Press.

Marshall, S. L. A. 1978. *Men against Fire: The Problem of Battle Command in Future War.* Gloucester, MA: Peter Smith.

Marx, Karl, and Friedrich Engels. 1978. *The Marx-Engels Reader,* second edition, ed. Robert C. Tucker. New York: Norton.

Mason, David S. 1996. *Revolution and Transition in East-Central Europe,* second edition. Boulder, CO: Westview.

Mattiuzzi, Paul. 2007. 'Why Do Kidnap Victims Sometimes Fail to Escape, Even When They Have the Chance to Run?' *Everyday Psychology,* January 18, http: //everydaypsychology.com/2007/01/why-do-kidnap-victims-sometimes- fail-to.html. Accessed July 20, 2010.

Milgram, Stanley. 2009. *Obedience to Authority: An Experimental View.* New York: Harper.

Mill, John Stuart. [1859] 1978. *On Liberty,* ed. Elizabeth Rapaport. Indianapolis: Hackett.

Miller, Donald L. 2001. *The Story of World War II.* New York: Simon & Schuster.

Montesquieu, Charles-Louis de Secondat. 1748. *The Spirit of the Laws.* Paris.

Mount, Steve. 2010. *Results of Presidential Elections,* www.usconstitution.net /elections.html. Accessed March 8, 2011.

Mueller, John. 2004. *Remnants of War*. Ithaca, NY: Cornell University Press.

Murphy, Liam, and Thomas Nagel. 2002. *The Myth of Ownership: Taxes and Justice*. Oxford: Oxford University Press.

Murphy, Mark. 1995. 'Philosophical Anarchism and Legal Indifference', *American Philosophical Quarterly* 32: 195–8.

Murray, Charles. 1984. *Losing Ground: American Social Policy, 1950–1980*. New York: Basic Books.

Murray, Charles, and Christopher Jencks. 1985. '"Losing Ground": An Exchange', *New York Review of Books* 32, 16 (October 24): 55–6.

Nader, Ralph. 1973. 'Introduction'. Pp. ix–xv in *The Monopoly Makers: Ralph Nader's Study Group Report on Regulation and Competition*, ed. Mark J. Green. New York: Grossman.

Nagel, Thomas. 1991. *Equality and Partiality*. New York: Oxford University Press.

——. 1995. 'Nozick: Libertarianism without Foundations'. Pp. 137–49 in *Other Minds: Critical Essays 1969–1994*. New York: Oxford University Press.

Namnyak, M., N. Tufton, R. Szekely, M. Toal, S. Worboys, and E. L. Sampson. 2008. '"Stockholm Syndrome": Psychiatric Diagnosis or Urban Myth?' *Acta Psychiatrica Scandinavica* 117: 4–11.

Narveson, Jan. 1988. *The Libertarian Idea*. Philadelphia: Temple University Press.

——. 1993. *Moral Matters*. New York: Broadview.

National Philanthropic Trust. 2011. *Philanthropy Statistics*, www.nptrust.org /philanthropy/philanthropy_stats.asp. Accessed February 15, 2011.

Norcross, Alastair. 2003. 'Killing and Letting Die'. Pp. 451–63 in *A Companion to Applied Ethics*, ed. R. G. Frey and Christopher Heath Wellman. Malden, MA: Blackwell.

Nozick, Robert. 1974. *Anarchy, State, and Utopia*. New York: Basic Books.

Oakeshott, Michael. 1962. *Rationalism in Politics and Other Essays*. London: Methuen.

Obama, Barack. 2004. *Dreams from My Father*. New York: Random House.

Olasky, Marvin. 1992. *The Tragedy of American Compassion*. Washington, D.C.: Regnery Gateway.

Opinion Research Business. 2008. *Update on Iraqi Casualty Data*, January, www. opinion.co.uk/Newsroom_details.aspx?NewsId=120. Accessed March 6, 2011.

Organski, A. F. K. 1968. *World Politics*, second edition. New York: Knopf.

Orwell, George. 1984. *1984*. New York: Signet.

Otsuka, Michael. 2003. *Libertarianism without Inequality*. Oxford: Oxford University Press.

Page, Benjamin I., and Robert Y. Shapiro. 1993. 'The Rational Public and Democracy'. Pp. 35–64 in *Reconsidering the Democratic Public*, ed. George E. Marcus and Russell L. Hanson. University Park: University of Pennsylvania Press.

Paoli, Letizia, and Cyrille Fijnaut. 2006. 'Organised Crime and Its Control Policies', *European Journal of Crime, Criminal Law and Criminal Justice* 14: 307–327.

Pape, Robert A., and James K. Feldman. 2010. *Cutting the Fuse: The Explosion of Global Suicide Terrorism and How to Stop It*. Chicago: University of Chicago Press.

Parker, Robert Alexander Clark. 1997. *The Second World War: A Short History*. Oxford: Oxford University Press.

Perry, Celia. 2008. 'My Bases Are Bigger Than Your Country', *Mother Jones*, August 22, http://motherjones.com/politics/2008/08/my-bases-are-bigger-your-country. Accessed October 18, 2011.

Pew Research Center. 2009. 'Mapping the Global Muslim Population: A Report on the Size and Distribution of the World's Muslim Population', Pew Forum on Religion & Public Life, http://pewforum.org/Mapping-the-Global-Muslim-Population.aspx. Accessed October 27, 2011.

Phinney, David. 1999. 'Dodging the Drug Question', *ABC News*, August 19, http://abcnews.go.com/sections/politics/DailyNews/prez_questions990819.html. Accessed October 24, 2002.

Pinker, Steven. 2011. *The Better Angels of Our Nature: Why Violence Has Declined*. New York: Viking.

Plato. 1974. *Plato's Republic*, tr. G. M. A. Grube. Indianapolis: Hackett.

——. 2000. *The Trial and Death of Socrates*, third edition, tr. G. M. A. Grube, rev. by John M. Cooper. Indianapolis: Hackett.

Pritikin, Martin H. 2008. 'Is Prison Increasing Crime?' *Wisconsin Law Review* 2008: 1049–1108.

Rachels, James. 2003. *The Elements of Moral Philosophy*, fourth edition. New York: McGraw-Hill.

Rand, Ayn. 1964. *The Virtue of Selfishness*. New York: Signet.

——. 1967. *Capitalism: The Unknown Ideal*. New York: Signet.

RAND Corporation. 2011. *RAND Database of Worldwide Terrorism Incidents*, http://smapp.rand.org/rwtid/search_form.php. Accessed October 2, 2011.

Rawls, John. 1964. 'Legal Obligation and the Duty of Fair Play'. Pp. 3–18 in *Law and Philosophy*, ed. Sidney Hook. New York: New York University Press.

——. 1974. 'Some Reasons for the Maximin Criterion', *American Economic Review* 64, 2 (Papers and Proceedings of the Eighty-sixth Annual Meeting of the American Economic Association): 141–46.

——. 1985. 'Justice as Fairness: Political Not Metaphysical', *Philosophy and Public Affairs* 14: 223–51.

——. 1999. *A Theory of Justice*, revised edition. Cambridge, MA: Harvard University Press.

——. 2001. *Justice as Fairness: A Restatement*. Cambridge, MA: Harvard University Press.

——. 2005. *Political Liberalism*, expanded edition. New York: Columbia University Press.

Raz, Joseph. 1986. *The Morality of Freedom*. Oxford: Clarendon Press.

Remak, Joachim. 1993. *A Very Civil War: The Swiss Sonderbund War of 1847*. Boulder, CO: Westview.

Reuters. 2007a. *U.S. CBO Estimates $2.4 Trillion Long-term War Costs*, October 24, www.reuters.com/article/2007/10/24/us-iraq-usa-funding-idUSN2450753720071024. Accessed April 11, 2011.

——. 2007b. *Factbox: Guns and Gun Ownership in the United States*, www.reuters.com/article/2007/04/17/us-usa-crime-shootings-guns-idUSN1743414020070417. Accessed September 7, 2011.

Ross, W. D. 1988. *The Right and the Good*. Indianapolis: Hackett. Originally published 1930.

Rothbard, Murray. 1978. *For a New Liberty*. Lanham, MD: University Press of America.

Ruggles, Steven. 2008. *Historical Bush Approval Ratings*, www.hist.umn. edu/~ruggles/Approval.htm. Accessed 17 March 2011.

Rummel, Rudolph J. 1998. *Statistics of Democide: Genocide and Mass Murder since 1900*. Piscataway, NJ: Transaction.

Russell, Bertrand. 1985. *The Philosophy of Logical Atomism*. LaSalle, IL: Open Court.

Russell, Jeffrey. 1991. *Inventing the Flat Earth: Columbus and Modern Historians*. New York: Praeger.

Russett, Bruce, and John Oneal. 2001. *Triangulating Peace: Democracy, Interdependence, and International Organizations*. New York: Norton.

Saad, Lydia. 2011. 'Self-Reported Gun Ownership in U.S. Is Highest since 1993', *Gallup*, October 26, www.gallup.com/poll/150353/Self-Reported-Gun-Owners hip-Highest-1993.aspx. Accessed October 27, 2011.

Sandburg, Carl. 1990. *The People, Yes*. Orlando, FL: Harcourt Brace.

Sanford, George. 2002. *Democratic Government in Poland: Constitutional Politics since 1989*. New York: Palgrave Macmillan.

Sarkar, Sumit. 1988. *Modern India 1885–1947*. New York: Saint Martin's Press.

Sartwell, Crispin. 2008. *Against the State: An Introduction to Anarchist Political Theory*. Albany: State University of New York Press.

Satloff, Robert. 2008. 'Just Like Us! Really?' *Weekly Standard*, May 12, www.weeklystandard.com/Content/Public/Articles/000/000/015/066chpzg.asp?pg=2. Accessed October 27, 2011.

Scanlon, Thomas M. 1998. *What We Owe to Each Other*. Cambridge, MA: Harvard University Press.

Schmidtz, David. 1998. 'Taking Responsibility'. Pp. 1–96 in *Social Welfare and Individual Responsibility*, ed. David Schmidtz and Robert E. Goodin.

———. 2000. 'Diminishing Marginal Utility and Egalitarian Redistribution', *Journal of Value Inquiry* 34: 263–72.

———. 2008. 'The Institution of Property'. Pp. 193–210 in *Person, Polis, Planet: Essays in Applied Philosophy*. Oxford: Oxford University Press.

Schumpeter, Joseph A. 1950. *Capitalism, Socialism, and Democracy*, third edition. New York: Harper.

Sen, Amartya. 1994. 'Population: Delusion and Reality', *New York Review of Books* 41, 15 (September 22): 62–71.

———. 1999. *Development as Freedom*. New York: Knopf.

Sharp, Gene. 1990. *Civilian-Based Defense: A Post-Military Weapons System*. Princeton, NJ: Princeton University Press.

Shaw, David R. 2009. *Special Report: The California Department of Corrections and Rehabilitation's Supervision of Parolee Phillip Garrido*, Office of the Inspector General, State of California, www.oig.ca.gov/media/reports/BCI/Special Report on CDCRs Supervision of Parolee Phillip Garrido.pdf. Accessed July 20, 2010.

Shaw, William. 1999. *Contemporary Ethics: Taking Account of Utilitarianism*. Malden, MA: Blackwell.

Simmons, A. John. 1979. *Moral Principles and Political Obligation*. Princeton, NJ: Princeton University Press.

———. 2001. *Justification and Legitimacy: Essays on Rights and Obligations*. Cambridge: Cambridge University Press.

Singer, Peter. 1993. *Practical Ethics*, second edition. Cambridge: Cambridge University Press.

———. 2005. 'Ethics and Intuitions', *Journal of Ethics* 9: 331–52.

Smith, Adam. 1979. *An Inquiry into the Nature and Causes of the Wealth of Nations*, vol. 1, ed. R. H. Campbell, A. S. Skinner, and W. B. Todd. Oxford: Clarendon. Originally published 1776.

Smith, John. 1986. *The Complete Works of Captain John Smith (1580–1631)*, vol. 2, ed. Philip L. Barbour. Chapel Hill: University of North Carolina Press.

Sobek, David. 2009. *The Causes of War*. Cambridge: Polity.

Somin, Ilya. 1998. 'Voter Ignorance and the Democratic Ideal', *Critical Review* 12: 413–58.

Stark, Cynthia. 2000. 'Hypothetical Consent and Justification', *Journal of Philosophy* 97: 313–34.

State of World Liberty Project. 2006. *The 2006 State of World Liberty Index*, www.stateofworldliberty.org/report/rankings.html. Accessed January 26, 2012.

Stiglitz, Joseph, and Linda Bilmes. 2008. 'The Three Trillion Dollar War', *The Times*, February 23, www.timesonline.co.uk/tol/comment/columnists/guest_contributors/article3419840.ece. Accessed April 11, 2011.

Stockholm International Peace Research Institute. 2012. *Recent Trends in Military Expenditure*, www.sipri.org/research/armaments/milex/resultoutput/trends. Accessed January 26, 2012.

Stove, David. 1995. *Cricket versus Republicanism and Other Essays*, ed. James Franklin and R. J. Stove. Sydney: Quakers Hill Press.

Stringham, Edward P., ed. 2007. *Anarchy and the Law: The Political Economy of Choice*. New Brunswick, NJ: Transaction.

Tetlock, Philip E. 2005. *Expert Political Judgment: How Good Is It? How Can We Know?* Princeton, NJ: Princeton University Press.

Thompson, Hugh C. n.d. *Moral Courage in Combat: The My Lai Story*, presentation to the U.S. Naval Academy, www.usna.edu/Ethics/Publications/ThompsonPg1-28_Final.pdf. Accessed August 1, 2010.

Tullock, Gordon. 1987. 'Rent seeking'. Pp. 147–9 in *The New Palgrave: A Dictionary of Economics*, vol. 4, ed. John Eatwell, Murray Milgate, and Peter Newman. London: Macmillan.

Tusty, James, and Maureen Castle Tusty, directors. 2006. *The Singing Revolution* (documentary film). 94 min. Mountain View Productions.

Tversky, Amos. 1969. 'Intransitivity of Preferences', *Psychological Review* 76: 31–48.

Tversky, Amos, and Daniel Kahneman. 1981. 'The Framing of Decisions and the Psychology of Choice', *Science* 211: 453–8.

———. 1982. 'Evidential Impact of Base Rates'. Pp. 153–60 in *Judgment under Uncertainty: Heuristics and Biases*, ed. Daniel Kahneman, Paul Slovic, and Amos Tversky. Cambridge: Cambridge University Press.

———. 1986. 'Rational Choice and the Framing of Decisions', *Journal of Business* 59: S251–S278.

———. 2002. 'Extensional versus Intuitive Reasoning: The Conjunction Fallacy in Probability Judgment'. Pp. 19–48 in *Heuristics and Biases: The Psychology of Intuitive Judgment*, ed. Thomas Gilovich, Dale Griffin, and Daniel Kahneman. Cambridge: Cambridge University Press.

Twenty-Fifth Aviation Battalion. n.d. *Vietnam War Statistics and Facts*, http://25thaviation.org/facts/id430.htm. Accessed May 23, 2011.

Unger, Peter. 1996. *Living High and Letting Die*. New York: Oxford University Press.

United Nations, Department of Economic and Social Affairs, Population Division. 2009. *World Population Prospects: The 2008 Revision*, http://esa.un.org/unpd /wpp2008/index.htm. Accessed March 3, 2011.

UN News Center. 2011. *Number of Private Security Guards Booming Worldwide, UN Survey Reveals*, July 6, www.un.org/apps/news/story.asp?NewsID=38957. Accessed January 26, 2012.

U.S. Census Bureau. 2011a. *Historical Estimates of World Population*, www.census. gov/ipc/www/worldhis.html. Accessed March 21, 2011.

———. 2011b. *Statistical Abstract of the United States*, www.census.gov/compendia /statab/2011edition.html. Accessed March 21, 2011.

———. 2011c. *Total Midyear Population for the World: 1950–2050*, www.census.gov /ipc/www/idb/worldpoptotal.php. Accessed March 21, 2011.

U.S. Central Intelligence Agency. 2011. *CIA World Factbook*, https://www.cia.gov /library/publications/the-world-factbook/index.html. Accessed March 4, 2011.

U.S. Congressional Budget Office. 2009. *Historical Effective Tax Rates: 1979 to 2006*, www.cbo.gov/ftpdocs/100xx/doc10068/effective_tax_rates_2006.pdf, Accessed March 25, 2010.

U.S. Department of Agriculture. 2011. *Farm Income and Costs: Farms Receiving Government Payments*, www.ers.usda.gov/briefing/farmincome/govtpayby-farmtype.htm. Accessed March 8, 2011.

U.S. Department of Defense. 2010. *Active Duty Military Personnel Strengths by Regional Area and by Country (309A)*, http://siadapp.dmdc.osd.mil/personnel /MILITARY/history/hst1009.pdf. Accessed September 29, 2011.

U.S. Department of Justice, Bureau of Justice Statistics. 2004. *Profile of Jail Inmates 2002*, http://bjs.ojp.usdoj.gov/content/pub/pdf/pji02.pdf, pub. July 2004, rev. October 12, 2004. Accessed May 27, 2010.

———. 2009. *Jail Inmates at Midyear 2008 – Statistical Tables*, http://bjs.ojp.usdoj. gov/content/pub/pdf/jim08st.pdf. Accessed May 27, 2010.

———. 2010a. *Criminal Victimization in the United States, 2007: Statistical Tables*, http://bjs.ojp.usdoj.gov/content/pub/pdf/cvus0701.pdf. Accessed April 12, 2011.

———. 2010b . *Prisoners in 2008*, http://bjs.ojp.usdoj.gov/content/pub/pdf/p08.pdf. Originally pub. December 2009, rev. April 1, 2010. Accessed May 27, 2010.

U.S. Department of State. 2011. *Background Note: Costa Rica*, www.state.gov/r/pa /ei/bgn/2019.htm. Accessed September 29, 2011.

U.S. Department of the Treasury. 2009. *Update on Reducing the Federal Tax Gap and Improving Voluntary Compliance*, www.irs.gov/pub/newsroom /tax_gap_report_-final_version.pdf. Accessed May 2, 2010.

U.S. Federal Bureau of Investigation. 2010. 'Offenses Cleared' in *Crime in the United States 2009*, www2.fbi.gov/ucr/cius2009/offenses/clearances/index. html. Accessed April 12, 2011.

U.S. Navy. 2009. *Information about Us*, www.public.navy.mil/usff/nctamspac /Pages/AboutUs.aspx. Accessed April 20, 2011.

U.S. Supreme Court. 2011. *Members of the Supreme Court of the United States*, www.supremecourt.gov/about/members.aspx. Accessed March 18, 2011.

Vastag, Brian. 2009. 'Five Years After: Portugal's Drug Decriminalization Policy Shows Positive Results', *Scientific American*, April 17, www.scientificamerican. com/article.cfm?id=portugal-drug-decriminalization. Accessed January 26, 2012.

Vegetius. 2001. *Vegetius: Epitome of Military Science*, tr. N. P. Milner. Liverpool: Liverpool University Press.

Ventrell-Monsees, Cathy. 2007. *Testimony on behalf of the National Employment Lawyers Association before the Subcommittee on Commercial and Administrative Law, House Judiciary Committee*, October 25, http://judiciary.house.gov/ hearings/pdf/Ventrell-Monsees071025.pdf. Accessed January 26, 2012.

Vinokur, Aaron, and Gur Ofer. 1987. 'Inequality of Earnings, Household Income, and Wealth in the Soviet Union in the 1970s'. Pp. 171–202 in *Politics, Work, and Daily Life in the USSR*, ed. James R. Millar. Cambridge: Cambridge University Press.

Wadhwa, Rakesh. 2005. 'When U.S. Tried Communism', *Himalayan Times*, January 24. Reprinted at www.ccsindia.org/article/people_rw_when_us_tried_ communism.asp.

Waldron, Jeremy. 1993. 'Theoretical Foundations of Liberalism'. Pp. 35–62 in *Liberal Rights: Collected Papers 1981–1991*. Cambridge: Cambridge University Press.

Walker, Nigel, and Mike Hough. 1988. 'Introduction: Developments in Methods and Perspectives'. Pp. 1–15 in *Public Attitudes to Sentencing: Surveys from Five Countries*, ed. Nigel Walker and Mike Hough. Aldershot, UK: Gower.

Wallace, Mike, and Paul Meadlo. 1969. 'Transcript of Interview of Vietnam War Veteran on His Role in Alleged Massacre of Civilians at Songmy', *New York Times*, November 25, 16.

Wall Street Journal. 2011. 'How the Presidents Stack Up', http://online.wsj.com /public/resources/documents/info-presapp0605–31.html. Accessed March 17, 2011.

Weber, Max. 1946. 'Politics as a Vocation. Pp. 77–128 in *From Max Weber: Essays in Sociology*, ed. H. H. Gerth and C. Wright Mills. New York: Oxford University Press.

——. 2000. 'Relational Facts in Liberal Political Theory: Is There Magic in the Pronoun "My"?' *Ethics* 110: 537–62.

——. 2005. 'Samaritanism and the Duty to Obey the Law'. Pp. 1–89 in Christopher Heath Wellman and A. John Simmons, *Is There a Duty to Obey the Law?* New York: Cambridge University Press.

White, Matthew. 2010. 'Deaths by Mass Unpleasantness: Estimated Totals for the Entire Twentieth Century', http://users.erols.com/mwhite28/warstat8. htm. Accessed February 13, 2012.

Wikileaks. 2010. *Collateral Murder* (video), www.collateralmurder.com/. Accessed March 10, 2011.

Williams, Juan. 1987. *Eyes on the Prize*. New York: Viking Penguin.

Wilson, Edward O. 2000. *Sociobiology: The New Synthesis*, 25th anniversary ed. Cambridge, MA: Harvard University Press.

Wilson, James Q. 1990. 'Against the Legalization of Drugs', *Commentary* 89: 21–8.

Wing, Nick. 2010. 'Mike Huckabee: WikiLeaks Source Should Be Executed', *Huffington Post*, November 30, www.huffingtonpost.com/2010/11/30/mike-h uckabee-wikileaks-execution_n_789964.html. Accessed March 10, 2011.

Wingo, Ajume. 2003. *Veil Politics in Liberal Democratic States*. Cambridge: Cambridge University Press.

Wittman, Donald. 1995. *The Myth of Democratic Failure: Why Political Institutions Are Efficient*. Chicago: University of Chicago Press.

Wolff, Jonathan. 1996. *An Introduction to Political Philosophy*. Oxford: Oxford University Press.

Wolff, Robert Paul. 1998. *In Defense of Anarchism*. Berkeley: University of California Press.

Zimbardo, Phillip. 2007. *The Lucifer Effect: Understanding How Good People Turn Evil*. New York: Random House.

Zimbardo, Phillip, Craig Haney, and Curtis Banks. 1973. 'Interpersonal Dynamics in a Simulated Prison', *International Journal of Criminology and Penology* 1: 69–97.

Index

CPSIA information can be obtained
at www.ICGtesting.com
Printed in the USA
FSOW02n0658120716
22636FS

9 781137 281654